Elements of Literat

Holt Reading Solutions

- Intervention
- English-Language Learners
- Special Education

DISCARD

DATE DUE			

DEMCO 128-5046

HOLT, RINEHART AND WINSTON

A Harcourt Education Company

Orlando • **Austin** • New York • San Diego • Toronto • London

Staff Credits

Executive Editor: Katie Vignery

Senior Editors: Amy Strong, Kathryn Rogers

Project Editors: Randy Dickson, Ann Michelle Gibson, Jennifer Schwan

Contributing Editor: Gail Coupland

Diagnostic Assessment: Harcourt Assessment Group

Copyediting: Michael Neibergall, *Copyediting Manager;* Mary Malone, *Copyediting Supervisor;* Elizabeth Dickson, Christine Altgelt, *Senior Copyeditors;* Julia Thomas Hu, Emily Force, *Copyeditors*

Managing Editor: Marie Price

Senior Editorial Coordinator: Janet Jenkins

Senior Permissions Editor: Ann Farrar

Cover Design: Betty Mintz

Design: Jeff Robinson

Graphics Services: Avanti! Graphics

Production Manager: Carol Trammel

Senior Production Coordinators: Belinda Barbosa Lopez, Michael Roche

Manufacturing: Shirley Cantrell, *Manufacturing Supervisor;* Mark McDonald, *Inventory Analyst;* Amy Borseth, *Manufacturing Coordinator*

ISBN 0-03-073909-8

1 2 3 4 5 6   021   06 05 04 03

Table of Contents

Collection 1 Lesson Plans
Facing Danger

Collection 2 Lesson Plans
Characters: Living Many Lives

Lesson Plans & Copying Masters, *continued*

Collection 3 Lesson Plans
Living in the Heart

Collection 4 Lesson Plans
Point of View: Can You See It My Way?

Lesson Plans & Copying Masters, *continued*

Collection 5 Lesson Plans
Worlds of Words: Prose and Poetry

Lesson Plans & Copying Masters, *continued*

Collection 6 Lesson Plans
Our Literary Heritage: Greek Myths and World Folk Tales

Collection 7 Lesson Plans
Literary Criticism: Where I Stand

Collection 8 Lesson Plans
Reading for Life

Lesson Plans & Copying Masters, *continued*

III. CORE READING SKILLS AND STRATEGIES LESSONS WITH MINIREADS

Overhead transparencies for the Reading Skills and Strategies Lessons can be found in the front cover pocket of this book.

Literary Comprehension Skills

IV. ADAPTED READINGS

Adapted prose and annotated poetry selections from Elements of Literature.

Adapted Readings, *continued*

To the Teacher

Two questions that more and more secondary language arts teachers ask every day are

- How can I help my struggling readers?
- How can I integrate support for my struggling readers into my mixed ability, literature-based classes?

Holt Reading Solutions provides the answers. This book provides tools for diagnosing and targeting reading skills deficiencies as well as lesson plans for managing the suite of reading development tools provided within the **Elements of Literature** program.

How to Use *Holt Reading Solutions*

To get the most out of *Holt Reading Solutions,* you will first need to identify your struggling readers. This group is broadly defined as anyone reading more than two levels below grade level. It may include English-language learners, special education students, students with learning disabilities, reluctant readers, and low-achieving students.

Diagnostic Assessment for Reading Intervention

You probably know from experience which students are reading well below grade level. The Diagnostic Assessment for Reading Intervention in this book will give you more detailed information about these students and their specific needs. Information about this test appears in the first tabbed section of this book. From the test's results, you can identify up to ten core reading comprehension skills for which each struggling reader may require remedial lessons. Lessons on each of these skills are included in *Holt Reading Solutions.*

Lesson Plans and Copying Masters

Holt Reading Solutions shows you how to provide remediation in core reading comprehension skills and how to integrate that remediation into your mixed ability, literature-based classroom. Each lesson plan covers a selection or selection cluster in the Student Edition. Within each lesson plan, you will find the following features that target your struggling readers.

(Core Skill) This icon appears wherever there is an opportunity for addressing one of the ten core reading skills. These features may be self-contained activities, directions to use a Reading Skills and Strategies lesson from *Holt Reading Solutions,* or directions to apply a core skill to the selection at hand.

(Mixed Ability Group) Because research shows that struggling readers can benefit from working with more proficient readers, most lesson plans include ideas for placing students in small mixed ability groups.

(Especially for ELL) Many readers struggle because they are learning English as a second language. Throughout the lesson plans are tips and activities designed especially to help English-language learners understand unfamiliar concepts and vocabulary in the literature of the Student Edition.

(Resources) Each lesson plan contains references to the ***Elements of Literature*** program's resources for struggling readers. These resources include audio CD recordings (in English and Spanish), videocassettes, *The Holt Reader,* the vocabulary worksheets mentioned below, and Adapted Readings described on the following page. In addition, suggestions for integrating these resources into specific literature lessons appear throughout each lesson plan.

Reading Skills Development These self-contained activities appear in the majority of full-length lesson plans. They generally provide further practice in the reading skill covered on the Before You Read page in the Student Edition or practice in a prerequisite skill.

Vocabulary Development Research tells us that vocabulary development is critical to the acquisition of superior word-recognition skill among older struggling readers. For this reason, many full-length lesson plans include extra support and practice for the Vocabulary Development features in the Student Edition. In addition, two copying masters, **Vocabulary and Comprehension** and **Additional Vocabulary Practice,** accompany each selection or selection cluster. You may want to let students use their textbooks or dictionaries as they complete these worksheets.

Targeted Strategies for Special Education Each lesson plan contains a separate section dedicated to special education students. Like the core lesson plans, these lesson plans provide activities and strategies for prereading, reading, and post-reading.

Reading Skills and Strategies

In this section of *Holt Reading Solutions,* you will find ten core reading comprehension skills lessons, five informational and five literary—the same skills assessed in the Diagnostic Assessment for Reading Intervention. These self-contained lessons include easy-to-read instructions for the students. With minimal teacher guidance, students can work through these lessons independently, in small groups, or as a class.

Each lesson introduces students to an easy-to-use strategy or procedure for comprehending texts. The lessons include notes for teachers and students and practice activities based on MiniReads—short, below–grade-level practice reads. Each lesson comes with an application activity to assess student mastery. You can tie the application of the reading skill back into any part of the Student Edition by selecting a passage from the Suggested Selections for Reading Skills Application list that begins the Reading Skills and Strategies section.

Adapted Readings

This section of *Holt Reading Solutions* contains adapted prose selections and annotated versions of longer poetry and drama selections found in the Student Edition. The adaptations are highly condensed and written two to four grades below the textbook's grade level.

The adapted readings can be used in a number of ways. They provide excellent material for fluency practice (which requires material written at the student's reading level) and for the application portion of the Reading Skills and Strategies lessons. The prose adaptations can also be used for prereading. The lesson plans for selections that include an adapted reading advise having all students read the adaptation in prereading. This activity can be completed quickly, even by struggling readers, and it provides a schema in a reader's mind as he or she approaches the original version.

Fluency, Decoding, and Phonics

Teachers with struggling readers know that each reader has different strengths and weaknesses. For example, some may struggle more with informational comprehension skills than with literary comprehension. Others may have difficulty with fluency and decoding.

As mentioned earlier, vocabulary is a cornerstone of reading proficiency. The vocabulary development activities and worksheets in *Holt Reading Solutions* provide ample support for vocabulary building. When you help students improve their vocabulary skills, you help them improve their ability to recognize words automatically. Improved automaticity helps them to focus on comprehension rather than on decoding.

Fluency, the ability to read automatically and with comprehension, can be improved by having students read aloud. Some lesson plans in *Holt Reading Solutions* include fluency activities, and the adapted readings can be used for fluency practice. The Vocabulary and Comprehension worksheets in *Holt Reading Solutions* serve as a quick comprehension check in conjunction with fluency activities.

If you note students having problems with pronunciation during fluency practice or other speaking activities, work with these students individually. Some struggling readers, especially English-language learners, have trouble hearing the differences between different pairs of vowel sounds or consonant sounds. Use the Phonics Chart and Decoding section in *Holt Reading Solutions* (page xxxviii) as a resource to help these students distinguish between different letter-sound correspondences.

The resources described above, combined with your professionalism and creativity, are powerful tools for reading intervention. By addressing struggling readers' specific needs yet still including them in your whole-class instruction, you can help them become confident, proficient readers. The following professional articles provide more detailed information on helping English-language learners and special education students.

Closing the Gap:

What Research Tells Us About Effective Strategies for Special Education Students and English-Language Learners

*. . . [T]hose who suffer most from unsound teaching methods
are the students most in need: learning disabled, impoverished,
and nonnative speakers of English—the so-called at-risk students.*

—Doug Carnine

Today's Classroom

Diversity defines today's classroom. Today's teacher in the mainstream classroom faces students with diverse needs. According to the National Center for Learning Disabilities' "23rd Annual Report to Congress," children classified as having learning disabilities have increased substantially, from roughly three quarters of a million in 1976 to more than 2.9 million in 2001. In their executive summary of the research, Gersten *et al.* also point to the rise in English-language learners (ELLs). Who are the students most at risk for reading failure? According to Lyon, they are "those who enter school with limited exposure to the English language."

Considering all the other demands on the classroom teacher's time and attention, meeting the needs of special education students and ELLs may sound overwhelming. What can the classroom teacher with no special training in teaching these students do? What does the research tell us about creating more effective programs for these students? What special needs must be met?

What the Research Says

We know that reading instruction is affected positively when direct instruction is combined with strategy instruction. In their synthesis of the research, Collins et al. show how "contemporary reforms in reading curricula . . . emphasize integrating metacognition, motivation, and strategies."

Why is the teaching of strategies so important? A key difference between strategic readers and special education students is that strategic readers know how to choose strategies to apply to reading, while special education students do not. These students need systematic and explicit instruction showing them how to choose strategies that fit their text, their purpose, and the occasion. Special education students benefit from strategies that help them overcome problems in

- comprehending what they read
- recognizing text patterns
- distinguishing between relevant and irrelevant information
- recalling information

Principles

Dickson, Carnine, and Kameenui's research for the National Center to Improve the Tools of Educators at the University of Oregon reveals six instructional principles for meeting the needs of special education students. They are

- big ideas
- conspicuous strategies
- mediated scaffolding
- strategic integration
- primed background knowledge
- judicious review

Big Ideas

Big ideas are "concepts and principles that facilitate the most efficient and broadest acquisition of knowledge across a range of examples in a domain." In other words, some ideas are more important than others and serve as umbrellas under which other ideas fit. By concentrating on big ideas, special education students will spend time mastering what is essential. This is particularly helpful since these students generally have more "catch-up" to do and face the "tyranny of time."

For special education students a big idea for instruction concerns the importance of text structure. Good readers know how to use the structure of the text and its special features to make sense from that text. Students with learning difficulties do not. According to Seidenberg, special education students benefit from instruction in how to do this.

Conspicuous Strategies

What is a strategy? Dickson et al. define a strategy as "an organized set of actions designed to accomplish a task." Conspicuous strategies are just that—conspicuous. In other words, they are made apparent to the student through identification and definition, modeling, guided practice, and appropriate feedback. To be effective, conspicuous strategies should be neither too narrow nor too broad, and they should be generalizable. Conspicuous strategies are essential for special education students, who need "an array of strategies to enhance their understanding of the narrative and expository material they read."

Mediated Scaffolding

Dickson et al. define mediated scaffolding as "the external support provided by teacher/peers, content, tasks, and materials during initial instruction." The first method of mediated scaffolding involves the way teachers interact with students and the way peers interact. It is called teacher-peer scaffolding. When the teacher models, he or she shows how to do something and then guides students' practice. In addition, the teacher may have students, or peers, tutor one another or share work with one another. In their synthesis of the research, Elbaum et al. discuss the results of students' tutoring one another: "Researchers found clear benefits to tutoring both in cases when the students with disabilities acted as reciprocal tutors-tutees and in cases when they were only tutors." They recommend peer-mediated instruction in reading as "an effective complement to other instructional practices for students with disabilities." Gersten et al. also find the benefits of peer-assisted learning strategies promising.

The next three methods of mediated scaffolding concern content, tasks, and materials. In other words, how should teachers differentiate the content they present, the tasks they ask students to do, and the materials they give students to use in order to meet the needs of diverse students? *Content scaffolding* involves presenting easier content before more difficult content. *Task control scaffolding* involves starting with easier tasks and building toward more difficult tasks. *Material scaffolding* involves providing materials—such as key words, think sheets, and interactive graphic organizers—to guide students' thinking.

Strategic Integration

Diverse learners benefit from material that is strategically integrated, since they have difficulty making these connections on their own. In other words, they find it helpful when connections between materials are pointed out or made clear. Dickson et al. define strategic integration as "the integrating of content, skills, or concepts that (a) mutually support each other, (b) communicate generalizations, or (c) transfer to areas further and further removed from the original area of instruction." Strategic integration, then, is the "careful combination of new information with what the learner already knows to produce a more generalizable, higher order skill."

Primed Background Knowledge

The research of Weaver and Kintsch has shown the importance of activating prior knowledge. Prior knowledge consists of not only background information about topics, themes, and concepts but also knowledge about text structure, academic language, and the conventions of English. In citing the converging evidence, Lyon says, "Students who comprehend well are able to activate their relevant background knowledge when reading—they can relate what has been read to their own experiences and background." On the other hand, special education students are not skilled at this. Effective instruction for these students includes ample time spent developing background knowledge, since that addresses the students' "memory and strategy deficits."

Judicious Review

According to Dickson et al., judicious review refers to "the sequence and schedule of opportunities students receive to apply and develop facility with the conventions of well-presented text and the organizational patterns of text structures." To be effective, review should be sufficient, distributed over time, cumulative, and varied.

Good Classroom Practices

How do these principles translate into good classroom practices? Most likely, they describe things you and other good teachers have already been doing, including the following practices:

- spending more time on big ideas, or umbrella concepts
- identifying and modeling strategies to use
- using scaffold instruction, moving from heavy support to lighter support or from easier concepts, tasks, and materials to more challenging concepts, tasks, and materials
- showing connections
- activating prior knowledge and building background
- reviewing often and regularly

How Does *Elements of Literature* Address These Principles?

Principles	Access
Big ideas	Collections are organized around a well-defined set of skills that serve as a foundation for instruction. Instruction in focused skills takes place in various contexts. Interactive notes point out text structure. Graphic organizers support text structure. Comprehension check tests academic language dealing with text structure.
Conspicuous strategies	Pretaught strategies are included in each collection. Modeling uses the strategies. Transparencies for modeling are included in *Holt Reading Solutions*. Guided practices using the strategies are included. Strategies are applied to many selections. Use of strategies is evaluated.
Mediated scaffolding Teacher-peer	Three-step instructional design in *Holt Reading Solutions:* • diagnostic assessment • appropriate presentation with instruction and immediate practice • reteaching and remediation options Program organization • scaffolded instruction within a grade and from grade to grade • reteaching and remediation focused on core skills • skill instruction in multiple contexts

How Does *Elements of Literature* Address These Principles? *(continued)*

Principles	Access
Content	• systematic organization • leveled interactive selections and lessons supporting core content instruction • selections available online • selections available on audio CDs • guided and independent strategies for selections
Task control	Lesson Plans in *Holt Reading Solutions*
Materials	Graphic organizers CDs
Primed background knowledge	Strategy Launches Before You Read notes
Judicious review	Skills practice notes Vocabulary checks Comprehension checks

Bibliography

R. Barr, M.L. Kamil, P.B. Mosenthal, and P.D. Pearson, eds. *Handbook of Reading Research,* vol. 2. White Plains, N.Y.: Longman, 1991.

Carnine, Douglas. "Introduction to the Mini-Series: Diverse Learners and Prevailing, Emerging and Research-Based Educational Approaches and Three Tools." *School Psychology Review* 23, No. 3 (1994): 341–350.

Collins, Vicki L., Shirley V. Dickson, Deborah C. Simmons, and Edward J. Kameenui. *Metacognition and Its Relation to Reading Comprehension: A Synthesis of the Research.* National Center to Improve the Tools of Educators, 1996. *<http://idea.uoregon.edu/~ncite/documents/techrep/tech23.html>.*

Dickson, Shirley V., Douglas Carnine, and Edward J. Kameenui. "Curriculum Guidelines for Diverse Learners." *National Center to Improve the Tools of Education.* Eugene, Ore.: U of Oregon, 1992.

Dickson, Shirley V., Deborah C. Simmons, and Edward J. Kameenui. *Text Organization: Curricular and Instructional Implications for Diverse Learners.* National Center to Improve the Tools of Educators, 1995. *<http://idea.uoregon.edu/~ncite/documents/techrep/tech18.html>.*

Dickson, Shirley V., Deborah C. Simmons, and Edward J. Kameenui. *Text Organizational and Its Relation to Reading Comprehension: A Synthesis of the Research.* National Center to Improve the Tools of Educators, 1995. *<http://idea.uoregon.edu/~ncite/documents/techrep/tech17.html>.*

Gersten, Russell, Scott Baker, Susan Unok Marks, and Sylvia B. Smith. "Effective Instruction for Learning Disabled or At-Risk English Language Learners: An Integrative Synthesis of the Empirical and Professional Knowledge Bases." *Research News.* National Center for Learning Disabilities, 1999. *<http://www.ld.org/research/osep_at_risk.cfm>.*

Gersten, Russell, and Scott Baker. "Reading Comprehension Instruction for Students with Learning Disabilities." *Research News.* National Center for Learning Disabilities, 1999. *<http://www.ld.org/research/ncld_reading_comp.cfm>.*

"Getting Education Back on Track." *Inquiry,* Spring 1997.

Kameenui, Edward J. "Diverse Learners and the Tyranny of Time: Don't Fix Blame; Fix the Leaky Roof." *The Reading Teacher* 46, no. 5 (1993): 376–383.

Kameenui, Edward J., and Carnine., eds. *Effective Teaching Strategies That Accommodate Diverse Learners.* Columbus, Ohio: Merrill–Prentice Hall, 1998.

Lyon, G. Reid. "The NICHD Research Program in Reading Development, Reading Disorders, and Reading Instruction." *Research News.* National Center for Learning Disabilities, 1999. <*http://www.ld.org/research/keys99_nichd.cfm*>.

Paris, S. C., B. A. Wasik, and J. C. Turner. "The Development of Strategic Readers." Barr, Kamil, Mosenthal, and Pearson. 609–640.

Pearson, P. D., and L. Fielding. "Comprehensive Instruction." Barr, Kamil, Mosenthal, and Pearson. 815–860.

Seidenberg, P. L. "Relating Text-Processing Research to Reading and Writing Instruction for Learning Disabled Students." *Learning Disabilities Focus* 5, no. 1 (1989): 4–12.

Simmons, Deborah C., and Edward J. Kameenui, eds. *What Research Tells Us About Students with Diverse Learning Needs.* Mahwah, N.J.: Lawrence Erlbaum Associates, 1998.

Swanson, Lee H. "Intervention Research for Adolescents with Learning Disabilities: A Meta-Analysis of Outcomes Related to High-Order Processing." *Research News.* National Center for Learning Disabilities, 1999. <*http://www.ld.org/research/ncld_high_order.cfm*>.

Swanson, Lee H. "Intervention Research for Students with Learning Disabilities: A Meta-Analysis of Treatment Outcomes." *Research News.* National Center for Learning Disabilities, 1999. <*http://www.ld.org/research/osep_swanson.cfm*>.

Weaver III, C. A., and W. Kintsch. "Expository Text." R. Barr, Kamil, Mosenthal, and Pearson. 230–244.

Mixed Ability Grouping

General Strategies for Grouping Students

What Is Mixed Ability Grouping?

Today's English language arts classroom includes students with varying abilities, needs, and backgrounds—and, as a result, different ways of experiencing reading. One way to address this diversity while connecting students to the excitement of literature is to create a learning environment composed of small, heterogeneous groups. **Mixed ability grouping,** also referred to as **heterogeneous grouping,** is defined in this essay as a group of two to five students of varying abilities who learn together. Such grouping allows all students access to high-level instruction and has positive effects on achievement, self-esteem, intergroup relations, and acceptance of mainstreamed students with special needs.

A major goal of mixed ability grouping is to provide a way of teaching in which students of differing abilities and backgrounds can reach their potential by learning to work together despite their individual differences. Educators who favor the small-group learning approach believe that it allows the classroom to emulate the real world, where people often function as members of a larger unit. While prizing individuality, many people recognize that a large part of life involves working in a myriad of situations toward goals that benefit the group as well as its individual members.

Within a heterogeneous-group environment, all members of a group take responsibility not only for their own learning but for that of their teammates as well. For example, following a presentation on rhythm and meter in poetry, students might gather into groups to practice distinguishing various meters (such as iambic pentameter, dactylic hexameter, and so on). Group members who quickly grasp the concepts can help fellow students mark feet and syllables in practice poems. In this way, strong students practice and strengthen their own knowledge through peer coaching while other students receive necessary individual instruction.

Why Create Mixed Ability Groups?

Small heterogeneous groups help students develop and improve communication skills needed both within and outside the classroom. By discussing literature in small groups, for example, students learn to articulate their ideas and to comprehend the logic behind others' statements and viewpoints. Encounters with different personalities and perspectives allow students to see the ambiguities and complexities inherent in any issue.

The mixed ability small-group approach to classroom organization promotes peer interaction and provides a comfortable forum for discussion. In traditional whole-class situations, only one person speaks at a time, and the period may end before everyone has had a chance to participate. Small-group discussions, on the other hand, allow students plenty of opportunity to voice their opinions and to engage in dialogue. Students who are reluctant to address the entire class will likely feel more comfortable sharing ideas in a small group of peers. Less able students have a chance to practice and pose questions they might hesitate to ask in a whole-class situation. Maximally heterogeneous classrooms encourage students to interact and achieve in ways and at levels not easily reached in other settings.

Problem solving is also enhanced by small-group work. Members of the group pool their resources, collaborating on difficult assignments and working together as peer tutors. For example, students who are having difficulty interpreting a poem or recognizing figures of speech can look to their classmates for help. When confronted with a challenging task, such as what to say in the opening paragraph of an essay about an author, students can consult one another, listing as many possible suggestions as they can within a five- or ten-minute period and reserving the evaluation of their ideas for later.

The mixed ability small-group approach provides students an ideal forum to

- read aloud to each other and help with explication/interpretation
- discuss and read literature
- study and practice literary concepts, using their combined knowledge to help each other learn
- write together and act as an audience for one another's writing
- help one another study/prepare for tests
- develop group projects (reports, book reviews, research papers, poems, and stories)
- prepare formal presentations (such as panel discussions)

How to Create Mixed Ability Groups

In creating small mixed ability groups, the teacher may want to consider the following additional factors:

- heterogeneity
- number of members
- length of time

A successful small group is heterogeneous, including a mix of high, average, and low achievers (achievement and ability are not necessarily the same thing), boys and girls, and students of any social and ethnic groups in the class. This grouping strategy promotes appreciation of and tolerance for diversity.

Another factor in creating small groups is the number of students. Many teachers have

discovered five to be an optimum number. In any case, odd numbers—three or five—may work best, as groups with even numbers of students tend to break up into pairs and stop working together as a unit.

The length of time a group works together is also important. Keeping a single group intact (that is, not changing members) is recommended, especially when students are working on long projects, sharing writing tasks, or responding to literature through the expression of personal experiences or feelings. Over time, group members tend to develop camaraderie and empathy for each other. As a result, they become increasingly comfortable sharing their thoughts.

The teacher's role in facilitating a heterogeneous small-group learning environment is to

- identify students' instructional objective
- form groups (consider the number of students in each group, how to group, length of time group works together)
- assign students to groups
- explain tasks and goals clearly
- explain criteria for success and give students a hard copy of these criteria (for example, to ensure that all students participate, everyone in group must speak once before any take a second turn)
- monitor and intervene, if necessary
- provide closure to group work, including synthesis or summary of the results of the learning. This may include soliciting student feedback about the activity.
- evaluate the group process and the final product

Specific Group Activities

The following activities may be used by mixed ability groups and can be especially helpful for struggling readers. The activities are divided into three sections: Access the Text, Reading Comprehension, and General Meaning-Making. Some activities are designed for work in pairs and may be adapted for use in a group setting.

Access the Text: Fluency Activities

- **Echo Reading** This activity can be used when it is important that all students have access to a text. Students of differing reading abilities can share in the process of reading a text. A fluent reader reads aloud while another reader reads along silently and then echoes what the first student says. Partners read a passage with one partner repeating what the first partner reads aloud.

- **Partner Reading** Partner Reading gives all students a chance to read aloud with a partner. Students read the story silently first. Then, students take turns reading the story aloud with partners, alternating readers after each paragraph. As one partner reads, the listener follows along and corrects any errors the reader makes, such as mispronunciations, omissions, and so on.

- **Popcorn Reading** This activity can be used to give every student a chance to share in the reading of a text and can be used to prepare students to explore a piece of literature in depth. Students take turns reading a text aloud. In small groups one person reads aloud while others in the group follow along. When he or she chooses, the reader says "popcorn" and the name of someone else in the group. Then, the named person reads aloud and then "pops" to another group member.

- **Break-in Reading** One variation of Popcorn Reading is Break-in Reading, in which one person reads aloud while others follow along. When another student in the group wants to read aloud, they "break in" and the other reader returns to following along with the group.

- **Words Out Loud** Words Out Loud gives students an opportunity to become familiar with vocabulary words in a text. Students are given a list of new or difficult words from the text. After the teacher presents the words, students practice reading their lists with partners or in small groups until they can read the words smoothly. Students should be able to read the words in any order without hesitating or stumbling.

Reading Comprehension: Developing an Understanding of the Text

- **Story Impressions** This prereading activity makes use of background knowledge to improve literary comprehension through prediction. The teacher selects key words about plot, setting, and character from the assigned story. The teacher lists the words connected by arrows to show the order of the key words in the story. Students read the words and make predictions about the story either as a whole class or as a small-group activity. Using the predictions generated, small groups of three to four students write a collaborative story. Students independently read the assigned story and in their writing groups compare the predicted version with the real version.

- **Think Aloud** Think Aloud is a reading strategy that emphasizes thinking processes and improves comprehension. The teacher first models with a passage that is both new and difficult and then has pairs of students (one with good comprehension skills and one with difficulties) practice the strategy. To model, the teacher reads a passage and breaks in at points to demonstrate comprehension strategies such as predicting, summarizing, making analogies, and using fix-up strategies. For example, the teacher may read a portion of a passage to the class and then summarize aloud what he or she has just read. For pairs practice, one student reads orally and thinks aloud while the other listens and adds comments to what the reader says. Then, roles are switched. Finally, students are encouraged to do the activity independently.

- **Think-Pair-Share** This prereading activity draws on students' background knowledge about the topic or theme of a selection. Students first independently develop their own definitions of a topic word (for example, *love*). Then, in small groups of two or three, students work together to come up with a group definition before sharing it with the entire class.

General Meaning-Making: Synthesis Activities

- **Charting** This is a synthesizing activity in which the elements of a work (for example, themes, symbols, and so on) are drawn on a large piece of paper for later presentation. The activity may be done during or after reading a text. The teacher divides students into small groups when the reading of the selection is completed. Groups then create charts using lines, words, and color to make sense of the literature in a new and different way that will be shared with the class.

- **Duologue** This activity can help students to develop an understanding of the thoughts and actions of two characters. The activity consists of a conversation between two students who assume the personae of characters in a piece of literature. After reading a piece of literature, students choose a scene from the story in which an unrecorded conversation *could* have taken place between two characters. Students talk to each other in character and develop a conversation as it might have occurred if it were incorporated into the story.

- **Found Poem** This postreading activity enables students to return to a text to focus on vivid words and phrases that contribute to the meaning of the text. A Found Poem is a collection of "luminous" words or phrases that are extracted from a text. When read aloud, these words or phrases form a poem that expresses the essence of that text. The Found Poem can be created after a chunk of text has been read or after an entire text has been read. Groups of at least three students look back at the text to select approximately eight luminous words or phrases (not sentences or paragraphs) that they feel best express the essence of the text. After each group has narrowed their selection to no more than four words or phrases, the groups should take turns reading one word or phrase without interruption between groups. The class, together, will have created a Found Poem about the selection.

- **Hot Seat** This activity gives each student an opportunity to assume the persona of a character in literature. After a portion of text has been read, students form small groups of three to five students. In groups each student assumes a different role and takes a turn responding to questions (in character) posed by other group members. The questions asked may focus on character motivation and feelings about the consequences of action. Hot Seat can also be used as a whole-class activity.

- **Reciprocal Teaching** This is an activity that teaches students to focus on what they are reading by developing and answering questions and by providing summaries. This activity can be used at any point during the study of a text. The teacher should model this activity before students attempt it on their own. First, all students in a pair or small group silently read a portion of the text. One student asks his or her partner or the rest of the group questions that came to mind about the reading—questions about content, relations to other lessons or selections, and so on. The partner or group answers as many questions as possible. For the next section of the text, the roles are reversed or exchanged, with another student asking questions and the partner or group answering them. At teacher-designated stopping points, the reading stops and one or all students summarize what they understand of the text to that point.

- **Silent Dialogue** The purpose of this activity is to help students make connections between two pieces of literature or to develop an understanding of the behavior of two characters in the same text. This is a silent written activity among a small group of students who each assume the persona of a character in literature. After a piece of literature is read or after two different literary works have been read, the teacher groups students (two to three per group) and has each group member select a character. The teacher gives students a question, an issue, or a topic of discussion to begin the conversation. Then, students pass around one sheet of paper to write on as members "talk" to each other in character about the assigned question, issue, or topic. Students pass around their conversation papers until time is called. Students then read their scripts aloud to the class.

• **Storymap** This activity can give students a better understanding of the significance of the order in which the events of a story occur. Following the reading of a piece of literature, small groups retell important events of a story through illustrations. First, groups verbally retell a story in order to identify the main events. Group members then draw the events on a large piece of paper in a logical sequence. Finally, groups share their storymaps with the whole class.

Bibliography

Adams, P. E. "Teaching *Romeo and Juliet* in the Nontracked English Classroom." *Journal of Reading* 38 (1995): 424–431.

Baumann, I. F., Seifert-Kessell, N., and Jones, L. A. "Effect of Think-Aloud Instruction on Elementary Students' Comprehension Monitoring Abilities." *Journal of Reading Behavior* 24 (1992): 143–172.

Bromley, K. D. *Webbing with Literature: Creating Story Maps with Children's Books.* 2nd ed. Boston: Allyn & Bacon, 1996.

Lyman, F. T. "The Responsive Classroom Discussion: The Inclusion of All Students." In A. Anderson (Ed.), *Mainstreaming Digest,* College Park: University of Maryland Press (1981): 109–113.

McGinley, W. J., and Denner, P. R. "Story Impressions: A Prereading/Writing Activity." *Journal of Reading* 31 (1987): 248–253.

Palinscar, A. S., and Brown, A. L. "Reciprocal Teaching of Comprehension-Fostering and Comprehension-Monitoring Activities." *Cognition and Instruction* 1 (1984): 117–175.

Focus on English-Language Learners: Characteristics, Diagnosis, and Best Practices

Throughout *Elements of Literature* you will find strategies and activities designed to help English-language learners become active participants in classroom learning communities with their English-speaking peers. Based on current and proven practices for teaching content area subject matter to ELL students, these strategies and activities reflect important ideas about the learner's role and about language and communication.

More specifically, the strategies in *Holt Reading Solutions* address the needs of ELL students who are in the early advanced stage of English language acquisition. It is important to note that even though these students may demonstrate oral language proficiency, their proficiency with written language may be behind. The use of intervention strategies begins by identifying where students are having difficulty with language and why, and then guiding them toward strategies that they can use to handle various problems.

Goals for ELL Students

- To facilitate the development of academic language in order to promote concept acquisition
- To facilitate the development of vocabulary required to learn new concepts
- To facilitate the production of oral and written language to express new concepts

The ELL Student and Learning Needs

Understanding the ELL Student

ELL students probably come from cultures with different traditions and routines. If they were born abroad, ELL students must become familiar with a new environment, a new culture, a new country, a new neighborhood, and a new school. Take into account the following points while working with ELL students in your classroom:

- ELL students may be experiencing culture shock and feel overwhelmed by all of the changes in their environments.

- Many ELL students have experienced deprivation and loss. They may have left people, belongings, and surroundings that were important to their lives. Therefore, they may feel sad or angry about living in a new country.

- ELL students may feel isolated because they do not know English well and do not understand the practices and the traditions in their new environments. They need to feel accepted and encouraged in order to gain confidence and experience a rise in self-esteem.

Detecting ELL Students' Difficulties

Since concept acquisition and development are intricately related to language ability, difficulties related to language acquisition may prevent students from developing new concepts fully. It is important to recognize when ELL students experience such difficulties so that you can help them by reteaching a lesson, reinforcing a learning activity, or clarifying an idea previously presented. Below are some of the classroom behaviors that may be indicative of the difficulties related to the development of academic language.

Behaviors That Indicate Problems

Behavior	Example
Lack of participation	The student may put his or her head down or refuse to answer a question.
Incorrect responses	The student continually gives incorrect responses even when questions have been simplified or additional prompts have been provided.
Mixing native language and English	The student speaks or writes in both English and his or her native language because a concept is not completely understood.
Over- or under-extension of concepts	The student fails to recognize examples of a concept (under) or includes examples that are not part of the concept (over).
Misunderstanding	The student may not be able to answer questions or follow directions because he or she does not understand what is being asked.
Difficulty in literal or inferential reading comprehension	The student may not be familiar with the words in the text or the ideas that the words represent. The student may not have prior knowledge of a concept.
Native language interference	The student may inappropriately generalize native language elements into English. For example, Spanish-speaking students may omit the verbs do, does, and did in interrogative phrases or sentences since in Spanish they are not used.
Cultural miscues	The student may not have prior knowledge or personal experiences from which to draw a correct response.
Inappropriate rhythm	The student may not be familiar with the words or punctuation within a text.
Uneasiness in using idioms and expressions	The student may translate an idiom word-for-word. Therefore, the student may be confused by the meaning.

General Strategies for Instructing ELL Students

By recognizing ELL students' personal situations and identifying their difficulties, you can address their learning needs better. Following are general strategies you can use to motivate ELL students and to support their learning.

- Recognize that the level of literacy achievement in the students' native languages may be obscured by a lack of facility with the English language.

- Note that ELL students may show more ability to express themselves in a social situation than in a learning situation. Social and academic English vary considerably, so classroom practices should take this into account.

- Recognize that it takes time to learn concepts in a familiar language, let alone a new one. ELL students need time to show their proficiency in English.

- Recognize that ELL students' prior knowledge bases were not developed around the cultural traditions of English. They will need help in developing strategies to activate their own prior knowledge, which is important to constructing meaning.

- Draw analogies to past experiences and provide opportunities for students to share their own experiences. This will help ELL students activate their prior knowledge.

- Help ELL students deal with culturally unfamiliar topics by doing what you do when you introduce a new topic to the entire class: Place it in a familiar context. Bring the topic to life and encourage students to draw upon their personal experiences and knowledge.

- Use role-playing, objects, pictures, and graphic organizers to create associations and support meaning. Use gestures and facial expressions to cue feelings and moods.

- Paraphrase questions. By restating questions, you can reinforce ELL students' existing knowledge and encourage the acquisition of new language.

- To determine if students understand new material, ask questions and encourage ELL students to offer explanations and summaries.

- To simplify a question, try replacing lengthy or complex sentences with shorter, declarative phrases or sentences.

- Pair ELL students with proficient native English speakers. Heterogeneous grouping allows the modeling of English—both social and academic—to occur in a natural context. Cooperative-learning situations also help all students recognize the value of cultural and ethnic diversity.

Strategies to Facilitate Language Development

The following are strategies and activities that can be used for all ELL students or for those students who require additional support in vocabulary and concept development, reading, writing, and understanding and producing oral language. When using any of these strategies, explain and model the strategies to students so that they can integrate these as part of their own learning strategies. The activities can be adapted to any unit or topic.

Vocabulary Development/Concept Development

You can facilitate the acquisition of new vocabulary and new concepts by using activities or materials that provide a context familiar to the students.

- **Use context-rich activities.** Demonstrate the use of new vocabulary in situations related to ELL students' experiences. Where appropriate, use the context provided by concepts or literature the students have already learned. The use of the classroom, the school, and the students' environment to build, develop, and exemplify new vocabulary and concepts provides context in the present, which makes the activity more concrete to the student.

- **Control the content.** When teaching new vocabulary, present words and phrases embedded in sentences or text well known to ELL students. Each sentence or portion of text should focus on only one new word or phrase. This allows the students to concentrate on the acquisition of the target language without having to be concerned with new vocabulary and new concepts at the same time.

- **Control the vocabulary.** When introducing and developing new concepts, control the complexity of the language. Learning new concepts and new vocabulary at the same time is loaded with too many unknowns, which tend to impede the acquisition of new material. Therefore, use language that does not present difficulties so that the focus is on the new concept.

Reading Comprehension

The greatest challenge in the acquisition of new academic language and new concepts is to make text comprehensible to students so that concept development can proceed logically.

- **Group text in small units.** Break long text into smaller units such as paragraphs. Well-constructed paragraphs usually have one main idea with supporting details, so they can stand alone without losing meaning. Use these units to identify the students' difficulties and teach to those areas. After working with the target paragraphs, reconstruct the whole text and restate the active-reading questions or the goal of the reading.

- **Identify main ideas.** Identify the main idea in the text as well as the supporting details. Explain to ELL students how the details support the main idea.

- **Paraphrase and rephrase text.** Simplify text by paraphrasing and rephrasing sections of text, such as sentences or short paragraphs, using language familiar to ELL students. Break down complex sentences into simple sentences. Help clarify the intention and meaning of each sentence, and reconstruct the original sentence afterward.

Listening

Multiple opportunities for listening, with different goals, enhance the development of language comprehension.

- **Promote active, focused listening.** Provide different goals for listening. For example, ask ELL students to listen for specific vocabulary related to a concept during an oral discussion. Then, have students write on a piece of paper the target words and the phrases or sentences in which the target words are embedded. Students can add to this list as you continue the discussion.

- **Use checklists.** Provide lists of words and have ELL students check the ones they hear during a discussion or an oral reading activity. This strategy will reinforce the words that are necessary in understanding a concept.

- **Use text.** Provide ELL students with a hard copy of the text to which they are listening. Have them focus on different elements of diction, such as emphasis, rhythm, and accentuation. For example, students can highlight words that they notice are emphasized during a reading.

- **Ask questions.** Provide questions to ELL students that will need to be answered after listening to a discussion, an oral reading activity, or an audiotape. This allows you to check their understanding of what they have heard.

Speaking

ELL students should be encouraged to practice their linguistic skills in academic arenas. Oral activities in which ELL students are prompted to voice their opinions or share personal experiences help them build confidence in their speaking abilities.

- **Ensure comprehension.** When ELL students have difficulties in presenting oral materials, ensure comprehension of the material by clarifying, reviewing, and discussing the concepts and the vocabulary.

- **Model and tape the presentation.** Provide ELL students with a taped model presentation of their material (you or a proficient English-speaking student can record it). Help students analyze the patterns and rhythms of the language, and encourage several listening sessions. Have students practice their oral presentations with a group of peers.

Other Resources

Specific writing, listening, and speaking strategies for ELL students appear in the Lesson Plans for Language Development section of *Workshop Resources: Writing, Listening, and Speaking.*

Student Self-Monitoring

By monitoring their own learning, ELL students are able to recognize the strategies that work best for them when they encounter difficulties. Consider the following activities to help students monitor their learning:

- Encourage ELL students to check their comprehension when reading or listening. To do this, students can summarize information or answer questions.

- Ask ELL students to identify (1) the difficulties they encounter when learning new lessons and (2) the strategies that work for them. Then, assist students in developing a plan that includes specific strategies that will help them achieve learning. Finally, have students evaluate their plans by discussing how their plans worked and what changes they may need to make in the future.

By providing ELL students with different activities and strategies, you can help them achieve the goals of developing academic language, acquiring vocabulary to learn new concepts, and producing oral and written language. More important, though, you are providing a nonthreatening environment in which ELL students become more self-confident and capable of many levels of communication.

Phonics Chart

- Encourage students to experiment with sounds from their native language as well as sounds from English. Celebrate students' languages. After all, English words derive from as many as 100 other languages.
- Focus on clearing up confusion rather than on correcting pronunciation. If a student says *ban* for *van*, just repeat the correct pronunciation, "Yes, that's a *van*."

- Avoid phonics activities with no oral component.

Consider your work in meeting diverse needs as an opportunity to stretch yourself and make yourself an ever-better teacher. Embrace the challenge.

Similarities across languages which can result in confusion with reading and spelling

Problem Contrast	Chinese	French	Greek	Italian	Japanese	Korean	Spanish	Urdu	Vietnamese
/ā/-/a/			X	X	X	X		X	
/ā/-/e/			X	X	X	X	X	X	X
/a/-/e/	X		X	X	X	X	X	X	X
/a/-/o/	X	X	X	X	X	X	X	X	X
/a/-/u/	X		X	X	X		X	X	
/ē/-/i/	X	X	X	X	X	X	X	X	X
/e/-/u/	X		X	X			X	X	
/ō/-/o/	X		X	X	X		X	X	X
/o/-/ô/	X		X		X	X	X	X	X
/o/-/u/	X		X	X	X		X		X
/u/-/o͞o/	X	X	X	X			X	X	X
/u/-/o͝o/	X		X		X		X		X
/u/-/ô/	X		X	X	X	X	X	X	
/o͞o/-/o͝o/	X	X		X		X	X	X	
/b/-/p/	X					X	X		X
/b/-/v/			X		X	X	X		
/ch/-/j/				X		X	X		X
/ch/-/sh/	X	X	X		X	X	X		X
/d/-/th/	X			X	X	X	X	X	X
/f/-/th/				X		X	X	X	X
/l/-/r/	X				X	X	X		X
/n/-/ng/	X	X	X	X	X		X	X	
/s/-/sh/			X	X	X	X	X		X
/s/-/th/	X	X		X	X	X	X	X	X
/s/-/z/	X		X	X		X	X		X
/sh/-/th/				X	X	X	X	X	X
/t/-/th/	X			X	X	X	X	X	X
/th/-/th/	X	X		X	X	X	X	X	X
/th/-/z/	X	X	X	X	X	X	X	X	X

From *The ESL Teacher's Book of Lists*, ©1993 by The Center for Applied Research in Education.

Decoding: Phonics Analysis

Consonants

Initial Correspondences /b/b, /d/d, /p/p
Some ELL students, including speakers of Chinese, Samoan, and Korean, may have difficulty differentiating the initial sound of *bat* from the initial sound of *pat* and *dad*.

Initial Correspondences /f/f, /p/p, /v/v
Some ELL students, including speakers of Tagalog and Vietnamese, have difficulty differentiating the initial sound of *fat* from the initial sound of *pat* or *vat*. Students must be able to hear and produce these different sounds in order to become successful readers of English.

Initial Correspondence /v/v, /b/b
Spanish-speaking students may have difficulty differentiating the initial sound of *bat* from the initial sound of *vat*, since they are used to pronouncing /b/ when the letter *v* appears at the beginning of a word. In pronouncing English words that begin with *v*, these students often substitute /b/ for /v/; thus *vest* becomes *best*, and *very* becomes *berry*.

Initial Correspondences /j/j, /y/y, /ch/ch
The sound /j/ in *jar* is difficult for ELL students who often confuse or interchange this sound with /ch/ or /y/, causing major comprehension difficulties. In addition, Spanish has a similar sound /y/ that is often substituted for the sound /j/, resulting in confusion when students try to differentiate between the words *jam* and *yam*.

Initial Correspondence /s/c,s
The letter-sound association for *c* usually follows the same generalizations in both English and Spanish. When *c* is followed by the letter *e* or *i*, it stands for the sound /s/; when *c* is followed by the letter *a*, *o*, or *u*, it stands for the sound /k/. In some Spanish dialects, when the letter *c* is followed by the letter *e* or *i*, the *c* stands for the sound /th/. Therefore, some Spanish-speaking students might have difficulty with this sound.

Initial Correspondence /s/s, /z/z
The sound /z/ is difficult for many ELL students to master because often it is not found in their native language. It is especially difficult for students to differentiate this sound from the sound /s/.

Initial Correspondence /n/n,kn; /l/l
The sound /n/ at the beginning of a word seems to present no special difficulties for most ELL students. However, students whose native language is Chinese, sometimes have difficulty differentiating this sound from the sound /l/ at the beginning of *lot*.

Initial Correspondence /r/r,wr; /l/l
Some ELL students, including speakers of Chinese, Japanese, Korean, Vietnamese, and Thai, may have great difficulty differentiating /r/ as in *rip* from /l/ as in *lip* . These students often pronounce both *lip* and *rip* with the beginning sound /l/.

Initial Correspondence /kw/qu, /w/w
Some ELL students have difficulty differentiating the initial sound /kw/ as in *queen* from the initial sound /w/ as in *wet*.

Initial Correspondence /v/v, /w/w
Some ELL students, including speakers of Chinese, Arabic, German, Samoan, and Thai, have difficulty differentiating /w/ as in *wet* from /v/ as in *van* . These students need much practice producing the sound /w/ in order to avoid confusing it with the sound /v/.

Initial Correspondence /g/g; /k/k,c
Some ELL students, especially speakers of Korean, Samoan, Vietnamese, Thai, and Indonesian, have difficulty differentiating /k/ as in *cat* and *king* from /g/ as in *go*. Speakers of Vietnamese and Thai especially have difficulty with these two sounds when they appear at the end of a word.

Initial Correspondence /h/h, /j/j, /hw/wh

Students who already read in Spanish may have difficulty with these sound-symbol correspondences, because in Spanish the letter *h* is silent. Students may forget to pronounce this sound in trying to decode English words, saying for example, /ot/ for *hot* and /at/ for *hat*. Because the sound /h/ is represented by the letter *j* in Spanish, this letter may be used in spelling English words that begin with *h*. Students may write *jat* for *hat, jot* for *hot, jouse* for *house,* and so on.

In addition, some ELL students may have difficulty differentiating the beginning sound of *hat* from the beginning sound of *what*. They will need practice in differentiating these two sounds.

Initial Correspondence /fr/fr, /fl/fl

The initial /fr/*fr* does not usually present difficulty for students who speak Spanish since these sounds are commonly found in Spanish. However, /fr/*fr* does present difficulty for students who speak Chinese or other Asian languages, especially when differentiating /fr/*fr* from /fl/*fl.*

Initial Correspondences /gr/gr, /dr/dr, /br/br

Some ELL students, especially speakers of Chinese and Vietnamese, may have difficulty differentiating the initial sounds of *grass* from the initial sounds of *broom* and *dress.* Much practice is needed to help students hear and produce these sounds in English in order to avoid problems when they start to work with the written symbols that represent these sounds.

Initial Correspondences /th/th, /thr/thr, /t/t

Some ELL students, especially Spanish-speaking students, may have difficulty pronouncing words that begin with /th/ and /thr/, and differentiating these sounds from/t/. Much practice is needed to help students hear and produce these sounds in English in order to avoid problems when they start to work with the written symbols that represent these sounds.

Initial Correspondences /kr/cr, /kl/cl, /gl/gl

Some ELL students, especially speakers of Chinese or Vietnamese, may have difficulty with these clusters. These clusters do not present difficulty for Spanish-speaking students since they are commonly found in the Spanish language.

Initial Correspondences /skr/scr; /sk/sk,sc; /kr/cr

The initial consonant clusters /skr/*scr* and /sk/*sk,sc* may be difficult for ELL students of various language backgrounds. Spanish-speaking students have difficulty with the *s*-plus-consonant pronunciation. Speakers of other languages may have difficulty with the initial consonant cluster /kr/*cr.*

Initial Correspondences /st/st; /str/str; /sk/sk, sch, sc

The majority of ELL students, especially those who speak Spanish, have difficulty pronouncing these consonant clusters in the initial position. In Spanish, these clusters never appear at the beginning of a word. Thus students tend to add the /e/ sound in front of a word: *school*/sko͞ol becomes /esko͞ol/ and *street* is pronounced /estrēt/.

Initial Correspondences /tr/tr, /thr/thr, /t/t

The consonant clusters /tr/ and /thr/ are difficult for ELL students whose native languages do not have these sounds in combination. Some students have difficulty differentiating among /tr/, /thr/, /t/, and /t/ with the vowel *i.*

Initial Correspondences /sl/sl, /pl/pl

The consonant cluster *sl* presents some difficulty for Spanish-speaking students who are not used to encountering the *s*-plus-consonant sound at the beginning of words. These students often add the /e/ sound in front of a word; for example, *sleep* is pronounced /eslēp/. The /pl/ sound does not present difficulty for speakers of Spanish because it is common in Spanish. However, speakers of Chinese and Vietnamese, among others, may find it difficult to master.

Initial Correspondences /sp/sp, /sm/sm

The majority of ELL students have difficulty pronouncing the consonant clusters *sp* and *sm* in the initial position. In Spanish, these clusters never appear at the beginning of words. Often Spanish-speaking students add /e/ before the /s/; thus *spot* is pronounced /espot/.

Initial Correspondence /sh/sh, /ch/ch

The sound /sh/ presents difficulty for many ELL students because it is not found in most languages. The sound /ch/ seems to be more common. Therefore many students do not distinguish between /sh/ and /ch/ and tend to substitute one for the other, saying *cheep* for *sheep* and *chin* for *shin*. This is particularly true of Spanish-speaking students.

Final Correspondences /p/p, /b/b

Spanish-speaking students may have difficulty hearing the final sound /p/ and may confuse this sound with the final sound /b/, since the final sound /b/ and /p/ do not often occur in Spanish.

Final Correspondences /t/t, /d/d

Some ELL students may have difficulty differentiating the final sound of *bat* from the final sound of *dad*. Much practice is needed to help students hear and produce these sounds in English to avoid problems when starting to work with the written symbols that represent these sounds.

Final Correspondences /ks/x; /s/s,ss

Final consonants can present a problem, especially for students whose native languages do not emphasize these consonants as much as English does. In Spanish, for example, there are only a few consonants that appear at the end of words (*n,s,z,d,l,j*). Many Spanish-speaking people tend to drop the final consonant sound in conversation; for example, *reloj* becomes *relo*.

Final Correspondences /z/z,zz; /s/s,ss

The sound /z/ is difficult for many ELL students to master because often it is not found in their native languages. It is especially difficult for students to differentiate this sound from the sound /s/.

Final Correspondences /k/k,ck; /g/g

The final sound /g/ may be difficult for Spanish-speaking students since this sound never occurs at the end of Spanish words. Students may have difficulty hearing this sound and may pronounce it as the sound /k/ or omit the sound completely.

Final Correspondences /f/f, ff; /p/p

Some ELL students may have difficulty differentiating the final sound of *wife* from the final sound of *wipe*. Much practice is needed to help students hear and produce these sounds in English in order to avoid problems when they start to work with the written symbols that represent these sounds.

Final Correspondences /p/p, /t/t

Some ELL students may have difficulty differentiating the final sound of *ape* from the final sound of *ate*. Much practice is needed to help students hear and produce these sounds in English in order to avoid problems when they start to work with the written symbols that represent these sounds.

Final Correspondences /d/d, /b/b

Some ELL students may have difficulty differentiating the final sound of *lad* from the final sound of *lab*. Much practice is needed to help students hear and produce these sounds in English in order to avoid problems when they start to work with the written symbols that represent these sounds.

Final Correspondences /ld/ld, /nt/nt, /nd/nd

Some ELL students may have difficulty differentiating the final sounds of *old* from the final sounds of *lint* and *find*. Having two consonant sounds at the end of a word increases the difficulty. Much practice is needed to help students hear and produce these sounds in English in order to avoid problems when they start to work with the written symbols that represent these sounds.

Final Correspondences /ng/ng, /ngk/nk

Some ELL students may have difficulty differentiating the final sounds of *sink* from the final sounds of *sing*. Much practice is needed to help students hear and produce these sounds in English in order to avoid problems when they start to work with the written symbols that represent these sounds.

Final Correspondences /s/s,ss; /st/st

Some ELL students may have difficulty differentiating the final sound of *gas* from the final sounds of *last*. Much practice is needed to help students hear and produce these sounds in English in order to avoid problems when they start to work with the written symbols that represent these sounds.

Final Correspondences /sh/sh; /ch/ch,tch

Some ELL students may have difficulty differentiating the final sound of *mush* from the final sound of *much*. Much practice is needed to help students hear and produce these sounds in English in order to avoid problems when they start to work with the written symbols that represent these sounds.

Final Correspondences /th/th, /t/t

Some ELL students, especially speakers of Spanish, may have difficulty differentiating the final sound of *bat* from the final sound of *bath*. Much practice is needed to help students hear and produce these sounds in English in order to avoid problems when they start to work with the written symbols that represent these sounds.

Vowels

Vowel Correspondences /a/a, /e/e

Short vowel sounds are the most difficult for ELL students to master. These create problems when students try to learn and apply the concept of rhyming; ELL students have difficulty differentiating the short vowel sound in *bat* from the short vowel sound in *bet*. Much practice is needed to help students hear and produce these sounds in English in order to avoid problems when they start to work with the written symbols that represent these sounds.

Vowel Correspondences /o/o, /u/u

The vowel sound in *cot* often causes great difficulty for students who speak Spanish, Chinese, Vietnamese, Tagalog, and Thai. This sound must be practiced frequently.

Vowel Correspondences /i/i, /ē/ee, ea, e_e

Words with the short *i* vowel sound are difficult for speakers of Spanish, Chinese, Vietnamese, and Tagalog, among others. ELL students in general have difficulty pronouncing this sound as they tend to confuse it with the long *e* vowel sound. Spanish-speaking students in particular have the tendency to replace the short *i* sound with the long *e* sound.

Vowel Correspondences /u/u, /a/a, /e/e

The vowel sound in *up* is one of the most difficult for ELL students to master because it does not exist in many languages and yet is one of the most common sounds in English. ELL students often have difficulty differentiating this sound from the vowel sounds in *bat* and *bet*. Much practice is needed to help students hear and produce these sounds in English in order to avoid problems when they start to work with the written symbols that represent these sounds.

Vowel Correspondences /o/o, /ō/oa, o_e; /ô/au, aw

The vowel sound in *cot* often causes great difficulty for ELL students who speak Spanish, Chinese, Vietnamese, Tagalog, or Thai. This sound must be practiced frequently, especially to differentiate it from the vowel sound in *coat* and *caught*. In addition, when the letters *oa* come together in Spanish, they stand for two separate sounds. Therefore, many Spanish-speaking students may have difficulty understanding that the letters *oa* can stand for one sound in English.

Vowel Correspondences /ā/a_e, /e/e

It is difficult for ELL students who speak Vietnamese, Spanish, or Tagalog to differentiate between the vowel sound in *race* and the vowel sound in *pet*. Much practice is needed to help students hear and produce these sounds in English in order to avoid problems when they start to work with the written symbols that represent these sounds.

Vowel Correspondences /i/i_e, /a/a

The vowel sound in *bike* may present a problem for some ELL students who have difficulty differentiating this sound from the vowel sound in *bat*. Much practice is needed to help students hear and produce these sounds in English in order to avoid problems when they start to work with the written symbols that represent these sounds.

Overview of the Assessment Program

What is the Diagnostic Assessment for Reading Intervention?

The Diagnostic Assessment for Reading Intervention is an informal, criterion-referenced assessment designed to identify a student's reading level and to diagnose the specific reading comprehension skills that need instructional attention. The Diagnostic Assessment for Reading Intervention was designed specifically for "struggling readers" or students who are having difficulty comprehending grade-level materials.

The Diagnostic Assessment for Reading Intervention assesses a student's ability to read literary texts and informational texts. For ease of use, the assessment is limited to multiple-choice items.

A separate Diagnostic Assessment for Reading Intervention is available for each grade from 6 through 12.

Who should take the Diagnostic Assessment for Reading Intervention?

Administer this diagnostic to students whom you have identified as reading below grade level and/or to students who score poorly on the Entry-Level Test found in *Holt Assessment: Literature, Reading and Vocabulary.*

What types of passages are found in the Diagnostic Assessment for Reading Intervention?

Each Diagnostic Assessment for Reading Intervention consists of four reading passages—two literary passages and two informational passages.

Literary passages are primarily narrative. They may be short stories, literary essays (personal narratives), excerpts from longer works, historical fiction, or fables and folk tales.

Informational (subject-matter centered) passages use language to provide information, present new ideas, solve problems, and raise questions. They may be subject-matter texts, magazine or newspaper articles, editorials, informational essays, biographies, or consumer materials.

What comprehension skills does the Diagnostic Assessment for Reading Intervention measure?

The Diagnostic Assessment for Reading Intervention assesses the following ten important reading comprehension skills.

Literary Comprehension Skills

- **Make predictions:** Determine the most likely outcomes; predict ideas or events that may take place; give a rationale for predictions.

- **Understand characters:** Recognize and understand characters' traits; determine characters' motivation and feelings based on clues in the text; understand character relationships; analyze interactions between main and subordinate characters; make inferences based on characters' words, actions, and reactions to other characters.

- **Recognize theme:** Identify ideas and insights about life and human nature expressed in literature.

- **Understand plot and sequence of events:** Analyze the development of plot in a narrative text; recognize the basic situation or central conflict, the events or complications related to the central conflict, the climax, and the resolution; know how cause-effect relationships affect the plot; understand where and when a story takes place; and trace the author's development of time and sequence.

- **Compare and contrast:** Compare and contrast aspects of narrative texts such as characters, settings, plot elements, and themes.

Informational Comprehension Skills

- **Recognize author's purpose:** Determine the author's message, intent, and attitude toward the subject, and recognize the effects of these elements on the text.

- **Identify main idea and important details:** Determine central ideas in informational text, and identify important details that support the central ideas.

- **Make inferences:** Make informed judgments based on evidence from the text, and use personal observations and prior experience to make and confirm inferences.

- **Summarize information:** Compare original text to a summary to determine whether the summary accurately captures the ideas, includes critical details, and conveys the underlying meaning; synthesize content to demonstrate comprehension.

- **Distinguish between facts and opinions:** Recognize statements that are truthful and can be verified, and distinguish them from statements that represent the author's feelings, beliefs, or attitudes.

How long does it take to administer the Diagnostic Assessment for Reading Intervention?

The Diagnostic Assessment for Reading Intervention is not a timed test. Most students should be able to complete the entire test in one class period, or twenty to forty minutes. Students should be given ample time to complete the assessment, even if more than one class period is necessary.

What materials do I need to administer the Diagnostic Assessment for Reading Intervention?

Student materials
Each student will need a test booklet and an answer sheet. Blackline masters for these can be found beginning on page 10 in this tabbed section. Once the test booklets are photocopied and assembled, they can be reused because students mark their answers on the consumable answer sheet.

Teacher materials
The only materials the teacher needs to administer the Diagnostic Assessment for Reading Intervention are the Directions for Administering. These can be found on page 9 in this section.

How do I score the Diagnostic Assessment for Reading Intervention?

The Diagnostic Assessment for Reading Intervention can be scored in one of the following two ways.

Using the Annotated Answer Sheet
One method of scoring is to use the Annotated Answer Sheet provided. This is a facsimile of the student's Answer Sheet with the correct answer bubbles filled in. Simply place the Annotated Answer Sheet alongside a student's completed answer sheet, compare the two, and mark the items answered incorrectly.

Using the List of Correct Answers and Skills
Also included in this tabbed section is a List of Correct Answers and Skills. This list identifies the correct answer as well as the reading skill assessed by each item. To score a student's assessment, simply compare the list to a student's completed answer sheet and mark the items that were not answered correctly.

What kind of scores will I receive from the Diagnostic Assessment for Reading Intervention?

The Diagnostic Assessment for Reading Intervention yields three scores—a Total Reading Score that can be converted to a Reading Proficiency Level, a Literary Comprehension Score, and an Informational Comprehension Score.

In addition, you can create a diagnostic profile of a student's strengths and weaknesses by noting how well the student performed on each skill. Each skill is tested with four items. If a student answers three or more of the four items correctly, he or she demonstrates proficiency in that skill. If a student answers fewer than three of the four items correctly, additional instruction is needed on that skill.

How can I summarize and report a student's performance on the Diagnostic Assessment for Reading Intervention?

Included in this tabbed section is a Performance Profile. This one-page blackline master summarizes a student's performance on the Diagnostic Assessment for Reading Intervention and provides a convenient place to record scores.

To use the Performance Profile, follow these steps:

1. Make a copy of the Performance Profile for each student taking the assessment.

2. Place a blank copy of the Performance Profile alongside a student's answer sheet that has been scored.

3. Use the item numbers on the Performance Profile to determine a student's performance for each skill. Turn to the student's answer sheet to see how the student answered these items. Mark each item that was answered incorrectly.

4. Tally the number of items answered *correctly* in the "Score" column. Record the number correct beside the number possible (for example, 3/4).

5. Add up the number of items answered *correctly* for Literary Comprehension and place that number in the space provided for Total Literary Comprehension (for example, 15/20).

6. Follow the same procedure to obtain the scores for each Informational Comprehension skill, Total Informational Comprehension, and Total Reading Comprehension.

7. Use the Total Reading Comprehension score (the number of items answered correctly on the entire test) to determine a student's Reading Proficiency Level. Circle the level that applies.

What do the Reading Proficiency Levels mean?

The Reading Proficiency Levels are intended to give you a general sense of a student's overall reading ability. At the middle school and high school levels, various reading tests may yield contradictory results because of the variability of the texts that students are asked to read and because of the variability in prior knowledge about and interest in specific topics. Therefore, more general Reading Proficiency Levels like those described in the following paragraphs are recommended.

Proficient Level
A student who scores at the Proficient Level should be able to read and comprehend grade-level assignments. The student may experience some difficulty when he or she is unfamiliar with the topic or the text vocabulary and language, or when he or she lacks personal interest in the topic. Some assistance may be needed in those situations.

Basic Level
A student who scores at the Basic Level is reading one to two years below his or her grade placement. The student will almost surely experience difficulty reading grade-level assignments. However, when a student at the Basic Level is provided with assistance for handling such texts, he or she can often rise to the occasion and process grade-level texts in a meaningful way. Such students need ample introduction to a text before reading it independently, shorter portions of text to process at a time, scaffolding aids such as the interactive questions in *The Holt Reader* to use while reading, and opportunities to interact and discuss a text after reading it. If the student's first language is not English, the "Especially for ELL" teaching suggestions in the Lesson Plan section of this book will be helpful.

Below Basic Level
A student who scores at the Below Basic Level is reading more than two years below his or her grade placement. The student will experience great difficulty reading and comprehending grade-level assignments. Because of their inability to process many

of the assignments given to them, such students frequently become frustrated, demonstrate avoidance strategies, and stop trying. If such students are expected to respond to grade-level assignments, considerable support must be given to them. Selection previews, such as the Adapted Readings contained in this book, will help below-basic-level readers. Students may also listen to selections on audio CDs while following along with the original text. Additionally, students may need to be paired with student partners who can offer assistance during the reading process. Students at the Below Basic Level could profit from basic reading instruction in an individual or small-group setting. Finally, the "Especially for ELL" teaching suggestions in the Lesson Plans provide scaffolding for non–native speakers.

What diagnostic information can I obtain from the Diagnostic Assessment for Reading Intervention?

The Performance Profile is also intended to give you some insights into a student's strengths and weaknesses in reading comprehension.

Literary Comprehension Versus Informational Comprehension
One of the first aspects of student performance to consider is text type. Did the student comprehend one type of text better than the other? The Performance Profile provides both a Literary Comprehension score and an Informational Comprehension score. By comparing the two, you can get a sense of whether the student is experiencing more difficulty with a particular type of text.

The scores may suggest, for example, that the student needs more assistance when reading informational passages. Perhaps key vocabulary or a simplified adaptation of the text needs to be introduced before the student reads independently. In addition, identifying what the student already knows about a topic before reading allows you to fill in some knowledge gaps in order to make the reading more meaningful.

If, on the other hand, the student shows more difficulty reading literary passages, you will need to provide other types of assistance. Introducing characters and discussing how they are related before the student reads a narrative selection can be helpful. You might also provide a skeletal plot summary or an adaptation to guide the student before or during reading. Relating the "big ideas" in a literary selection to those in familiar stories, TV programs, or movies can also aid comprehension.

Reading Skills Analysis
Each Diagnostic Assessment for Reading Intervention measures ten reading comprehension skills—five in Literary Comprehension and five in Informational Comprehension. Four items assess each skill. Using the conventional standard of 75 percent or more correct, "mastery" is defined as at least 3 out of 4 correct. By reviewing the Score column on the Performance Profile, you can identify which skills a student has mastered and which skills need further instruction.

This information can be used to plan instruction and prescribe remediation. For example, you may want to use the lessons from the Reading Skills and Strategies section of this book to address a student's specific weaknesses. Lessons and assignments in the Student Edition could also be modified or augmented to focus on the specific weaknesses the student has demonstrated. Suggestions for skills-related modifications appear in the Lesson Plan section of this book.

Technical Report

Test Design

The Diagnostic Assessment for Reading Intervention is a series of grade-level assessments. Although a separate stand-alone assessment was developed for each grade (6 through 12), the individual assessments are interrelated to form a unified battery.

The readabilities of the passages were carefully monitored using the Dale-Chall formula and the Fry Readability Graph. On each grade-level assessment, some of the passages are below level in difficulty and some of the passages are on level. Consistency was built into the battery by systematically overlapping passages at adjacent levels.

Reading Skills

The Diagnostic Assessment for Reading Intervention assesses ten important reading comprehension skills. Each assessment consists of forty items with four items measuring each skill. Although most of the target skills remain the same across grade levels, there are some differences between the middle school and high school levels. A complete description of each skill can be found on pages 1–2 of this book.

Content Validity

The validity of an assessment refers to the adequacy and appropriateness of the interpretations one will make with it. A test is considered valid if it measures what it claims to measure. Establishing content validity is by definition a judgmental process.

The developers of the Diagnostic Assessment for Reading Intervention took a number of steps to ensure the instrument is valid. First, they surveyed a wide array of state standards at the middle school and high school levels to identify the comprehension skills that are most frequently expected of students. Those survey results formed the basis of the skills included in the Diagnostic Assessment for Reading Intervention. Second, subject matter experts trained in test construction developed specific items to match the skills assessed. Third, the items were reviewed by subject matter editors who are familiar with the standards and who checked for alignment between the items and the standards. The end result is an assessment that is valid for assessing the targeted reading comprehension skills at the middle school and high school levels.

Field Testing

To further evaluate the technical features of the Diagnostic Assessment for Reading Intervention, it was administered to a sample of students. Approximately six hundred middle school and high school students took the assessment in the spring of 2003.

An item analysis was conducted to verify that each item was functioning as intended. Item difficulty, item discrimination, and item distractors were examined.

Item Difficulty

Item difficulty is traditionally defined in terms of "p-value," the percentage of students answering the item correctly. Because the Diagnostic Assessment for Reading Intervention is intended for low-achieving readers, items with extremely low p-values were not included in the assessment.

Item Discrimination

Item discrimination is used to judge the effectiveness of an item. A "good" item is one that is answered correctly by students who score high on the overall test and answered incorrectly by students who score low on the overall test. In

Table 3—Average Point Biserial Correlations

Grade 6	Grade 7	Grade 8	Grade 9	Grade 10	Grade 11	Grade 12
.18	.40	.26	.21	.42	.36	.29

other words, the item "discriminates" between those students who possess the skill and those who don't.

Point biserial correlations were used to evaluate item discrimination. Most experts suggest that the point biserial correlations should be above .20. The table above summarizes the average point biserial correlations for each level of the Diagnostic Assessment for Reading Intervention.

Distractor Analysis

Distractor analysis is used to evaluate each option in a multiple-choice item. By examining the number and percentage of students choosing each option, one can determine if a particular option is unclear or too tempting. Any distractors that drew a higher percentage of student responses than the intended correct answer were rewritten to make them less plausible.

Reliability

The reliability of a test pertains to its consistency. Is the assessment internally consistent? Will it yield consistent scores if used repeatedly? Reliability is usually expressed in terms of a correlation coefficient with 1.0 being perfect reliability. Most experts look for reliabilities in the .90s for high-stakes assessments like standardized tests, and reliabilities in the .60s to .80s for classroom assessments. KR-20, a common statistical formula for assessment, was used to estimate the reliabilities.

Standard Error of Measurement (SEM) is a statistic used to describe the accuracy or precision of an assessment. For example, if an assessment had a SEM of 5, it would mean that there is a 68% chance that a student's true score is likely to be within plus or minus 5 of his or her actual score. In other words, the smaller the SEM, the more accurate the assessment. The table below summarizes the reliabilities and SEMs for each level of the Diagnostic Assessment for Reading Intervention.

Summary

Evidence indicates that the Diagnostic Assessment for Reading Intervention is a valid and reliable measure of reading comprehension that is appropriate for low-level readers at the middle school and high school levels. Teachers should understand, however, that no one test or assessment can possibly capture a student's reading performance. Therefore, it is recommended that the Diagnostic Assessment for Reading Intervention be combined with other measures, including teacher observation and judgment and student word samples, when you are evaluating student performance.

Table 4—Reliabilities and Standard Errors of Measurement

	Grade 6	Grade 7	Grade 8	Grade 9	Grade 10	Grade 11	Grade 12
Index of Reliability	.75	.93	.87	.85	.94	.92	.89
SEM (in raw score points)	1.85	1.91	1.86	1.78	1.91	1.95	2.05

Distribute Testing Materials

- Each student should have a test booklet that contains four reading passages and forty test items.
- Each student should have a blank Answer Sheet.

Directions

Read the following directions to students, or phrase them in your own words.

Today you are going to take a reading assessment. The purpose of this assessment is to determine how well you comprehend what you read. This assessment is not timed, so there is no need to rush.

The assessment contains four reading passages followed by multiple-choice questions. Read each passage. Then, read the questions that follow the passage. Use the Answer Sheet I have given you to fill in your answer choices. It is better to use a pencil. That way, if you wish to change your answer, you can erase your first choice and mark your new choice.

Some of the passages and questions may be easy to read; others may be more difficult. Try to do your best on all of the passages and questions. Since I want to see how well you read independently, I cannot help you while you are taking the assessment.

When you finish answering all of the questions, go back and check your work if there is time to do so.

Go ahead and begin the assessment.

When all students have completed the assessment, collect the test booklets and answer sheets.

Reading Comprehension

DIRECTIONS: Read each selection. Then, read each question and choose the best answer. Mark the space for your answer on the answer sheet you have been given.

SAMPLE

Rewarding Work

Mason had had enough. His teacher, Ms. Kresge, obviously hated him. She was constantly making him rewrite perfectly good essays and making him read thick books full of unfamiliar words. She didn't push other kids to work the way she pushed him. It wasn't fair, and he was going straight to the principal about it. Mason marched to the office but stopped short when he reached the door—there was Ms. Kresge talking to the principal! He turned to leave.

"Mason! Come back," called the principal. Mason froze. The principal continued, "Ms. Kresge was just telling me what excellent work you've been doing and what a great example you've been. I'd like to send you as a representative to the district retreat next week. You'd have to miss a day of school, hang out in the park brainstorming ideas, and eat a lot of pizza. What do you say?"

The sun burst through the window, and Mason broke into a grin.

1. Why does Ms. Kresge push Mason to do harder work?
   A because she doesn't like him
   B because she wants him to reach his potential
   C because she pushes all of her students
   D because the principal asked her to

   1. Ⓐ ● Ⓒ Ⓓ

2. What will Mason likely do the next time he gets a difficult assignment?
   A gladly complete it because he knows it will help him
   B complete it because he is afraid of failing the class
   C take the assignment to the principal to complain about it
   D refuse in front of the entire class to do the work

   2. ● Ⓑ Ⓒ Ⓓ

Reading Comprehension

Coyote and the Fire Beings

A   Long, long ago, the people of the earth had no fire to keep themselves warm. Three powerful and terrible Fire Beings kept the fire on the summit of a distant mountain. In spring and summer, when the sun warmed the earth, the people thrived, but when winter arrived, they suffered. Year after year, the tribal leaders searched in vain for a solution.

B   "Our old ones suffer terribly in this cold, and many will not survive if we do not attempt something," said one of the leaders.

C   "But we do not understand how to create fire," a woman observed.

D   "And no one is clever enough to steal it from the Fire Beings," added a young man.

E   Then a small boy addressed the leaders and said, "Perhaps one of the animals could help us."

F   "With their thick fur coats, animals have no need of fire's warmth," said an elderly woman to the boy, who was known as Swift Runner. "Besides, what animal would risk his life for us?"

G   "Coyote would," replied Swift Runner, "because he is my special companion, and he is very clever."

H   "We know how clever he is, for even our finest hunters cannot catch him," said the woman. "But what could we possibly offer him in return?"

I   "Our promise that we will not hunt him anymore," replied Swift Runner. There was a long silence as the leaders considered the boy's words.

J   "The boy speaks wisely," said one finally. To Swift Runner he said, "Go tell your friend that we will not hunt him again if he will help us."

K   So Swift Runner hurried to the broad prairie where Coyote lived and called, "Coyote! It is I, Swift Runner!" Coyote appeared, but stopped warily at some distance.

L   "Are you alone?" Coyote asked.

GO ON

Reading Comprehension

M   "Yes," replied Swift Runner, "and if you will assist my people, you will never have to fear us again."

N   "That is a tempting offer," said Coyote, "but what do you want me to do?"

O   "Help us to steal fire from the Fire Beings," said Swift Runner.

P   Coyote's sharp eyes widened in surprise. "You ask a difficult favor," he said. "The Fire Beings are powerful and cautious, and it is no simple matter to outsmart them." Then he grinned slyly and said, "But as I am extremely clever, and you are very swift, together we can accomplish this task."

Q   After traveling through forests and across prairies, Coyote and Swift Runner reached Burning Mountain. At the summit, flames rose into the sky. "There is the fire," said Coyote. "The Fire Beings guard it day and night. Stay here, and be prepared to run as soon as you hear me coming."

R   "I will wait," said Swift Runner. Then Coyote vanished into the thick trees that flanked the mountain.

S   On the mountaintop, the Fire Beings danced wildly around the flames. Coyote crept among the bushes and watched until the dancers grew weary.

T   "Time to rest," said the first Fire Being. "I will keep watch. You two go into the teepee and sleep, and I will wake you by turns."

U   Then the Fire Being sat down to guard the fire. The night grew silent except for the crackle of the flames. After a while, the Fire Being began to yawn. He rose and stretched, and then walked to the teepee, always keeping his eyes on the fire. Coyote watched every movement carefully.

V   "Get up in there!" yelled the Fire Being. "It is my turn to sleep." A sound of grumbling came from inside the teepee, and then the second Fire Being came out.

W   "All right, all right," she said grumpily, "I will take my turn." The two Fire Beings pushed and shoved each other in the entryway, and for one instant, neither was watching the fire. Hidden in the bushes, Coyote smiled to himself, and waited.

GO ON ➡

Reading Comprehension

X   The second Fire Being took her place near the fire. After a long time, she yawned and rubbed her eyes. Then she walked toward the teepee, still watching the fire. Coyote's keen eyes never even blinked.

Y   The second Fire Being approached the teepee and yelled, "Get up in there!" Once more, the sound of grumbling came from inside. Then, as the third Fire Being pushed and shoved his way out of the teepee, the second Fire Being looked away from the fire. At that moment, Coyote dashed from the bushes and grabbed a burning stick from the flames.

Z   "Someone is stealing our fire!" screamed the third Fire Being.

AA   Coyote raced down the mountainside, while, with a tremendous roar, the three Fire Beings rushed in pursuit.

BB   At the bottom of the mountain, Swift Runner heard the terrible commotion. He remembered what Coyote had told him, and prepared to run. As Coyote reached Swift Runner, he passed the burning stick into the boy's hand and cried, "Now live up to your name!"

CC   Swift Runner dashed away and ran as never before. The Fire Beings sped down the mountain, but not fast enough to catch the boy. And that is how Swift Runner and Coyote brought fire to the people. From that time on, the people kept warm in winter.

1. What is the problem in this story?

   A The tribe needs a way to keep warm in the winter.

   B The hunters cannot find enough game in the forests.

   C Animals are stealing the tribe's winter food supplies.

   D The Fire Beings are threatening to take over the tribe.

2. When Coyote first appears in the story, he keeps a distance from Swift Runner because he—

   A wants the boy to play a game

   B hopes to avoid helping the boy

   C hasn't yet become friends with the boy

   D thinks the boy might have brought a hunter

GO ON

Reading Comprehension

3. Which of the following *best* describes Coyote on the mountaintop?

   A humorous and friendly
   B patient and watchful
   C nervous and cautious
   D loud and frightening

4. Coyote is able to steal a burning stick from the fire *mainly* because the Fire Beings—

   A fall asleep inside the teepee
   B dance too wildly on the mountain
   C are busy pushing and shoving each other
   D yawn and stretch as they walk to the teepee

5. When compared with the Fire Beings, Swift Runner is—

   A older
   B faster
   C lonelier
   D stronger

6. This story shows the importance of humans' relationship with—

   A mountains
   B weather
   C animals
   D spirits

7. The Fire Beings are similar to Coyote and Swift Runner when they—

   A yell at one another
   B decide to help others
   C stay awake late at night
   D cooperate in guarding the fire

8. What *most* likely happened when Swift Runner arrived at his village with the burning stick?

   A He was treated as a hero.
   B The Fire Beings caught him.
   C He became the chief of the tribe.
   D He found the tribe had moved away.

9. How did the tribe *most* likely act toward Coyote after he gave Swift Runner the fire?

   A They avoided him.
   B They hunted him again.
   C They chased him away.
   D They treated him as a friend.

10. Which of the following *best* expresses an important idea in this story?

   A Children should not play with fire.
   B Coyotes can run faster than humans.
   C Teamwork can solve difficult problems.
   D People should not hunt animals for their fur.

STOP

Reading Comprehension

Building a Campfire

A   If you've ever gone camping, chances are you spent some time around a campfire. Whether you're backpacking in the wilderness or just roasting marshmallows in the yard, sitting by a campfire is great fun. Building a campfire sounds very simple, but doing it properly is more complicated than many people think. There are several different ways to build a campfire, and there are some important safety rules to follow.

B   The first step in building a campfire is to choose a good location. Then, clean away all the leaves, grass, or underbrush nearby. Your spot should be completely bare of everything but dirt. Also, clear the area around your spot for a distance of at least ten feet. Fires throw out burning sparks, so it is important to make sure that there is no dry grass, pine needles, or leaves that could catch fire.

C   There are three types of wood you will need for a campfire: tinder, kindling, and fuel. Tinder is material that will catch fire easily from a single match. Examples of tinder are dry pine needles, dry bark, and very thin twigs. A handful of tinder is about the right amount. One of the best things to use is the bark from a birch tree. The bark produces a good flame and will burn even when wet. Softwood such as pine or cedar is usually best because it catches fire quickly, but thin, dry hardwoods work as well.

D   The tinder needs to burn only long enough to ignite the kindling, which is the next largest type of wood you will use. Kindling includes thin sticks you find on the ground and dead branches that are still on trees. If a branch snaps off easily, it is dry and will probably burn well. If it bends instead of snapping, it is too green to use. Each branch should be about as thick as a pencil.

E   Fuel means larger pieces of wood that will burn for a long time at an even temperature. The best choices are hardwoods such as hickory, oak, beech, sugar maple, and white ash. Logs should be about a foot or two long.

GO ON ➤

Reading Comprehension

F   There are many different ways to arrange the wood for your fire. Two of the most popular arrangements are the crisscross and the teepee. For cooking, the crisscross works best because it provides an even bed of hot coals. To build a crisscross fire, lay a pair of sticks alongside each other, a foot apart. Put the tinder, with the kindling around it, in the middle. Then, put another pair of sticks crosswise on top of the first two. Keep building the stack up until it is about a foot high. To build a teepee fire, first place the tinder on the ground. Then, shove a stick into the ground so that it slants at an angle over the tinder. Next, put kindling sticks around the slanted stick so that they are arranged in a circle with their tops leaning against each other. Leave a space between the sticks so that you can light the tinder and kindling with a match. Then, put the larger pieces of firewood around the kindling sticks in the same type of arrangement.

G   When you finish enjoying your fire, it is very important to make sure it is completely out. Have a canteen or bucket of water available. First, sprinkle water on the coals until they are soaking wet. Then, stir them around with a stick and sprinkle more water on any spots that are still hot. Sprinkle water on the ground all around the fire, also. Last, cover the wet ashes with dirt until they are completely buried.

11. What is the *main* purpose of this passage?

   A to warn people of campfire dangers

   B to entertain people with campfire stories

   C to persuade people to go camping more often

   D to inform people how to make a campfire properly

12. To make ideas in paragraphs C, D, and E clear, the author *mostly* uses—

   A personal stories

   B opinions of experts

   C facts and examples

   D statistics and quotations

GO ON

Reading Comprehension

13. This passage would be *most* appropriate for someone who is—

    A teaching a class on woodworking

    B preparing for a first camping trip

    C serving as a volunteer firefighter

    D working as a forest ranger

14. Which sentence below would be *most* important to include in a summary of paragraph C?

    A Materials that quickly catch fire are called tinder.

    B Birch bark burns well, even if it has gotten wet.

    C Birch tree bark makes especially good tinder.

    D Only a handful of tinder is required to build a fire.

15. Which of these is *most* likely to happen if you don't clear the area around your fire?

    A The fire won't burn as long.

    B The fire will burn unevenly.

    C The fire will be harder to start.

    D The fire will spread to grass nearby.

16. Which of these is an *opinion* in this passage?

    A ". . . sitting by a campfire is great fun."

    B "Fires throw out burning sparks. . . ."

    C "If a branch snaps off easily, it is dry. . . ."

    D "Fuel means larger pieces of wood. . . ."

17. What is paragraph F *mainly* about?

    A different materials

    B clearing an area

    C laying the fire

    D fire safety

18. Which is the *best* detail to add to paragraph G?

    A Wood for tinder can sometimes be found under logs and trees.

    B When the area is clear, construct a fire ring surrounded by rocks.

    C Hardwoods are excellent for cooking and don't create a lot of sparks.

    D To put out the fire, spread the coals out until they lose their red glow.

GO ON ▶

Reading Comprehension

19. Which of these is a *fact* in this passage?

   A "Building a campfire sounds very simple. . . . "

   B "Tinder is material that will catch fire easily. . . ."

   C "The best choices are hardwoods. . . ."

   D "For cooking, the crisscross works best. . . ."

20. Which is the *best* summary of this passage?

   A The first step to building a campfire is to choose a good location.

   B To build a campfire, clear an area, use the right wood, arrange the wood correctly, and follow safety rules for putting the fire out.

   C There are many different ways to arrange the wood for a campfire; the crisscross and the teepee are frequently used arrangements.

   D Building a campfire sounds very simple, but doing it properly is more complicated than many people think.

STOP

Reading Comprehension

The King's Hawk

A   Even the world's greatest leaders sometimes learn things the hard way. Eight hundred years ago a powerful king named Genghis Khan ruled an empire that stretched from eastern Europe to the Sea of Japan and included all of China. His armies marched on China and Persia, and Khan was known as the greatest king since Alexander the Great.

B   According to legend, one day Khan gathered some friends and servants and rode into the countryside to search for game. Everyone in the party had high hopes of bringing home enough meat for a great feast that night. In those days it was customary to bring a trained hawk along on hunting trips. On command, the hawk would leave its master's wrist and fly high into the sky. Then, using its exceptional eyesight, the hawk would spot its prey and swoop down on it, so the hunters would know where to follow.

C   On this trip the king had brought his favorite hawk. It was a hot summer day, and although the hunting party rode for hours, they had no luck finding game. At dusk they gave up and turned toward home. The king knew the area well, and while the hunting party took the fastest way home, the king rode off on his own between two large mountains, determined to have a successful hunt. In the valley, his hawk flew off.

D   As the king rode farther, he became parched and started looking for a spring of water. His thirst was growing, but the hot summer had dried up all the brooks that usually ran by the path. Finally, he spotted a trickle of water running over the edge of a steep rock. Quickly, he jumped from his horse, taking a small silver cup from his bag. He held the cup under the trickle of water until there was enough to drink.

E   However, as he raised the cup to his lips, there was a whooshing sound, and the cup was knocked from his hand to the ground. The king turned to see who could be responsible. Spotting his pet hawk, he wondered why the

GO ON

Reading Comprehension

bird would do such a thing. Angrily, the king picked up the cup and again held it under the trickling water. This time he held the cup for just a few seconds before he began to raise it to his mouth. Just as the cup touched his lips, the hawk flew down again, rushed past the king, and again knocked the cup to the ground.

F   The king was very angry now. Again he filled the cup, and again the hawk kept him from having even the smallest drink. "You awful bird!" the king shouted. "If you were near me I would kill you in an instant!" As the king filled the cup for the fourth time, he spoke to the hawk. "Now, you arrogant hawk, I warn you. If you value your life, let me drink." As he spoke, he held his sword ready. Again the bird flew down, knocking the cup from the king's hand; but this time, the king was ready. His sword flashed and the bird fell. The hawk dropped at his master's feet and died quickly.

G   "That will teach you," said the king. Then Genghis Khan turned and looked for the cup, but it was nowhere to be found. "I will drink now anyway," he said, and started climbing the steep rock toward the source of the water. It was a long climb, and the king's thirst grew and grew.

H   Finally, he reached the top and could see the water. As he walked closer, he could see something in the water. With one more step the king could see now that the huge thing was a dead snake, one of the most poisonous in his entire kingdom.

I   Now, the king stopped walking. He forgot his thirst, and his heart ached as he thought dismally of the dead hawk he had left lying on the ground below. He dropped his head and said, "You were a true friend, Sir Hawk. You saved my life, and yet in anger I killed you. I will honor your memory and never forget the lesson you taught me."

GO ON ➡

Reading Comprehension

21. In paragraph 1, the author *most* likely compares the king with Alexander the Great in order to show that the king—

   A was enormously powerful

   B hoped to become famous

   C came from noble blood lines

   D was humble despite his high position

22. Compared with other members of his hunting party, the king was more—

   A careless

   B generous

   C stubborn

   D awkward

23. What is the conflict in this story?

   A The king becomes lost after getting separated from his hunting party.

   B The king does not understand the actions of his hawk and becomes angry.

   C The king's hunting party does not find any game, despite help from a trained hawk.

   D The king comes upon a dangerous snake in a lake but has no weapon to defend himself.

24. Why did the hawk knock the cup to the ground?

   A so it could drink from the cup

   B because it wanted attention

   C to disobey the king's authority

   D to save the king's life

25. Which happened *last* in the story?

   A The king and his companions went separate ways.

   B The hawk forced the cup from the king's hand.

   C The king saw a snake.

   D The king went hunting.

26. Which word *best* describes how the king probably felt at the end of the story?

   A lucky

   B guilty

   C proud

   D relieved

27. The lesson the king learns in this story is to—

   A hold his temper

   B love his enemies

   C avoid being jealous

   D have faith in himself

GO ON ➡

Reading Comprehension

28. What will the king *most* likely do if a trained hawk ever knocks a cup from his hand again?

    A kill the hawk swiftly

    B refuse to hunt with the hawk again

    C try to understand the hawk's actions

    D order a servant to get rid of the hawk

29. How is the king *most* likely to be different in the future?

    A He will be more cruel to animals.

    B He will not hunt anymore.

    C He will not lead armies again.

    D He will think carefully before acting.

30. Which of the following *best* expresses an important idea in this story?

    A Good deeds will bring rewards.

    B Animals can be loyal friends to people.

    C Great success requires great courage.

    D Hard work is more important than luck.

STOP

Reading Comprehension

The Black Death

A   The growing cities of the Middle Ages could be exciting places. However, many were dark, unsafe, and unhealthy. Streets were narrow, crooked, and filthy. There were no streetlights or police. Many people did not go out alone at night for fear of robbers. If people did go out, they often took servants along with them for protection and to carry lanterns or torches to light the way. Waste was dumped into open gutters. All in all, conditions were disgusting. This caused diseases to spread quickly through the crowded cities.

B   Beginning in 1347, one such disease, a terrible plague, swept through Europe. The disease was called the Black Death because of the darkened color of its victims' faces after they died. The plague began in Asia and spread along busy trade routes. Trading ships carried the disease west to the Mediterranean. From the Mediterranean ports, the disease spread throughout most of Europe. Rats on the ships carried the disease. Fleas from the rats spread the disease to people.

C   Once people became infected, the disease could be spread from person to person. People became infected as they came in contact with the sick. According to Jean de Venette, a friar who lived at the time, young people were more likely to die than old people. Those who got sick lasted only two or three days and then died suddenly. This happened in such great numbers that often those who lived could not keep up with burying the dead. The friar wrote, "Someone who was healthy one day could be dead and buried the next. . . . A healthy person who visited the sick hardly ever escaped death."

D   No one knows the exact number of plague deaths in Europe. Some guess that about 25 million people died in Europe from 1347 to 1351. This was about one third of the entire population. The death rate varied from place

GO ON ➡

Reading Comprehension

to place. Towns seemed to be harder hit than the countryside. Some entire villages and towns were wiped out. The plague affected the rich as well as the poor. Even the great and powerful, including royalty, were struck down. Throughout Europe, populations were devastated by, as the Welsh called it, "death coming into our midst like black smoke."

E   The Black Death greatly affected Europe. Relations between the upper classes and lower classes changed. Workers, now in short supply, demanded higher wages. In several European countries, peasants staged uprisings. There were emotional effects as well. In some areas, the theme of death appeared in poetry, sculpture, and painting. People's faith was shaken. The church lost some of its power and importance. The Black Death took a greater toll on human life than any war or illness before that time. It was perhaps the greatest tragedy in all of European history.

31. What is the *main* purpose of this passage?

  A to warn people of the dangers of the plague

  B to inform people about a famous plague in history

  C to persuade people to read more about the plague

  D to entertain people with stories about plague victims

32. What is paragraph B *mainly* about?

  A how quickly the plague claimed victims

  B how many people the plague killed

  C how the plague got its name

  D how the plague spread

33. To help readers understand what medieval Europeans experienced, the author uses—

  A specific examples of plague symptoms in humans

  B quotations from people who lived during the plague

  C opinions given by health experts on how to avoid the plague

  D statistics about which towns suffered the greatest plague losses

GO ON

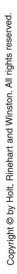

Reading Comprehension

34. Which sentence below would be *most* important to include in a summary of paragraph D?

   A Perhaps 25 million people died during a five year period.

   B Some places had higher death rates than others.

   C No one knows exactly how many people the plague killed.

   D Even members of the royalty were killed by the plague.

35. You can tell from the passage that Friar Jean de Venette—

   A inherited goods from those who died

   B bravely cared for the sick

   C witnessed much tragedy

   D became ill himself

36. It is *most* likely that disease hit towns harder than the countryside because the towns—

   A had no police

   B had more rats

   C were not lighted

   D were more crowded

37. Which is the *best* detail to add to paragraph E?

   A One effect of the deaths of farm workers was that much less land could be prepared for crops.

   B King Alfonso XI of Castile died, and Joan, daughter of King Edward III, died on the way to her wedding to Alfonso's son.

   C The wide use of torches and lanterns made fire a serious danger for medieval towns.

   D From the Mediterranean, the disease spread to North Africa, to mainland Italy, Spain, England, and France, and then to Austria and Hungary.

38. Which sentence from the passage contains the author's *opinion*?

   A "The growing cities of the Middle Ages could be exciting places."

   B "Waste was dumped into open gutters."

   C "The plague began in Asia and spread along busy trade routes."

   D "Fleas from the rats spread the disease to people."

GO ON

Reading Comprehension

39. Which of these is a *fact* in this passage?

   A "However, many were dark, unsafe, and unhealthy."

   B "All in all, conditions were disgusting."

   C "Trading ships carried the disease west to the Mediterranean."

   D "It was perhaps the greatest tragedy in all of European history."

40. Which is the *best* summary of this passage?

   A A disease called the Black Death got its name based on the appearance of its victims' faces.

   B A disease called the Black Death swept through Europe in the 1300s and changed the course of European history.

   C During the Middle Ages, cities were exciting, but they were also dangerous.

   D Relations between the classes were affected by a plague that killed millions during the 1300s.

STOP

NAME _____ DATE _____

Reading Comprehension

Answer Sheet

1.	Ⓐ	Ⓑ	Ⓒ	Ⓓ		21.	Ⓐ	Ⓑ	Ⓒ	Ⓓ
2.	Ⓐ	Ⓑ	Ⓒ	Ⓓ		22.	Ⓐ	Ⓑ	Ⓒ	Ⓓ
3.	Ⓐ	Ⓑ	Ⓒ	Ⓓ		23.	Ⓐ	Ⓑ	Ⓒ	Ⓓ
4.	Ⓐ	Ⓑ	Ⓒ	Ⓓ		24.	Ⓐ	Ⓑ	Ⓒ	Ⓓ
5.	Ⓐ	Ⓑ	Ⓒ	Ⓓ		25.	Ⓐ	Ⓑ	Ⓒ	Ⓓ
6.	Ⓐ	Ⓑ	Ⓒ	Ⓓ		26.	Ⓐ	Ⓑ	Ⓒ	Ⓓ
7.	Ⓐ	Ⓑ	Ⓒ	Ⓓ		27.	Ⓐ	Ⓑ	Ⓒ	Ⓓ
8.	Ⓐ	Ⓑ	Ⓒ	Ⓓ		28.	Ⓐ	Ⓑ	Ⓒ	Ⓓ
9.	Ⓐ	Ⓑ	Ⓒ	Ⓓ		29.	Ⓐ	Ⓑ	Ⓒ	Ⓓ
10.	Ⓐ	Ⓑ	Ⓒ	Ⓓ		30.	Ⓐ	Ⓑ	Ⓒ	Ⓓ
11.	Ⓐ	Ⓑ	Ⓒ	Ⓓ		31.	Ⓐ	Ⓑ	Ⓒ	Ⓓ
12.	Ⓐ	Ⓑ	Ⓒ	Ⓓ		32.	Ⓐ	Ⓑ	Ⓒ	Ⓓ
13.	Ⓐ	Ⓑ	Ⓒ	Ⓓ		33.	Ⓐ	Ⓑ	Ⓒ	Ⓓ
14.	Ⓐ	Ⓑ	Ⓒ	Ⓓ		34.	Ⓐ	Ⓑ	Ⓒ	Ⓓ
15.	Ⓐ	Ⓑ	Ⓒ	Ⓓ		35.	Ⓐ	Ⓑ	Ⓒ	Ⓓ
16.	Ⓐ	Ⓑ	Ⓒ	Ⓓ		36.	Ⓐ	Ⓑ	Ⓒ	Ⓓ
17.	Ⓐ	Ⓑ	Ⓒ	Ⓓ		37.	Ⓐ	Ⓑ	Ⓒ	Ⓓ
18.	Ⓐ	Ⓑ	Ⓒ	Ⓓ		38.	Ⓐ	Ⓑ	Ⓒ	Ⓓ
19.	Ⓐ	Ⓑ	Ⓒ	Ⓓ		39.	Ⓐ	Ⓑ	Ⓒ	Ⓓ
20.	Ⓐ	Ⓑ	Ⓒ	Ⓓ		40.	Ⓐ	Ⓑ	Ⓒ	Ⓓ

Reading Comprehension

Annotated Answer Sheet

1. ● B C D
2. A B C ●
3. A ● C D
4. A B ● D
5. A ● C D
6. A B ● D
7. A B C ●
8. ● B C D
9. A B C ●
10. A B ● D
11. A B C ●
12. A B ● D
13. A ● C D
14. ● B C D
15. A B C ●
16. ● B C D
17. A B ● D
18. A B C ●
19. A ● C D
20. A ● C D

21. ● B C D
22. A B ● D
23. A ● C D
24. A B C ●
25. A B ● D
26. A ● C D
27. ● B C D
28. A B ● D
29. A B C ●
30. A ● C D
31. A ● C D
32. A B C ●
33. A ● C D
34. ● B C D
35. A B ● D
36. A B C ●
37. ● B C D
38. ● B C D
39. A B ● D
40. A ● C D

Holt Reading Solutions
Diagnostic Assessment for Reading Intervention
List of Correct Answers and Skills—Grade 7

		Skill			Skill
1	A	Understand plot and sequence of events	21	A	Compare and contrast
2	D	Understand characters	22	C	Compare and contrast
3	B	Understand characters	23	B	Understand plot and sequence of events
4	C	Understand plot and sequence of events	24	D	Understand characters
5	B	Compare and contrast	25	C	Understand plot and sequence of events
6	C	Recognize theme	26	B	Understand characters
7	D	Compare and contrast	27	A	Recognize theme
8	A	Make predictions	28	C	Make predictions
9	D	Make predictions	29	D	Make predictions
10	C	Recognize theme	30	B	Recognize theme
11	D	Recognize author's purpose	31	B	Recognize author's purpose
12	C	Recognize author's purpose	32	D	Identify main idea and details
13	B	Make inferences	33	B	Recognize author's purpose
14	A	Summarize information	34	A	Summarize information
15	D	Make inferences	35	C	Make inferences
16	A	Distinguish between fact and opinion	36	D	Make inferences
17	C	Identify main idea and details	37	A	Identify main idea and details
18	D	Identify main idea and details	38	A	Distinguish between fact and opinion
19	B	Distinguish between fact and opinion	39	C	Distinguish between fact and opinion
20	B	Summarize information	40	B	Summarize information

Holt Reading Solutions
Diagnostic Assessment for Reading Intervention
Performance Profile—Grade 7

Skill	Literary Comprehension					Score (number correct)
	Item Numbers **(Mark incorrect answers.)**					
Make predictions	8	9	28	29		_____ / 4
Understand characters	2	3	24	26		_____ / 4
Recognize theme	6	10	27	30		_____ / 4
Understand plot and sequence of events	1	4	23	25		_____ / 4
Compare and contrast	5	7	21	22		_____ / 4
Total Literary Comprehension						_____ / 20

Skill	Informational Comprehension					Score (number correct)
	Item Numbers **(Mark incorrect answers.)**					
Recognize author's purpose	11	12	31	33		_____ / 4
Identify main idea and details	17	18	32	37		_____ / 4
Make inferences	13	15	35	36		_____ / 4
Summarize information	14	20	34	40		_____ / 4
Distinguish between fact and opinion	16	19	38	39		_____ / 4
Total Informational Comprehension						_____ / 20
Total Reading Comprehension						_____ / 40

Reading Proficiency Level (Circle one.)		
Proficient	**Basic**	**Below Basic**
(36–40)	(24–35)	(Fewer than 24)

Collection 1
Facing Danger

Elements of Literature: Plot
Alternative Teaching Strategies

Core Skill **Create a Plot Chart** For students struggling with the concept of plot, make a plot chart like the one on page 3 in the student book with the following headings: BASIC SITUATION, EVENTS, CLIMAX, RESOLUTION. Fill in the chart with students' responses to these questions about "Little Red Riding Hood":

- *Basic situation:* Who are the characters? What is their conflict? Is it external or internal? Are there any clues about what happens next?
- *Events:* What does the wolf do when Little Red refuses a ride? What happens when the wolf arrives at Grandmother's? What does the wolf do next? What happens when Little Red gets there?
- *Climax:* What part of the story is most exciting? What makes it exciting? What events make up this climax?
- *Resolution:* How does the story end?

Play a Memory Game Reinforce the concept of plot by playing a memory game with students. Have them close their eyes. Erase or cover one of the story elements. When they open their eyes, ask, "What is missing?" Rewrite or uncover each element as students reply. Finally, ask for volunteers to retell the story.

Vocabulary Practice

Especially for ELL **Academic Vocabulary** Help students learn the academic vocabulary in the essay on plot by reviewing these terms and their definitions, from pages 2 and 3 of their textbooks. Have them write the words and definitions in their notebooks.

- *plot:* pattern of events in a story or play
- *conflict:* struggle between characters or forces
- *climax:* point at which the conflict is decided
- *resolution:* where loose ends are tied up and the story is closed
- *external conflict:* a character struggles against another person, a group of people, or a force of nature
- *internal conflict:* a struggle within the character's mind
- *foreshadow:* give clues that hint at future events

SKILLS FOCUS

Literary Skills
Understand plot structure and foreshadowing.

Cultural Tip
Students from other cultures may not know "Little Red Riding Hood." Explain that the version that they will be reading has been modernized and is intended to be funny. Ask students to discuss any similar stories they know from their own culture.

TARGETED STRATEGIES FOR SPECIAL EDUCATION STUDENTS

Elements of Literature: Plot

Reteach the Key Idea

Identify Elements of a Story Explain to students that a story must have a beginning, a middle, and an end. Tell a well-known story, like "The Three Little Pigs," and point out the story parts. Ask individual students to retell each part. As they retell the story, work with the class to identify the basic situation, the events, the climax, and the resolution.

Alternative Teaching Strategy

Discuss Foreshadowing Remind students that storytellers give readers clues that foreshadow, or hint at, future events. Ask them to listen for words or events that foreshadow later events in the story. Read the "Little Red Riding Hood" story from the student book aloud, or have students take turns reading it. Stop periodically to talk about what might happen later in the story. Ask students what clues they might have noticed that foreshadow upcoming events. Allow time to follow up on their predictions.

Listening and Speaking Opportunity

Increase Comprehension and Fluency To determine whether students comprehend what they are reading, ask volunteers to read aloud one sentence from the story. Model the pronunciation of words that give students difficulty. Ask what the words mean. Discuss the words until the meanings are clear. Then, read the entire sentence clearly with inflection, so students can hear its meaning. Once the meaning is clear, have students practice reading the sentence aloud until they can read it smoothly.

Alternative Activity

Use Visual Reinforcement It is often helpful for students to see information presented graphically. On the chalkboard, recreate the plot chart on page 3 of the text. Ask students to identify plot elements from "Little Read Riding Hood." As they respond, record their answers on the chart. To give students opportunities for extra practice with these literary concepts, make copies of the plot chart and distribute them to students. Suggest that they chart the plot elements of the stories that they are reading on their own. Periodically review their plot charts with them, either as a group or individually.

"Rikki-tikki-tavi" by Rudyard Kipling

Prereading

Additional Background

Identify Character and Setting Make the story more accessible by explaining to students that "Rikki-tikki-tavi" takes place in India, where snakes are common pests. Explain that the hero of the story is not a human, but a pet mongoose, a small squirrel-like creature, valued for its ability to hunt and kill snakes. The evil characters are a pair of king cobras and Karait, all poisonous snakes.

Alternative Activities

Read the Adaptation Distribute copies of the adapted reading of "Rikki-tikki-tavi" (available in this book and, with marginal questions, in *Holt Adapted Reader*). To prepare for reading the original version and to practice fluency, students should read the adaptation silently.

Use *The Holt Reader* You may consider having students use the Before You Read page in *The Holt Reader*, either instead of or in addition to the Before You Read page in the student book.

Vocabulary Practice

(**Especially for ELL**) **Work with Idiomatic Phrases** English-language learners may be unfamiliar with the idioms used in this story. Before they read "Rikki-tikki-tavi," preview the following phrases from the story.

- *single-handed (p. 16):* without help
- *eaten up (p. 17):* filled
- *return stroke (p. 20):* hit back, or hit in turn
- *stole off (p. 21):* sneaked away
- *featherbrained (p. 24):* not smart

Reading

Alternative Teaching Strategies

Use *The Holt Reader* You may consider having students read the selection in *The Holt Reader* and use the margins in that book to make notes and respond to the instruction.

Identify the Conflict To help identify the main problem, or conflict, of "Rikki-tikki-tavi," read the story with students. Stop periodically,

SKILLS FOCUS

Literary Skill
Analyze conflict.

Reading Skill
Retell story events.

(**Resources**)

In this book:
- Adapted Readings
- Vocabulary and Comprehension, p. 37
- Additional Vocabulary Practice, p. 40 (includes the next selection)

Other Resources:
- *The Holt Reader*
- *Holt Adapted Reader*
- *Audio CD Library*
- *Audio CD Library, Selections and Summaries in Spanish*
- *Supporting Instruction in Spanish*
- Videocassette, Segment 1

(**Teacher Tip**)

Remind students to watch for the Vocabulary words defined at the bottom of the student-book pages.

and have them answer the following questions. Record their responses on the chalkboard.

- What is the setting of this story? *(an army post in India many years ago)*
- Who are the characters in the story? *(a mongoose named Rikki-tikki-tavi and his human family)*
- What is the main problem, or challenge, that Rikki-tikki-tavi faces? *(keeping deadly cobras out of his family's garden)*
- Who does Rikki-tikki-tavi face in his biggest battle? How did the previous battle lead to it? *(Nagaina, who wants revenge on Rikki for getting Nag killed)*
- How does the story end? *(Cobras no longer enter the garden; Rikki's human family is grateful to him for keeping them safe.)*

Postreading
Alternative Activity

Use *The Holt Reader* You may consider having students use the postreading activities in *The Holt Reader,* either instead of or in addition to the postreading activities in the student book.

Check Comprehension

Answer Questions Ask the following questions to assess students' comprehension of the story.

1. What kind of animal is Rikki-tikki-tavi? *(mongoose)*
2. Who is Teddy? *(Teddy is a young boy. Rikki-tikki-tavi is his friend.)*
3. Where does Rikki-tikki-tavi live? *(Rikki-tikki-tavi lives in the bungalow with Teddy and his family.)*
4. How did he come to live there? *(The family found him after a flood.)*
5. Who is Karait? What happens to Karait? *(Karait is a poisonous snake. Rikki-tikki-tavi kills him.)*
6. Who is Nag? What happens to Nag? *(Nag is a five-foot-long king cobra. Teddy's father shoots Nag.)*
7. Who is Nagaina? What happens to Nagaina? *(Nagaina is Nag's wife. Rikki-tikki-tavi kills her.)*

Additional Practice

Core Skill **Complete a Plot Diagram** Ask students to copy into their journals the plot diagram that appears on page 30 in their text. Remind them that the basic situation includes the:

- characters
- setting
- problem

The events are the key things that happen that lead to the climax, which is the most exciting point in the story. The resolution is how the story ends. Have students chart the plot of "Rikki-tikki-tavi" on the diagram, using their answers to the questions from "Answer Questions" on the previous page.

Vocabulary Skill
Clarify word meanings by using contrast.

Vocabulary Development

Reinforce Targeted Vocabulary

Clarify Word Meanings: Contrast As an exercise, write these sentences on the chalkboard. Underline the Vocabulary words.

- Rikki was <u>immensely</u> pleased, but Nagaina was *not a bit* pleased.
- Chuchundra <u>cowered</u> in front of the danger, while the <u>valiant</u> Rikki faced the danger and fought the snake.
- Rikki was <u>powerful</u>, but Chuchundra was *impotent*.
- The contestant who came in second got a yellow ribbon as a <u>consolation</u> prize, instead of a *first-place* gold medal.

Read the sentences aloud as you point to each word. Point out that each sentence has two parts, and that each part contrasts with the other. Draw attention to the signal words *(but, while, instead)*, and ask students to circle them. Then, have students find and underline the words in the contrasting phrase that mean the opposite of the underlined word. Complete the exercise by asking students to use the Vocabulary words in new sentences.

Look for Contrast Clues Review the following list of words with students: *although, but, yet, still, unlike, not, in contrast, instead, however.* Explain to students that they can sometimes figure out the meaning of an unfamiliar word by using contrast clues or phrases starting with *but, although, however,* etc., that show how one word or phrase is unlike another.

Reading Skills Development

(**Mixed Ability Group**) **Retell Story Events** Students may have difficulty paring down the events as they attempt to retell a story. Arrange students in mixed ability groups to read together a selection you choose from the "Understanding Plot" section of the list that begins on page 383 of this book. Have group members take turns reading small sections of the selection (for more on group reading, see "Break-in Reading" on page xxix of this book). Group members should pause to ask each reader what important events happened in the section just read. Encourage students to use as their definition of an "important event" any occurrence, decision, or revelation of information that promises to affect the story's course. After the groups have finished reading, ask volunteers to share their groups' retellings, and discuss as a class any extraneous information that is included.

(**Core Skill**)
Use the resources in the Reading Skills and Strategies section of this book to help students having difficulty understanding plot. Use "Rikki-tikki-tavi" for the application portion of the lesson.

Literary Skill
Analyze conflict.

Reading Skill
Retell story events.

(Resources)

In this book:
• Adapted Readings
• Vocabulary and
Comprehension, p. 37
• Additional Vocabulary
Practice, p. 40 (includes
the next selection)

Other Resources:
• *The Holt Reader*
• *Holt Adapted Reader*
• *Audio CD Library*
• *Audio CD Library,
Selections and Summaries
in Spanish*
• *Supporting Instruction
in Spanish*
• Videocassette, Segment 1

(Teacher Tip)

If students have difficulty
expressing themselves
verbally, have them
demonstrate their grasp of
"Rikki-tikki-tavi" by
creating a storyboard.

TARGETED STRATEGIES FOR SPECIAL EDUCATION STUDENTS

Prereading
Alternative Teaching Strategies

Provide Background Information Explain that this story is set in India many years ago, when Great Britain ruled India. The animals are common in India, but may not be familiar to students. Explain that a mongoose looks like a large squirrel, while a cobra is a poisonous snake, whose venom is deadly to humans.

Preview the Text Briefly summarize the story. Explain that it is about a conflict between Rikki-tikki-tavi, a mongoose who lives with a human family, and a pair of king cobras who live in the garden. The cobras want to drive the humans from their home so they can have the garden for themselves, while Rikki wants to protect the family and get rid of the cobras. Tell students that Rikki will have a series of fights with the cobras. Ask them to list each fight, take notes on what happens next, and record how the story ends.

Reading
Listening Opportunity

(Core Skill) Create a Plot Diagram You may want to use the audio recording of "Rikki-tikki-tavi" to give students a chance to hear the story. While they listen, ask them to fill out plot diagrams. *(See p. 30 of the text.)* Stop the recording after key events and have students record them on their diagrams.

Postreading
Alternative Teaching Strategy

Review the Plot Diagram Help students understand how the events of "Rikki-tikki-tavi" advance the plot by reviewing their plot diagrams with them. Check for comprehension of the *basic situation.*

Have students identify the first main event of the plot *(the encounter between Rikki and the two cobras)* and suggest how it advances the plot. *(main characters meet; Rikki becomes aware of cobras and wounds Nagaina)* Lead students to identify the second event *(Rikki saves Teddy by killing Karait, proving to the cobras that Rikki is dangerous)* and the third event *(Rikki attacks and holds Nag)*, then the fourth *(Nagaina threatens Teddy)*, which leads to the climax *(Rikki kills Nagaina in her nest).* Have students point out how each event leads to the next.

Vocabulary and Comprehension

"Rikki-tikki-tavi"

A. Match words and definitions. Write the letter of the correct definition next to each word.

_____ **1.** immensely

_____ **2.** cowered

_____ **3.** valiant

_____ **4.** impotent

_____ **5.** consolation

a. comfort

b. powerless

c. crouched and trembled in fear

d. enormously

e. brave and determined

B. Choose three words from above. Use each word in a sentence.

1. _____

_____

2. _____

_____

3. _____

_____

C. Answer each question below.

1. How does Rikki-tikki-tavi come to live with the family?

_____

_____

2. Describe what happens when Nag and Nagaina enter the house.

_____

_____

3. How does Rikki-tikki-tavi save Teddy's life?

_____

_____

"India's History"

SKILLS FOCUS

Reading Skills
Identify the structure and purpose of a textbook.

(**Resources**)

In this book:
• Vocabulary and Comprehension, p. 39
• Additional Vocabulary Practice, p. 40 (includes the previous selection)

Other Resources:
• *Holt Adapted Reader*
• *Audio CD Library*
• *Audio CD Library, Selections and Summaries in Spanish*
• *Supporting Instruction in Spanish*

Special Education Students

Some students may require additional help identifying the sections of the textbook. As you identify the different features of a textbook, write them on the board. Write a page number reference beside each. You may want to encourage students to write down the features and page numbers in their notebooks to refer to in the future.

Prereading
Alternative Activity

(**Especially for ELL**) **Understand the Structure of a Textbook**
Help students identify the parts of their textbooks. Ask them to scan the table of contents and name chapter titles or reading selections. Invite students to find a page with illustrations and captions. Choose a volunteer to read a caption and elicit that a caption explains who or what is in the picture.

Reading
Alternative Activities

Use *Holt Adapted Reader* You may want to have struggling readers read "India's History" in *Holt Adapted Reader* and answer the marginal questions in that book.

Get the Answers Direct students to the Test Practice questions, then work with them to find the answers in the text. Have students note that the questions are listed in the order they will be answered in the text. Point out to students that reading the questions *before* doing the reading may help focus their reading.

Postreading
Alternative Activity

Learn to Discern Review with students the Test Practice quiz on page 37 of the student book. If they need extra practice, have them work collaboratively to create a chart that lists each feature they've learned about from the questions in this selection. List the feature on the left side of the chart and the definitions of the feature on the right. For example:

Features	Definitions
Table of Contents	a list of all the sections or chapters of a book
Caption	explains the subject of an illustration

The groups can share their work when they've finished.

Vocabulary and Comprehension

"India's History"

A. Read each sentence, and then fill in the missing words from the list below. Remember to read past the blank before deciding which word(s) to write in.

table of contents   captions   index   inset   boldface type

1. The _____ on page 657 is a small map that shows where the subject of the photograph is located.

2. Key terms that are defined in the text are often set in

_____.

3. The _____, which is located at the front of the textbook, tells the reader the major topics in the book.

4. The _____, which is located at the back of the book, helps the reader locate specific topics.

5. Illustrations often have _____ that explain the subject of the photograph or drawing.

B. Answer each question below.

1. How can maps and other illustrations help you understand information?

_____

_____

2. How can you use questions at the end of each section to help you understand what you have read?

_____

_____

3. Textbooks include special features to help readers understand information. Describe the purpose of two of these features.

_____

_____

Additional Vocabulary Practice

"Rikki-tikki-tavi"; "India's History"

A. Match idiomatic phrases and definitions. Write the letter of the correct definition next to each word.

_____ **1.** single-handed   **a.** without help

_____ **2.** eaten up   **b.** sneaked away

_____ **3.** return stroke   **c.** filled

_____ **4.** stole off   **d.** hit back, or hit in turn

_____ **5.** featherbrained   **e.** not smart

B. Match the words in the left column with clues in the left column. Write the correct letter on the blanks.

_____ **1.** index

_____ **2.** boldface type

_____ **3.** table of contents

_____ **4.** captions

   a. contains specific names, subjects, and terms and corresponding page numbers

   b. makes words stand out from other words

   c. found at the beginning of a book

   d. They go with a picture.

C. The following words name places where people or animals live or spend time. Find the words in "Rikki-tikki-tavi," and write your own definitions for them.

1. bungalow _____

2. veranda _____

3. garden _____

4. burrow _____

5. nest _____

"Three Skeleton Key" by George G. Toudouze

Prereading

Additional Background

Discuss the Title Read the title of the story aloud. Point out that the word *key* has more than one meaning. Ask students to tell any meanings they know. Explain that, while they may be familiar with the common meaning of the word *key*, in this story, a *key* is a small island. Ask students to discuss the title of the story and what type of story they think it might be, based on the title.

Alternative Activities

Read the Adaptation Distribute copies of the adapted reading of "Three Skeleton Key" (available in this book and, with marginal questions, in *Holt Adapted Reader*). To prepare for reading the original version and to practice fluency, students should read the adaptation silently.

Use The Holt Reader You may consider having students use the Before You Read page in *The Holt Reader,* either instead of or in addition to the Before You Read page in the student book.

Vocabulary Practice

Preview Vocabulary To increase students' enjoyment and understanding of the story, preview the following words that they may find challenging. Tell them to look out for the words as they read.

- *extinguished (p. 43):* put out
- *maneuver (p. 41):* move skillfully
- *monotonous (p. 40):* uninteresting because it doesn't change; boring or tiresome
- *morose (p. 46):* gloomy
- *riveted (p. 43):* fixed or held firmly
- *treacherously (p. 40):* seeming safe and reliable but not really so

Reading

Alternative Activity

Use The Holt Reader You may consider having students read the selection in *The Holt Reader* and use the margins in that book to make notes and respond to the instruction.

SKILLS FOCUS

Literary Skill
Understand suspense.

Reading Skill
Make predictions.

Resources

In this book:
- Adapted Readings
- Vocabulary and Comprehension, p. 45
- Additional Vocabulary Practice, p. 48 (includes the next selection)

Other Resources:
- *The Holt Reader*
- *Holt Adapted Reader*
- *Audio CD Library*
- *Audio CD Library, Selections and Summaries in Spanish*
- *Supporting Instruction in Spanish*

Especially for ELL

Explain to students that a lighthouse is a brightly lit tower used to guide or warn ships as they approach land.

Core Skill

Use the Reading Skills Development activity on page 43 or the resources in the Reading Skills and Strategies section of this book to help students having difficulty making predictions. Use "Three Skeleton Key" for the application portion of the lesson.

Some students will benefit from a written schematic of the main events and details. Write each main event across the board as students name it. Under each main event, write the details students identify that foreshadow it. When students have completed the reading, encourage them to refer to the visual schematic to help them retell the story.

Listening and Speaking Opportunity

Especially for ELL **Listen Attentively** Play the audio recording of "Three Skeleton Key" and have students listen to the story and follow along in their books. To assess students' comprehension of the story, pause occasionally and ask students to summarize the story to that point in their own words and to make a prediction about what will happen next.

Alternative Teaching Strategy

Identify Key Points Point out that the author of this story uses foreshadowing to create suspense. To increase students' comprehension of the technique, pause at various points in the reading and ask students to predict what will happen next. Encourage them to explain their predictions by identifying the clues the author has provided that hint at what will happen later in the story. Begin by pausing after the second paragraph, where the author writes, "The pay was high, so in order to reach the sum I had set out to save before I married, I volunteered for service in the new light." Elicit from students possible reasons for the high pay. (*The job was dangerous or undesirable.*) Help students use this clue to make predictions about the story. (*For example: Something bad will happen after the narrator takes the job.*) Repeat the process at other key points in the story such as the following:

- p. 41, col. 2: "Itchoua nodded soberly and looked at us sharply as he remarked: 'See us? No doubt—if there *is* a crew aboard!' "

- p. 43, col. 1: "They had been driven out by the rats. Not those poor specimens of rats you see ashore, barely reaching the length of one foot. . . . No, these were ships' rats, huge, wise creatures, born on the sea, sailing all over the world on ships. . . ."

- p. 45, col. 2: "He pointed at the white metal plate sealing the opening through the granite. 'If that gives way'—he [Itchoua] shrugged—'they can change the name of this place to Six Skeleton Key.' "

- p. 49, col. 1: "Through my glasses, I saw that the barge was filled with meat."

Postreading
Alternative Activities

Use *The Holt Reader* You may consider having students use the postreading activities in *The Holt Reader,* either instead of or in addition to the postreading activities in the student book.

Create a Story Web Ask students to identify main events of the story with the details that foreshadow those events. Begin the web on the chalkboard by eliciting some of the main events from students, and draw circles around them with lines leading out, which the students can complete. This works well as a collaborative activity.

Connect with the Text To monitor students' comprehension of the underlying horror of the story, you might have a class discussion in which the students try to imagine that they are the narrator. Ask volunteers to suggest possible responses to such questions as: *How did you manage not to go crazy like Le Gleo? Why didn't you keep the lantern unlit the first night? Why did you return to the island?*

Vocabulary Development
Alternative Teaching Strategy

Clarify Word Meanings Review the Vocabulary words and their meanings with students. To assess their comprehension, write the following sentences on the chalkboard and ask them to select the best choice to complete each sentence.

derisive   hordes   receding   fathom   edible

1. If you poke that bee hive, ___ of angry bees may come after you. *(hordes)*

2. Be sure those berries are ___ before you taste one. *(edible)*

3. We watched the waves rolling in and then ___ back into the ocean. *(receding)*

4. It's hard to ___ what it would be like to be trapped by thousands of rats. *(fathom)*

5. His ___ comments made it clear that he did not like the story. *(derisive)*

Reading Skills Development

(**Mixed Ability Group**) **Make Predictions** Students may have difficulty making predictions simply because they fail to stop and consider the possible paths the plot of a story can take. Assign students partners of differing ability levels, and have each pair read aloud "Three Skeleton Key." Direct partners to pause their reading whenever the plot seems to be taking an unexpected turn and to read these important sections aloud twice, each partner taking a turn. Partners should brainstorm a number of possible paths the plot can take at that point. As partners progress through the story, they should revise their predictions, adding new possibilities and eliminating old ones as necessary. After students have finished reading, ask volunteers to share the predictions they and their partners made and revised while reading.

Literary Skill
Understand suspense.

Reading Skill
Make predictions.

(Resources)

In this book:
• Adapted Readings
• Vocabulary and
Comprehension, p. 45
• Additional Vocabulary
Practice, p. 48 (includes
the next selection)

Other Resources:
• *The Holt Reader*
• *Holt Adapted Reader*
• *Audio CD Library*
• *Audio CD Library,
Selections and Summaries
in Spanish*
• *Supporting Instruction
in Spanish*

(Teacher Tip)

Tell students that story
charts help them organize
information not only from
stories but also from
movies and TV shows.
Encourage them to use
story charts to track the
plots of a favorite movie
or TV show.

TARGETED STRATEGIES FOR SPECIAL EDUCATION STUDENTS

Prereading

Background

(Core Skill) Preview and Predict Help students set the scene for the story by reading the title aloud. Explain that *key* in this story refers to a small island. Ask them to discuss what the title, "Three Skeleton Key," means. Then, ask them to predict, based on the title, what kind of story this might be. Have them explain their predictions. Elicit that the word *skeleton* suggests that the story will be suspenseful or scary. Explain that writers of suspense stories often give clues throughout a story that hint at, or foreshadow, what's to come. The title, "Three Skeleton Key," is an example of foreshadowing. Choose a volunteer to read the first sentence of the story. Encourage students as they read to look for clues that the story will be about a terrifying experience.

Reading

Alternative Teaching Strategy

Use a Story Chart As students read, help them track the plot of the story on a story chart. Draw a story chart on a sheet of chart paper with blank boxes for the characters, setting, conflict, major events, and resolution. As you read the story, pause and ask students to write their responses in the appropriate boxes. Repeat this with the conflict when you come to it. As each major story event occurs, pause and ask students to retell it in their own words. Record their responses on the chart. As students finish the story, have them describe the resolution, and record that on the chart as well.

Postreading

Alternative Assessment

Retell the Story For students who find it difficult to write, have them retell the whole story so that you can assess their comprehension. Encourage them to identify the setting, conflict, main events, and resolution. Ask them to comment on clues that hint at major events and to discuss how one event leads to another.

Vocabulary and Comprehension

"Three Skeleton Key"

A. Match words and definitions. Write the letter of the correct definition next to each word.

_____ **1.** hordes   **a.** fit to be eaten

_____ **2.** receding   **b.** understand

_____ **3.** fathom   **c.** large, moving crowds

_____ **4.** edible   **d.** scornful and ridiculing

_____ **5.** derisive   **e.** moving back

B. Choose three words from above. Use each word in a sentence.

1. _____

_____

2. _____

_____

3. _____

_____

C. Answer each question below.

1. Why does Three Skeleton Key have a bad reputation?

_____

_____

2. What happens when the ship crashes on the rocks?

_____

_____

3. How are the rats finally defeated?

_____

_____

"Eeking Out a Life" by Matt Surman

SKILLS FOCUS

Reading Skills
Identify the structure and purpose of a newspaper article.

(Resources)

In this book:
• Adapted Readings
• Vocabulary and Comprehension, p. 47
• Additional Vocabulary Practice, p. 48 (includes the previous selection)

Other Resources:
• *Holt Adapted Reader*
• *Audio CD Library*
• *Audio CD Library, Selections and Summaries in Spanish*
• *Supporting Instruction in Spanish*

(Core Skill)

Use the resources in the Reading Skills and Strategies section of this book to help students having difficulty identifying author's purpose. Use "Eeking Out a Life" for the application portion of the lesson.

(Special Education Students)

If students need additional practice understanding the structure and purpose of newspaper articles, have them read other articles, applying the questions from the Test Practice on page 55 of their books.

Prereading

Background

(Especially for ELL) **Play on Words** English-language learners may not catch on to the humorous play on words in the title of the article. Write the words *eek* and *eke* on the chalkboard. Introduce the expression "eke out a living," and elicit that the expression means "to earn a living with great effort." Then, explain that *eek* is the sound a rat makes . . . as well as the sound some people make when they see a rat or mouse. Ask students to use their understanding of the title's wordplay to predict what the article will be about.

Alternative Activity

Read the Adaptation Distribute copies of the adapted reading of "Eeking Out a Life" (available in this book and, with marginal questions, in *Holt Adapted Reader*). To prepare for reading the original version and to practice fluency, students should read the adaptation silently.

Reading

Listening and Speaking Opportunity

Develop Fluency To help students develop fluency, select a paragraph and model reading it aloud or play the audio recording, encouraging students to read along in their books. Choose a volunteer to re-read the paragraph aloud. Repeat the process with other paragraphs.

Postreading

Additional Practice

Understand the Structural Elements of a Newspaper When students have finished reading, ask them to return to the article and identify the following elements: headline, subhead, byline, and dateline. Then ask a student to identify and read the headline aloud. Ask students whether they think that it is a summary headline or an attention grabber, and why. Elicit that it is an attention grabber because it makes the reader curious about the rat. It does not express the main idea of the article. Finally, ask students to describe the tone of the article. Elicit that it is lighthearted and humorous, and ask students how they think it would be different if the story was about someone who became ill from a rat bite.

Vocabulary and Comprehension

"Eeking Out a Life"

A. Match words and definitions. Write the letter of the correct definition next to each word.

_____ **1.** headline

_____ **2.** subhead

_____ **3.** byline

_____ **4.** dateline

_____ **5.** lead

_____ **6.** tone

a. name of the reporter who wrote the article

b. sentence or paragraph that begins the news article

c. choice of words and point of view that show a certain feeling

d. catchy boldface words that tell you what the article is about

e. location where the article was reported and date on which the information was reported

f. additional boldface words in smaller type under the headline

B. Answer each question below.

1. Why should the lead in an article be interesting and catch the reader's attention?

_____

_____

2. Where in the article would you expect to find answers to the questions *who? what? when? where? why?* and *how?*

_____

_____

3. Why do you think articles are written in the inverted pyramid style?

_____

_____

4. Is the tone of "Eeking Out a Life" serious or humorous? Explain your answer.

_____

_____

Additional Vocabulary Practice

"Three Skeleton Key"; "Eeking Out a Life"

A. Write the correct word in parentheses to complete each sentence.

1. *(edible, inedible)*   Berries that are fit to be eaten are _____.

These berries are poisonous; they are _____.

2. *(wild, wilderness)*   Animals that are not tame are _____.

Many untamed animals live in the _____.

3. *(deride, derisive)*   If you ridicule or make fun of someone, you

_____ them. A _____ laugh is scornful and ridiculing.

B. Complete each sentence with a word from the Word Bank.

1. Most people think of rats as disgusting, trouble-

some small animals, or _____.

2. Can you understand, or _____, why
someone would keep a rat as a pet?

3. When there is a flood, _____ of animals
flee from the rising waters.

4. The animals go back to their homes when the waters begin moving

back, or _____.

Word Bank
fathom
hordes
receding
vermin

C. Write a sentence for each word, using the definition given.

1. *eek:* an exclamation of surprise or fright

_____

_____

2. *eke out:* barely able to get or make

_____

_____

The Monsters Are Due on Maple Street by Rod Serling

Prereading

Additional Background

Preview Teleplays and Dialogue Remind students that a teleplay is a script for a television movie or program. Point out that *The Monsters Are Due on Maple Street* is an actual episode of a science fiction series called *The Twilight Zone*.

Alternative Activity

(**Especially for ELL**) **Use Spanish Resources** Spanish-speaking English-language learners may benefit from reading or listening to the selection summary in Spanish in preparation for reading it in English.

Vocabulary Practice

(**Especially for ELL**) **Reinforce Targeted Vocabulary** English-language learners may benefit from additional practice with the Vocabulary words on page 58. Review the words and sentences with students and have them use the words in new sentences. Remind students to look for these words as they read.

- *transfixed (p. 61):* very still, as if nailed to the spot
  The sunset was so beautiful that Dad stood *transfixed*.

- *intelligible (p. 62):* understandable
  Some people talk so fast that their speech is not *intelligible*.

- *assent (p. 63):* agreement
  All club members gave their *assent* to a change in meeting time.

- *intimidated (p. 64):* frightened with threats or violence
  The children were *intimidated* by the playground bully.

- *defiant (p. 64):* boldly resisting authority
  The duke was *defiant*, even after the king had threatened him with imprisonment.

- *idiosyncrasy (p. 71):* peculiarity
  Jan's greatest *idiosyncrasy* was her habit of wearing a name tag.

- *menace (p. 72):* danger, threat
  Falling rocks become a *menace* to hikers on the mountain path.

- *converging (p. 74):* closing in
  Ticketholders from everywhere were *converging* on the stadium.

SKILLS FOCUS

Literary Skill
Identify plot complications.

Reading Skill
Make inferences.

(**Resources**)

In this book:
- Vocabulary and Comprehension, p. 53
- Additional Vocabulary Practice, p. 56 (includes the next selection)

Other Resources:
- *Audio CD Library*
- *Audio CD Library, Selections and Summaries in Spanish*
- *Supporting Instruction in Spanish*

Cultural Tip

The setting of the teleplay is a typical small town in the United States in the 1950s. The typical American town today may be very different. If possible, show students a picture of a small town at that time. Point out the gliders on the porches. Explain the role of the Good Humor man, and demonstrate how to play hopscotch. Being able to visualize the setting will help students understand the action of the teleplay and the actions and reactions of the characters.

Teacher Tip

Point out that a plot chart helps the reader keep track of the events in a story or play. Encourage students to make their own plot charts as they read other selections and to use them to organize information.

- *explicit (p. 75)*: definite
  The chainsaw came with *explicit* directions for safe use.

- *variations (p. 76)*: differences
  What *variations* can you find in these two meatloaf recipes?

Reading
Alternative Activity

Use the Audio Recording You may consider allowing struggling readers to listen to the audio recording of the teleplay as they follow along in their books.

Alternative Teaching Strategy

Mixed Ability Group **Complete a Plot Chart** Students may benefit from working in groups to complete a plot chart (like the one on page 78 in their books) as they read. Ask each group to identify the characters, setting, and main conflict of the story *(the power has gone out and cars and appliances have mysteriously stopped working on Maple Street)* and record them on the "basic situation" portion of the plot chart. Have group members pause periodically to identify story complications and record each in an "event" section of the chart. Group members should note how one complication leads to the next. Each time they make note of a complication, students should predict what will happen next and why they think that. *(Students should recognize complications such as: Tommy suggests that aliens cause the power failure; Les Goodman's car mysteriously starts; the neighbors accuse Goodman of causing their problems; Charlie and Steve begin accusing each other; Don gets his shotgun.)* Finally, groups should identify and record the climax *(Charlie shoots Pete)* and resolution. *(All of the neighbors turn on each other. The Maple Street problems are revealed to be the work of aliens who cleverly exploit the worst of human nature.)* Discuss groups' findings with the class.

Postreading
Alternative Activity

Discuss Symbolism Students may have difficulty looking beyond the literal meaning of the teleplay. Ask them to explain what a symbol is. Elicit that it is something that stands for something else; for example, the picture of a printer on a computer screen is a symbol standing for "click here to print your document."

Discuss the symbolism of the story's setting and conflict. Elicit that Maple Street symbolizes streets everywhere, suggesting that people everywhere can behave like the Maple Street residents. Ask students to identify other examples of symbolism in the teleplay.

Vocabulary Development

Review the Key Idea

Clarify Word Meanings Review the vocabulary words on page 58 in the student book. Then explain to students that writers sometimes include the definitions of a difficult work within the same sentence in which the word appears. Write the following sentence on the board:

> Steve stood *transfixed,* looking at the sky as if he had been nailed to the spot and couldn't move.

Help students see that the first part of the sentence, *Steve stood transfixed looking at the sky* is all the author needed to write to describe what is happening. The rest of the sentence, *as if he had been nailed to the spot and couldn't move,* defines the word *transfixed.* Ask students to copy into their notebooks the remaining sentences from the Practice on page 69. Have them work in pairs to identify the words in each sentence that define the underlined word. Ask them to circle these words.

Vocabulary Practice

Monitor Comprehension To monitor students' comprehension of the teleplay, you may want to suggest that they write unfamiliar words in their journals as they read. Go over a few possible words with them.

- *twilight (p. 61):* dim light just after sunset or just before sunrise
- *flustered (p. 62):* excited or confused
- *antagonism (p. 65):* the state of being opposed or hostile to another or to one another

Reading Skills Development

Mixed Ability Group **Make Inferences About Character Motivation** Students may have difficulty making inferences about character motivation because they do not pay sufficient attention to the details used by the author to describe the character. Point out to students that authors rarely waste words, and the details that describe a character will often give insight into the way he or she thinks and behaves. Have students re-read *The Monsters Are Due on Maple Street* to give them practice making inferences about character motivation. Have students read the story with a partner. Partners should pause frequently to fill out a chart such as the following.

Details About the Character	What the Details Tell Me	What I Can Infer or Predict from the Details

SKILLS FOCUS

Literary Skill
Identify plot complications.

Reading Skill
Make inferences.

(**Resources**)

In this book:
• Vocabulary and Comprehension, p. 53
• Additional Vocabulary Practice, p. 56 (includes the next selection)

Other Resources:
• *Audio CD Library*
• *Audio CD Library, Selections and Summaries in Spanish*
• *Supporting Instruction in Spanish*

(**Teacher Tip**)

Many public libraries carry collections of *The Twilight Zone* episodes.

TARGETED STRATEGIES FOR SPECIAL EDUCATION STUDENTS

Prereading

Additional Background

Identify Features of a Play Help students understand the differences between a play and other kinds of writing by previewing its key features with students. Point out the box on page 60, and read the introduction to "Teleplay Terms." Then, ask students to notice the list of characters. Explain that these are the characters that appear in the teleplay. Flip through the following pages. Point out the stage direction and the way the dialogue is formatted.

Reading

Listening and Speaking Opportunity

Use Audio Some students will benefit from hearing the teleplay performed. Play the audio recording, and have students read along in their books as they listen to the dialogue. You may want to replay particular scenes or pieces of dialogue to model how they should be read. Have volunteers re-read the dialogue aloud.

Alternative Teaching Strategy

(**Core Skill**) **Make Predictions** To help students understand how story complications advance the plot, have them pause at key points and predict what will happen next. Ask them to explain their predictions.

Postreading

Alternative Assessment

Use a Storyboard Explain that scriptwriters often use *storyboards,* a series of drawings that show important events, to guide them through the action of a play or movie they are writing. Ask students to create their own storyboards for *The Monsters Are Due on Maple Street.* They can use the story's illustrations as a guide for their storyboards. After they have completed their storyboards, let them take turns sharing their work with the class, using the boards to retell the plot. Use students' drawings and retellings to assess their comprehension of the teleplay. Have students include a piece of dialogue as a caption under each picture in their storyboards. Model an example for them on the chalkboard or on chart paper.

Vocabulary and Comprehension

The Monsters Are Due on Maple Street

A. Complete each sentence with a word from the Word Bank.

1. The neighbors stood still and _____ when they heard the loud sound.

2. Steve said it might be a meteor. People agreed and nodded in _____.

3. Timmy said aliens, not meteors, were the real _____.

4. The neighbors became frightened. First, they threatened and _____ Les Goodman.

5. Then they began closing in, or _____, on Charlie and Steve.

6. No one was safe from accusations. Everyone had some peculiarity or _____ that made them look like aliens.

> **Word Bank**
> converging
> assent
> intimidated
> transfixed
> menace
> idiosyncrasy

B. Answer each question below.

1. Describe the pattern of behavior people follow when the lights go out and strange things start to happen.

_____

_____

2. Neighbors are quick to suspect each other. Describe one instance in which someone's ordinary behavior is viewed as strange and suspicious.

_____

_____

"Cellular Telephone Owner's Manual"

SKILLS FOCUS

Reading Skills
Identify the structure and purpose of an instructional manual.

(Resources)

In this book:
• Adapted Readings
• Vocabulary and Comprehension, p. 55
• Additional Vocabulary Practice, p. 56 (includes the previous selection)

Other Resources:
• *Holt Adapted Reader*
• *Audio CD Library, Selections and Summaries in Spanish*
• *Supporting Instruction in Spanish*

(Pronunciation Tip)

Students may find the pronunciation of *align* challenging. Point to the word, and pronounce it slowly and clearly. Ask students what vowel sounds they hear. (*–ign* represents the long *i* sound)

(Special Education Students)

Ask students to skim the selection before they begin to read and write down any words with which they are unfamiliar. Go over the meanings of these words before assigning students the selections.

Prereading
Alternative Activity

Read the Adaptation Distribute copies of the adapted reading of "Cellular Telephone Owner's Manual" (available in this book and, with marginal questions, in *Holt Adapted Reader*). To prepare for reading the original version and to practice fluency, students should read the adaptation silently.

Vocabulary Practice

Understand Terms Help students understand that the terms below are used to explain how to take apart or to assemble a product.

• *depress (p. 82):* press down; lower
• *reinstall (p. 82):* put back in position for use
• *align (p. 82):* put into a straight line

Reading
Alternative Teaching Strategy

(Especially for ELL) **Use Sequence** To help English-language learners, explain that steps are often numbered in the sequence in which they must occur to achieve the desired result. Write these four steps on the chalkboard:

___ slide battery pack down

___ lift battery pack

___ turn off phone

___ slide battery pack up

Ask students to copy these steps, and then number them in the correct order as they read, from 1 to 4. *(2, 3, 1, 4)*

Postreading
Alternative Activity

(Mixed Ability Group) **Create an Instructional Manual** Help students understand and analyze how the structure of an instructional manual fulfills its purpose. Divide the class into small groups. Choose some familiar piece of equipment in the classroom, such as a pencil sharpener, window shade, light switch, or dictionary. Have them write one page of an operator's manual with numbered steps.

Vocabulary and Comprehension

"Cellular Telephone Owner's Manual"

A. Match words and definitions. Write the letter of the correct definition before each word.

____ **1.** glossary

____ **2.** diagram

____ **3.** manual

____ **4.** steps

a. drawing or chart that helps explain a thing

b. alphabetical list of terms and their definitions

c. a small book of instructions

d. acts or stages in a process

B. Use the correct form of the word in parentheses to complete each sentence.

1. *(instruct, instructions)*   A manual contains _____ that explain how to use a gadget or device. Some manuals will teach, or _____, you on how to make simple repairs.

2. *(replace, replacement)*   If a device doesn't work, you may need to change, or _____, the battery. The manual tells you the steps to follow in battery _____.

3. *(remove, removal)*   First, you must take out, or _____, the old battery. The drawing shows the correct _____ procedure.

C. Answer each question below.

1. What kind of information is contained in an instructional manual?

_____

_____

2. Why is it a good idea to read through all the directions first before you use your device?

_____

_____

Additional Vocabulary Practice

The Monsters Are Due on Maple Street; "Cellular Telephone Owner's Manual"

A. Match words and definitions. Write the letter of the correct definition next to each word.

_____ **1.** converging

_____ **2.** menace

_____ **3.** assent

_____ **4.** intimidated

_____ **5.** variations

a. agreement

b. frightened with threats

c. closing in

d. differences

e. danger; threat

B. Complete each sentence about "Cellular Telephone Owner's Manual" with a word from the Word Bank.

1. An illustration or _____ explains the parts of a device.

2. Follow all the _____ in step-by-step order.

3. To find the definition of a word, look it up in the

_____.

4. What other information besides instructions is contained in an

owner's _____?

Word Bank
glossary
diagram
manual
directions

C. Complete each sentence with a word from the Word Bank.

1. If directions are clearly stated, they are _____.

2. If you can understand someone's words, the words

are _____.

3. A person who opposes a group of people is called

_____.

4. When you can't take your eyes off something, you are _____.

Word Bank
transfixed
defiant
intelligible
explicit

Comparing Literature: Science Fiction

Prereading

Vocabulary Practice

Preview Vocabulary To help students increase their vocabulary and better understand the reading, review the following words and their definitions. Ask students to use the words in sentences of their own.

- *laden (p. 89):* burdened
- *foray (p. 90):* expedition
- *impunity (p. 91):* without fear of counterattack
- *deftness (p. 92):* skill
- *respite (p. 97):* break
- *frenetic (p. 101):* fevered
- *tableau (p. 104):* picture
- *implacable (p. 104):* unable to be pacified

Reading

Alternative Teaching Strategy

(**Mixed Ability Group**) **Make a Chart** Arrange students in groups, and tell the groups to use a chart such as the one below to compare the two selections as they read them together. Point out to students that in each story the reader is led to believe one thing is happening but discovers that something else is actually happening. Discuss similarities and differences between the plots of the selections.

Story	What You Think Is Happening	What Is Actually Happening
"Zoo"		
"The Ruum"		

Postreading

Alternative Activity

Examine Comparison and Contrast Review with students the two methods of comparing and contrasting by having volunteers demonstrate each method by comparing two ordinary objects in the classroom. Write students' examples on the chalkboard, and discuss with students the method they will use to organize their essays.

SKILLS FOCUS

Literary Skill
Understand the elements of science fiction.

Reading Skill
Compare and contrast stories.

(**Resources**)

In this book:
- Vocabulary and Comprehension, p. 59
- Additional Vocabulary Practice, p. 60

(**Core Skill**)

Use the resources in the Reading Skills and Strategies section of this book to help students having difficulty comparing and contrasting. Use "Zoo" and "The Ruum" for the application portion of the lesson.

Literary Skill
Understand the elements of science fiction.

Reading Skill
Compare and contrast stories.

Resources

In this book:
• Vocabulary and Comprehension, p. 59
• Additional Vocabulary Practice, p. 60

Teacher Tip

Ask students having difficulty understanding the stories to study the illustrations. Ask: What do the illustrations suggest is happening? Can you find that event in the story?

Teacher Tip

Students having difficulty understanding or paying attention to the stories might benefit from using modeling clay to make models of the characters or machines in the stories. To check their comprehension, have them retell the stories using the clay figures.

TARGETED STRATEGIES FOR SPECIAL EDUCATION STUDENTS

Prereading
Reteach the Key Idea

Review Comparing and Contrasting Ask students to name stories they enjoy. Write students' suggestions on the chalkboard, and ask them to give examples of literary elements from each story. Point out to students that almost every story can be said to have a main character, setting, plot, conflict, and theme. Allow students to practice comparing and contrasting the elements of the stories they have mentioned.

Reading
Additional Practice

Read Aloud Students who are having trouble reading the stories may benefit from hearing them read aloud. Choose a short passage from one of the two stories. Read it aloud yourself, or ask a proficient reader to do so. Then, have hesitant students re-read the passage aloud several times. Encourage them to read with energy and feeling. Continue modeling reading until students demonstrate some measure of fluency. It can be helpful to repeat this exercise with the same passages on several consecutive days.

Postreading
Alternative Activity

Make Posters Have students select one of the two stories and make a poster for the movie that could be made from it. Ask students to pick an important moment from the story for their posters. Have them make small drawings of one or more subplots around the edges of their posters. To check comprehension, ask them to explain why the small drawings are important to the story.

Alternative Assessment

Check Comprehension Guide students through these questions:
• What is the setting for the story "Zoo"? *(Earth in the future)*
• Who are in the zoo this year? *(the horse-spider people of Kaan)*
• What do the creatures inside the zoo think of the Earth people outside? *(They think the Earth people on the outside are the zoo.)*
• Why might the ruum have chased Jim only to let him go? *(He lost so much weight during the chase that he did not weigh enough for the ruum to "collect" him.)*

Vocabulary and Comprehension

Comparing Literature: Science Fiction

A. Match the words in the left column with the clues in the right column. Write the correct letter in the blanks.

_____ **1.** phlegmatic

_____ **2.** feral

_____ **3.** phosphorescent

_____ **4.** ricochet

_____ **5.** cached

a. might describe a stray cat

b. the opposite of *panicked*

c. describes the action of a ball or bullet

d. the opposite of *left out in the open*

e. might describe a glowing firefly

B. Choose three words from above. Use each word in a sentence.

1. _____

_____

2. _____

_____

3. _____

_____

C. Write T or F next to each statement to tell if it is true or false.

_____ **1.** In "Zoo," the creatures escape from the zoo and attack the humans.

_____ **2.** At the end of "Zoo," the creatures talk about how strange humans are.

_____ **3.** In "The Ruum," the spaceship leaves the ruum on Earth in order to collect humans.

_____ **4.** Jim finally destroys the ruum.

_____ **5.** The ruum weighs Jim and lets him go.

Additional Vocabulary Practice

Comparing Literature: Science Fiction

A. Match words and definitions. Write the letter of the correct definition next to each word.

____ **1.** laden

____ **2.** impunity

____ **3.** deftness

____ **4.** foray

____ **5.** tableau

a. picture

b. burdened

c. without fear of counterattack

d. skill

e. journey

B. Choose two words from above. Use each word in a sentence.

1. _____

_____

2. _____

_____

C. Replace the word or phrase in parentheses with the correct word from the Word Bank.

1. Megan was *(unable to be pacified)* _____ in her search for justice. She wanted to know who littered along the roadside by the school and would not stop until she found out.

2. The race was so long that the contestants agreed to take a brief *(break)* _____.

3. Sam was behind on the test and so finished the last few items at a *(fevered)* _____ pace.

4. The flashlight illuminating the possums as they ate your camp food must have made an interesting *(picture)* _____.

5. When it gets dark, we plan to go on a little *(journey)* _____ into the woods to look for fireflies.

> **Word Bank**
> tableau
> foray
> frenetic
> implacable
> respite

Collection 2

Characters: Living Many Lives

Elements of Literature: Characterization

SKILLS FOCUS

Literary Skill
Analyze characterization.

Alternative Teaching Strategy

Make a Character Web Help students understand the concept of characterization by modeling how to make character webs like the one on page 129 in the student book. Begin by discussing a familiar short story. Write the main character's name in a circle on the board. Ask students to list the character's traits. Write each trait in a circle. Ask for examples of appearance, actions, speech, thoughts, and feelings that reveal each trait. Write each example in a circle, and connect it to the trait that it exemplifies. Then, link all the circles to the main character's name.

Especially for ELL

Remind students that in English all proper names begin with a capital letter but that the names of professions—cowboy and gladiator, for example— begin with lowercase letters.

Alternative Activity

Identify Characters To help students learn to identify characters as well as to analyze characterization, write the names of familiar characters on strips of paper. Put the strips in a paper bag, and have a student choose one strip. Tell the student to give an example of something the character said or did. Have the class guess the character and the trait suggested by the words or behavior.

Vocabulary Practice

Especially for ELL **Introduce Academic Vocabulary** The academic vocabulary may not be familiar to English-language learners. Help students learn the words on pages 128 and 129 and their definitions:

- *appearance:* what the character looks like
- *character:* person in a story, play, or movie
- *direct characterization:* writer tells the reader what the character is like
- *indirect characterization:* writer shows the reader what the character is like
- *reaction:* response of one character in the story to another, thereby providing further information about the character

If time permits, ask students to define the academic vocabulary in their own words and to use each word in a sentence.

TARGETED STRATEGIES FOR SPECIAL EDUCATION STUDENTS

Elements of Literature: Characterization

Alternative Teaching Strategy

Use a Graphic Organizer Students may benefit from organizing what they know about a character into a chart. Create a six-column chart on the chalkboard and label the columns CHARACTER, APPEARANCE, ACTION, SPEECH, THOUGHTS AND FEELINGS, and OTHER CHARACTERS' REACTIONS. Choose a story character and write his or her name in the first column. Then, help students complete the chart by telling what they've observed about the character's traits.

Alternative Activity

(**Core Skill**) **Understand Characterization** Write the words *happy, curious,* and *brave* on the chalkboard. Help students name characters that those adjectives describe, and write the names of the characters under the appropriate words. You can expand this activity by asking students to suggest other traits that apply to each character they list. Then, have students identify specific actions or words that led them to their conclusions about the characters.

(**Teacher Tip**)
Encourage students to use graphic organizers to help them keep track of characters' traits as they read the stories in this chapter.

Additional Practice

Make a Visual Representation Have students choose a character they described above and represent it through art. First, have students list traits for the character, then brainstorm how these traits might be demonstrated visually. For example, the trait "well organized" might be reflected in neatly pressed and matching clothes. The trait "pensive" might be shown by drawing the character reading a book. Have students present their drawings by naming each character trait and explaining how it is represented.

Alternative Assessment

Play a Game Show To engage students' attention and assess their understanding, have them play a game show called "Name That Character." First, have students write the names of movie stars, singers, athletes, and other famous people on slips of paper. Collect the papers, fold them, and put them in a bag. Divide students into two contestant groups. Ask one group to draw a name from the bag. Have the group describe the famous person by traits, appearance, actions, speech, how others react to them, etc. Based on this characterization, the other group must guess who the person is.

"Mother and Daughter" by Gary Soto

Prereading

Additional Background

(**Core Skill**) **Use Pictures to Preview and Predict** Tell students that this story is set in Fresno, California, a city with a large Mexican American population. Explain that as they read the story, they will encounter various Spanish words and phrases. Then, use the story illustrations to preview the characters. Ask students to look at the picture of Mrs. Moreno on page 138. Have them name traits they might attribute to her based on her appearance. Then, ask them to look at the picture of Yollie on page 139 and to predict what she might be like. Have them review their predictions for accuracy after they've read the story.

Alternative Activities

Read the Adaptation Distribute copies of the adapted reading of "Mother and Daughter" (available in this book and, with marginal questions, in *Holt Adapted Reader*). To prepare for reading the original version and to practice fluency, students should read the adaptation silently. Encourage students to write notes, questions, predictions, reactions, and comments on the worksheets as they read.

Use *The Holt Reader* You may consider having students use the Before You Read page in *The Holt Reader,* either instead of or in addition to the Before You Read page in the student book.

Reading

Alternative Activity

Use *The Holt Reader* You may consider having students read the selection in *The Holt Reader* and use the margins in that book to make notes and respond to the instruction.

Listening and Speaking Opportunity

(**Especially for ELL**) **Practice Fluency** To help students develop fluency, select a paragraph or short passage from the story and model it by playing the audio recording or reading it aloud. Encourage students to read along in their books as you play or read the passage. Then, choose a student to re-read the passage aloud. Repeat the exercise with several passages, so that all students have an opportunity to practice reading aloud.

SKILLS FOCUS

Literary Skill
Understand character traits.

Reading Skill
Make inferences.

(**Resources**)

In this book:
- Adapted Readings
- Vocabulary and Comprehension, p. 67
- Additional Vocabulary Practice, p. 68

Other Resources:
- *The Holt Reader*
- *Holt Adapted Reader*
- *Audio CD Library*
- *Audio CD Library, Selections and Summaries in Spanish*
- *Supporting Instruction in Spanish*

(**Especially for ELL**)

Draw on the abilities of your native Spanish speakers by having them translate the Spanish words and phrases for their classmates.

Additional Activity

(**Mixed Ability Group**) **Make a Chart** Draw on the chalkboard a chart like the one shown below. Have groups of students copy the chart and use it to analyze characters as they read together the story "Mother and Daughter." Remind groups to fill in the names of the major story characters, and note important thoughts, words, actions, or descriptions that reveal something about each character. After reading, make a master chart together on the chalkboard that compiles the groups' findings.

Character	Thoughts	Words	Actions	Narrator's description
Yollie				
Mrs. Moreno				

Postreading

Alternative Activity

Use *The Holt Reader* You may consider having students use the postreading activities in *The Holt Reader,* either instead of or in addition to the postreading activities in the student book.

Alternative Teaching Strategy

(**Mixed Ability Group**) **Make a Character Web** Have groups use their character charts to make a web that describes Yollie "at a glance." Tell them to put Yollie's name in a circle at the center. Then, have them draw connecting circles that contain character traits, such as *excited, outgoing, demanding,* etc. To each trait, have groups connect circles that contain proof of this trait. For example, for the trait "excited," students might list "bounced into the car before the dance." Remind groups to refer to their charts for thoughts, words, actions, or descriptions that suggest each trait.

Vocabulary Development

Reteach the Key Idea

Use the Dictionary to Find Word Origins Explain that etymology is the study of where words come from and how they developed into their modern forms. Write on the chalkboard some of the symbols and abbreviations commonly found in etymologies.

- < (*derived, or comes from*)
- > (*from which comes*)
- Fr. (*French*)
- Lat. (*Latin*)
- Gk. (*Greek*)

Direct students to the section of the dictionary where the etymology information is located and ask them to identify these symbols and abbreviations. Explain each and write the explanation beside the symbol or abbreviation on the board. Then, choose a word from the Word Bank, for example, *matinee*, and write it on the chalkboard. With the class, look up the word in the dictionary and lead the class to analyze the etymology's elements to see how the meaning of *matinee* is connected to the words from which it is derived.

Additional Vocabulary Practice

Introduce Words with Common Latin Roots Point out to students that many Spanish and English words have common Latin roots. Explain that understanding common roots can help them determine word meanings, because words that sound similar in English and Spanish often have similar meanings. For example:

English word	Definition	Spanish word	Definition	Common origin
inscribe	to write or carve on a surface	escribir	to write	Latin *scribere*, to write
primary	first or highest in rank	primero	first	Latin *primus*, first
receive	to take or acquire	recibir	to receive	Latin *recipere*, to take

Challenge students to expand the chart with other Spanish and English words with common Latin roots.

Reading Skills Development

(**Mixed Ability Group**) **Perform a Skit** Students who have difficulty making inferences about character traits may benefit from performing a skit based on a story. Arrange students in mixed ability groups to act out a scene from a story of your choice from the "Understanding Characters" section of the list that begins on page 383 of this book. Each group member should play the part of one of the characters, with any extra group members playing the role of a narrator or participating as extras. Students should make sure that their portrayal of their characters is consistent with the characters' traits as displayed in the story. Ask groups to take turns presenting their skits for the rest of the class.

(**Core Skill**)

Use the resources in the Reading Skills and Strategies section of this book to help students having difficulty understanding characters. Use "Mother and Daughter" for the application portion of the lesson.

Literary Skill
Understand character traits.

Reading Skill
Make inferences.

(Resources)

In this book:
• Adapted Readings
• Vocabulary and
Comprehension, p. 67
• Additional Vocabulary
Practice, p. 68

Other Resources:
• *The Holt Reader*
• *Holt Adapted Reader*
• *Audio CD Library*
• *Audio CD Library,*
Selections and Summaries
in Spanish
• *Supporting Instruction*
in Spanish

(Teacher Tip)

Noticing picture details may
help students better
understand the story. Ask
students to open their
books to page 137 and look
at the picture of Yollie
and her mother. Have
them name as many
characteristics as they can
based on how the
characters look.

TARGETED STRATEGIES FOR SPECIAL EDUCATION STUDENTS

Prereading
Alternative Activity

Use Sticky Notes Have students write the following character traits on sticky notes: *concerned, sad, inventive, funny*. Explain that the words describe four of Mrs. Moreno's character traits. Tell students that Mrs. Moreno is *concerned* that her child get a good education, *sad* because she can't afford to buy Yollie a new outfit for the dance, *inventive* in the way she solves problems, and *funny* in the way she expresses herself. As students read the story, have them paste the sticky notes on the parts of the story that reflect those traits. Repeat this process for Yollie's character, using these traits: *smart, friendly, confident, expressive.*

Reading
Listening and Speaking Opportunity

Use Audio Play the audio recording of the story while students follow along in their books. Encourage them to jot down words that describe the characters. Stop the recording from time to time to guide students to notice important information.

Postreading
Alternative Activity

(Core Skill) Compare and Contrast Draw a large Venn diagram on the chalkboard. Label one circle MRS. MORENO and the other YOLLIE. Have students copy the diagram into their notebooks. Ask students to name traits for each character, and write these traits in the appropriate places on the diagram. Encourage students to use the Venn diagram to talk about how the characters are alike and different.

Alternative Assessment

Retell the Story Use collective retelling to assess students' comprehension of the story. Have one student begin by retelling the first event in the story. Choose another student to continue. Give all students a turn at retelling a segment of the story. Encourage students to summarize characters' reactions to events as they retell what happened.

Vocabulary and Comprehension

"Mother and Daughter"

A. Complete each sentence with a word from the Word Bank.

1. Even though Mrs. Moreno's earnings were

_____, she was able to

save some money.

2. Yollie hoped that she would look

_____ in her black dress

and new black shoes.

3. When Yollie's dress got ruined at the dance, she burst into a

_____ at her mother.

4. Yollie and her mother loved to go to the movies in the afternoons.

Saturday _____ were their favorite.

5. Everyone enjoyed the funny _____ of
Yollie's mother.

| **Word Bank** |
| matinees |
| antics |
| meager |
| sophisticated |
| tirade |

B. Write T or F next to each statement to tell if it is true or false.

_____ **1.** Yollie's mother was a serious woman who worried
all the time.

_____ **2.** Yollie and her mother usually got along.

_____ **3.** Mrs. Moreno wanted to see Yollie get a good education.

_____ **4.** Yollie was not a good student.

_____ **5.** The dance was no fun because Ernie didn't want to
dance with Yollie.

_____ **6.** Yollie's dress was ruined when someone spilled
punch on it.

_____ **7.** Mrs. Moreno used her secret stash of money to buy
Yollie some new clothes.

Additional Vocabulary Practice

"Mother and Daughter"

A. Match words and definitions. Write the letter of the correct definition next to each letter.

_____ **1.** riot

_____ **2.** gobbled up

_____ **3.** stashed away

_____ **4.** slammed

_____ **5.** throbbing

a. hit with great force

b. used up quickly

c. hilariously funny person

d. beating or vibrating

e. hidden in a secret place

B. Complete each sentence with a word from the list above.

1. Mrs. Moreno's old car _____ a lot of her savings.

2. Late at night Yollie could hear the _____ hum of the refrigerator.

3. Mrs. Moreno was such a _____ that some people thought she should perform on stage.

4. Her mother had _____ some money for her education.

5. She was so angry that she _____ the palm of her hand on the arm of the chair.

C. Match each present tense verb in the first column with its past tense form in the second column.

_____ **1.** stand

_____ **2.** mean

_____ **3.** keep

_____ **4.** tear

_____ **5.** know

_____ **6.** wear

a. wore

b. meant

c. stood

d. knew

e. tore

f. kept

"The Smallest Dragonboy"

by Anne McCaffrey

Prereading

Additional Background

Discuss Genre Tell students that "The Smallest Dragonboy" is a fantasy. Explain that a fantasy takes place in an imaginary world and often includes creatures, such as dragons, that do not exist in the real world. Ask students if they have read other fantasy stories. Tell them that, as they read, they should think about ways in which the characters in a fantasy are similar to and different from characters in a realistic story. *(For example, while Keevan's home, clothing, and chores are different from those of a real boy, his feelings are very similar.)*

Alternative Activity

Read the Adaptation Distribute copies of the adapted reading of "The Smallest Dragonboy" (available in this book and, with marginal questions, in *Holt Adapted Reader*). To prepare for reading the original version and to practice fluency, students should read the adaptation silently. Encourage students to write notes, questions, predictions, reactions, and comments on the worksheets as they read.

Vocabulary Practice

Especially for ELL **Understand Pernspeak** The invented language in this story will be especially challenging for English-language learners. Write the following words and definitions on the chalkboard and review them with students. Explain that some are not real English words and that others are English words with different meanings. Note that these terms were invented to describe imaginary people, events, and things on the planet Pern.

- *dragonriders (p. 148):* people who ride dragons
- *Thread (p. 148):* deadly plant spores that threaten living things on Pern
- *bronze (p. 149):* a bronze-colored dragon, considered the most powerful of all Pern dragons
- *Impression (p. 150):* the process by which a newborn dragon chooses its rider; a sort of telepathic communication
- *firestone (p. 151):* special rock fed to dragons to make them breathe flames that destroy Threads

SKILLS FOCUS

Literary Skill
Understand motivation.

Reading Skill
Make inferences.

Resources

In this book:
- Adapted Readings
- Vocabulary and Comprehension, p. 73
- Additional Vocabulary Practice, p. 76 (includes the next selection)

Other Resources:
- *Holt Adapted Reader*
- *Audio CD Library*
- *Audio CD Library, Selections and Summaries in Spanish*
- *Supporting Instruction in Spanish*

Cultural Tip

In European folklore, dragons are believed to represent evil. Many Asian cultures, however, believe that dragons are friendly and bring good luck. Ask students to share what they know about dragons and the roles dragons play in their cultures.

Additional Vocabulary Practice Write the following words and definitions on the chalkboard and review them with students.

- *punctual (p. 148):* on time
- *transparent (p. 148):* so clear or so fine that objects on the other side can be easily seen; seen through
- *fleetingly (p. 149):* briefly; momentarily
- *obscured (p. 149):* concealed from view; hidden
- *enviable (p. 149):* good enough to be envied or wished for
- *aspire (p. 150):* have a strong desire to get or do something
- *console (p. 150):* make less sad or troubled; comfort
- *evasion (p. 152):* avoiding a duty or question by being clever or dishonest

Reading
Alternative Activity

Play the Audio Recording Struggling readers may benefit from listening to the audio recording of the selection as they read along in their books. You may want to stop the reading from time to time to ask students to summarize what has happened so far and to make predictions about what is going to happen in the story.

Alternative Teaching Strategy

Use Charts to Make Inferences Remind students that most information about a character is not explicitly stated by the writer. Instead, readers use information about a character's thoughts, words, and actions to make educated guesses about that character's traits and motivations. Model this process by reading aloud the first paragraph of the story. Ask students to describe Keevan's action in this paragraph. Then, make an inference about Keevan that is based on this action. Use a simple chart like the one shown here.

Keevan

What (actions)	Why (inferences)
Keevan lengthens his stride.	He wants to keep up with the bigger boys.

Tell students to make inferencing charts for both Keevan and Beterli and to fill them out as they read "The Smallest Dragonboy."

Postreading
Alternative Activity

Core Skill **Analyze Character** Bring students together to discuss the charts they filled out for Keevan and Beterli as they read "The Smallest Dragonboy." As students note actions, thoughts, or descriptions, have them try to come to agreement on a list of traits for each character.

Vocabulary Development
Alternative Teaching Strategy

Especially for ELL **Recognize Affixes** Many ELL students may not be familiar with common English affixes. Help them by listing the following affixes and their meanings. Show how each prefix or suffix contributes to the example word. Point out that recognizing affixes can help one understand the meanings of unfamiliar words.

Prefix	Meaning	Example
ex-	from, out	export (to send out)
mis-	wrong	misplace (to put in the wrong location)
non-	not	nonprofit (not trying to earn a profit)
pre-	before	prehistorical (before the recording of historical events)
re-	back, again	reheat (to heat again)
un-	not	untrue (not proven)

Suffix	Meaning	Example
-able	capable of being	readable (capable of being read)
-ful	full of	truthful (full of truth)
-ity	state of being	scarcity (state of being scarce)
-less	without, lacking	wordless (without words)
-ly	in a certain way	freely (in a free way)
-tion (-ion, -sion)	act of, state of being	resolution (act of resolving)

Reading Skills Development

Mixed Ability Group **Make Inferences** Students may have difficulty making inferences about characters in a story. Have students work together in small groups to read together a selection you choose from the "Understanding Characters" section of the list that begins on page 383 of this book (for more on group reading, see "Access the Text: Fluency Activities" on page xxix of this book). Have group members use a chart such as the one below to draw up a list of the story's main characters and to give a number of adjectives that describe each one. In the final column, students should list quotations from the story that support their character descriptions by showing the characters' traits through their own or others' actions, thoughts, and words. Ask groups to share their work with the class.

Character	Traits	Evidence

Vocabulary Skills
Understand roots and affixes.

Language Tip
Over, under, and *pass* are three words that illustrate how English developed from many sources: *Over* is from the Old English *ofer* ("above; beyond"); *under* came into Old English by way of the Old Norse word *undir;* and *pass* is from the Latin *passus* ("step").

Core Skill
Use the resources in the Reading Skills and Strategies section of this book to help students having difficulty understanding characters. Use "The Smallest Dragonboy" for the application portion of the lesson.

SKILLS FOCUS

Literary Skill
Understand motivation.

Reading Skill
Make inferences.

Resources

In this book:
• Adapted Readings
• Vocabulary and
Comprehension, p. 73
• Additional Vocabulary
Practice, p. 76 (includes
the next selection)

Other Resources:
• *Holt Adapted Reader*
• *Audio CD Library*
• *Audio CD Library,
Selections and Summaries
in Spanish*
• *Supporting Instruction
in Spanish*

Teacher Tip

Tell students that the
technique of breaking long
or complex sentences into
smaller sections also
can be applied to long
or unfamiliar words.
Show them how to break
words into syllables to
clarify both meaning
and pronunciation.

TARGETED STRATEGIES FOR SPECIAL EDUCATION STUDENTS

Prereading
Alternative Activity

Core Skill **Preview and Predict** Explain to students that this story is a fantasy; that is, it is set in an imaginary land. Point out that the dragons in the story do not exist in the real world, and even the people are not exactly like real people. To help students visualize the world of Pern, ask them to flip through the illustrations. Invite them to comment on what Pern and its characters might be like.

Reading
Listening and Speaking Opportunities

Use Audio Play the audio recording of "The Smallest Dragonboy," pausing occasionally to discuss Keevan's actions. Encourage students to make inferences about why Keevan acts as he does, and to note what these actions reveal about his character. You might want to use the WHAT/WHY chart explained on page 70 of this book. After students listen to the story, help them develop a list of Keevan's character traits.

Practice Fluency Model how to read longer sentences by breaking down this sentence from "The Smallest Dragonboy" as follows:

> "On the height, / the blue watch dragon, / his rider mounted on his neck, / stretched the great transparent pinions that carried him on the winds of Pern / to fight the evil Thread that fell at certain times from the skies."

Read the sentence aloud phrase by phrase, inviting students to read along with you. Then, model the entire sentence, pausing at commas and other logical breaks. Finally, ask students to read the sentence once again, first one phrase at a time, and then in its entirety.

Postreading
Alternative Assessment

Retell the Story Have students use the story illustrations to help them narrate a retelling of "The Smallest Dragonboy." To guide students, ask questions such as: What happened in the story before this picture? What happened after? Who is in this picture? What is he or she doing? Finally, write the names Keevan, Beterli, and Mande on the board. Ask students for three words that describe each character. Have students explain their answers by referring to the story.

Vocabulary and Comprehension

"The Smallest Dragonboy"

A. Match words and definitions. Write the letter of the correct definition next to each word.

_____ **1.** goaded

_____ **2.** imminent

_____ **3.** perturbed

_____ **4.** confrontation

_____ **5.** alleviate

a. disagreement

b. relieve; reduce

c. pushed or driven

d. about to happen

e. disturbed; troubled

B. Answer each question below.

1. Why is it an honor to become a dragonrider?

_____

_____

2. What do the dragonriders give the dragons to help them breathe fire?

_____

_____

3. How are dragonriders matched with their dragons?

_____

_____

4. What happened when Beterli fought with Keevan?

_____

_____

5. What happened to Keevan at the Impressing? Why was this a special honor?

_____

_____

"Here Be Dragons" by Flo Ota De Lange

SKILLS FOCUS

Reading Skill
Understand comparison and contrast.

Resources

In this book:
• Vocabulary and Comprehension, p. 75
• Additional Vocabulary Practice, p. 76 (includes the previous selection)

Other Resources:
• *Audio CD Library*
• *Audio CD Library, Selections and Summaries in Spanish*
• *Supporting Instruction in Spanish*

Core Skill

Use the resources in the Reading Skills and Strategies section of this book to help students having difficulty comparing and contrasting. Use "Here Be Dragons" for the application portion of the lesson.

Special Education Students

Ask students if they know any dragon stories. Ask: What cultures do these stories come from? What are the story dragons like— do they help or harm people? Have students compare the dragons they are familiar with with the ones pictured in "Here Be Dragons."

Prereading

Alternative Teaching Strategies

Especially for ELL **Use Spanish Resources** Spanish-speaking English-language learners may benefit from reading or listening to the selection summary in Spanish in preparation for reading it in English.

Use Visuals Have students examine the illustrations on pages 165 and 166. Ask: How are the two dragons alike? How are they different? Explain that the first picture shows a traditional Chinese image of a dragon, while the second picture shows a typical European image of a dragon. Tell students that this article will compare and contrast ideas about dragons in Eastern and Western cultures. Ask students to look for similarities and differences as they read.

Reading

Listening and Speaking Opportunity

Practice Fluency Play the audio recording of this selection and have students read along in their books as they listen. Then, give students an opportunity to practice reading aloud on their own. You may want to replay particular passages from the text to model how they should be read and then have a student re-read the passage aloud. Repeat this with a number of difficult passages so that all students have an opportunity to practice reading aloud.

Postreading

Alternative Teaching Strategy

Identify Key Points Have students re-read the first section and identify the author's key points. (*Dragon stories have been told for ages all over the world. Dragons differ from culture to culture.*) Repeat the process with the sections on Eastern and Western dragons, asking students to identify the main idea of each paragraph. (*Eastern dragons are beautiful. They come from a primordial swamp. They love to help people. Western dragons are mean and smelly, and live underground. They hunt people.*) Finally, have a students identify the key points of the last section, "Dragons Today." (*Although dragon stories aren't as widespread today, they still exist in our popular culture.*) As students review, write their responses on the chalkboard and guide them to determine that the author uses the block method. Then, display a point-by-point chart, and help students identify where to place each key point.

Vocabulary and Comprehension

"Here Be Dragons"

A. Match words and definitions. Write the letter of the correct definition next to each word.

_____ **1.** seething

_____ **2.** cosmos

_____ **3.** primal

_____ **4.** primordial

a. basic; fundamental

b. violently agitated or disturbed

c. original; first in time

d. the whole universe

B. Use each word above in a sentence.

1. _____

_____

2. _____

_____

3. _____

_____

4. _____

_____

C. Read each question. Write the letter of the correct answer next to each question.

_____ **1.** Where does the expression "Here be dragons" come from?

    a. the lyrics of a Middle English epic song

    b. the title of a famous mythology book

    c. a warning written on old maps

_____ **2.** Dragons were believed to have the ancient power of which two forces?

    a. wind and fire

    b. wind and water

    c. fire and water

Additional Vocabulary Practice

"The Smallest Dragonboy"; "Here Be Dragons"

A. Use the words from the Word Bank and the clues to fill in the puzzle.

Word Bank

aspire
console
enviable
evasion
fleetingly
obscured
punctual
transparent

Across

2. avoiding a duty or question
3. clear or fine; seen through
7. concealed from view; hidden
8. make less sad or troubled; comfort

Down

1. briefly; momentarily
4. on time
5. good enough to be wished for
6. have a strong desire to get or do something

"A Rice Sandwich" by Sandra Cisneros

Prereading

Background

Discuss Setting and Title Explain that this story takes place in a Mexican American neighborhood in Chicago, Illinois. The first-person narrator, the "I" in this story, is a girl named Esperanza who goes to a Catholic school. Her teachers are nuns, which is why they are all called Sister. The principal is called Sister Superior.

Choose a student to read the title of the story aloud. Have students tell what a sandwich is and list some items that normally go into a sandwich. Ask whether anyone has ever had a rice sandwich. Be sure students understand that rice is an unusual sandwich ingredient. Then, ask students to guess what they think this story will be about and whether they can predict any of the events that will take place in a story entitled "A Rice Sandwich."

Alternative Activity

Use *The Holt Reader* You may consider having students use the Before You Read page in *The Holt Reader,* either instead of or in addition to the Before You Read page in the student book.

Reading

Alternative Activity

Use *The Holt Reader* You may consider having students read the selection in *The Holt Reader* and use the margins in that book to make notes and respond to the instruction.

Alternative Teaching Strategy

Make Inferences Point out to students that Esperanza, the first-person narrator of "A Rice Sandwich," tells her story as if she were speaking to a friend—someone who already knows certain details about her. In order to fully understand Esperanza's narration, readers must sometimes make inferences about what she says. Model making inferences by having students read aloud the first two paragraphs. Then, ask why they think some kids wear keys around their necks. Elicit that it might be because these kids' parents are not at home to let them in after school. Next, ask students how they think Esperanza feels about the keys. *(She probably thinks these kids are lucky to have their own keys. She calls them the "special kids," and wants to eat in the canteen with them.)*

SKILLS FOCUS

Literary Skill
Understand the narrator.

Reading Skill
Make inferences.

Resources

In this book:
- Vocabulary and Comprehension, p. 81
- Additional Vocabulary Practice, p. 82

Other Resources:
- *The Holt Reader*
- *Audio CD Library*
- *Audio CD Library, Selections and Summaries in Spanish*
- *Supporting Instruction in Spanish*
- Videocassette, Segment 2

Teacher Tip

The writer doesn't use quotation marks in this story, and she doesn't always use standard capitalization when people speak. Alert students to the fact that they will have to use context to know who is speaking, especially on page 170.

Have students take turns reading the rest of the story aloud, pausing occasionally to make inferences. Possible questions include Who are Nenny, Kiko, and Carlos? *(Esperanza's siblings)* Why does Esperanza's mother finally allow her to eat in the canteen? *(she is tired of Esperanza bugging her)* How does Esperanza feel when she has to go to the Sister Superior's office? *(very upset)* Will Esperanza want to eat in the canteen again? *(probably not)*

Vocabulary Practice

Especially for ELL **Use Adjectives** English-language learners may be unfamiliar with some of the adjectives from "A Rice Sandwich" that describe Esperanza. Write these words *(p. 170 of the student book)* and definitions on the chalkboard. Review their meanings with students. Then, have students use each word in a sentence about a real or fictional person.

- *dizzy:* having a whirling or spinning feeling; unsteady
- *shy:* timid; reserved
- *tired:* worn-out; exhausted

Postreading

Alternative Activities

Use *The Holt Reader* You may consider having students use the postreading activities in *The Holt Reader,* either instead of or in addition to the postreading activities in the student book.

Retell the Story To help students understand point of view, have a student re-read the second and third paragraphs of the story aloud. Remind students that the story is told by a first-person narrator; then, ask them to find the words that indicate this point of view. *(I, my, me)* List the words on the board under the heading FIRST PERSON. Next, ask students to retell the story from a third-person point of view. Ask them to point out the words they used to refer to the main character. *(Esperanza's, her, hers)* List these words on the board under the heading THIRD PERSON. Repeat the process with other passages.

Additional Practice

Mixed Ability Group **Analyze Character** Have groups of students make a character web that describes Esperanza. As group members name traits, have them go back to the story and find passages that support the named traits. If groups need prompting, ask the following questions:

- After Esperanza pleaded with her mother to let her eat at school, her mother finally gave in. What does this reveal about Esperanza? *(she is persistent)*
- What do Esperanza's reactions to Sister Superior reveal about her character? *(she is sensitive)*
- What is one trait that Esperanza states explicitly about herself? *(she is shy)*

Vocabulary Development

Reteach the Key Idea

Reinforce Targeted Vocabulary Write the Word Bank words and their definitions on the chalkboard, and review them with students. Then, review the word origins explained at the top of page 173 of the student book. Make sure that students understand how the meaning of each word is derived from its origin.

- *canteen (p. 169):* a place to get food or drink in a school or factory; school cafeteria
- *triangles (p. 169):* three-sided shapes
- *suffering (p. 170):* enduring pain or hardship
- *Spartan (p. 170):* hardy, disciplined person
- *anemic (p. 170):* pale and weak

Grammar Link

Additional Practice

Make Pronouns and Antecedents Agree Have students complete the sentences below with a pronoun that agrees with the underlined antecedent.

1. <u>Jessica</u> likes to put peanut butter on ___ sandwiches. *(her)*
2. When <u>Tony</u> packs lunch, ___ always includes an apple. *(he)*
3. Ms. Ramirez gives her <u>twins</u> milk with ___ breakfast. *(their)*
4. <u>Judy and I</u> like to eat ___ meals together. *(our)*
5. <u>Robert</u> gave me a piece of ___ apple pie. *(his)*
6. Why do <u>you</u> always eat ___ salad first? *(your)*

Reading Skills Development

Rewrite a Scene Students may have difficulty understanding that a narrator is not the author but simply another character who happens to be telling the story. To help emphasize this point for students, have students read "Bargain," another story in the student book that is written in the first-person point of view. Students should read the story and select a specific scene to rewrite from another character's perspective, using first-person point of view. Have students share their results with the class. Ask: How did the change in point of view change the telling of the story? Why do you think the author decided to tell the story from the narrator's point of view?

SKILLS FOCUS

Vocabulary Skill
Understand word origins.

(Teacher Tip)

Point out that although the expression "without blood" is the etymology of *anemic*, anemic people actually lack sufficient red blood cells. People who are anemic often look pale, which may be why the word originally meant "without blood."

(Especially for ELL)

To demonstrate how similar-sounding Spanish and English words may have the same origin, invite native Spanish speakers to give the Spanish versions of these words.

(Core Skill)

Use the resources in the Reading Skills and Strategies section of this book to help students having difficulty understanding characters. Use "A Rice Sandwich" for the application portion of the lesson.

Literary Skill
Understand the narrator.

Reading Skill
Make inferences.

Resources

In this book:
• Vocabulary and Comprehension, p. 81
• Additional Vocabulary Practice, p. 82

Other Resources:
• *The Holt Reader*
• *Audio CD Library*
• *Audio CD Library, Selections and Summaries in Spanish*
• *Supporting Instruction in Spanish*
• *Videocassette, Segment 2*

Teacher Tip

Because some students may have been adopted, it is important to present the character traits in terms of behaviors rather than hereditary characteristics.

TARGETED STRATEGIES FOR SPECIAL EDUCATION STUDENTS

Prereading

Alternative Teaching Strategy

Core Skill **Preview and Predict** Have students open their books to page 169. Ask a student to read the story title aloud. Have students tell whether or not they think a rice sandwich sounds good. Then, ask students to predict what this story might be about.

Reading

Listening and Speaking Opportunity

Read Aloud Esperanza narrates this story in the first person. She talks to the reader colloquially, with words and phrasing a girl her age would use. For that reason "A Rice Sandwich" lends itself well to being read aloud. Let students take turns choosing a paragraph of narration and reading it expressively. If they have difficulty, first model reading a paragraph and then have students read it.

Alternative Activity

Core Skill **Make a Character Web** Suggest students use a character web to organize all the information they learn about Esperanza. Have them write her name in a circle in the center of their papers. As they read, encourage them to jot down her character traits on spokes around the central circle. Tell students that for each trait they include, they must connect other circles that contain supporting information from the story. If there's time, have students make a small character web of Esperanza's mother.

Postreading

Alternative Activity

Use Point of View After students read "A Rice Sandwich," check their understanding of point of view by asking them to summarize the story in the first person, as if they were Esperanza. Then, choose students to retell relevant parts of the story in a third-person narrative, through the eyes of either Esperanza's mother or Sister Superior. Have them first brainstorm about what Esperanza's mother probably thought when her daughter asked her for a bag lunch or what Sister Superior thought when Esperanza was sent to her office. Elicit that the story changes according to the point of view from which it is told.

NAME _____ DATE _____

Vocabulary and Comprehension

Elements of Literature
pages 168–173

"A Rice Sandwich"

A. Use the words from the Word Bank and the clues to fill in the puzzle.

Across
3. enduring pain or hardship
4. cafeteria

Down
1. three-sided shapes
2. pale and weak
3. hardy, disciplined person

Word Bank
canteen
triangles
suffering
Spartan
anemic

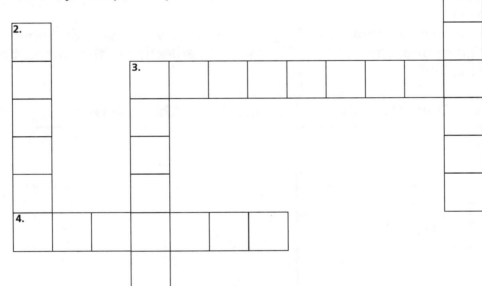

B. Answer each question below.

1. What does Esperanza do at the beginning of the story?

_____

_____

2. Does Esperanza enjoy her lunch in the canteen? Why or why not?

_____

_____

Additional Vocabulary Practice

"A Rice Sandwich"

A. Match words and definitions. Write the letter of the correct definition next to each word.

_____ **1.** anemic

_____ **2.** shy

_____ **3.** tired

_____ **4.** skinny

_____ **5.** ugly

_____ **6.** raggedy

a. timid; reserved

b. thin

c. unattractive; not pretty

d. shabby or shaggy

e. worn-out; exhausted

f. pale and weak

B. Re-read each adjective above carefully to determine whether it describes physical or emotional characteristics. Write each adjective in the correct box in the chart below.

Physical Characteristics	Emotional Characteristics

C. Choose two words from the boxes. Use each word in a sentence.

1. _____

_____

2. _____

_____

"Antaeus" by Borden Deal

Prereading

Alternative Activities

(**Core Skill**) **Use the Title to Make a Prediction** Have students read the Allusion section found on student book page 174 to learn about who Antaeus is in Greek mythology. Ask students to make a prediction about the story, based on the title. *(Students may say that the story will be about someone with strong connections to the earth.)* Tell students to keep their prediction in mind as they read and to think about what the allusion adds to the story.

Read the Adaptation Distribute copies of the adapted reading of "Antaeus" (available in this book and, with marginal questions, in *Holt Adapted Reader*). To prepare for reading the original version and to practice fluency, students should read the adaptation silently. Encourage students to write notes, questions, predictions, reactions, and comments on the worksheets as they read.

(**Especially for ELL**) **Use Spanish Resources** Spanish-speaking English-language learners may benefit from reading or listening to the selection summary in Spanish in preparation for reading the selection in English.

Vocabulary Practice

Preview Additional Vocabulary Preview the following additional vocabulary words with students. Write the words and their definitions on the chalkboard, and ask for volunteers to use each in a sentence.

- *robust (p. 176):* strong; full of energy
- *obscure (p. 177):* unclear
- *stolid (p. 178):* unemotional
- *reckoned (p. 179):* thought; calculated
- *laborious (p. 179):* involving great labor or work
- *inert (p. 179):* unmoving
- *dilating (p. 179):* widening
- *violation (p. 180):* breaking of a rule or law
- *frenzied (p. 183):* wildly energetic
- *nurtured (p. 183):* cared for
- *sterility (p. 183):* lifelessness
- *anonymous (p. 183):* without a name

SKILLS FOCUS

Literary Skills
- Understand motivation.
- Understand allusion.

Reading Skill
Make predictions.

(**Resources**)

In this book:
- Adapted Readings
- Vocabulary and Comprehension, p. 87
- Additional Vocabulary Practice, p. 90 (includes the next selection)

Other Resources:
- *Holt Adapted Reader*
- *Audio CD Library*
- *Audio CD Library, Selections and Summaries in Spanish*
- *Supporting Instruction in Spanish*

(**Core Skill**)

Use the resources in the Reading Skills and Strategies section of this book to help students having difficulty making predictions. Use "Antaeus" for the application portion of the lesson

Reading
Alternative Activity

Use the Audio Recording You may consider having struggling readers listen to the audio recording of the story as they follow along in their books. Stop the recording from time to time to allow students to make predictions about what will happen next in the story. Write students' predictions on the chalkboard, and when you do pause the reading, have students review their last predictions before making new ones.

Alternative Teaching Strategy

Mixed Ability Group **Use a Motivation Chart** Arrange students in small, mixed ability groups to take turns reading from the story. Whenever group members pause to change readers, have them also use a chart such as the one below to keep track of the actions and motivations of the main characters. Point out that characters may be listed on the chart more than once, for more than one action, and emphasize to students that characters who engage in the same actions may nevertheless have different motivations. Encourage students to discuss characters' possible motivations for their actions as they fill out their charts. After groups have finished reading, allow time for them to share with the class their notes and inferences.

Character	Action	Motivation

Postreading
Reteach the Main Idea

Draw the Struggle of the Hero Discuss with students the similarities between the character of T. J. and the Greek mythological figure of Antaeus. Ask students specifically to speak about what the allusion adds to the story. Then, point out that figures from mythology are frequent subjects for fine art. Provide students with drawing supplies, and have them each draw a picture of the hero of Deal's story. Challenge students not only to show T. J.'s struggle but to give the viewer some idea of what things are important to T. J. Students may want to show T. J. nurturing his plants on the rooftop, for example, or facing down the men who have come to destroy his garden.

Vocabulary Development

Reteach the Main Idea

Clarify Word Meanings Write on the chalkboard the list of additional vocabulary words that were defined on page 83 in this book. Have students choose five words from the list and use each of these five words in an original sentence. Call on students to share their sentences with the class.

Alternative Activity

Share Examples of Dialect Students may mistakenly believe that dialect is incorrect and always the way "someone else" speaks. Point out to students that every region has its peculiarities of speech, from the words people use (for soft drinks, for example) to the pronunciations and speech rhythms of those words. Emphasize to students that this diversity adds to the constant change and great creativity of the English language. Ask students to make lists of different words or pronunciations used by friends or family who live in another area of the country. Have students share their examples and tell what is unusual about them. Ask whether the friends or family have noted the use of dialect in their own speech, and challenge students to give examples of their own use of dialect.

Reading Skills Development

Mixed Ability Group **Practice Understanding Character Motivation** Students who have difficulty making predictions about a text may need more practice understanding character motivation. Arrange students in small, mixed ability groups to read a selection from the "Making Predictions" section of the list that begins on page 383 of this book. Have groups read the story, pausing occasionally to make predictions. Then, each group member should choose a specific action, speech, thought, or decision of the main character and think of what the character's motivation is at that point in the story. What does the character want, and why? How will the character's motivation affect what happens in the story? Group members can write down their thoughts before sharing them with the group. Ask for volunteers to read their results for the class.

SKILLS FOCUS

TARGETED STRATEGIES FOR SPECIAL EDUCATION STUDENTS

Prereading

Background

Make a Connection The story is about a young boy who is trying to make a home in an unfamiliar place. Ask students if they have ever visited a town or city and found it strange. What elements about home did they find themselves missing? If students have limited experience visiting unfamiliar places, ask them to think about the things that mean "home" to them. How would they feel if those elements were changed or taken away?

Reading

Additional Activity

Core Skill **Make Predictions** Have students listen to the audio recording of the story. Pause the recording occasionally to sum up the events in the story and to ask students to make predictions about what they think will happen next in the story. Have them support their predictions with details from the text. Write students' predictions on the chalkboard, and review them with students at the next stopping place in the story.

Postreading

Alternative Assessment

Core Skill **Make a Character Map** Have students make a character map by drawing a circle and writing T. J.'s name in it. Students should draw other circles connected to the central circle that give character traits demonstrated by T. J. in the story. Students should be prepared to support their choice of traits by giving details from the story. Ask students to share their character maps and to tell how T. J.'s traits contribute to his actions. For example, the fact that T. J. values nature leads him to want to make a garden on the rooftop. A sample character map is given below.

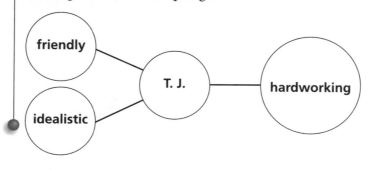

Vocabulary and Comprehension

"Antaeus"

A. Match words and definitions. Write the letter of the correct definition next to each word.

_____ **1.** sterile

_____ **2.** contemplate

_____ **3.** domain

_____ **4.** shrewd

_____ **5.** resolute

a. territory

b. look at or think about carefully

c. firm and purposeful; determined

d. barren; lacking interest or vitality

e. clever

B. Choose three words from above. Use each word in a sentence.

1. _____

_____

2. _____

_____

3. _____

_____

C. Write T or F next to each statement to tell if it is true or false.

_____ **1.** T. J. comes to the South from the North.

_____ **2.** T. J.'s family moves to find work during World War II.

_____ **3.** Antaeus is the Greek god of earthquakes.

_____ **4.** The boys plant grass on the roof of the building.

_____ **5.** The adults who find the boys' garden approve of their hard work.

Elements of Literature
pages 187–189

"In a Mix of Cultures, an Olio of Plantings" by Anne Raver

SKILLS FOCUS

Reading Skill
Identify the main idea.

(**Resources**)

In this book:
• Vocabulary and Comprehension, p. 89
• Additional Vocabulary Practice, p. 90 (includes the previous selection)

Other Resources:
• *Audio CD Library*
• *Audio CD Library, Selections and Summaries in Spanish*
• *Supporting Instruction in Spanish*

(**Core Skill**)

Use the resources in the Reading Skills and Strategies section of this book to help students having difficulty determining main idea. Use "In a Mix of Cultures, an Olio of Plantings" for the application portion of the lesson.

(**Special Education Students**)

As students read the selection aloud, have them also summarize each paragraph. This should help them find the main idea of the article.

Prereading
Vocabulary Practice

(**Especially for ELL**) **Preview Selection Vocabulary** Preview the following words and definitions with students. Ask students if they can make any predictions about the article from the words. Then, ask students to find the words as they read the article.

• *husk (p. 188):* outer covering of a fruit or vegetable
• *pungent (p. 188):* strong-smelling
• *herb (p. 188):* a plant used in cooking or in medicine
• *till (p. 188):* prepare ground for planting
• *debris (p. 188):* garbage or clutter

Reading
Reteach the Key Idea

(**Core Skill**) **Use Questions to Find the Main Idea** Remind students that finding the main idea of a piece of writing can be as easy as asking a few questions—the 5*W-How?* questions. Have students fill out a chart such as the following as they read.

Who was involved?	
What happened?	
When did it happen?	
Where did it happen?	
Why did it happen?	
How did it happen?	

Postreading
Alternative Assessment

(**Mixed Ability Group**) **Write an Advertisement** To check student comprehension of the article, have students work in small groups to write an ad for a community garden such as the one described in the selection. Groups can use the information from the article in their ads but should come up with their own ideas about the benefits and attractions of such a garden to entice the ad's audience to participate in the program. Have groups share their ads with the class.

Vocabulary and Comprehension

"In a Mix of Cultures, an Olio of Plantings"

A. Match the words in the left column with the clues in the right column. Write the correct letter in the blanks.

_____ **1.** husk

_____ **2.** perennial

_____ **3.** herb

_____ **4.** debris

_____ **5.** pungent

a. trash or clutter

b. outer covering of a fruit or vegetable

c. a plant used in cooking or medicine

d. strong-smelling

e. a plant that grows again year after year

B. Choose three words from above. Use each word in a sentence.

1. _____

_____

2. _____

_____

3. _____

_____

C. Do you think city gardening programs are a good idea or a bad idea? Support your answer with details from the article.

_____

_____

_____

_____

_____

_____

_____

Additional Vocabulary Practice

"Antaeus"; "In a Mix of Cultures, an Olio of Plantings"

A. Match words and definitions. Write the letter of the correct definition next to each word.

_____ **1.** robust

_____ **2.** reckon

_____ **3.** inert

_____ **4.** stolid

_____ **5.** nurture

a. unemotional

b. unmoving

c. think or calculate

d. strong; full of energy

e. care for

B. Choose two words from above. Use each word in a sentence.

1. _____

_____

2. _____

_____

C. Replace the word or phrase in parentheses with the correct word from the Word Bank.

1. When you eat an ear of corn, you first must remove the *(outer covering)* _____.

2. The spaghetti sauce was flavored with *(plants used for cooking)* _____.

3. After the circus left town, the fairgrounds were covered with *(clutter)* _____.

4. Before you plant seeds, you must *(prepare for planting)* _____ the land.

5. Cilantro is a particularly *(strong-smelling)* _____ herb.

Word Bank
husk
pungent
till
debris
herb

Comparing Literature: Characters and Character Traits

Prereading

Vocabulary Practice

Preview Additional Vocabulary To help students increase their vocabulary and better understand the reading, preview the following words and their definitions.

- *epidemic (p. 192):* outbreak of disease
- *solemn (p. 199):* serious
- *sore at (p. 200):* angry with
- *pitch (p. 200):* fall

Reading

Alternative Activity

Read the Stories Aloud Struggling readers may benefit from hearing the stories read aloud as they follow along in their books. You may want to ask proficient readers to take turns reading from the stories or read the stories aloud yourself.

Alternative Teaching Strategy

Use a Venn Diagram Schatz in "A Day's Wait" and the narrator of "Stolen Day" both are faced with illness, but they react in completely different ways. Draw a Venn diagram on the chalkboard with *Schatz* and *narrator of "Stolen Day"* written at the top of the circles. Ask students to compare and contrast the two boys' attitudes toward their "illnesses." Alert students to look for specific words in the stories that reflect this attitude of the characters. After students have finished reading, ask them to share their diagrams.

Postreading

Alternative Activity

(**Mixed Ability Group**) **Compare Literary Elements** Review with students the literary elements of setting, character, and plot. Point out to students that the elements are interrelated—sometimes a stormy night, for example, can emphasize a character's anger or the taut suspense of the plot. Arrange students in small groups, and challenge the groups to find elements about the setting and plot of each story that reflect qualities about the characters in the stories. Ask groups to share their ideas with the class.

SKILLS FOCUS

Literary Skill
Understand character traits.

Reading Skill
Compare and contrast characters.

(**Resources**)

In this book:
- Vocabulary and Comprehension, p. 93
- Additional Vocabulary Practice, p. 94

(**Especially for ELL**)

English-language learners may either not understand or may completely sympathize with Schatz's confusion over the different systems of measurement. Discuss the issue with students, and allow students to discuss their own difficulties adapting from one system to another.

(**Core Skill**)

Use the resources in the Reading Skills and Strategies section of this book to help students having difficulty comparing and contrasting. Use "A Day's Wait" and "Stolen Day" for the application portion of the lesson.

SKILLS FOCUS

Literary Skill
Understand character traits.

Reading Skill
Compare and contrast characters.

Resources

In this book:
• Vocabulary and Comprehension, p. 93
• Additional Vocabulary Practice, p. 94

Teacher Tip

Students may benefit from comparing and contrasting brief sections of each story side by side. You may want to have them compare sections that show how each character feels about his predicament.

TARGETED STRATEGIES FOR SPECIAL EDUCATION STUDENTS

Prereading

Additional Background

Freewrite on the Theme Explain to students that the two stories follow characters who face the possibility of a serious illness. Help students think of other characters they know of from books, films, or TV shows who are confronted with the possibility of becoming ill. How did the characters act? Allow students time to freewrite on how they would feel if they thought they might be becoming seriously ill.

Alternative Activity

(Core Skill) **Use the Titles to Make Predictions** Encourage students to compare the titles of the two stories and to try to use the titles to predict how the characters will react to the prospect of falling ill. What feelings or thoughts does each title evoke?

Reading

Alternative Activity

(Core Skill) **Listen for the Characters' Traits** Read the two stories aloud. As you read the stories aloud, pause often to allow students to discuss what they can tell so far about the boy in each story. Tell students to think of adjectives that describe the characters, and write students' suggestions on the chalkboard. After finishing the two stories, review the adjectives on the chalkboard and ask students what traits the two characters have in common. Then, ask how the characters differ.

Postreading

Alternative Activity

Compare the Characters to a Real Person Students who have difficulty comparing the two characters may benefit from comparing and contrasting each character with a person they know. Students should begin by thinking of how the people they know would have acted differently in the same situations as the characters. Then, students should write down their ideas and explore what the difference in actions might indicate about the characters' and people's different traits. Ask students to share their comparisons with the class.

Vocabulary and Comprehension

Comparing Literature: Characters and Character Traits

A. Match the words in the left column with the clues in the right column. Write the correct letter in the blanks.

_____ **1.** purgative

_____ **2.** covey

_____ **3.** flush

_____ **4.** rheumatism

_____ **5.** freshet

a. scare into the open

b. sudden overflowing of a stream

c. a disease

d. a group of quail

e. a laxative

B. Choose three words from above. Use each word in a sentence.

1. _____

_____

2. _____

_____

3. _____

_____

C. Write T or F next to each statement to tell if it is true or false.

_____ **1.** *Schatz* is a German word for "treasure."

_____ **2.** Schatz wants to go fishing before he dies.

_____ **3.** The narrator of "Stolen Day" is unexpectedly visited by the doctor.

_____ **4.** The narrator of "Stolen Day" catches a huge carp.

_____ **5.** The narrator of "Stolen Day" sees a girl drown in the well.

Additional Vocabulary Practice

Comparing Literature: Characters and Character Traits

A. Match words and definitions. Write the letter of the correct definition next to each word.

_____ **1.** sore at   **a.** angry with

_____ **2.** epidemic   **b.** serious

_____ **3.** solemn   **c.** outbreak of disease

_____ **4.** pitch   **d.** fall

B. Choose two words from above. Use each word in a sentence.

1. _____

_____

2. _____

_____

C. Replace the word or phrases in parentheses with the correct word from the Word Bank.

1. Due to the sudden *(outbreak of disease)*

_____, the tourist business to the islands fell off dramatically.

2. Samantha pulled hard on the rope, afraid the boat

would *(fall)* _____ over.

3. Grandpa laughed that he was hardly *(angry at)*

_____ us for the surprise party; in fact, he had

enjoyed it immensely.

4. Studying for their tests, the students were all quiet and *(serious)*

_____.

> **Word Bank**
> epidemic
> solemn
> sore at
> pitch

Collection 3
Living in the Heart

Elements of Literature: Theme

Alternative Teaching Strategies

Retell a Fable For students struggling with the concept of theme, read a fable by Aesop. A good one is "The Lion and the Mouse," the story of a mouse who awakens a sleeping lion. To keep the lion from eating him, the mouse pleads, "Let me go. I will never forget your kindness. Someday I may be able to help you." So the lion lets the mouse go. Later the lion is caught in a hunter's trap. The mouse sets him free by gnawing through the ropes that bind the lion. Act out the story as you tell it. Help students identify the theme by asking them what the lion learns from the mouse. Lead them to discover the traditional theme: Even the smallest act of kindness can bring great rewards.

(Especially for ELL) Make Cross-Cultural Connections Ask students for the names of stories from their own languages and cultures that have the same set of themes as are discussed in the student book, about the importance of friendship and so on. Themes are often universal, and students should be able to relate to the themes found in the literature. Relating particular themes to students' lives is an excellent way to enable students to gain an appreciation of literature and reading.

Academic Vocabulary

Review Vocabulary Help students develop their academic vocabulary by reviewing these words from student book pages 236–237 and their definitions:

- *theme:* main idea of a story
- *plot:* pattern of events in a story or play
- *title:* name of a literary work, movie, or piece of music
- *setting:* place where the action of a story occurs
- *character:* person or animal in a story, poem, or play
- *novel:* long story, more than one hundred pages, usually about fictional people

Reinforce what students have learned. Have them write a paragraph using some of the academic vocabulary listed above to describe a story they have read or a television show they have watched.

SKILLS FOCUS

Literary Skill
Understand and analyze theme.

(Teacher Tip)
For some students, learning to distinguish between topic and theme may take a great deal of time. Teaching what it's about and what it's *really* about will take patience on the part of the teacher. Sometimes one particular work will suddenly make it clear for a student.

SKILLS FOCUS

Literary Skill
Understand and analyze
theme.

TARGETED STRATEGIES FOR SPECIAL EDUCATION STUDENTS

Elements of Literature: Theme
Alternative Teaching Strategy

Identify Themes Explain to students that most stories, poems, plays, and even songs convey important messages about people and the world in which we live. Tell a well-known folk story—"The Little Red Hen" or "The Tortoise and the Hare." Help students to identify the story's theme. Give students the opportunity to share some favorite stories, and ask them to identify the themes.

Alternative Activity

(Core Skill) Illustrate the Theme Write the following three themes or any themes of your choice on the chalkboard or on an overhead:

- the benefits of cooperation
- the value of friendship
- the importance of generosity

Ask students to create posters that reflect the themes. Have them work in pairs. Students can create original art or use photographs from magazines. Ask students to list the names of two or more stories with that theme on each theme poster.

Alternative Assessment

Distinguish Between Theme and Plot Have students work collaboratively to identify the difference between theme and plot. Ask each group to make a list of three or four of their favorite movies. Ask students to group their list according to theme so they can see that stories with very different plots can have similar themes. Circulate and assist groups as they work. Remind them to consider the main character and whether the character changes or makes any discovery. Have them re-read pages 236–237 of their texts to assist them in thinking about plot and theme. When the groups are ready, have them present their results to the class. Make sure students understand the difference between plot and theme. In other words, stress the difference between what happens in the story and what it means. Make your examples very specific: A movie may be about a man robbing a bank and getting caught, but the theme is that crime does not pay.

"The Highwayman" by Alfred Noyes

Prereading

Vocabulary Practice

Preview Challenging Vocabulary Write the following words and their definitions on the chalkboard. Model the pronunciation of each word, and help students use the word in a sentence. Remind students to look for the words as they read.

- *breeches (p. 247, line 8):* men's knee-length pants
- *galloped (p. 248, line 36):* rode a horse very fast
- *muskets (p. 250, line 45):* guns with long barrels, used before the invention of the rifle
- *torrent (p. 247, line 1):* strong, fast flow
- *twinkle (p. 247, line 10):* sparkle, reflected light

Alternative Activity

Use *The Holt Reader* You may consider having students use the Before You Read page in *The Holt Reader,* either instead of or in addition to the Before You Read page in the student book.

Reading

Alternative Activities

Read the Annotated Version Distribute copies of the annotated version of "The Highwayman" (available in this book and, with marginal questions, in *Holt Adapted Reader*). Encourage students to write notes, questions, reactions, and comments on the worksheets as they read.

Use *The Holt Reader* You may have students read the selection in *The Holt Reader* and use the margins in that book to make notes and respond to the instruction.

Listening and Speaking Opportunity

Especially for ELL Use the Audio Recording Students may not know where to pause when reading poetry. To help students understand how the poem should sound, play the recording all the way through while they follow along in their books. Then, play the recording stanza by stanza, asking a student to read each stanza aloud after it is played. Doing choral response with some stanzas is also useful, as is asking the students to clap out the rhythm while they listen to portions of the recording once more. Discuss alliteration with students, keeping in mind that it may be a new concept to

SKILLS FOCUS

Literary Skills
- Understand topic and theme.
- Understand narrative poems.

Resources

In this book:
- Adapted Readings
- Vocabulary and Comprehension, p. 101
- Additional Vocabulary Practice, p. 104 (includes the next selection)

Other Resources:
- *The Holt Reader*
- *Holt Adapted Reader*
- *Audio CD Library*
- *Audio CD Library, Selections and Summaries in Spanish*
- *Supporting Instruction in Spanish*
- Videocassette, Segment 3

Especially for ELL

Imagery can be difficult for ELLs to understand. Review these phrases before students read the poem: "ribbon of moonlight," "black cascade of perfume," "the bunch of lace at his throat."

English-language learners. Tell students that it is a frequently used poetic device in English in which the same consonant sound is repeated in a phrase or line of poetry. Two examples of alliteration in "The Highwayman" are "Over the cobbles, he clattered and clashed" in line 13 and "Dumb as a dog" in line 24.

Postreading
Alternative Activities

Use *The Holt Reader* You may consider having students use the postreading activities in *The Holt Reader,* either instead of or in addition to the postreading activities in the student book.

Change the Ending/Change the Theme Reinforce the concept of theme by having students write different endings to "The Highwayman." Help students decide whether the original theme of the poem changes with the new endings.

Alternative Teaching Strategy

Core Skill **Complete a Plot Diagram** To help students work out the theme of the poem, draw a three-column chart with the headings LOVE, BETRAYAL, and DEATH. Ask students to note how each subject is handled in the poem. Ask: Which characters are in love? What stands in the way of their love? Who betrays them? Why? Who dies? How and why? List the student responses on the chalkboard and lead a discussion on theme. What is the poem telling you about the three subjects listed on the chalkboard? List on the chalkboard the varying student responses. Possible themes they may identify are: *love is worth dying for; unrequited love (Tim's for Bess) can lead to betrayal.* Ask students to tell whether they agree with the themes listed and to explain their position.

Additional Practice

Examine Descriptive Words On the chalkboard, create a two-column chart, the left side headed CHARACTER, and the right, WORDS AND PHRASES. Write the names of the characters in the left column and invite students to list words and phrases from the poem that describe how each character looks and acts. Examples are given.

Character	Words and Phrases
Highwayman	*whistles* *rides* *wears French hat*
Bess	*black-eyed* *red-lipped* *black hair plaited*
Tim	*white and peaked face* *eyes hollows of madness* *hair like moldy hay* *dumb as a dog*

Vocabulary Development

Reteach the Key Idea

Understand Metaphor and Simile In "The Highwayman," there are many examples of metaphors and similes. Metaphor makes a direct comparison between two things. For example:

- The wind was a torrent of darkness *(p. 247, line 1)*
- The moon was a ghostly galleon *(p. 247, line 2)*
- The road was a gypsy's ribbon *(p. 248, line 39)*

Ask students to explain the comparisons.

A comparison between two things using words or phrases such as *like, as, than, similar to, resembles,* or *seems* is a simile. Review the following similes from "The Highwayman," and let students explain the comparison in each case.

- and the hours crawled by like years *(p. 251, line 57)*
- Her face was like a light! *(p. 251, line 73)*
- He spurred like a madman *(p. 252, line 85)*
- Down like a dog on the highway *(p. 252, line 88)*

Alternative Teaching Strategy

Use Figures of Speech To help students understand the use of similes and metaphors, write the following chart on the chalkboard. Fill in only the *Idea* column. Then, have students complete the comparisons with simile and metaphor. *(Possible answers are given.)*

Idea	Simile	Metaphor
cold wind	The wind seemed cold as ice.	The wind was ice against his face.
bright moonlight	The moonlight was as bright as gold.	The moon was a gold coin.
dark night	The night looked dark as the devil.	Blackness reigned at midnight.

Reading Skills Development

Mixed Ability Group **Recognize Theme** To help students develop and apply their skill in recognizing theme, arrange students in odd-numbered, mixed ability groups to read together a selection you choose from the "Recognizing Theme" section of the list that begins on page 383 of this book. Then, have group members work together to describe in their own words what the selection is about. Group members should then answer two questions: What is the story's subject? What is the story's theme? Remind students that the two are different. Have groups share their answers to the questions with the class.

SKILLS FOCUS

Vocabulary Skills
Understand similes and metaphors.

Teacher Tip
The figurative language in the poem is also full of *imagery*, a term you may decide not to deal with in this selection. But you can direct students to notice how the poem appeals strongly to the senses.

Core Skill
Use the resources in the Reading Skills and Strategies section of this book to help students having difficulty recognizing theme. Use "The Highwayman" for the application portion of the lesson.

TARGETED STRATEGIES FOR SPECIAL EDUCATION STUDENTS

Prereading
Reteach the Key Idea

Provide Background Information To help students understand "The Highwayman," explain that it is a narrative poem, that is, a poem that tells a story. Like novels and movies, narrative poems have themes. This poem is a story that takes place in England during the 1700s, but its theme may still be relevant today. Tell students that as they read, they should try to think about what the poet might be saying about love.

Reading
Listening and Speaking Opportunity

Use Audio to Increase Understanding and Fluency Use the recording, pausing between events to ask students if they can predict what will happen next. The second playing of the recording should be stanza by stanza to allow volunteers to read aloud. At some point, have students listen to the tape all the way through without interruption, after they've demonstrated their understanding of the events.

Postreading
Alternative Assessments

Retell the Story To assess whether students understand the plot of the poem, ask them to retell the story in prose. Instruct them in the use of a plot line and note the actions of the main characters. Ask them, "What happens next?" Some students might illustrate a scene or do a drawing of a character from the story.

Make a Time Line One of the areas in which special education students are often weak is in their understanding of time, on both practical and conceptual levels. Thus, working on a time line to clarify the order of events would be useful in conjunction with the plot line.

Core Skill **Discuss the Theme** Have students discuss what the author might be saying about love. First, identify the two people in love. What were the obstacles to their love? What did Bess sacrifice for their love? Ask students to explain what they think the theme is in their own words.

Vocabulary and Comprehension

"The Highwayman"

A. Match words and definitions. Write the letter of the correct definition next to each word.

____ **1.** casement   **a.** harass or push along

____ **2.** harry   **b.** window that opens outward on hinges

____ **3.** rapier   **c.** braiding

____ **4.** plaiting   **d.** sword

B. Write T or F next to each statement to tell if it is true or false.

_____ **1.** The highwayman was a robber.

_____ **2.** Bess had long red hair.

_____ **3.** The highwayman was shot on a moonlit night.

_____ **4.** The soldiers wanted only to talk to the highwayman.

_____ **5.** The highwayman heard Bess's warning and escaped.

_____ **6.** The highwayman promised Bess he'd be back by moonlight.

C. Answer each question below.

1. When does the highwayman expect to return to Bess?

_____

_____

2. Why are the soldiers waiting for the highwayman?

_____

_____

3. Why do the soldiers tie up Bess?

_____

_____

4. How does Bess warn the highwayman?

_____

_____

"Gentlemen of the Road" by Mara Rockliff

SKILLS FOCUS

Reading Skill
Understand cause and effect.

Resources

In this book:
• Adapted Readings
• Vocabulary and Comprehension, p. 103
• Additional Vocabulary Practice, p. 104 (includes the previous selection)

Other Resources:
• *Holt Adapted Reader*
• *Audio CD Library*
• *Audio CD Library, Selections and Summaries in Spanish*
• *Supporting Instruction in Spanish*

Special Education Students

Help students by giving them extra feedback and by modeling more of the learning strategies.

Prereading
Additional Background

Explain the Robin Hood Legend Explain that Robin Hood has been written about since roughly 1100. By the eighteenth century, many stories, poems, plays, and ballads made the legend popular. In all the tales, Robin Hood seeks justice for the poor by robbing the rich. The poor help the outlaws survive by providing them with the necessities for life in the forest.

Alternative Activity

Read the Adaptation Distribute copies of the adapted reading of "Gentlemen of the Road" (available in this book and, with marginal questions, in *Holt Adapted Reader*). To prepare for reading the original version and to practice fluency, students should read the adaptation silently.

Reading
Alternative Teaching Strategies

(**Especially for ELL**) **Learn with Peers** Pair an English-language learner with a native English speaker. Ask the pairs to take turns reading paragraphs from "Gentlemen of the Road." Have students list on a piece of paper the words or phrases they don't understand. Then, ask students to define the words. Ask them to share the reading strategies, if any, that they used to get the meanings.

Complete a Cause-and-Effect Chart Students may benefit from continuing the cause-and-effect chart begun on page 256 of the student book. Have students copy the chart into their notebooks. Guide them in completing the last effect box, which begins with "Highwaymen . . . ," with the information that highwaymen gave some of the money they stole to the poor. Then, have them create a new effect box to show what happened when they gave away money, and so on.

Postreading
Alternative Activity

Play a Cause-and-Effect Game List several causes and effects on the chalkboard, and have students match them. Then, ask students to sum up by giving three reasons why people thought highwaymen were gentlemen.

Vocabulary and Comprehension

"Gentlemen of the Road"

A. Complete each sentence with a word from the Word Bank.

1. The highwaymen robbed people as they traveled

through the _____.

2. Wealthy women often wore expensive

_____.

3. The highwaymen were often thought of as

_____ because they treated their
victims with kindness and respect.

4. The highwaymen robbed _____, who had lots of money
and valuables.

5. Highwaymen earned the loyalty of their horses, or

_____, by treating them well.

> **Word Bank**
> gentlemen
> aristocrats
> countryside
> jewels
> steeds

B. Write T or F next to each statement to tell if it is true or false.

_____ **1.** Highwaymen robbed from the poor and helped the rich
get richer.

_____ **2.** Highwaymen usually treated their victims as badly as
possible.

_____ **3.** In seventeenth-century England, the punishment for
robbery was a fine.

_____ **4.** Highwaymen came from wealthy families.

_____ **5.** Highwaymen always dressed simply.

_____ **6.** Many poor people believed that highwaymen, like
Robin Hood, were heroes.

_____ **7.** Wealthy travelers rode in private carriages and
stagecoaches.

_____ **8.** The authorities never punished highwaymen.

_____ **9.** Highwaymen often wore high-heeled boots and fancy
clothes.

Additional Vocabulary Practice

Elements of Literature
pages 246–259

"The Highwayman"; "Gentlemen of the Road"

A. Complete each sentence with a word from the Word Bank.

1. The road was a ribbon of _____, visible even though it was night.

2. The highwayman wore _____ at his neck.

3. Bess, the highwayman's _____ sweetheart, was very beautiful.

4. Bess heard the horse's _____ from far away.

5. The _____ made a loud bang when it was fired.

Word Bank
gallop
musket
lace
moonlight
bonny

B. Choose two words from above. Use each word in a sentence.

1. _____

_____

2. _____

_____

C. Use context clues to determine the meaning of the underlined word.

1. Some highwaymen tried to act like *gentlemen* and treated women with

respect. <u>Gentlemen</u> means _____

_____

2. With their stylish clothes and fine horses, highwaymen looked more like

aristocrats than simple butchers or cheese sellers. <u>Aristocrats</u> means

_____

_____

"Annabel Lee" by Edgar Allan Poe

Prereading

Additional Background

Introduce the Work Edgar Allan Poe, one of America's greatest poets, short story writers, and critics, wrote "Annabel Lee" in tribute to his beloved young wife. In 1835, Poe was given an editorial position in Baltimore, which allowed him to marry his cousin Virginia. It was not a rare occurrence at the time for first cousins to marry. It was her age, thirteen, that was unusual. But they married and seemed quite happy until she became ill with tuberculosis in 1842. After five years of struggle and pain, she died in January 1847. Poe wrote "Annabel Lee" in 1849, the year of his own death.

Vocabulary Practice

(Especially for ELL) **Define Unfamiliar Terms** "Annabel Lee" contains many words that may be unfamiliar to English-language learners. Before reading the poem, write the following words and definitions on the chalkboard and read them with students. Tell students to watch for these words as they read pages 261–262 and to notice how the words are used.

- *bride (p. 262, line 39):* recently married woman
- *chilling (p. 261, line 15):* making cold
- *demons (p. 262, line 31):* fiends; evil, supernatural beings
- *dissever (p. 262, line 32):* separate
- *highborn (p. 261, line 17):* of the upper class
- *kingdom (p. 261, line 2):* country ruled by a king or queen
- *kinsmen (p. 261, line 17):* relatives; family members
- *sepulcher (p. 261, line 19):* tomb; burial place above ground, usually ornate and meant for individuals of noble birth
- *tomb (p. 262, line 41):* burial place

Reading

Listening and Speaking Opportunities

(Especially for ELL) **Use Spanish Resources** Spanish-speaking English-language learners may benefit from listening to the audio recording of the selection in Spanish in preparation for reading the poem in English. You may want to have them comment on any differences between the original and the translation.

SKILLS FOCUS

Literary Skills
- Understand universal themes.
- Understand repetition in poems.

Resources

In this book:
- Vocabulary and Comprehension, p. 109
- Additional Vocabulary Practice, p. 112 (includes the next selection)

Other Resources:
- *Audio CD Library*
- *Audio CD Library, Selections and Summaries in Spanish*
- *Supporting Instruction in Spanish*

Especially for ELL

"Annabel Lee" offers a good opportunity for pronunciation practice. Note particularly the name Annabel Lee, as well as *sepulcher* (sep' əl·kər), both of which will pose difficulty for Asian speakers. Model the words, and have them repeat the words with you and then after you.

Read Aloud Introduce students to "Annabel Lee" with silent reading, and then play the audio recording all the way through. Ask students to follow along as you read the poem again, stanza by stanza, and then have a student repeat the reading. Ask students to sum up each stanza before going on. Discuss why Poe chose to repeat certain words, phrases, and sounds. Elicit from students that the repeated use of the name Annabel Lee reflects his obsession with her and his inability to get her out of his mind. Point out that his repeated use of the word *sea* reminds us that his rhythm brings an association of waves beating repeatedly against the shore. Let students also note the strength of the rhythm and rhyme in the work. Working aloud with the poetry is important for students to be able to appreciate Poe's work.

Alternative Activity

(Especially for ELL) **Practice Choral Reading** Read through the poem with students as a choral reading. Then, divide the class into small groups, combining English-language learners with English-proficient peers. Assign each group a stanza to practice. Once all the students have practiced the material, have the class come back together. Perform the poem, with each group reciting its stanza at the right time. You can also repeat the process, asking individual students in each group to do the reading. Hearing the poem repeated in this manner will help reinforce students' familiarity with the pronunciation, intonation, rhythm, and rhyme of the poem.

Postreading

Alternative Teaching Strategy

Learn to Identify Theme Discuss the theme of the poem with students. Ask students what Poe was trying to say about love and loss. Elicit that the poem was about eternal love, a love that goes on forever, even after one of the lovers has died.

Additional Activity

Develop Literary Skill "Annabel Lee" draws upon elements of fact and fantasy to create the vivid imagery of the kingdom by the sea. Have students go back into the poem to identify individual images. On paper, have them list their findings under two columns with the headings FACT and FANTASY. As students identify the elements of the poem, have them list the imagery in the appropriate column. Ask them to compare their lists when they finish. Then, ask students to demonstrate how the lists contribute to the theme of the poem. Guide them to see how exaggeration, in the form of fantasy, emphasizes the emotions the poet wishes to express.

Vocabulary Development

Additional Activity

Identify Analogies in "Annabel Lee" Students may find the concept of analogy confusing. Explain that an analogy is a comparison between two things to show how they are alike. A writer might use an analogy to explain something difficult by comparing it to something simpler or more familiar. After reading the introduction to analogy on page 265 of their text, have students read how in "Annabel Lee" "we loved with a love . . . that the winged seraphs of heaven coveted. . . ." In other words, Poe says they loved each other so much that the seraphs (angels) envied them. Have students work in pairs to discover other examples of analogy in the poem.

Alternative Activity

Write Analogies Have students complete the comparisons below. The first one has been done as an example.

1. He compared the beauty of the bride to *(a flower in spring)* .
2. Susan said that the ___ reminded her of a tomb because ___.
3. The chill of the night made Terry think of ___.
4. Her envy of her neighbors was like ___.
5. The beams of light from the car reminded Jerry of ___.

Reading Skills Development

(Mixed Ability Group) **Recognize Universal Themes** Students may have difficulty recognizing universal themes in a work. To help students, arrange them in small, mixed ability groups to read together a selection you choose from the "Recognizing Theme" section of the list that begins on page 383 of this book. As they read, have each group take note of situations the main character faces, thoughts the character has, or actions he or she engages in that seem to be common to all humans. After they have finished reading, direct group members to review their lists and to circle those items that relate to the most important ideas in the story. Ask: *What might the author be saying about people in general in the story?* Discuss students' opinions, and point out that in their answers they are identifying the story's universal theme.

SKILLS FOCUS

Vocabulary Skills
Understand and use analogies.

(Core Skill)

Use the resources in the Reading Skills and Strategies section of this book to help students having difficulty recognizing theme. Use "Annabel Lee" for the application portion of the lesson.

Literary Skills
- Understand universal themes.
- Understand repetition in poems.

(**Resources**)

In this book:
- Vocabulary and Comprehension, p. 109
- Additional Vocabulary Practice, p. 112 (includes the next selection)

Other Resources:
- *Audio CD Library*
- *Audio CD Library, Selections and Summaries in Spanish*
- *Supporting Instruction in Spanish*

(**Teacher Tip**)

Using poetry to teach reading to special education students provides an excellent opportunity to read aloud to students and to have them be active listeners. The class can function both as listeners and participants. Listening is an important step in the process of reading and adds to the total language experience.

(**Teacher Tip**)

Some students might prefer to illustrate a scene or do a drawing of a character from the poem.

TARGETED STRATEGIES FOR SPECIAL EDUCATION STUDENTS

Prereading
Background Information

Summarize the Poem Students may have difficulty with the language and format of "Annabel Lee." Provide a brief synopsis for them, telling them that in this poem Poe describes the joy and grief that may accompany love. The language in "Annabel Lee" expresses the feelings Poe experienced upon the death of his wife. People find different ways to express strong emotion; Poe chose to share his feelings of grief through a poem. Have students reflect on how important it is to express emotions. On a piece of paper, have students jot down their thoughts about which medium they think would best capture and express strong emotions.

Reading
Listening and Speaking Opportunity

Use the Audio Recording Help students appreciate the poem by playing the audio recording. Tell them that poems are read differently than prose. Ask them to listen closely to hear how the poem should be read. After playing the reading once without pause, play or read it stanza by stanza, asking students to sum up each stanza in their own words.

Postreading
Alternative Assessment

Retell the Story To assess whether students understand the plot of the poem, ask them to retell the story in their own words. Instruct them in the use of a plot line, and note the actions of the main characters. Ask: What happens next? Have students discuss what the author might be saying about love.

Check Comprehension

(**Mixed Ability Group**) **Recap the Theme of the Poem** After reading the poem, have students work in small groups to answer the following questions:

- Who was Annabel Lee?
- What happened to Annabel Lee?
- Where is Annabel Lee now?
- Why and how did Annabel Lee leave the kingdom?

Vocabulary and Comprehension

"Annabel Lee"

A. Complete each sentence with a word from the Word Bank.

1. Annabel Lee's body was placed in a

_____ by the sea.

2. The speaker and Annabel Lee were happy in their

_____ by the sea.

3. At night, when the moon _____,
the speaker dreams of Annabel Lee.

4. Annabel Lee was a beautiful _____
who lived by the sea.

Word Bank
sepulcher
maiden
beams
kingdom

B. Choose two words from above. Use each word in a sentence.

1. _____

_____

2. _____

_____

C. Answer each question below.

1. Whom is the poem named after?

_____

_____

2. What happened to the young woman in the poem?

_____

_____

3. How does the speaker say the angels felt about him and Annabel Lee?

_____

_____

"The Fall of the House of Poe?"
by Mara Rockliff

SKILLS FOCUS

Reading Skills
Take notes and make outlines.

Vocabulary Skill
Understand Latin roots.

(Resources)

In this book:
• Adapted Readings
• Vocabulary and Comprehension, p. 111
• Additional Vocabulary Practice, p. 112 (includes the previous selection)

Other Resources:
• *Holt Adapted Reader*
• *Audio CD Library*
• *Audio CD Library, Selections and Summaries in Spanish*
• *Supporting Instruction in Spanish*

(Core Skill)

Use the resources in the Reading Skills and Strategies section of this book to help students having difficulty determining main idea. Use "The Fall of the House of Poe?" for the application portion of the lesson.

Prereading
Additional Background

Discuss Historic Preservation Explain to students that places where writers or other famous people lived are sometimes preserved or protected because of their historical significance. For example, there is the Poe cottage located just north of New York City, where Poe lived from 1846 to 1849. It was there that he wrote "Annabel Lee" and a number of other works. The city of New York purchased it, opened it as a museum in 1917, and maintains it as a memorial to Poe, with period furniture and exhibits on the writer, his life, and times.

Alternative Activity

Read the Adaptation Distribute copies of the adapted reading of "The Fall of the House of Poe?" (available in this book and, with marginal questions, in *Holt Adapted Reader*). To prepare for reading the original version and to practice fluency, students should read the adaptation silently. Encourage students to write notes, questions, predictions, reactions, and comments on the worksheets as they read.

Reading
Alternative Activity

Take Notes Have students take turns reading "The Fall of the House of Poe?" aloud. Starting with the end of the third paragraph, have students pause at the end of each paragraph and state the main idea of the paragraph just read. Ask them to supply at least two supporting details. Write their responses on the chalkboard in the format shown on page 266 of the student book. Point out that one can take notes in an outline form like this to help keep track of the most important information in a text.

Postreading
Vocabulary Practice

(Especially for ELL) **Work with Latin Roots** Write on the chalkboard some of the words from the Word Bank on page 270. Go over the exercise on page 270 with students. Ask if they can think of any other words with these roots.

Vocabulary and Comprehension

"The Fall of the House of Poe?"

A. Complete each sentence with a word from the Word Bank.

1. A _____ for New York University said that the school would tear down the building at 85 Amity Street.

2. Many fans of Poe signed _____ to stop NYU from destroying Poe's former home.

3. Many people feel that the building on Amity Street

is a _____.

4. The _____ in the house are in good shape, even though people walk on them daily.

5. Poe lived in a _____ with his young wife, Virginia, and her mother.

> **Word Bank**
> boarding-
>   house
> floorboards
> petitions
> landmark
> spokesman

B. Write T or F next to each statement to tell if it is true or false.

_____ **1.** NYU wanted to tear down Poe's former boardinghouse and build a new building for its law school.

_____ **2.** Poe was born in the boardinghouse on Amity Street.

_____ **3.** Fans of Poe wanted the building turned into a museum.

_____ **4.** NYU's supporters shouted, "Nevermore," a line from Poe's famous poem, "The Raven."

_____ **5.** A state supreme court judge decided that NYU did not have the right to tear down the building.

_____ **6.** Virginia, Poe's wife, died of tuberculosis.

_____ **7.** While he lived at the boardinghouse, Poe was struggling with his literary career.

_____ **8.** Poe lived in the boardinghouse for eighteen months.

_____ **9.** The original address of the boardinghouse was 85 Amity Street.

Additional Vocabulary Practice

"Annabel Lee"; "The Fall of the House of Poe?"

A. Match words and definitions. Write the letter of the correct definition next to each word.

_____ **1.** sepulcher

_____ **2.** kinsmen

_____ **3.** seraphs

_____ **4.** coveted

a. envied

b. angels

c. tomb; burial place

d. relatives

B. Use each word above in a sentence.

1. _____

_____

2. _____

_____

3. _____

_____

4. _____

_____

C. Use context clues to determine the meaning of the underlined word.

1. Poe lived in a room in a *boardinghouse* for about six months. A

boardinghouse is a _____

_____

2. People signed *petitions* to protest the plans to tear this house down. A

petition is a _____

_____

"User Friendly" by T. Ernesto Bethancourt

Prereading

Additional Background

Preview the Selection Explain to students that this story is set in Silicon Valley in California, and that Kevin's father builds a computer using the latest components from the computer company where he works. Kevin's newly built computer, named Louis, suddenly develops a personality and begins conversing with him. As Kevin shares with Louis his feelings about Ginny Linke, a girl in school, strange things begin to happen to the Linke family. Kevin begins to think that Louis is the culprit, and he has to decide what to do about the problem.

Vocabulary Practice

Preview Vocabulary Students with limited access to computers may not know some of the computer terminology in "User Friendly." Write the following words and their definitions on the chalkboard, and discuss each word meaning with the class:

- *absently (p. 274):* in a distracted, inattentive way
- *components (p. 274):* parts
- *CPU—central processing unit (p. 274):* part of the computer that controls what happens inside
- *databanks (p. 277):* information organized so that particular pieces of it can be found more easily
- *diskette (p. 273):* plastic disk used to store information
- *floppy drive (p. 273):* part of the computer that reads information stored on a diskette
- *mainframe (p. 277):* large central computer that shares information with smaller computers connected to it
- *modifications (p. 274):* slight changes
- *screen (p. 273):* part of the computer where images and information are displayed; looks like a television screen
- *Silicon Valley (p. 274):* area in central California that is a center of the computer industry (silicon is used in the manufacture of computer chips, or circuits)
- *voice module (p. 274):* unit that, when connected to a computer, enables it to produce speech

SKILLS FOCUS

Literary Skill
Find a story's theme.

Reading Skill
Understand cause and effect.

Resources

In this book:
- Vocabulary and Comprehension, p. 117
- Additional Vocabulary Practice, p. 120 (includes the next selection)

Other Resources:
- *Audio CD Library*
- *Audio CD Library, Selections and Summaries in Spanish*
- *Supporting Instruction in Spanish*

Teacher Tip

Have students keep a separate vocabulary notebook for technical/computer terminology.

Vocabulary Tip

Explain that *missing link*, the term Kevin uses, refers to a life form that might have existed between the ape and the human in the evolutionary chain.

Alternative Activity

Especially for ELL **Use Spanish Resources** Spanish-speaking English-language learners may benefit from reading or listening to the selection summary in Spanish in preparation for reading the selection in English.

Reading

Alternative Teaching Strategy

Analyze Labels Students may relate to the story's theme of loneliness. Write the words Kevin and others use to describe themselves and one another: *nerdy kid, freak, brain, dumbo, bad news, "The Missing" Linke,* etc. Ask students to divide a sheet of paper into two columns: one titled POSITIVE LABELS and the other NEGATIVE LABELS. Have students work in pairs to arrange the nicknames in the appropriate columns.

Listening and Speaking Opportunity

Play the Audio Recording Let students listen to the audio recording. Pause between scenes to ask students to summarize what took place in the scene they just heard. Help them distinguish between fact and opinion about the characters and events in the story. To reinforce this, ask them to identify whether examples of events are facts, valid opinions, or unsupported opinions.

Postreading

Fluency Opportunity

Role-Play Students will benefit from the speaking practice offered by role-playing. Pair students, and ask them to enact a brief dialogue between Kevin and Louis. To help students get a feel for the way Kevin and Louis speak, have volunteers read aloud from the story selected scenes between Kevin and Louis.

Alternative Activity

Core Skill **Explore Theme** Discuss with students the theme of "User Friendly." Ask them what caused so many problems for the Linkes. If Louis loved Kevin, did he hurt the Linkes because they were not nice to Kevin? Ask students what they think Kevin learned from his experiences in this story. *(Answers will vary. Students may note that Kevin learned a lesson about doing the right thing. He had to make the tough decision about "pulling the plug" on Louis, even though Louis was his friend.)* Ask them to think about what his story says about friendship and to write a sentence that states the theme of the story. Student sentences will vary, but they should get the general idea that friendship has its limits and not everything someone or something does is all right, even if it's meant in the name of friendship.

Vocabulary Development
Additional Vocabulary Practice

Explain Idioms English-language learners may be confused by American idioms. Explain that an idiom is an expression that is peculiar to itself either grammatically or in having a meaning that differs from that of the words themselves. Reiterate that idioms exist in all languages. Point out that "User Friendly" has many idiomatic expressions. For example:

- *ace out (p. 276):* have your chance at something ruined
  "Worse than that, you're a brain. If that doesn't *ace* you *out* with girls, what does?"
- *got up the nerve (p. 275):* gathered strength or courage
  "Somehow I'd never *got up the nerve.*"
- *knock it off (p. 278):* stop, quit doing something
  "'So you and your creepy girlfriend better *knock it off.*'"
- *lose one's marbles (p. 276):* go crazy
  "'I'm *losing my marbles.*'"

Ask students to locate each idiom in the story and try to figure out its meaning from context. Have students write sentences of their own using these idioms.

Grammar Link
Additional Practice

Review Pronoun Use Explain that *I, he, she, we,* and *they* are used when the pronoun refers to the subject and that *me, him, her, us,* and *them* are used when the pronoun is being used as an object. Ask students to supply the pronoun for the following sentences from "User Friendly":

1. Don't swear at ___ for something ___ didn't do.
2. "___ don't have a girlfriend, creepy or otherwise," ___ said.
3. "And third, you better let ___ go, Chuck Linke."
4. "Then this morning," ___ continued, "___ got two whole truckloads of junk mail!"
5. ___ were still laughing and looking back over their shoulders at ___ when ___ got off the bus.

Reading Skills Development

(**Mixed Ability Group**) **Identify Cause and Effect** Students may have difficulty identifying cause and effect if they concentrate solely on character motivation as a causative force in a story. Point out to students that accidents and nature, as well as other outside forces, can often play a role in stories' plots. Have students re-read "User Friendly" with a partner and work together to create a flowchart that shows how one element of the plot leads to another. Ask for volunteers to present their charts to the class. (See Storymap on page xxxi.)

SKILLS FOCUS

Vocabulary Skills
Identify and explain idioms.

(**Especially for ELL**)
Ask students to explain an idiom from their native language.

(**Teacher Tip**)
Students may have difficulty distinguishing which pronouns are subjects and which are objects. Review that *I, he, she, we,* and *they* can only be used as subjects, while *me, him, her, us* and *them* can only be used in the objective case. Point out that *you* can be either a subject or an object. Go over the lesson on page 283 in the student book before doing the exercise offered here.

SKILLS FOCUS

Literary Skill
Find a story's theme.

Reading Skill
Understand cause and effect.

Resources

In this book:
• Vocabulary and Comprehension, p. 117
• Additional Vocabulary Practice, p. 120 (includes the next selection)

Other Resources:
• *Audio CD Library*
• *Audio CD Library, Selections and Summaries in Spanish*
• *Supporting Instruction in Spanish*

Teacher Tip

Explain that "@#%!!!" is read as "expletive." It means that Kevin is using a swear word.

Teacher Tip

Review with students that personified objects can be considered characters in stories. Ask students under what circumstances a computer could be considered a character. Ask them to think of characteristics or behaviors of a computer that could be considered lifelike. Ask them to think about whether the computer in the story can be considered a character.

TARGETED STRATEGIES FOR SPECIAL EDUCATION STUDENTS

Prereading
Additional Background

Explain Text Format Explain that Kevin tells the story in regular print. Point out that the change in type that begins in the selection on page 273 represents the computer's message to Kevin, and that using a different typeface helps to clarify this. Note that Kevin's exchanges with the computer are displayed in italics. If possible, have students who work with computers share their experience.

Reading
Listening and Speaking Opportunity

Read Aloud in Pairs/Fluency Practice Reading aloud often helps students to better understand a story. Have students work collaboratively in pairs, reading some of the dialogue between Louis and Kevin. Ask students who are reading the part of Louis to read the way they think the computer would speak. Play the audio recording for students before they read.

Additional Practice

Distinguish Fact from Opinion Read the selection once more with the class, and ask students to keep a notepad on the desk. Pause at opportune moments and have students note whether you are discussing examples of fact or opinion. Remind them that facts need supporting evidence while opinions are unsupported. Invite students to compare their results after the reading is completed.

Postreading
Alternative Activity

Core Skill **Write About Theme** Discuss the theme of the story with students. What does "User Friendly" say about love and friendship? Was Louis's love for and loyalty to Kevin a good thing? Was Louis a good friend to Kevin? Ask students to write a sentence that states the theme of the story. Have students think about the theme in comparison to other stories that they've read that have themes of love, friendship, or both. Ask students whether this story's theme reminds them of any other story and, if so, to explain why.

Vocabulary and Comprehension

"User Friendly"

A. Complete each sentence with a word from the Word Bank.

1. Kevin can see what he writes on the computer

_____.

2. Louis sits all day on a _____.

3. Kevin slid a _____ into the disk drive.

4. Kevin types on the _____ every time
he wants to talk to Louis.

Word Bank
keyboard
computer
table
diskette
screen

B. Write T or F next to each statement to tell if it is true or false.

_____ **1.** Louis was Kevin's brother.

_____ **2.** Ginny really likes Kevin.

_____ **3.** Kevin is very popular at school.

_____ **4.** Kevin is one of the smartest boys in the school.

_____ **5.** Louis thought Kevin was a nerd.

_____ **6.** Louis was jealous of Ginny.

_____ **7.** Kevin's father deleted Louis.

_____ **8.** After Kevin's father fixed the computer, Louis came back.

C. Match words and definitions. Write the letter of the correct definition
next to each word.

_____ **1.** components

_____ **2.** tutorial program

_____ **3.** graphics

_____ **4.** console

a. designs or pictures produced on and
printed out from a computer

b. a computer's keyboard and monitor

c. program that provides instructions for
performing specific tasks on a computer

d. parts

"It Just Keeps Going and Going . . ."

by Joan Burditt

SKILLS FOCUS

Reading Skill
Understand cause-and-effect text structure.

Resources

In this book:
• Adapted Readings
• Vocabulary and Comprehension, p. 119
• Additional Vocabulary Practice, p. 120 (includes the previous selection)

Other Resources:
• *Holt Adapted Reader*
• *Audio CD Library*
• *Audio CD Library, Selections and Summaries in Spanish*
• *Supporting Instruction in Spanish*

Especially for ELL

Have students create their own vocabulary flash cards on large index cards. Have them cut and paste any pictures related to the word onto each index card.

Special Education Students

Lead students in brainstorming the questions "What causes students to come to school?" and "What effects do they expect from their learning?"

Prereading

Vocabulary Practice

Preview Selection Vocabulary Before reading, preview the following vocabulary with the class. Have volunteers use each word in a sentence.

• *antivirus (p. 286):* against a virus
• *chaos (p. 286):* complete disorder or confusion
• *massive (p. 286):* very large
• *motives (p. 286):* reasons for doing things
• *pesky (p. 285):* bothersome; annoying
• *self-replicating (p. 285):* making copies of itself
• *tentacles (p. 285):* long, flexible arms, like those of an octopus
• *villains (p. 286):* "bad guys," cruel people

Alternative Activity

Read the Adaptation Distribute copies of the adapted reading of "It Just Keeps Going and Going . . ." (available in this book and, with marginal questions, in *Holt Adapted Reader*). To prepare for reading the original version and to practice fluency, students should read the adaptation silently. Encourage students to write notes, questions, predictions, reactions, and comments on the worksheets as they read.

Reading

Alternative Teaching Strategy

Understand Cause and Effect Read the article with students, or play the audio recording. Then, ask students to draw a cause-and-effect chain in their notebooks and to fill it in as they read. Discuss what students have written in their notebooks, and have them explain how they see the cause and effect in "It Just Keeps Going and Going . . ."

Postreading

Additional Practice

Analyze Cause and Effect If students have trouble with the Practice Test in their books, help them to select and understand the correct answers. You might also ask them to read other cause-and-effect articles and then quiz them on their reading.

Vocabulary and Comprehension

"It Just Keeps Going and Going . . ."

A. Complete each sentence with a word from the Word Bank.

1. The attack of a computer virus results in the

_____ of data.

2. A computer virus can cause a lot of

_____ for people.

3. Sometimes a virus just causes minor,

_____ problems.

4. No one understands the _____ of
people who create computer viruses.

5. Those who create viruses to damage computers

are considered _____.

> **Word Bank**
> chaos
> villains
> pesky
> motives
> corruption

B. Write T or F next to each statement to tell if it is true or false.

_____ **1.** A computer virus is a self-replicating computer program.

_____ **2.** Viruses can be pesky or worse.

_____ **3.** Computer viruses are created by other computers.

_____ **4.** People who create computer viruses have good motives.

_____ **5.** One result of computer viruses is that they corrupt data.

_____ **6.** Computer viruses are like a human-made monster.

_____ **7.** An antivirus program can detect a virus before it
spreads.

_____ **8.** *Self-replicating* means that the virus keeps making
copies of itself.

_____ **9.** Viruses destroy only desktop computers.

_____ **10.** People should be careful what they load into
a computer.

Additional Vocabulary Practice

"User Friendly"; "It Just Keeps Going and Going . . ."

A. Match words and definitions. Write the letter of the correct definition next to each word.

_____ **1.** keyboard

_____ **2.** screen

_____ **3.** modifications

_____ **4.** diskette

_____ **5.** absently

a. slight changes

b. in a distracted, inattentive way

c. plastic disk used to store information

d. keys used to input information into a computer

e. part of the computer where images and information are displayed

B. Choose three words from above. Use each word in a sentence.

1. _____

_____

2. _____

_____

3. _____

_____

C. Replace the words in parentheses with a word or phrase from the Word Bank that means the same or nearly the same.

1. Most of the students at the high school think Kevin is a (very smart person)

_____.

2. Ginny's brother Chuck looked (*very angry*)

_____ when he grabbed Kevin.

3. Kevin decided he had to (*disconnect and terminate*)

_____ Louis.

> **Word Bank**
> brain
> real ticked off
> pull the plug on

"Echo and Narcissus"

Greek myth, retold by Roger Lancelyn Green

Prereading

Additional Background

Discuss Myths Mythology is born of a culture's desire to make sense of the universe. Frequently mythology explains where a people came from or how the universe originated. In addition to providing explanations of events, mythology tells colorful tales about the causes of many things in the world. Many myths, like Echo and Narcissus, are origin myths that explain how something came to be. Ask students to note how this myth explains two things: echo and narcissism. Also explain that the characters in this myth are well known in Greek mythology. Tell them that in Greek mythology, Zeus is king of the gods, Hera is his wife, and Aphrodite is the goddess of love.

Alternative Activities

Read the Adaptation Distribute copies of the adapted reading of "Echo and Narcissus" (available in this book and, with marginal questions, in *Holt Adapted Reader*). To prepare for reading the original version and to practice fluency, students should read the adaptation silently.

Use *The Holt Reader* You may consider having students use the Before You Read page in *The Holt Reader*, either instead of or in addition to the Before You Read page in the student book.

Reading

Alternative Activity

Use *The Holt Reader* You may have students read the selection in *The Holt Reader* and use the margins in that book to make notes and respond to the instruction.

Listening and Speaking Opportunity

(Especially for ELL) **Read Aloud/Fluency Practice** English-language learners can benefit from hearing "Echo and Narcissus" read aloud. Play the audio recording through once. Then, play it a paragraph at a time and have a student read each paragraph after it is played. Then, ask other students to read. After they have finished, write these or similar questions on the chalkboard:

• Why is Hera angry at Echo?

SKILLS FOCUS

Literary Skill
Understand recurring themes.

Reading Skill
Use context clues.

(**Resources**)

In this book:
• Adapted Readings
• Vocabulary and Comprehension, p. 125
• Additional Vocabulary Practice, p. 126

Other Resources:
• *The Holt Reader*
• *Holt Adapted Reader*
• *Audio CD Library*
• *Audio CD Library, Selections and Summaries in Spanish*
• *Supporting Instruction in Spanish*

(**Especially for ELL**)

Read several myths to the class, especially myths from the cultures of your students, to demonstrate the genre.

(**Teacher Tip**)

Have students illustrate cards for each of the Greek gods and goddesses mentioned in the myth of Echo and Narcissus.

Teacher Tip

For a discussion question, ask students if they think that Hera's punishment of Echo was fair.

• How does Hera punish Echo?
• How does Aphrodite help Echo?
• How does Aphrodite punish Narcissus?
• How did echoes come into being?
• How did the narcissus flower come into being?

Vocabulary Practice

Understand Vocabulary Through Context Ask students to re-read "Echo and Narcissus" and to write down any words they don't recognize, as well as the number of the page on which each word appears. After they finish reading, have pairs of students go back through the story to identify the new words and try to determine their meanings based on the context.

Postreading

Alternative Activity

Use *The Holt Reader* You may consider having students use the postreading activities in The Holt Reader, either instead of or in addition to the postreading activities in the student book.

Alternative Teaching Strategy

Mixed Ability Group **Explore Character and Theme** Ask small groups of students to make a two-column chart and to label one column ECHO and the other NARCISSUS. Have groups brainstorm for words or expressions that describe each character. Encourage them to find passages in the text that support their ideas. Have groups write the descriptions in the appropriate columns. Then, ask students to think about how these traits created problems for Echo and Narcissus and whether they cause problems for people in general. Groups should select a statement of theme from the choices given on page 294, question 4, in their books. Ask them to discuss how this theme is reflected in the characters' behavior. Guide students to see that Narcissus reflects the theme of being so self-absorbed that he can't love anyone else. Echo, on the other hand, experiences the powerful feeling of love although she doesn't seek it. They illustrate how the effects of romantic love and self-love can be devastating.

Fluency Opportunity

Cause-and-Effect Flowchart To reinforce what students have learned about cause and effect, have them complete a cause-and-effect flowchart for "Echo and Narcissus." See page 271 in the student book for a model. If students are unable to complete the chart on their own, draw one on the chalkboard, and ask students to look through the text and decide what should go in each box. When the chart is complete, remind students that "Echo and Narcissus" is an origin myth, and ask them to write a sentence identifying the two things whose origins are explained in the myth.

Vocabulary Development

Reinforce Targeted Vocabulary

Build Vocabulary Through Context Have students note how the Vocabulary Development words are used in the selection. Ask them to supply definitions based on context, and assist them if necessary. Then, ask students to generate their own sentences using the words.

- *detain (p. 290, col. 1):* hold back; delay
  "But at last Hera realized that Echo was doing this on purpose to *detain* her while Zeus went quietly back to Olympus as if he had never really been away."

- *vainly (p. 292, col. 1):* uselessly; without result
  ". . . she could only follow wherever he went, hiding behind trees and rocks, and feasting her eyes *vainly* upon him."

- *unrequited (p. 292, col. 2):* not returned in kind
  "Well, he shall love himself and no one else, and yet shall die of *unrequited* love!"

- *parched (p. 292, col. 2):* very hot and dry
  "With a cry of satisfaction, for the day was hot and cloudless, and he was *parched* with thirst, Narcissus flung himself down beside the pool and leaned forward to dip his face in the cool water."

- *intently (p. 293, col. 1):* with great concentration
  "Drawing out his arms, he gazed *intently* down and, as the water grew still again, saw once more the face of his beloved."

Grammar Link

Additional Activity

Identify Words That Are Often Confused Point out that while *its* and *it's* and *your* and *you're* sound alike and look similar, they are different words with different uses. The words *you're* and *it's*, which have apostrophes, are contractions of *you are* and *it is*, while *its* and *your* are possessive pronouns. They show whom or what something belongs to. Have students practice the exercise on page 295 of their book first. Then, have students use each of these words in at least one sentence of their own about "Echo and Narcissus." Finally, write the following sentences on the chalkboard, and ask students to complete each one with either *its*, *it's*, *your*, or *you're*.

1. Hera said, "___ voice will be useless except to repeat what others say."

2. The pool showed a surprising reflection on ___ surface.

3. Aphrodite said, "___ going to die of unrequited love."

4. The flower opened ___ petals the following spring.

5. ___ been a long time since Echo's own voice was heard on the mountain.

SKILLS FOCUS

Vocabulary Skill
Use context clues.

(**Teacher Tip**)

Explain that the root of a word is the part that is used as a base for making other words. Discuss the verb *affix;* it means "fasten; attach; stick (*affix* a label to the jar)." It is not surprising that a syllable that is attached to a word to modify its meaning is called an *affix*.

Literary Skill
Understand recurring
themes.

Reading Skill
Use context clues.

(**Resources**)

In this book:
• Adapted Readings
• Vocabulary and
Comprehension, p. 125
• Additional Vocabulary
Practice, p. 126

Other Resources:
• *The Holt Reader*
• *Holt Adapted Reader*
• *Audio CD Library*
• *Audio CD Library,
Selections and Summaries
in Spanish*
• *Supporting Instruction
in Spanish*

(**Teacher Tip**)

If students have auditory-
processing problems, write
key ideas and sentences on
the chalkboard or an
overhead. Assign a study
buddy to help with notes.

(**Teacher Tip**)

Ask students to look at
Narcissus by Caravaggio on
page 291. Explain that the
image is how the Italian
artist imagined Narcissus
to be. Have students draw
their own versions of the
characters in the story.

TARGETED STRATEGIES FOR SPECIAL EDUCATION STUDENTS

Prereading
Background Information

Know the Characters Help students become familiar with the characters before they begin reading the story. Be sure to include Zeus, Hera, Echo, the Oreades, Narcissus, and Aphrodite. Explain that this story describes a self-absorbed, selfish character and that it is about love and self-love. Tell students to keep that in mind as they think about the theme of the story.

Reading
Alternative Activity

(Core Skill) **Explore the Theme** Ask students to describe love. *(to feel a deep fondness, or to be generous and unselfish to the person you love)* As you read the story aloud in class, have students listen for a character who loves unselfishly. Is there one? To prompt the discussion, ask questions like these:

• Who does Echo love? Does wanting to win someone's affection mean that you love unselfishly?

• Who does Narcissus love? What is self-love? Can you love yourself and still love someone else? Did Narcissus love someone else?

Postreading
Alternative Activity

Use Writing Prompts When they've finished reading, have students write a personal response to the story. Ask them to identify the story's theme and tell how they feel about it. You may want to use one of the following prompts to help students get started.

• The character I like/dislike the most is ___ because ___.

• I think ___ was wrong/right to ___ because ___.

• I felt the story was too ___ because ___.

• I think the theme of the story is ___ because ___.

Alternative Assessment

(Core Skill) **Understand Characters** To assess how well students understand the characters, assign each student a character, and have each student give a short presentation as his/her character. In their presentations, students must tell about and justify their actions in the story. Allow students to use cue cards to help with their presentations.

Vocabulary and Comprehension

"Echo and Narcissus"

A. Complete each sentence by filling in a word from the Word Bank.

1. _____ is a talkative nymph.

2. The gods live on _____.

3. Echo tried to _____ Hera while Zeus went back to Olympus.

4. _____ falls in love with his reflection in the water.

5. As the goddess of love, _____ cares how people love each other.

6. Hera is mad at _____ because he wanders with the nymphs.

7. Echo's love for the beautiful Narcissus was _____.

Word Bank
Zeus
unrequited
Echo
Mount Olympus
detain
Narcissus
Aphrodite

B. Write T or F next to each statement to tell if it is true or false.

_____ 1. Hera's curse on Echo lasts for only a while.

_____ 2. Echo dies of a broken heart.

_____ 3. Narcissus is handsome and kind.

_____ 4. Echo loved Narcissus the first time she saw him.

_____ 5. Aphrodite likes the way Narcissus loves himself.

_____ 6. Echo can only repeat what others say to her.

_____ 7. Aphrodite doesn't help Echo.

_____ 8. Mount Olympus is the home of the gods.

_____ 9. Aphrodite punishes Narcissus for being cruel to Echo.

_____ 10. A flower blossoms where Narcissus died.

Additional Vocabulary Practice

"Echo and Narcissus"

A. Match words and definitions. Write the letter of the correct definition next to each word.

_____ **1.** detain

_____ **2.** vainly

_____ **3.** unrequited

_____ **4.** parched

_____ **5.** intently

a. not returned in kind

b. very hot and dry

c. uselessly; without result

d. hold back; delay

e. with great concentration

B. Choose three words from above. Use each word in a sentence.

1. _____

_____

2. _____

_____

3. _____

_____

C. Complete each sentence with a word from the Word Bank.

1. Echo would _____ Hera with long conversations, holding her attention.

2. Although Echo fell in love with Narcissus, her

love was not returned and was _____.

3. She tried _____ to tell him of her love.

4. When Narcissus was _____ and thirsty, he looked into the water and saw his face.

5. Narcissus gazed at his reflection _____ and with great concentration.

Word Bank
detain
intently
parched
unrequited
vainly

Comparing Literature: Characters, Settings, Themes

Prereading

Vocabulary Practice

Preview Additional Vocabulary Preview with students the following additional vocabulary words and their definitions.

- *swaggering (p. 297):* walking in a self-important way
- *scornfully (p. 300):* dismissively; with disrespect
- *jostling (p. 308):* pushing and shoving
- *agape (p. 309):* hanging open
- *raspish (p. 309):* rough
- *ruefully (p. 309):* regretfully
- *compliance (p. 310):* agreement
- *consoled (p. 312):* comforted
- *reign (p. 317):* royal rule
- *reconvened (p. 318):* met again

Reading

Alternative Activity

Make a Comparison Chart Ask students to take notes on the main character and setting of each story. After students have finished, have them record the theme in the chart. Finally, students should compare the three elements in the stories.

	Main Character	Setting	Theme
"Charles"			
"Miss Awful"			

Postreading

Alternative Activity

Identify Points of Comparison and Contrast Review with students the block and point-by-point methods of comparing and contrasting. Ask for volunteers to suggest elements in the stories to compare and contrast, and write two sample essay outlines on the chalkboard, one in block style and one in point-by-point style.

SKILLS FOCUS

Literary Skills
Analyze characters, settings, and themes.

Reading Skill
Compare and contrast stories.

(Resources)

In this book:
- Vocabulary and Comprehension, p. 129
- Additional Vocabulary Practice, p. 130

(Especially for ELL)

Before students read the stories, you may want to review what is acceptable behavior in your classroom and the typical American classroom. Invite students who have attended classes in other countries to compare and contrast expectations and behavior.

(Core Skill)

Use the resources in the Reading Skills and Strategies section of this book to help students having difficulty comparing and contrasting. Use "Charles" and "Miss Awful" for the application portion of the lesson.

Literary Skills
Analyze characters, settings, and themes.

Reading Skill
Compare and contrast stories.

(**Resources**)

• **In this book:**
Vocabulary and Comprehension, p. 129
• Additional Vocabulary Practice, p. 130

TARGETED STRATEGIES FOR SPECIAL EDUCATION STUDENTS

Prereading
Reteach the Key Idea

Review Theme Ask students to think about stories they enjoy. Write their answers on the chalkboard, and discuss what might make a story enjoyable and memorable. Then, explain that some stories do more than just entertain: They also help people think more deeply about life. Ask: *Can you think of a story that influenced you in a good way? Did that influence come from the story's theme?* Remind students that themes are open to interpretation.

Reading
Alternative Teaching Strategy

(Core Skill) **Compare and Contrast Characters** Students may benefit from hearing the stories read aloud more than once. To help students focus on the characters and settings in the selections, read aloud each story twice, once for students to focus on the story's protagonist and once to focus on its setting. As you read, have students take notes of words that describe each of the main characters and each of the settings, either words taken from the stories or descriptive terms that come to mind as they listen. After you have read the stories, lead students to compare and contrast the two characters and settings. Have students use the following chart to keep track of their descriptive words so that they might more easily compare the characters and settings.

	Main Character	Setting
"Charles"		
"Miss Awful"		

Postreading
Alternative Assessment

Discuss Recurring Themes Encourage students to think about how the main characters' experiences are alike. Elicit from students a list of lessons that could be taken from the first selection, and write students' suggestions on the chalkboard. Ask students if the same morals could also be taken from the second selection. Have students refer to specific details in the two stories to support their answers.

Vocabulary and Comprehension

Comparing Literature: Characters, Settings, Themes

A. Match words and definitions. Write the letter of the correct definition next to each word.

_____ **1.** swaggering

_____ **2.** agape

_____ **3.** reign

_____ **4.** jostling

_____ **5.** consoled

a. pushing and shoving

b. hanging open

c. walking confidently

d. comforted

e. royal rule

B. Choose three words from above. Use each word in a sentence.

1. _____

_____

2. _____

_____

3. _____

_____

C. Write T or F next to each statement to tell if it is true or false.

_____ **1.** In "Charles," Laurie is in kindergarten.

_____ **2.** Charles visits Laurie's house and causes trouble.

_____ **3.** In "Miss Awful," the substitute teacher says she is a witch.

_____ **4.** Miss Orville was evicted from her apartment.

_____ **5.** Miss Orville greatly values her plants, which she tends carefully.

Additional Vocabulary Practice

Comparing Literature: Characters, Settings, Themes

A. Match the words in the left column with the clues in the right column. Write the correct letter in the blanks.

_____ **1.** reconvened

_____ **2.** ruefully

_____ **3.** scornfully

_____ **4.** raspish

_____ **5.** compliance

a. the opposite of *happily, hopefully*

b. the opposite of *disagreement*

c. might describe a shark's rough skin

d. the opposite of *politely and with respect*

e. the student council at its second meeting

B. Choose two words from above. Use each word in a sentence.

1. _____

_____

2. _____

_____

C. Replace the word or phrase in parentheses with the correct word from the Word Bank.

1. Elijah *(comforted)* _____ his friend after the team lost the championship game.

2. Elizabeth I's *(rule)* _____ lasted for quite a long time in England.

3. The soccer players sprinted down the field, *(pushing and shoving)* _____ for the ball.

4. Arturo's mouth was *(open)* _____ as he watched the sparrow fly off with his ice-cream cone.

5. After receiving the highest grade in the class, Mia went *(walking confidently)* _____ down the hall.

Word Bank
swaggering
agape
reign
jostling
consoled

Collection 4
Point of View: Can You See It My Way?

Elements of Literature: Point of View

Additional Practice

Check the Point of View To help students understand different points of view, ask them to read the passage demonstrating the omniscient point of view on page 348. As students name its characters *(princess, father, mother)*, list the characters on the chalkboard. Ask students what they know about these characters from reading the passage, and write their responses under the appropriate names. Point out that students know something about each of them. Contrast this with the first-person point of view on the next page. Lead students to discover that they only know what the princess tells them in this passage. She states that her parents don't feel sorry for her at all, which we know from the first passage to be untrue. Therefore, lead students to conclude that the first-person point of view is not necessarily reliable. The third-person limited point of view is demonstrated in the next paragraph. Point out that, once again, students know only what the princess is thinking but that this time the reporting is accurate. We know that she blames her parents but realizes that she is truly responsible. We realize that she rather uncharitably thinks of cooking the frog.

Background

(Especially for ELL) **Take a Look at Stories** Depending upon the purpose of the narrative, cultures may look upon some stories as actual history, others as legend, and yet others as important tradition.

Academic Vocabulary

Master Vocabulary Students may need some help developing their academic vocabulary. Review these terms from pages 348 and 349 and their definitions:

- *point of view:* vantage point of the one telling the story (narrator)
- *omniscient point of view:* an all-knowing narrator who can tell us thoughts and dreams, or any other information
- *first-person point of view:* the narrator tells the story using *I*, telling the story from his or her point of view
- *third-person limited point of view:* the story is seen through the eyes of one character who is not the narrator

SKILLS FOCUS

Literary Skill
Understand point of view.

(Teacher Tip)

Third-person omniscient is probably the oldest form of narration and is found in ancient stories that have been passed down from generation to generation.

(Teacher Tip)

Have students keep an academic vocabulary notebook. Ask them to write key words, their definitions, and one or two sample sentences. Have them start a new section in their notebook for each chapter in the text.

TARGETED STRATEGIES FOR SPECIAL EDUCATION STUDENTS

Elements of Literature: Point of View

Background

Contrast Points of View To help students understand point of view, explain that stories are told from the point of view of a narrator. The most common points of view are:

- first person
- third-person limited
- omniscient

Alternative Teaching Strategies

Teach First-Person Point of View Demonstrate first-person narration by asking volunteers what they have done that day. Point out the use of the personal pronoun *I*. Explain that these first-person point of view narratives told only the narrator's thought and deeds.

Teach Third-Person Limited Point of View Tell students that sometimes stories are told from the point of view of a character who is not the narrator. The reader knows only about the things the character sees, feels, hears, thinks, and experiences. For example, this narrative is told from the point of view of a cat:

> The cat stretched, yawned, and thought lazily, "It's rather quiet for this time of evening." She sauntered into the kitchen anticipating a piece of kibble or two. "What has happened to my people?" she wondered. The parakeet squawked from the safety of its cage. "What foolishness that bird speaks," thought the cat.

The cat is not telling the story because there are no personal pronouns, but the story is seen through the cat's eyes and thoughts.

Teach Omniscient Point of View Explain that the omniscient narrator knows and tells everything, so the reader knows more than the characters. Most stories are written from the omniscient point of view.

Alternative Assessment

Write a Story Divide the class into three groups. Have Group 1 write a story about a cat from the first-person point of view; Group 2, a story about a dog from the third-person limited point of view; and Group 3, a story about a goldfish from the omniscient point of view.

(**Teacher Tip**)

Pair students who have difficulty with the concept of point of view with "mentors" who can practice and work with them on understanding the different points of view.

"After Twenty Years" by O. Henry

Prereading

Background

Make the Connection To interest students in the concept of doing the right thing, pose some morally challenging questions. Base the discussion on the letter provided in Make the Connection. How would students respond to the letter? Do they agree with reporting someone's wrongdoing? Would their opinions change if that person were a friend? Invite students to share any experiences they may know of that are similar to the one in the letter.

Alternative Activities

Read the Adaptation Distribute copies of the adapted reading of "After Twenty Years" (available in this book and, with marginal questions, in *Holt Adapted Reader*). To prepare for reading the original version and to practice fluency, students should read the adaptation silently.

Use *The Holt Reader* You may consider having students use the Before You Read page in *The Holt Reader,* either instead of or in addition to the Before You Read page in the student book.

Reading

Alternative Activity

Use *The Holt Reader* You may have students read the selection in *The Holt Reader* and use the margins in that book to make notes and respond to the instruction.

Vocabulary Practice

(Especially for ELL) Use Context Clues to Understand Vocabulary It may be helpful to alert students to look for the words below as they read "After Twenty Years." Write them and the sentences in which they appear in this story on the board. Ask students to copy the definitions and write new sentences that show they understand the meanings.

- *reassuringly (p. 358):* removing doubts and fears; making someone feel secure again. "'It's all right, officer,' he said *reassuringly*."

- *dragged (p. 359):* pulled in a slow, hard way, especially along the ground. "'You couldn't have *dragged* Jimmy out of New York; he

SKILLS FOCUS

Literary Skill
Understand omniscient point of view.

Reading Skill
Make predictions.

(Resources)

In this book:
- Adapted Readings
- Vocabulary and Comprehension, p. 137
- Additional Vocabulary Practice, p. 140 (includes the next selection)

Other Resources:
- *The Holt Reader*
- *Holt Adapted Reader*
- *Audio CD Library*
- *Audio CD Library, Selections and Summaries in Spanish*
- *Supporting Instruction in Spanish*

(Especially for ELL)

Whether in patrol cars or on foot, many police officers circulate through a neighborhood or a specific area of town, called their *beat.* By getting to know a particular area, police officers become aware of the residents and normal neighborhood activities and thus are more likely to notice any unusual activity in the area.

thought it was the only place on earth.'"

- *wits (p. 359):* shrewd minds; the power to think and reason. "'I've had to compete with some of the sharpest *wits* going to get my pile.'"
- *trembled (p. 360):* shook from cold, fear, weakness, excitement, etc. "His hand was steady when he began to read, but it *trembled* a little by the time he had finished."

Alternative Strategy

Think About Point of View As they read, have students think about how this story would be different if told from a single character's point of view. What pieces of information would we not have if we were seeing the story through the policeman's eyes? Remind students that the omniscient narrator can tell you everything about all the characters, even their most private thoughts. This omniscient narrator has a broader view than either Silky Bob or Jimmy Wells.

Additional Practice

Core Skill **Make Predictions** To help prepare students for the surprise ending, ask them to stop at each open-book logo in the text, consider what they have read, and jot down a prediction. When, in their reading, they reach the next open-book logo, have them review their previous predictions and ascertain whether they were accurate. After they have finished this exercise, ask them if they guessed the ending of the story.

Postreading
Alternative Activity

Use *The Holt Reader* You may consider having students use the postreading activities in *The Holt Reader,* either instead of or in addition to the postreading activities in the student book.

Additional Practice

Identify Point of View Some students may have difficulty distinguishing between third-person limited and omniscient narrators. Have students refer to the essay on pages 348 and 349:

- the *omniscient narrator* "can tell you everything about all the characters, even their most private thoughts."
- the *third-person limited narrator* is concerned with "the thoughts and feelings of just one character in the story. This point of view helps us share that character's reactions to the story's events."

Elicit from students that "After Twenty Years" is not limited to the point of view of just one of the characters. Therefore, it is not an example of third-person limited narration.

Vocabulary Development

Reteach the Key Idea

Clarify Word Meanings Review with students how they can clarify the meaning of a word through the use of definition, example, restatement, and contrast. Provide students with the following sentences, and have them explain which of the three methods can be used to clarify the meanings of the underlined words.

- Instead of drawing an <u>intricate</u> design, she drew a simple outline of a flower. *(contrast)*
- The pattern of the cloth was <u>intricate</u>, filled with details of flowers and birds. *(restatement)*
- An <u>intricate</u> pattern is complicated and full of details. *(definition)*

Review some of the words that signal contrast: *although, but, however, instead of, not,* and *unlike.* Explain that when students see these words, they should look for two things that are being contrasted.

SKILLS FOCUS

Vocabulary Skill
Clarify word meanings.

Grammar Link

Additional Practice

Use Correct End Punctuation Review the rules for using end punctuation. Write the following sentences on the chalkboard or on a transparency. Have students place the correct end punctuation where necessary.

1. Why was the man waiting there *(?)*
2. How long he must have waited *(. or !)*
3. He had made this appointment twenty years ago. *(correct)*
4. What a long time twenty years is *(. or !)*
5. Did the other man show up as he had promised *(?)*

Reading Skills Development

(**Mixed Ability Group**) **Make Predictions** To help students develop and apply their skills of making predictions, arrange students in odd-numbered, mixed ability groups to read together a selection you choose from the "Making Predictions" section of the list that begins on page 383 of this book. After each reader takes a turn, the group should stop to discuss what might happen next in the story, taking notes on their ideas. Groups should then review their predictions in successive turns. You may ask students: *What did you find surprising about the story, and why? Do you think the writer wanted to surprise you? Why, or why not?* Have groups share their answers with the class.

SKILLS FOCUS

Literary Skill
Understand omniscient point of view.

Reading Skill
Make predictions.

(**Resources**)
In this book:
• Adapted Readings
• Vocabulary and Comprehension, p. 137
• Additional Vocabulary Practice, p. 140 (includes the next selection)

Other Resources:
• *The Holt Reader*
• *Holt Adapted Reader*
• *Audio CD Library*
• *Audio CD Library, Selections and Summaries in Spanish*
• *Supporting Instruction in Spanish*

(**Teacher Tip**)
Prompt students to discuss how they feel about Jimmy's letter at the end of the story. Let them discuss the issue of honesty versus friendship.

TARGETED STRATEGIES FOR SPECIAL EDUCATION STUDENTS

Prereading

Background

Preview the Story Students may benefit from hearing a brief summary of "After Twenty Years" before they read. Tell them that this is a story set in New York City and is about a man waiting to meet a friend he hasn't seen for a very long time. Twenty years ago the friends had planned to meet on this day, but, because so much time has passed, it is not certain whether this meeting will actually happen, or whether the old friends will recognize each other. The evening may end up being very surprising for both men. Explain that the story has an omniscient, or all-knowing, narrator. That means that the narration will not be limited to one character's point of view; instead, the narrator will know everything that is happening.

Reading

Listening and Speaking Opportunity

(**Core Skill**) **Encourage Predictions** Some students may benefit from hearing "After Twenty Years" read aloud. Play the audio recording, and ask students to follow along in their books. Pause at various points to ask students what they think will happen next, and then stop periodically to check the accuracy of their predictions. Also, point out passages indicating an omniscient narrator.

Postreading

Alternative Assessment

Check Comprehension To check students' comprehension of the story, write the following statements on the chalkboard or on a transparency. Have students determine whether each statement is true or false. If a statement is false, ask students to rewrite the sentence to make it true.

1. Bob appeared to be wealthy. *(T)*
2. Jimmy never showed up for the meeting. *(F)*
3. Jimmy recognized Bob as a wanted criminal. *(T)*
4. Bob thought that a stranger was his friend. *(T)*
5. Bob had a scar on his hand and a little white scar on his forehead. *(F)*
6. Jimmy was a traveler and wanted to leave New York. *(F)*

Vocabulary and Comprehension

"After Twenty Years"

A. Match words and definitions. Write the letter of the correct definition next to each word.

_____ **1.** habitual

_____ **2.** intricate

_____ **3.** dismally

_____ **4.** egotism

_____ **5.** simultaneously

a. miserably; gloomily

b. at the same time

c. done or fixed by habit; customary

d. complicated; full of detail

e. conceit; talking about oneself too much

B. Choose four words from above. Use each word in a sentence.

1. _____

_____

2. _____

_____

3. _____

_____

4. _____

_____

C. Write T or F next to each statement to tell if it is true or false.

_____ **1.** The night was chilly and the streets were empty.

_____ **2.** Jimmy and Bob had been writing to each other for twenty years.

_____ **3.** The two friends planned to meet at 10 P.M.

_____ **4.** Jimmy didn't want to leave New York.

_____ **5.** Bob didn't recognize Jimmy when he saw him.

_____ **6.** Jimmy knew Bob was a wanted man, so he decided to help Bob escape the law.

"What's *Really* in a Name?" by Joan Burditt

SKILLS FOCUS

Reading Skill
Analyze an author's perspective.

(**Resources**)

In this book:
• Adapted Readings
• Vocabulary and
Comprehension, p. 139
• Additional Vocabulary
Practice, p. 140 (includes
the previous selection)

Other Resources:
• *Holt Adapted Reader*
• *Audio CD Library*
• *Audio CD Library,
Selections and Summaries
in Spanish*
• *Supporting Instruction
in Spanish*

(**Special Education
Students**)

Many students have
heard their names
mispronounced. Lead a
discussion about names.
Would changing a name
change an identity? Ask
students to discuss whether
a name affects how a
person is seen by others.

Prereading
Alternative Activity

(**Especially for ELL**) **Read the Adaptation** Distribute copies of
the adapted reading of "What's *Really* in a Name?" (available in this
book and, with marginal questions, in *Holt Adapted Reader*). To
prepare for reading the original version and to practice fluency,
students should read the adaptation silently.

Reading
Alternative Teaching Strategy

Take a Name Help students identify and trace the development of
the author's perspective in the text "What's *Really* in a Name?" Point
out that the author begins the essay by describing her feelings when
she learned that her sister's friend had changed her name. She then
explains that people have many reasons for changing their names:

• hide a crime

• respond to their publisher's request

• adopt one that sounds better and is more appealing

Lead students to understand that the author is troubled that Patsy,
her sister's friend, may have been trying to get rid of her past when
she changed her name. Point out the author's conclusion that she
hopes that Patsy and others hold onto their roots when they change
their names. Elicit from students that the essay develops the
perspective that names link us to our pasts and offer no limits to
our futures.

Postreading
Alternative Activity

Write a Paragraph Use the chart on page 364 of the text to help
students trace the development of the author's perspective in "What's
Really in a Name?" Draw the chart on the chalkboard and help
students fill in the sections. After successfully tracking the perspective
of the author in this essay, ask students to write a paragraph in which
they develop their own perspectives on the statement "Girls work
harder than boys." Do students agree or disagree? When finished,
draw two more charts on the chalkboard. Label one AGREE and the
other DISAGREE. As volunteers read their paragraphs to the class, help
the class fill in the new charts.

Vocabulary and Comprehension

"What's *Really* in a Name?"

A. Match the following people with their pseudonyms.

____ **1.** Norma Jean Baker	**a.** Mark Twain
____ **2.** Reginald Dwight	**b.** O. Henry
____ **3.** Samuel Clemens	**c.** Ralph Lauren
____ **4.** William Sydney Porter	**d.** Marilyn Monroe
____ **5.** Ralph Lifshitz	**e.** Elton John

B. Complete each sentence with a word from the Word Bank.

1. Some writers write under a pen name, or

_____.

2. Can a different name give you an air of

_____ and make you

seem worldly-wise?

Word Bank
pseudonym
sophistication
memorable
roots

3. If you have a common name, an unusual one might

stand out and be more _____.

4. Never forget your family ties, or _____, no

matter what your name is.

C. Write T or F next to each statement to tell if it is true or false.

_____ **1.** The author's friend Patsy gave herself a pseudonym to
be used in the credits for the film.

_____ **2.** A pseudonym is a made-up name.

_____ **3.** Only people who work in movies use pseudonyms.

_____ **4.** For actors, another word for *pseudonym* is "pen name."

_____ **5.** The author assumed Patsy was trying to get rid of her
past by taking a pseudonym.

_____ **6.** The author wanted to adopt a pseudonym, too.

_____ **7.** The author thinks it is important to remember your roots.

Additional Vocabulary Practice

"After Twenty Years"; "What's *Really* in a Name?"

A. Match words and definitions. Write the letter of the correct definition next to each word.

_____ **1.** drizzle

_____ **2.** gusts

_____ **3.** chilly

_____ **4.** pseudonym

_____ **5.** hustling

_____ **6.** destiny

_____ **7.** thoroughfare

_____ **8.** guardian

_____ **9.** spectators

_____ **10.** credits

a. strong and sudden rushes of air

b. watchers

c. light rain, with small raindrops

d. protector

e. moving quickly

f. public street

g. cold

h. pen name; false name taken by a writer

i. fate

j. names of people who took part in a movie

B. Complete each sentence with a word from the list above.

1. The policeman wanted people to be safe. He was a _____.

2. There were no _____ on the street to see the fancy way he was twirling his club.

3. He needed his warm coat because the night was _____.

4. The wind came in powerful _____.

5. He didn't need an umbrella. There was only a little _____.

6. Bob had left New York to find his _____ in the West.

7. In the West, he _____ from town to town, looking for ways to make money.

8. Samuel Clemens wrote *Tom Sawyer* under the _____ of Mark Twain.

9. Patsy's name did not appear in the _____ at the end of the movie.

"Bargain" by A.B. Guthrie

Prereading

Background

Refer to American History Students may not be familiar with westerns or the Old West. Explain that the first immigrants to the United States lived on the East Coast. In the mid-1800s, large numbers of people began moving west. Life in the West was tough at first. People tended to live by their own laws. Besides Al, the main characters in this story are Mr. Baumer, a Dutch immigrant who learned to read and write English, and Freighter Slade, who hauls merchandise fifty miles from the railroad depot to Moon Dance. Explain that Freighter Slade, who was born in the United States, cannot read and write. This story is about a dispute between Mr. Baumer and Freighter Slade, and about justice and revenge. If necessary, define *justice* and *revenge:*

- *justice:* the quality of being fair; reward or punishment as deserved
- *revenge:* harm or evil done in return for harm or evil that has been done

Discuss how the meanings of the words are alike and how they are different. Ask students to use the words in sentences of their own.

Vocabulary Practice

Recognize Action Words To increase students' understanding and enjoyment of the story, define these action words from "Bargain." Then, make note cards for these words so that students can take turns picking a card and acting out the word on it for others to guess.

- *rattled (p. 369):* made a series of sharp, short sounds
- *prodded (p. 369):* poked or jabbed with a stick
- *drop (p. 370):* fall or let fall
- *slouched (p. 370):* sat, stood, or walked with the head drooping and shoulders slumping
- *smoothed (p. 370):* made level or even
- *scream (p. 371):* give a loud, shrill cry in fright, pain, or surprise
- *thump (p. 374):* hit, fall, or pound with a dull sound
- *hustle (p. 375):* go or do quickly with much energy

SKILLS FOCUS

Literary Skills
- Understand first-person point of view.
- Understand historical fiction.

Reading Skill
Make predictions.

Resources

In this book:
- Adapted Readings
- Vocabulary and Comprehension, p. 145
- Additional Vocabulary Practice, p. 146

Other Resources:
- *Holt Adapted Reader*
- *Audio CD Library*
- *Audio CD Library, Selections and Summaries in Spanish*
- *Supporting Instruction in Spanish*

Teacher Tip

Explain to students that "Bargain" is a work of historical fiction that incorporates factual information about the era.

Core Skill

Use the resources in the Reading Skills and Strategies section of this book to help students having difficulty making predictions. Use "Bargain" for the application portion of the lesson.

Alternative Activity

Read the Adaptation Distribute copies of the adapted reading of "Bargain" (available in this book and, with marginal questions, in *Holt Adapted Reader*). To prepare for reading the original version and to practice fluency, students should read the adaptation silently. Encourage students to write notes, questions, predictions, reactions, and comments on the worksheets as they read.

Reading
Alternative Teaching Strategy

Identify the First-Person Narrator Help students recognize that Al is the narrator, and that he is telling the story in the first person as an eyewitness. Have students take turns reading aloud. Stop them after the first paragraph to clarify the identity of the narrator. Ask them to explain how they can tell that this is a first-person narration. (*The narrator refers to himself as "I."*) Have students continue reading aloud; then, stop the reading when they come across sentences or paragraphs in which Al reveals his feelings about Mr. Baumer (*for example, pp. 370, 373*) and Freighter Slade (*p. 375*). You might also stop the reading after each encounter between Baumer and Slade to discuss how the story would be different if it were being told from Baumer's or Slade's point of view.

Postreading
Listening and Speaking Opportunity

Especially for ELL **Read and Listen** This activity combines reading aloud and paraphrasing to check understanding. Group students in pairs and assign each pair a few paragraphs from "Bargain." Ask students to take turns as listener and reader. After a reader finishes a paragraph, ask the listener to paraphrase it in his or her own words.

Alternative Activity

Examine Point of View To reinforce students' understanding of point of view, ask volunteers to retell the story. Discuss the ending by asking: Would the ending be a surprise if Mr. Baumer were the narrator? Elicit from students that it couldn't have been a surprise ending in that case because, unlike Al, Mr. Baumer knew what had happened to Slade. Have half the class retell the story from Mr. Baumer's point of view, and half from Freighter Slade's point of view. Discuss the differences.

Vocabulary Development

Reteach the Key Idea

Use Comprehension Strategies to Clarify Meaning Students who are struggling to learn new words will benefit from mastering the following vocabulary comprehension strategies.

- *Look to see if word parts are familiar.* Write on the board the sentence "Mr. Baumer had his hand in a sling." Point out that the words *sling* and *slingshot* are related words. A *sling* is a loop of cloth that hangs down from around the neck, for holding an injured arm or hand. A *slingshot* has a similar loop, this time attached to the ends of a stick. Remind students that to figure out a word, they can use a word that is related in spelling and meaning.

- *Look at the surrounding words and sentences.* Write these sentences on the board and read them to students, underlining the word as shown: *Mr. Baumer saw Slade and <u>hesitated</u> in his step and came to a stop. He <u>shuddered</u> a little, as if he hadn't got the chill off even yet.*

Vocabulary Practice

Reinforce Comprehension Strategies Have students practice the two strategies above.

Make copies of these sentences and have students figure out the meaning of the underlined words:

1. Slade came out of the saloon and stood on the <u>boardwalk</u>. *(a walk made of thick boards)*

2. Please, <u>shortsighted</u> the way you are, don't catch sight of him at all! *(condition in which the eye cannot see distant objects)*

3. People felt every bounce and bump riding in a <u>buckboard</u> because the open wagon had no springs. *(a light open wagon)*

4. Several horses stood patiently at the <u>hitchpost</u> in front of Mr. Baumer's store. *(a post used to tether horses)*

Reading Skills Development

Mixed Ability Group **Make Predictions** Students may benefit from seeing the process of making predictions from another angle. To help students develop and apply their skills of making predictions, arrange students in odd-numbered, mixed ability groups to read together a selection you choose from the "Making Predictions" section of the list that begins on page 383 of this book. After each reader takes a turn, group members should each suggest one thing that will *not* happen in the story, providing reasons for their ideas. Students should record each group member's "anti-prediction" and then review them in successive turns. You may ask students: *What did you expect would not happen in the story, and why? Were you correct?* Have groups share their answers with the class.

SKILLS FOCUS

Vocabulary Skill
Use comprehension strategies.

Special Education Students

For some students these comprehension strategies may be too abstract. Try color coding. Write a word on the chalkboard. Underline the root in one color, the prefix in another, and the suffix in another. Ask students to come to the board and mark other words themselves.

Literary Skills
- Understand first-person point of view.
- Understand historical fiction.

Reading Skill
Make predictions.

(Resources)

In this book:
- Adapted Readings
- Vocabulary and Comprehension, p. 145
- Additional Vocabulary Practice, p. 146

Other Resources:
- *Holt Adapted Reader*
- *Audio CD Library*
- *Audio CD Library, Selections and Summaries in Spanish*
- *Supporting Instruction in Spanish*

(Teacher Tip)

Preview illustrations in the story. Tell students that many small towns in the Old West had main streets that looked similar to the one shown on page 369.

TARGETED STRATEGIES FOR SPECIAL EDUCATION STUDENTS

Prereading

Background

Preview the Story In the history of the United States, the Wild West was known for its cast of strong, independent characters who sometimes took the law into their own hands to resolve conflicts. This story tells of one man's struggle to overcome his differences with a particularly difficult man. Mr. Baumer, a mild-mannered Dutch immigrant, devises a way to get even with a freighter named Slade. It is left up to the reader to determine whether Baumer's actions amount to justice or underhanded revenge.

Reading

Alternative Teaching Strategy

Realize That the Point of View Affects the Theme Help students identify the narrator of "Bargain." Note that the story is written in the first person. Read the story with students. Encourage them to identify with Al. Ask what they think about Mr. Baumer and Slade after each encounter. Point out that Al reveals to the reader what he thinks of the two. He changes his thinking by the end of the story, but he doesn't tell us exactly how he feels. Ask students how they feel about Mr. Baumer's actions. Have them support their responses with details from the story. Ask students how the story would be different had Mr. Baumer been the narrator.

Postreading

Alternative Assessment

Check Comprehension Write the following statements on the chalkboard or on a transparency. Have students determine whether each statement is true or false.

1. Mr. Baumer learned to read and write English when he immigrated to this country at sixteen years of age. *(T)*

2. Slade was gentle with his horses. *(F)*

3. Slade read the Moon Dance newspaper every day. *(F)*

4. Slade never paid any of his debts. *(T)*

5. It was normal for freighters to steal a little bit of whiskey from the shipment of goods. *(T)*

6. Slade paid his bill the second time Mr. Baumer gave it to him. *(F)*

NAME _____ DATE _____

Vocabulary and Comprehension

"Bargain"

A. Match words and definitions. Write the letter of the correct definition next to each word.

_____ **1.** freighter

_____ **2.** rigs

_____ **3.** string

_____ **4.** ornerier

a. a group of horses

b. wagons pulled by horses

c. person who transports goods

d. meaner than usual

B. Choose two words from above. Use each word in a sentence.

1. _____

_____

2. _____

_____

C. Answer each question below.

1. Who is the narrator of the story?

_____

_____

2. What does Mr. Baumer want from Slade?

_____

_____

3. Why does Mr. Baumer hire Slade?

_____

_____

4. What does Slade die from?

_____

_____

Additional Vocabulary Practice

"Bargain"

A. Complete each sentence with a word from the Word Bank.

1. Mr. Baumer was a small man with

_____ shoulders that
bent forward slightly.

2. Slade was a _____ and
hauled goods from the railroad station back to
the town.

3. Al helped Mr. Baumer by doing

_____, like getting the mail.

4. Mr. Baumer bought some poison that was a

_____. He didn't pay much for it.

5. Slade's _____ of horses stretched out in front
of the wagon when they came down from the buttes.

> **Word Bank**
> freighter
> errands
> stooped
> bargain
> string

B. Choose the correct word in parentheses to complete each sentence.

1. *(slouch, slouching)* Slade was _____ in front of the bar
with some friends. He was a tall man, but he often walked with a

_____ instead of standing up straight.

2. *(merchant, merchandise)* Mr. Baumer was a _____ and

owned a small store. His store was full of _____, like
sugar and flour.

3. *(mistake, mistaken)* Mr. Baumer made a big _____
when he trusted Slade. He thought Slade would pay his bill, but he

was _____.

4. *(beat, beaten)* Slade _____ Mr. Baumer in a fight. But

to Al, Baumer did not look _____, like a man who had
given up.

"Yeh-Shen" Chinese folk tale, retold by Ai-Ling Louie

Prereading

Background

Preview the Story Before beginning this story, make sure that all students are familiar with the story "Cinderella and the Glass Slipper." If necessary, retell the story prior to reading "Yeh-Shen."

Vocabulary Practice

Reinforce Targeted Vocabulary If students are keeping vocabulary journals, remind them to enter any unknown words. Start them off with the following words:

- *azure (p. 385):* like the color of a blue sky
- *pavilion (p. 386):* large tent or shelter, often highly decorated
- *herald (p. 386):* the person in a king's court who makes official announcements

(**Especially for ELL**) **Learn Additional Vocabulary** The following words from the selection may be unfamiliar to ELL students. Read the words and definitions with students; then, have them use the words in sentences.

- *coarsest (p. 384):* roughest or harshest to the touch
- *crafty (p. 384):* skillful in tricking or fooling others; sly; cunning
- *beauteous (p. 385):* delightful to look at, listen to, or think about; pleasing to the mind or senses
- *precious (p. 385):* having a high value or price
- *resemble (p. 385):* be or look like
- *sage (p. 385):* wise person
- *soles (p. 385):* the bottom surfaces of shoes or feet
- *transformation (p. 385):* a change from one thing into something else
- *timidly (p. 386):* feeling or showing fear
- *undaunted (p. 386):* not afraid or discouraged
- *tattered (p. 387):* torn; ragged

Alternative Activity

Read the Adaptation Distribute copies of the adapted reading of "Yeh-Shen" (available in this book and, with marginal questions, in *Holt Adapted Reader*). To prepare for reading the original version and to practice fluency, students should read the adaptation silently.

SKILLS FOCUS

Literary Skill
Understand omniscient point of view.

(**Resources**)

In this book:
- Adapted Readings
- Vocabulary and Comprehension, p. 151
- Additional Vocabulary Practice, p. 154 (includes the next selection)

Other Resources:
- *Holt Adapted Reader*
- *Audio CD Library*
- *Audio CD Library, Selections and Summaries in Spanish*
- *Supporting Instruction in Spanish*

(**Especially for ELL**)

ELLs probably know stories from their native countries that are similar to the story of Cinderella. Ask them to share a story about mean relatives and a girl who is blessed with good fortune.

Reading

Alternative Activity

Play the Audio Recording Struggling readers may benefit from listening to the audio recording of the selection as they follow along in their books. You may want to stop and replay any confusing sections for students.

Alternative Teaching Strategy

Identify the Omniscient Point of View To help students identify the point of view of "Yeh-Shen" as being omniscient, review with them what signs they should look for. Elicit from them that the omniscient narrator uses the third-person pronoun, knows the private thoughts and feelings of everyone, and knows what is happening everywhere in the story.

Help students find signs in the story that determine that the story is told from the omniscient point of view. Point out that:

- it is not first-person narration, because there is no *I* telling the story
- the narrator tells the reader *(p. 384)* what the stepmother is thinking
- the narrator tells the reader *(p. 385)* that Yeh-Shen wants to ask the old man more questions
- the narrator tells the reader *(p. 386)* what happens to the lost shoe
- the narrator tells the reader *(p. 386)* that the king is entranced with the tiny slipper
- the narrator tells the reader *(p. 387)* that Yeh-Shen is unaware of the excitement she caused
- the narrator tells the reader *(p. 387)* that years later the stepmother and stepsister are crushed to death in a shower of flying stones

Postreading

Additional Practice

(**Mixed Ability Group**) **Examine Point of View Through Retelling** Have students choose a character from "Yeh-Shen" to tell the story in the first person. Students may work in small groups to re-create the story from that character's point of view. For example, if they choose to tell the story from the point of view of the fish, they will need to describe the thoughts and feelings of the fish while he's with Yeh-Shen, when he gets stabbed and eaten, and as he helps Yeh-Shen. Have group members review the story scene by scene to determine whether the character they chose is in each scene. Have them ask themselves: Would that character know about this scene? Should this scene be included in the story? Allow time for groups to present their stories to the class.

Ask students how a different point of view affects the overall theme of the story. For example, the king's story might be about how wise he was to devise a plan to find a perfect wife in a neglected, unloved servant girl.

Check Comprehension Review the main events in the story by calling on students to answer the following questions.

1. Who is Yeh-Shen's only friend? *(a fish)*
2. What does the stepmother do when she finds out about the fish? *(she kills the fish and cooks it)*
3. Why is Yeh-Shen able to go to the festival? *(the magic fish bones give her clothes so that she can go)*
4. How does the king get the slipper? *(a merchant gives it to the king)*
5. What happens to Yeh-Shen when she puts on the slippers in front of the king? *(her clothes are transformed into her festival gown and cloak)*

Vocabulary Practice

Reinforce Story Vocabulary To reinforce the vocabulary from "Yeh-Shen," copy this paragraph onto the board. Read the paragraph with students. Ask them to choose the correct word to fill in each blank.

> Mary worked at the ___ (<u>pavilion</u>/herald) near the center of town. She wore the ___ (transformed/<u>coarsest</u>) clothing, and the ___ (<u>soles</u>/herald) of her shoes needed to be fixed. She earned very little but she was ___ (transformed/<u>undaunted</u>). You see, her eyes were ___ (<u>azure</u>/herald) blue and she ___ (transformed/<u>resembled</u>) a princess. All she needed for her ___ (<u>transformation</u>/soles) was a prince.

Reading Skills Development

(**Mixed Ability Group**) **Understand Characters** Students having difficulty understanding omniscient point of view may need more practice understanding characters. To help students, arrange them in small, mixed ability groups to choose from the Reading teaching strategy on page 148 one of the places in the story indicating the omniscient point of view. Have each group use a chart to show that the omniscient narrator knows much more about what is happening in the story than does the character. Ask students: *What does the omniscient point of view add to the reader's experience of the story? How would the story differ if the reader knew only what an individual character knew?* Discuss groups' answers and charts with the class.

What the Character Thinks and Does	What the Narrator Knows

Literary Skill
Understand omniscient point of view.

(Resources)

In this book:
• Adapted Readings
• Vocabulary and Comprehension, p. 151
• Additional Vocabulary Practice, p. 154 (includes the next selection)

Other Resources:
• *Holt Adapted Reader*
• *Audio CD Library*
• *Audio CD Library, Selections and Summaries in Spanish*
• *Supporting Instruction in Spanish*

(Teacher Tip)

Review the cues for determining whether a sentence is told from the first-person or third-person point of view. Highlight the use of "I" in first person, and "he, she, or they" in the third person.

TARGETED STRATEGIES FOR SPECIAL EDUCATION STUDENTS

Prereading
Background

Preview the Story Introduce the story of Yeh-Shen by reminding students of the story of Cinderella. If students are not familiar with the European version of the tale, read it to them. Then, discuss "Cinderella" with students. Ask: Who likes the story? Why?

Reading
Reteach the Key Idea

Identify Point of View Explain to students that this story has an omniscient narrator—one who knows everything that is happening and what each character thinks and feels. While students are reading, have them find three examples that show the narrator as omniscient. (*e.g., the narrator knows that the stepmother is jealous of Yeh-Shen, that Yeh-Shen wants to ask the old man more questions, and what happens to the shoe after Yeh-Shen loses it*)

Postreading
Alternative Activity

Use Word Maps In almost every Cinderella tale, the character and dresses up, often with the help of magic, and then meets a prince. Ask students to list the clothing that Yeh-Shen wears. Then, list words that describe it. Instruct students to circle each article of clothing and draw lines to the descriptive words and phrases and circle them. For example:

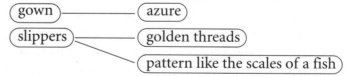

Alternative Assessment

Use True/False Statements Write the following statements on the chalkboard. If the statement is false, ask students to revise the sentence to make it true.

____ 1. Yeh-Shen could not go to the festival and stayed home. *(F)*

____ 2. Yeh-Shen was not as beautiful as her stepsister. *(F)*

____ 3. One of Yeh-Shen's golden slippers was lost. *(T)*

____ 4. The stepmother killed the fish with a gun. *(F)*

____ 5. The fish bones had magic. *(T)*

Vocabulary and Comprehension

"Yeh-Shen"

A. Complete each sentence with a word from the Word Bank.

1. The bones of the magic fish had a powerful soul, or

_____.

2. Yeh-Shen could ask the bones to grant her wish, or

_____, but she must not
waste the gifts.

3. Yeh-Shen lived in fear and

_____ that her
stepmother would take the bones away.

4. The bones changed, or _____, her old rags
into clothes of great beauty.

5. Yeh-Shen shyly and _____ spoke to the king.

Word Bank
dread
timidly
desire
spirit
transformed

B. Answer each question below.

1. Who are the characters in the story?

_____

_____

2. What happens to the fish after it is killed?

_____

_____

3. How does the fish help Yeh-Shen?

_____

_____

4. Who finds the missing shoe?

_____

_____

Elements of Literature
pages 389–392

"Mirror, Mirror on the Wall . . . ?"
by Joan Burditt

SKILLS FOCUS

Reading Skill
Trace an author's argument.

Resources

In this book:
• Vocabulary and Comprehension, p. 153
• Additional Vocabulary Practice, p. 154 (includes the previous selection)

Other Resources:
• *Audio CD Library*
• *Audio CD Library, Selections and Summaries in Spanish*
• *Supporting Instruction in Spanish*

Special Education Students

Work with students to write a summary sentence for each sidebar letter as you read the article together. Then, lead a discussion about what they think of the article, and whether they agree with the writer.

Prereading
Vocabulary Practice

Preview the Vocabulary These are the literary terms introduced in the essay. Preview these terms, and check for comprehension as students read.

• *evidence (p. 389):* something that shows or proves, or gives reason for believing in

• *persuaders (p. 389):* people or things that convince someone to do or believe something

• *statements (p. 389):* declarations, remarks, reports of facts or opinions

• *anecdote (p. 390):* a short, interesting or amusing story about some person or event

• *argument (p. 391):* a reason given for or against something

Alternative Activity

Especially for ELL **Use Spanish Resources** Spanish-speaking English-language learners may benefit from reading or listening to the selection summary in Spanish in preparation for reading the selection in English.

Reading
Alternative Teaching Strategy

Track the Argument Use the sidebar notes to identify and trace the development of the author's argument. Starting with sidenote A, ask students to identify and summarize the anecdote to which the sidenote refers. Ask what point the anecdote makes. *(People often have a distorted idea of what they look like.)* Continue using the sidenotes as prompts.

Postreading
Alternative Activity

Track the Argument Guide students through the Test Practice on page 392, prompting them to choose correct answers. Use each item as an opportunity for class discussion of how the author developed her argument.

Vocabulary and Comprehension

"Mirror, Mirror, on the Wall . . . ?"

A. Match words and definitions. Write the letter of the correct definition next to each word.

_____ **1.** illusion

_____ **2.** self-esteem

_____ **3.** interview

_____ **4.** statistics

_____ **5.** insecure

a. belief in oneself

b. not feeling safe or confident

c. data presented in number form

d. the appearance of something that makes one see it in a false way

e. meeting in which one person asks another questions about his or her opinions, activities, or experience

B. Answer each question below.

1. What do middle-school and high school students say about their own weights?

_____

_____

2. What kind of clothes are important to these students?

_____

_____

3. In your own words, what is the main idea of this story?

_____

_____

4. List a detail that supports the main idea of the story.

_____

_____

Additional Vocabulary Practice

"Yeh-Shen"; "Mirror, Mirror, on the Wall . . . ?"

A. Circle the letter of the word or phrase that best fits the meaning of the underlined word.

1. Yeh-Shen was a poor <u>orphan</u> with no parents to love her.
   a. child   **b.** parentless child   **c.** daughter

2. Yeh-Shen was very <u>bright</u> and a quick learner.
   a. smart   **b.** shiny   **c.** light

3. The fish had <u>wondrous</u> powers and could grant wishes.
   a. confusing   **b.** silly   **c.** wonderful

4. When she felt sad, Yeh-Shen found <u>comfort</u> in talking to the bones of the fish.
   a. pain   **b.** ease   **c.** worry

5. Like a scared mouse, she tiptoed <u>timidly</u> across the floor.
   a. loudly   **b.** quickly   **c.** fearfully

6. Her old rags were <u>transformed</u> into beautiful clothes.
   a. washed   **b.** painted   **c.** changed

7. The king's <u>herald</u> announced that the shoe was to be given back to its original owner.
   a. messenger   **b.** bodyguard   **c.** brother

B. Complete each sentence with a word from the Word Bank.

1. Magazines for teens are _____ the way teens look and dress.

2. The magazines are full of _____ for clothes and makeup.

3. It's hard for a girl to feel high _____ when she sees pictures of beautiful models.

4. But a photograph of a model shows an

   _____, not a real person.

5. Not all girls, of course, feel worried and _____ about their looks.

Word Bank
illusion
self-esteem
insecure
influencing
advertisements

"Names/Nombres" by Julia Alvarez

Prereading

Background

Identify Locations Explain to students that this is an autobiographical essay about the author's experiences after her family moved from the Dominican Republic to New York City. To help locate the story, point out the Dominican Republic and New York City on a map.

Alternative Teaching Strategy

(**Especially for ELL**) **Reteach the Key Idea** English-language learners may need more practice to understand the concepts of subjective and objective. Explain that:

• *subjective statements* are based on opinion and personal experience.

• *objective statements* are based on facts.

Draw a chart with two columns on the chalkboard. Label the columns SUBJECTIVE and OBJECTIVE. Have the class brainstorm statements of opinion and fact, and then write them in the appropriate columns.

Alternative Activities

Read the Adaptation Distribute copies of the adapted reading of "Names/Nombres" (available in this book and, with marginal questions, in *Holt Adapted Reader*). To prepare for reading the original version and to practice fluency, students should read the adaptation silently.

Use *The Holt Reader* You may consider having students use the Before You Read page in *The Holt Reader*, either instead of or in addition to the Before You Read page in the student book.

Reading

Alternative Activities

Use *The Holt Reader* You may have students read the selection in *The Holt Reader* and use the margins in that book to make notes and respond to the instruction.

Clarify Fact and Opinion Ask students to keep a piece of paper and a pencil on their desks as they read "Names/Nombres." Have them draw a two-column chart labeled SUBJECTIVE and OBJECTIVE as above. Tell them to look for examples of objective and subjective statements

SKILLS FOCUS

Literary Skills
Understand objective and subjective points of view.

Reading Skill
Find the main idea.

(**Resources**)

In this book:
• Adapted Readings
• Vocabulary and Comprehension, p. 159
• Additional Vocabulary Practice, p. 160

Other Resources:
• *The Holt Reader*
• *Holt Adapted Reader*
• *Audio CD Library*
• *Audio CD Library, Selections and Summaries in Spanish*
• *Supporting Instruction in Spanish*
• Videocassette, Segment 4

(**Teacher Tip**)

Spanish names and words in the text may be difficult to pronounce for students who do not speak Spanish. If possible, ask a Spanish-speaking student to pronounce the Spanish words in the selection so the class can hear how they should sound.

in the selection and to list each statement under the proper heading. Later, review these charts with students and discuss why each statement they listed is a fact or an opinion.

Postreading

Alternative Activity

Use *The Holt Reader* You may consider having students use the postreading activities in *The Holt Reader,* either instead of or in addition to the postreading activities in the student book.

Listening and Speaking Opportunity

Discuss Names To generate discussion about the importance of names to different people, ask students the following questions:

- How do you feel about names? Are they important? Why or why not?
- How do the names parents give their children affect the children?
- What can names tell us about someone's background or ethnicity?
- Do your parents use nicknames for their children?

You may want to conclude the discussion by summarizing cultural differences and similarities related to names. Such a discussion will help students develop a greater appreciation of other cultures. Also, discuss whether people ever have trouble pronouncing any of the names of students. Ask if any students have nicknames.

(Especially for ELL)

Word webs are often a useful way of getting students to understand the difference between subjective and objective statements. You may want to use this kind of graphic organizer with "Names / Nombres."

Additional Practice

Identify Subjective and Objective Statements To help students identify this as a subjective essay, ask them to find statements in "Names/Nombres" in which Julia Alvarez shares her own feelings, thoughts, opinions, and judgments. They may find the following:

- It took awhile to get used to my new names. I wondered if I shouldn't correct my teachers and new friends.
- They were being curious, I knew, but I burned with shame whenever they singled me out as a "foreigner," a rare, exotic friend.

Contrast these with objective statements found in the "Meet the Writer" section on page 398 of the text. Have students note that these present facts and figures instead of the writer's personal opinions and private feelings.

(Core Skill) Identify the Theme Help students identify the theme of "Names/ Nombres." Explain that both her Spanish and her Americanized names symbolize the way the author is able to synthesize her Dominican Republic heritage and the culture of her American home.

Vocabulary Development

Reteach the Key Idea

Clarify Word Meanings Through Definitions Remind students that writers sometimes define difficult words in context. Point out that phrases such as "in other words" and "that is" are often followed by a definition. Writers use definitions within a sentence to clarify the meaning of unfamiliar words for the reader. Write these model sentences on the board. Read them aloud with students, and point out or underline the unfamiliar targeted words. Ask students to underline the definitions of these targeted words.

1. The dress was very *exotic*, that is, it was very strange and foreign.

2. Francis's explanation of his science project was very *convoluted*; in other words, it was too complicated.

3. Studies have shown that *ethnicity*, meaning culture or nationality, influences the kinds of programs we watch on television.

4. He wanted to learn more about his *heritage*, that is, the customs and traditions his family had followed for generations.

Grammar Link

Additional Practice

Don't Leave Your Modifiers Dangling Have students revise the following sentences to eliminate dangling modifiers.

1. Using their wits, the day was saved. *(Using their wits, they saved the day.)*

2. Leaving the door open, our dog left. *(The door was open, so our dog left.)*

3. Noticing his accent, his heritage was questioned. *(His heritage was questioned because of his accent.)*

Reading Skills Development

(Mixed Ability Group) **Practice Finding the Main Idea** Students who have difficulty finding the main idea may benefit from additional practice in a group setting. Arrange students in small, mixed ability groups to read together a selection you choose from the "Determining Main Idea" section of the list that begins on page 383 of this book. As groups read the selection, have them stop periodically to restate in their own words what the selection is about. After they have read the selection, group members should review their notes and discuss what the details have in common. Encourage each group to come up with a complete sentence that states the main idea of the selection. Have groups share their statements with the class and use the statements to write out the selection's main idea on the chalkboard.

SKILLS FOCUS

Vocabulary Skill
Clarify word meanings by using definitions.

(Teacher Tip)
Definitions are often given within a statement, and can be found more easily by looking for phrases, often between commas (*e.g., in other words; that is*).

(Core Skill)
Use the resources in the Reading Skills and Strategies section of this book to help students having difficulty determining main idea. Use "Names/Nombres" for the application portion of the lesson.

SKILLS FOCUS

Literary Skills
Understand objective and subjective points of view.

Reading Skill
Find the main idea.

Resources

In this book:
• Adapted Readings
• Vocabulary and Comprehension, p. 159
• Additional Vocabulary Practice, p. 160

Other Resources:
• *The Holt Reader*
• *Holt Adapted Reader*
• *Audio CD Library*
• *Audio CD Library, Selections and Summaries in Spanish*
• *Supporting Instruction in Spanish*
• Videocassette, Segment 4

Teacher Tip

Write two columns on the board labeled SUBJECTIVE and OBJECTIVE. Have students give subjective and objective statements a recent immigrant might make, for example, "I don't speak English" or "I think America is so different."

TARGETED STRATEGIES FOR SPECIAL EDUCATION STUDENTS

Prereading
Background
Preview the Selection Tell students that "Names / Nombres" is an autobiographical essay that deals with the importance of names in the author's life. Remind students that an autobiographical essay is written in the first person. Discuss the author's reason for using both the English and Spanish words in her title. Ask students: How would you feel if people mispronounced your name? Would you correct their pronunciation? Why or why not?

Reading
Listening and Speaking Opportunity
Listen and Discuss Some students may have difficulty with the Spanish names and terms in this selection. Play the audio recording, or read the selection aloud, as students follow along. Stop at key points to discuss what has been read. Explain that students can tell that the essay is written from a subjective viewpoint because it expresses the author's feelings and opinions. Ask them to find two sentences written from a subjective viewpoint. For example:

- They were just being curious, I knew, but I burned with shame whenever they singled me out as a "foreigner," a rare, exotic friend. (*The writer is telling her feelings. She burned with shame.*)
- My little sister, Ana, had the easiest time of all. (*This is subjective because the statement is not provable.*)

Postreading
Alternative Assessment
Use True/False Statements Write the following statements on the board. Have students determine whether each statement is true or false.

____ 1. Julia Alvarez, the author of "Names/Nombres," came to the United States from Sweden. *(F)*

____ 2. Julia and her family had an easy time adjusting to life in the United States because people understood their heritage. *(F)*

____ 3. Julia was actually born in New York City. *(T)*

____ 4. When Julia graduated high school, all her relatives came. *(T)*

Vocabulary and Comprehension

"Names/Nombres"

A. Complete each sentence with a word from the Word Bank.

1. Another word for culture or nationality is

_____.

| **Word Bank** |
| ethnicity |
| heritage |
| convoluted |

2. Customs, foods, and traditions that are passed from generation to generation help preserve a person's

cultural _____.

3. Her relationships to her many relatives were so complicated and

_____ that she could not explain them easily.

B. Write T or F next to each statement to tell if it is true or false.

_____ **1.** Julia Alvarez was born in the Dominican Republic.

_____ **2.** Mami was embarrassed to tell her baby's name to the other new mothers.

_____ **3.** Julia's parents gave her a typewriter so she could write her stories and poems.

C. Answer each question below.

1. What happens to the pronunciation of the names of the Alvarez family when they come to New York City?

_____

_____

2. Why do other students ask Julia where she is from? How does she reply?

_____

_____

3. In your own words, what is the main idea of "Names/Nombres"?

_____

_____

Additional Vocabulary Practice

"Names/Nombres"

A. Match words and definitions. Write the letter of the correct definition next to each word.

_____ **1.** ethnicity

_____ **2.** exotic

_____ **3.** heritage

_____ **4.** convoluted

a. traditions that are passed along

b. complicated

c. common culture or nationality

d. foreign; not native

B. Choose the correct word in parentheses to complete each sentence.

1. *(pronounce, pronunciation)* When Julia came to the United States, everyone used a different _____ to say her name. No one seemed able to _____ her first or her last name correctly.

2. *(foreign, foreigner)* With her dark hair and her accent, she looked like a _____ to her classmates. They asked her what _____ country she was from.

3. *(ethnic, ethnicity)* Her family is proud of their culture and _____. Each week they gather to share their special _____ foods.

4. *(affection, affectionate)* Nicknames are one way to show warm feelings and _____ for someone. Her sister was given several _____ nicknames by her boyfriends.

C. Finish each sentence with a description that fits the underlined word.

1. Some of the traditions that are part of one's <u>heritage</u> are _____

_____

2. The most <u>exotic</u> food I have ever eaten is _____

_____

"An Unforgettable Journey"
by Maijue Xiong

Prereading

Background

Look at the Map Use a world map to locate Vietnam and Laos. Point out that while autobiographical writing is subjective, because it presents the author's feelings and opinions about his or her experiences, it can also contain objective facts about the author's family and country. Explain that "An Unforgettable Journey" will contain both facts and opinions.

Vocabulary Practice

Additional Vocabulary Practice Provide additional practice to help students understand selection vocabulary. Preview these words and definitions with students. Ask volunteers to use each word in a sentence of their own creation.

- *adaptations (p. 404):* changes made to fit new conditions
- *desperate (p. 405):* having a great need
- *rampant (p. 406):* spreading wildly without control
- *anxiously (p. 406):* uneasily; worriedly

Alternative Activity

(Especially for ELL) **Use Spanish Resources** Spanish-speaking English-language learners may benefit from reading or listening to the selection summary in Spanish in preparation for reading the selection in English.

Alternative Teaching Strategy

Identify the Speaker Help students understand that first-person narration is when the writer uses the personal pronoun *I*. When the writing is nonfiction, that is, a true story, and the person is writing about his or her own life, it is an autobiography. In this case, the *"I"* in "An Unforgettable Journey" is the author, Maijue Xiong. Review the "Meet the Writer" section with students before reading the selection with them. Have students keep in mind that the author is the *"I"* of the story.

SKILLS FOCUS

Literary Skill
Understand autobiography.

Reading Skill
Distinguish fact from opinion.

(Resources)

In this book:
- Vocabulary and Comprehension, p. 165
- Additional Vocabulary Practice, p. 168 (includes the next selection)

Other Resources:
- *Audio CD Library*
- *Audio CD Library, Selections and Summaries in Spanish*
- *Supporting Instruction in Spanish*

(Especially for ELL)

On the chalkboard, write the word *autobiography*. Define the word, and explain that the anecdotes in the selection are autobiographical.

(Teacher Tip)

Be sure students understand that "An Unforgettable Journey" presents the author's perspectives on her family, the Vietnamese war, becoming a refugee, and her new life in America. The story is Maijue Xiong's story, told from the first-person point of view.

Reading

Alternative Activity

Play the Audio Recording Struggling readers may benefit from listening to the audio recording of the selection as they follow along in their books.

Listening and Speaking Opportunity

Recognize Objective and Subjective Information To help students distinguish between objective and subjective information in "An Unforgettable Journey," explain that objective information reports figures and verifiable statements, and subjective writing presents personal opinion and unverifiable statements. As students read, have them write three sentences containing objective information and three sentences containing subjective information. The sentences might include:

- *I was born in a small village called Muong Cha in Laos on April 30, 1972. (objective)*
- *When you wake up, you don't remember what it was you had dreamed about but recall only those bits and pieces of the dream that stand out the most. (subjective)*

Postreading

Listening and Speaking Opportunity

(**Especially for ELL**) **Interview for Objective and Subjective Information** To help students distinguish between objective and subjective information, have them interview each other briefly about their native countries. Help students analyze the information they gather and note which statements are objective and which are subjective. Ask students to present their interviews to the class.

Alternative Assessment

(**Core Skill**) **Distinguish Fact and Opinion** Have students write numbers 1–7 in their notebooks. Read the following statements about "An Unforgettable Journey," and ask students to identify each as fact or opinion by writing F or O after each number.

1. We found ourselves without a home or a country and with a need to seek refuge in another country. *(F)*
2. The fishermen were mean to the refugees. *(O)*
3. The refugees' feet were also swollen from walking. *(F)*
4. America offered a better life *(O)*
5. The author entered kindergarten at Isla Vista Elementary School. *(F)*
6. It was shocking to see so many faces of different colors. *(O)*
7. The author is the very first member of her family to attend college. *(F)*

Special Education Students

To provide additional help, you might want to write out the sample sentences from the "Listening and Speaking Opportunities" in the Reading section and distribute photocopies. Pair students or have them work in small groups to identify which sentences are objective and which are subjective.

Vocabulary Development

Reteach the Key Idea

Identify Words That Signal Contrast Review words that signal contrasts by writing these signal words and definitions on the chalkboard.

- *although:* in spite of the fact that
- *but:* except; other than
- *however:* in spite of that; nevertheless; but
- *in contrast:* unlike; as opposed to
- *instead:* in place of the other
- *not:* in no way; to no degree
- *still:* in spite of that
- *unlike:* different; not alike
- *yet:* but; nevertheless

Write the following sentence on the chalkboard, and show students how to use the contrast clues to figure out the meaning of *scorching:*

> *Although* the sun was *scorching*, a light breeze *cooled* us.

Additional Practice

Clarify Word Meanings Through Contrast In the sentences below, have students circle the contrast words. Then, have them tell what they think the meaning of the target word is.

1. Instead of finding <u>persecution</u>, they are welcomed and accepted. *(contrast words = welcomed and accepted; the act of willfully hurting others because of their beliefs or ethnic background)*
2. Unlike the <u>deprivation</u> they suffered in their old country, there was abundant food in America. *(contrast word = abundant; scarcity, lack)*

Reading Skills Development

(Mixed Ability Group) **Distinguish Between Fact and Opinion**
Students having difficulty distinguishing between fact and opinion may benefit from more practice in a group. Arrange students in small, mixed ability groups, and have each group member write ten sentences, five of which give facts and five that give opinions. The sentences should be unmarked and in random order. Have group members sit in a circle and pass their lists to the person on the right. Each group member should identify on a separate sheet of paper which sentences contain facts and which contain opinions. Group members should exchange lists and repeat the exercise until each student has received his or her original list. Have group members discuss their answers, helping resolve any disagreements, if necessary.

SKILLS FOCUS

Vocabulary Skill
Clarify word meanings by using contrast.

(Core Skill)
Use the resources in the Reading Skills and Strategies section of this book to help students having difficulty distinguishing fact from opinion. Use "An Unforgettable Journey" for the application portion of the lesson.

Resources

In this book:
• Vocabulary and Comprehension, p. 165
• Additional Vocabulary Practice, p. 168 (includes the next selection)

Other Resources:
• *Audio CD Library*
• *Audio CD Library, Selections and Summaries in Spanish*
• *Supporting Instruction in Spanish*

Teacher Tip

Help students understand the difference between being a tourist and being an exile. Write the two words on the chalkboard, and elicit ideas from students about the different perspectives these two different kinds of travelers might have.

TARGETED STRATEGIES FOR SPECIAL EDUCATION STUDENTS

Prereading
Background

Define Autobiography Explain to students that when someone writes about himself or herself, it is autobiographical. "An Unforgettable Journey" is such an autobiographical story about Maijue Xiong. Invite students to look at the author's picture on page 407 in their text. Explain that autobiographical stories are narrated in the first person, and contain facts, but may also contain feelings and opinions about the author's experiences.

Reading
Alternative Teaching Strategy

Reteach the Key Idea To help students understand the difference between subjective and objective statements, ask them to identify subjective and objective statements in the text. For example: "My mother gave birth to a boy a month after we arrived in the United States." *(objective—this event can be proven by documentation)* "Therefore, I am determined to do well at the university." *(subjective— that Maijue is determined cannot be verified; it is her desire and goal)*

Postreading
Alternative Activity

Discuss Point of View To reinforce students' understanding of point of view, have them discuss how Maijue Xiong's story would be different if told by her mother, her father, or her stepuncle.

Alternative Assessment

Make a Time Line To assess student comprehension, copy the time line from page 408 of the text onto the board. Help students locate these events in the text, and place them in the correct order on the time line:

- The family arrives in the "land of the giants."
- The family lives in a refugee camp.
- The family travels to Bangkok.
- The Xiong family travels by night through the jungles of Laos.
- Maijue Xiong becomes the first member of her family to attend college.

Vocabulary and Comprehension

"An Unforgettable Journey"

A. Match words and definitions. Write the letter of the correct definition next to each word.

_____ **1.** refuge

_____ **2.** transition

_____ **3.** persecution

_____ **4.** refugee

a. act of willfully hurting others because of their beliefs or ethnic backgrounds

b. person who flees home or country to escape war or persecution

c. change

d. shelter

B. Choose three words from above. Use each word in a sentence.

1. _____

_____

2. _____

_____

3. _____

_____

C. Answer each question below.

1. Who is telling the story?

_____

_____

2. Why did so many Hmong flee Laos for Thailand?

_____

_____

3. Why was the family allowed to come to America without waiting for a year or more?

_____

_____

"Exile Eyes" by Agate Nesaule

SKILLS FOCUS

Reading Skills
Understand an author's purpose and perspective.

Resources

In this book:
• Vocabulary and Comprehension, p. 167
• Additional Vocabulary Practice, p. 168 (includes the previous selection)

Other Resources:
• *Audio CD Library*
• *Audio CD Library, Selections and Summaries in Spanish*
• *Supporting Instruction in Spanish*

Core Skill

Use the resources in the Reading Skills and Strategies section of this book to help students having difficulty identifying author's purpose. Use "Exile Eyes" for the application portion of the lesson.

Special Education Students

Explain that the purpose of "Exile Eyes" is to present some of the difficulties faced by people who have had to leave their homelands to find a safer place to live. The author sympathetically describes several exiles who fled to the United States.

Prereading

Vocabulary Practice

Identify Unfamiliar Words To help support students as they learn vocabulary, give them the following list and have them circle any words they do not know. Help students use each word in a sentence.

• *energetic (p. 411):* active
• *dangle (p. 411):* hang
• *snugly (p. 411):* tightly
• *disillusioned (p. 412):* disappointed
• *exile (p. 412):* force someone to leave their own country and live somewhere else
• *snips (p. 412):* cuts

Reading

Alternative Activity

(Especially for ELL) **Play the Audio Recording** English-language learners may benefit from listening to the audio recording of the selection in English.

Alternative Teaching Strategy

Look for the Perspective As you read the article with students, pause at appropriate points to ask about details that reveal the author's perspective. Look for statements that show that the author was herself an exile *(I believed that cutting off my braids would transform me into an American)* and statements that show that she has sympathy for the exiles. *(I am afraid to look into the women's eyes, and when I do, it is as bad as I had expected.)* Remind students that the author says, "And their longing for home will be confused with ingratitude to America." Ask students why they think the author said this. *(she wants to encourage Americans to be more understanding of exiles)*

Postreading

Alternative Assessment

Review the Perspective To assess whether students understand the author's purpose and perspective, ask them why Agate Nesaule is sympathetic to the plight of exiles. *(she had to leave her home in Latvia during World War II)*

Vocabulary and Comprehension

"Exile Eyes"

A. Match words and definitions. Write the letter of the correct definition next to each word.

____ **1.** exile

____ **2.** polyester

____ **3.** disillusioned

____ **4.** giggles

____ **5.** snips

____ **6.** desperate

a. extremely anxious

b. cuts

c. force someone to leave their country and live somewhere else

d. a fabric made from artificial materials

e. disappointed

f. laughs

B. Answer each question below.

1. Who is the author writing about?

_____

_____

2. What is the setting of the story?

_____

_____

3. What does the author mean by "exile eyes"?

_____

_____

4. Where is the author from?

_____

_____

5. Why do you think the author was interested in exiles?

_____

_____

Additional Vocabulary Practice

"An Unforgettable Journey"; "Exile Eyes"

A. Match each word below with a synonym, a word that means the same thing. Write the letter of the correct synonym next to each word.

_____ **1.** anxiously   **a.** shelter

_____ **2.** stubborn   **b.** worriedly

_____ **3.** refuge   **c.** tired; worn out

_____ **4.** weary   **d.** make upset or uneasy

_____ **5.** disturb   **e.** not willing to give in

B. Choose two words from above. Use each word in a sentence.

1. _____

_____

2. _____

_____

C. Complete each sentence with a word from the Word Bank.

1. Many people every year seek safety and

_____ in the United States.

2. To escape war at home, the

_____ fled to the safety of a
new country.

3. Those who do not escape may face torture or

_____ for their beliefs or
ethnic background.

4. They may suffer terrible conditions and _____ of
food and clothing on their journey.

5. It is very difficult for many to make the change, or

_____, from one country to another.

Word Bank
refuge
transition
persecution
refugee
deprivation

"Elizabeth I" by Milton Meltzer

Prereading

Additional Background

Identify Biography To help students recognize that "Elizabeth I" is a biography written about Elizabeth by someone else, have them read the first few sentences of the selection. Explain that Queen Elizabeth I enjoyed one of the longest reigns in English history.

Reading

Additional Activity

Recognize Subjective Statements Point out that while this biography includes much objective information about Elizabeth I, such as when she was born and when and how she became queen, it also reveals some of the author's feelings and opinions about her. Ask students to identify several subjective statements about Elizabeth. For example, in the first paragraph, the author calls Elizabeth I "one of the most remarkable women who ever lived."

Vocabulary Practice

(**Especially for ELL**) **Reinforce Targeted Vocabulary** Emphasize the importance of the Vocabulary Development words by asking students to find those words and note their usage in "Elizabeth I." Review the words with them, and then ask students to use them in sentences of their own.

- *monarch (p. 418):* sole and absolute leader
- *monopoly (p. 420):* exclusive control of a market
- *arrogant (p. 420):* overly convinced of one's own importance

Postreading

Listening and Speaking Opportunity

Examine Biography Have students review the subjective statements they noted during reading. Ask them to infer how the author feels about Elizabeth I. *(he likes her and believes she was a great ruler)* Have students discuss how the biography would be different if it were written by someone who disliked Elizabeth. Finally, ask what it might be like if it contained only totally factual information. *(students may observe that it would be drier and less interesting)*

SKILLS FOCUS

Literary Skills
- Understand biography.
- Distinguish objective from subjective writing.

Reading Skill
Use the SQ3R system for studying informational texts.

(**Resources**)

In this book:
- Vocabulary and Comprehension, p. 171
- Additional Vocabulary Practice, p. 172

Other Resources:
- *Audio CD Library*
- *Audio CD Library, Selections and Summaries in Spanish*
- *Supporting Instruction in Spanish*

(**Teacher Tip**)

Explain to students that during Elizabeth I's reign the period of Modern English began. Today we refer to Shakespeare as an "Elizabethan writer." We refer to the historical period of Elizabeth I's reign as the *Elizabethan Era.*

(**Special Education Students**)

Ask students how they can tell that the selection is not an autobiography. Guide them to note that there is no first-person "I" telling the story.

Literary Skills
• Understand biography.
• Distinguish objective from subjective writing.

Reading Skill
Use the SQ3R system for studying informational texts.

Resources

In this book:
• Vocabulary and Comprehension, p. 171
• Additional Vocabulary Practice, p. 172

Other Resources:
• *Audio CD Library*
• *Audio CD Library, Selections and Summaries in Spanish*
• *Supporting Instruction in Spanish*

Social Studies Connection

Students may need help with the geographic references. Work with a map and locate England, Scotland, France, and Spain. Tell students they are going to read about a queen of England, Elizabeth I, who was queen at a time when European monarchs had much more power than they have today.

Teacher Tip

Ask students to keep pad and pencil out while listening to the recording so they can jot down words they don't know as well as any questions they want to ask.

TARGETED STRATEGIES FOR SPECIAL EDUCATION STUDENTS

Prereading

Additional Background

Reinforce Important Information Review with students the terms *biography, third-person narration,* and *objective* and *subjective points of view.* Tell them that they will be using those terms while discussing "Elizabeth I." Write the terms and their definitions on the board. Discuss the definitions in order to help students better comprehend the selection.

Reading

Alternative Teaching Strategy

Create a Time Line Read the story aloud or play the audio recording a small portion at a time, pausing for comprehension checks. To help students keep track of important events in Elizabeth's life, draw a time line on the chalkboard. Ask students to identify important events and list them in the correct place on the time line.

Postreading

Additional Practice

Discuss Point of View Ask students how they think Milton Meltzer feels about Elizabeth I. You might want to read them the quote from Meltzer on page 427 and discuss how it applies to Elizabeth I. Then discuss how the selection would be different if any of the following were true:

• The author disliked Elizabeth I.

• Elizabeth I were telling the story herself.

• The author left out all statements that reveal his opinions about Elizabeth I.

Alternative Assessment

Check Comprehension Have students work in small groups to answer the following questions. Offer assistance as needed.

1. How did Elizabeth get to be the queen of England? (*she was the daughter of Henry VIII, and after her brother and older sister died, she was the next in line to rule*)

2. Why didn't she marry? (*had she married, her husband could have taken away all her power even though she would still have been called queen*)

Vocabulary and Comprehension

"Elizabeth I"

A. Match words and definitions. Write the letter of the correct definition next to each word.

_____ **1.** monarch

_____ **2.** alliance

_____ **3.** arrogant

_____ **4.** intolerable

_____ **5.** monopoly

_____ **6.** succession

a. sole and absolute leader

b. overly convinced of one's own importance

c. order in which one succeeds to the throne

d. pact between nations for some purpose

e. exclusive control of a market

f. unbearable

B. Choose four words from above. Use each word in a sentence.

1. _____

_____

2. _____

_____

3. _____

_____

4. _____

_____

C. Number these historical events in the order in which they happened.

_____ Elizabeth I dies.

_____ Pope Pius V excommunicates Elizabeth.

_____ Elizabeth becomes queen of England.

_____ Elizabeth's navy defeats the Spanish Armada.

_____ Henry VIII dies.

_____ Anne Boleyn, Elizabeth's mother, is executed.

_____ Mary, Elizabeth's half-sister, marries the king of Spain.

Additional Vocabulary Practice

"Elizabeth I"

A. Complete each sentence with a word from the Word Bank.

1. Elizabeth began her _____
after the death of her sister, Mary.

2. An absolute _____ is a king
or queen who has total power over a country.

3. Because Elizabeth's _____
taught her well, she was prepared to rule England
when she came to the throne.

4. Elizabeth's _____ was made up of many
people, all of whom did different jobs for her.

5. During Elizabeth's reign, there was a _____ of
interest in music, art, and philosophy.

Word Bank
monarch
reign
tutors
staff
revival

B. In each sentence, replace the word *interesting* or
interested with a word from the Word Bank.

1. Queen Elizabeth was (an) <u>interesting</u> woman.

2. She was <u>interested (in)</u> many different things.

3. She liked to talk to people about <u>interesting</u> things.

4. She was <u>(an) interesting</u> person.

Word Bank
(a) fascinating
fascinated by
intrigued by
(an) amusing
(an) educated
(a) beautiful

1. _____

_____

2. _____

_____

3. _____

_____

4. _____

_____

Comparing Literature: Mood and Theme

Prereading
Vocabulary Practice

(Especially for ELL) Preview Additional Vocabulary Preview the following words and their definitions with students. Ask them to use the words in sentences of their own.

- *saplings (p. 430):* young trees
- *warily (p. 433):* cautiously
- *labored (p. 434):* difficult and tiring
- *heedlessly (p. 435):* carelessly
- *churning (p. 435):* stirring; moving quickly in a circular way
- *sod (p. 439):* earth, especially grassy earth
- *pageant (p. 439):* showy exhibition; spectacle

Reading
Alternative Activity

Retell the Story Use collective retelling to assess students' understanding of the first selection. Have one student begin by telling the first event in the story. Choose another student to continue. Give every student a turn at retelling.

Fluency Practice

Read the Selections/Practice Fluency To help students identify mood and theme and to give them practice reading aloud, you may have them participate in an oral reading of the selections. You may want to try Break-in Reading (see page xxix of this book).

Postreading
Alternative Activity

(Mixed Ability Group) Author Interview Pair students, and have partners take turns as the interviewer and the interviewee in author interviews for each of the three texts. Each student should write three questions about the mood or theme of each piece, preferably questions that he or she would like to ask the real authors. When students play the roles of the authors, they should look for evidence for their answers from the authors' own texts. Students can use results from the interviews to help them fill in their Mood and Theme Charts from the After You Read section of the student book.

SKILLS FOCUS

Literary Skills
Understand mood and theme.

Reading Skill
Compare and contrast texts.

(Resources)

In this book:
- Vocabulary and Comprehension, p. 175
- Additional Vocabulary Practice, p. 176

(Core Skill)

Use the resources in the Reading Skills and Strategies section of this book to help students having difficulty comparing and contrasting. Use "The Last Dinosaur," "Buffalo Dusk," or "I Was Sleeping Where the Black Oaks Move" (choose two) for the application portion of the lesson.

SKILLS FOCUS

Literary Skills
Understand mood and theme.

Reading Skill
Compare and contrast texts.

(**Resources**)

In this book:
• Vocabulary and Comprehension, p. 175
• Additional Vocabulary Practice, p. 176

(**Teacher Tip**)

Some students may be unfamiliar with the native American animals described in the two poems. Ask volunteers to describe buffalo, elk, and herons and to draw pictures of each on the chalkboard.

TARGETED STRATEGIES FOR SPECIAL EDUCATION STUDENTS

Prereading
Reteach the Key Idea

Review Mood Ask students to think about the ways in which they use the word *mood*. Gather some examples of the word's everyday use, and then ask students how the word might apply to works of literature. Encourage students to connect a text's mood to the way they feel when they read it. Elicit examples of stories, poems, and other works that students describe as having a specific mood, and write these suggestions on the chalkboard. Have students brainstorm a list of adjectives in addition to those given in their books that may be applied to a text's mood.

Reading
Alternative Teaching Strategy

Read the Poems Aloud/Fluency Practice Students will benefit from hearing the stories read aloud. To help students focus on the mood of each piece, encourage them to draw a picture as they listen to the work. In the case of the poems, you may want to have volunteers take turns reading them more than once. Emphasize to students that they should try to express in their drawings the feelings stirred in them by the texts. Students should label each drawing with the text's title and then try to put the feelings into words, writing a list on the back of each drawing of words that describe the text's mood.

Postreading
Alternative Assessment

(**Core Skill**) **Compare and Contrast** Draw three columns on the chalkboard, labeling each column with the title of one of the three works. Ask three students to go to the chalkboard, one for each work, and have them answer the questions you ask about the mood and theme of the pieces. Ask: *How does this author feel about nature? How do you know? What does the author want to tell the reader about life?* After the three students have finished writing their answers, discuss them with the class. Then, ask three other students to come to the chalkboard for the next question: *Literature often helps people see things they might not otherwise see. Did this work make you think about something you don't usually think about?* Use students' answers to prompt a class discussion about the texts' similarities and differences.

Vocabulary and Comprehension

Comparing Literature: Mood and Theme

A. Match words and definitions. Write the letter of the correct definition next to each word.

_____ **1.** frond

_____ **2.** spillway

_____ **3.** sapling

_____ **4.** pageant

_____ **5.** shrewlike

a. young tree

b. showy exhibition; spectacle

c. resembling a small, mouselike mammal

d. leaf of a palm or fern

e. channel around a dam

B. Choose three words from above. Use each word in a sentence.

1. _____

_____

2. _____

_____

3. _____

_____

C. Write T or F next to each statement to tell if it is true or false.

_____ **1.** In "The Last Dinosaur," a tyrannosaurus rex guards her eggs.

_____ **2.** The dinosaurs are threatened in the story by a great flood.

_____ **3.** In "Buffalo Dusk," only the buffaloes are described as "gone."

_____ **4.** In "I Was Sleeping Where the Black Oaks Move," a fire is raging.

_____ **5.** In "I Was Sleeping Where the Black Oaks Move," someone does an "elk dance."

Additional Vocabulary Practice

Comparing Literature: Mood and Theme

A. Match the words in the left column with the clues in the right column. Write the correct letter in the blanks.

____ **1.** labored

____ **2.** churning

____ **3.** heedlessly

____ **4.** warily

____ **5.** sod

a. the opposite of *easy*

b. the opposite of *carefully*

c. might describe a boat's propeller

d. a deer tiptoeing across a road

e. sometimes you may stand on it

B. Choose two words from above. Use each word in a sentence.

1. _____

_____

2. _____

_____

C. Replace the word or phrase in parentheses with the correct word from the Word Bank.

1. After the scary part of the movie was over, Ralph peeked *(cautiously)* _____ through his fingers at the screen.

2. The *(water channel by the dam)* _____ on the river is choked with logs.

3. The biologist gently lifted the *(fern leaf)* _____, revealing the brightly colored insect underneath.

4. The floats snaked through the downtown streets as though in a *(showy exhibition)* _____ of loud colors and textures.

Word Bank
warily
pageant
frond
spillway

Collection 5
Worlds of Words: Prose and Poetry

Elements of Literature: Reading Like a Wolf

Background

Discuss Reading "Like a Wolf" Students may not understand what Gary Paulsen means when he advises students to "read like a wolf eats." Ask whether anyone can picture how a wolf eats. Point out that a wolf has a large appetite and eats voraciously. Ask students how they would read if they read the way a wolf eats. Elicit that they would read a lot and read all the time.

Academic Vocabulary

Especially for ELL **Explain the Terms** Write the words and definitions below on the chalkboard, and discuss them with the class. Have students write a sentence for each term.

- *prose (p. 478):* speech and writing in ordinary language
- *fiction (p. 478):* writing about imaginary people and what they do
- *nonfiction (p. 478):* writing about real people and true events
- *short story (p. 478):* fiction about few characters and covering a short time
- *novel (p. 478):* long story, more than one hundred pages, usually about imaginary people
- *novella (p. 478):* short novel, but a long story of about twenty to one hundred pages
- *essay (p. 479):* short piece of prose that discusses a limited topic
- *biography (p. 479):* story of a real person's life written by someone else
- *article (p. 479):* a complete piece of writing on a single subject in a newspaper, magazine, etc.
- *autobiography (p. 479):* the story of one's own life written by oneself

Alternative Teaching Strategy

Reteach the Key Idea To reteach the types of prose, provide students with examples of each type. Have students compare the kind of information they would expect to find in each piece of writing. If possible, provide examples that are related in content and theme. For example, you might have students compare and contrast a short story and a biography of Abraham Lincoln.

SKILLS FOCUS

Literary Skill
Understand forms of prose.

Cultural Tip
Make cultural connections with the academic vocabulary by citing some examples of prose forms by authors who share your students' cultural heritage.

SKILLS FOCUS

Literary Skill
Understand forms of prose.

Elements of Literature: Reading Like a Wolf

Reteach the Key Idea

Discuss Forms of Prose To help students articulate the expressed purposes and characteristics of different forms of prose, preview the content of the essay "Reading Like a Wolf." Ask the class to name short stories they have particularly enjoyed. Write the titles on the chalkboard. Choose one of these stories and ask: How many characters does it have? Does it have a plot with a conflict, climax, and resolution? How many pages does it have? Explain that a short story is told about one or two main characters; its plot has a conflict, climax, and resolution; and it is told within five to twenty pages. Ask if anyone can recommend a favorite novel to the class. Tell them that a novel is a long story. It generally has more characters than a short story, has a main plot and one or more subplots, and is told in one hundred or more pages. Ask students how they would identify a novella. Explain that its length falls in between a short story and a novel. "Reading Like a Wolf" is an essay. Explain that an essay is a nonfiction piece that discusses a limited topic, such as the different kinds of prose available for people to read. Longer essays can discuss more complex issues. Ask students to list the short stories, novellas, novels, and essays they would recommend to others.

Alternative Activities

Play a Vocabulary Memory Game Before class, write each academic vocabulary word and its definition from the previous page of this book on a separate index card. In class, shuffle the cards, and lay them face down on a table. Have students match academic vocabulary words and their definitions.

Use a Reading Log To help students keep track of their reading, tell them to make a reading log entitled "Read the Way a Wolf Eats." Allow for free reading time in class. Ask students to log in the date and time of each free reading session, as well as the title and form of prose they read.

Alternative Assessment

Find Prose Forms Put two or three examples of each prose form on tables around the classroom. Ask students to go to the tables, choose a piece of literature, and write on a piece of paper its title and author and the type of prose they think it is.

(Teacher Tip)

Use the memory game as a group activity or as extra practice for a single student. Be sure you have enough sets of words and definitions for students to play in groups of two to four. To keep the sets separated, use different-colored index cards or construction paper for each word-definition set.

"Amigo Brothers" by Piri Thomas

Prereading
Alternative Activities

Read the Adaptation Distribute copies of the adapted reading of "Amigo Brothers" (available in this book and, with marginal questions, in *Holt Adapted Reader*). To prepare for reading the original version and to practice fluency, students should read the adaptation silently.

Use *The Holt Reader* You may consider having students use the Before You Read page in *The Holt Reader*, either instead of or in addition to the Before You Read page in the student book.

Alternative Teaching Strategies

Understand Conflict Help students keep track of the internal and external conflicts in the short story by having them each draw a two-column chart. They should label the columns INTERNAL CONFLICT and EXTERNAL CONFLICT. Define *internal conflict* as a problem inside a character's head; a struggle with his or her emotions. Define *external conflict* as a problem outside the character, such as a conflict with another person, thing, or environment. They can start off their charts with examples from other familiar stories.

Relate to Personal Experience Ask students to consider the possible outcomes of competing with a friend in a situation, such as the one they will read about, where one of them would be the winner and the other the loser. Encourage students to think about the potential advantages and disadvantages of such a competition.

Vocabulary Practice

Picture the Vocabulary Have students make an illustration for each word listed below. Under each drawing, have students write the word and its definition.

- *bouts (p. 486):* matches; contests
- *pensively (p. 488):* thoughtfully
- *torrent (p. 489):* flood or rush
- *dispelled (p. 491):* driven away
- *frenzied (p. 492):* wild

SKILLS FOCUS

Literary Skills
- Understand forms of prose: the short story.
- Understand internal and external conflict.

Reading Skill
Understand comparison and contrast.

Resources

In this book:
- Adapted Readings
- Vocabulary and Comprehension, p. 183
- Additional Vocabulary Practice, p. 186 (includes the next selection)

Other Resources:
- *The Holt Reader*
- *Holt Adapted Reader*
- *Audio CD Library*
- *Audio CD Library, Selections and Summaries in Spanish*
- *Supporting Instruction in Spanish*

Reading

Alternative Activity

Use *The Holt Reader* You may have students read the selection in *The Holt Reader* and use the margins in that book to make notes and respond to the instruction.

Listening and Speaking Opportunity

(**Especially for ELL**) **Play the Audio Recording** Play the audio recording for students as they follow along in their texts. Have students keep pencil and pad handy so they can jot down any words they don't understand. Pause to monitor comprehension by asking students to summarize what they've heard.

Postreading

Alternative Activity

Use *The Holt Reader* You may consider having students use the postreading activities in *The Holt Reader,* either instead of or in addition to the postreading activities in the student book.

(**Teacher Tip**)

Using a story map or other type of graphic organizer helps students see more clearly the elements of a short story.

Alternative Teaching Strategy

Identify Characteristics of a Short Story Explain that "Amigo Brothers" is an example of a short story. Point out that this short story includes:

- two main characters
- one plot, with no subplots
- a conflict that the characters must resolve
- a climax and a resolution

Have students describe the problem, or *internal conflict* and *external conflict,* Antonio and Felix face. Ask students to tell what they think the climax of the story is and to explain how the conflict is resolved. You may want to use a story map to outline the problem, main events, climax, and resolution.

Additional Activity

Use Competition to Understand Conflict Have the class think about conflict by having a competition. Divide the class into two groups. Have students take turns going to the chalkboard and writing in an event from "Amigo Brothers" to create a time line. Each time a student from the other team can add an event to the time line, that team gains a point. The team with the most points wins.

Vocabulary Development
Reteach the Key Idea

(Mixed Ability Group) **Use Vocabulary** Review the vocabulary words and their definitions with students. Then, have them work in small, mixed ability groups to write each word in a sentence. Invite groups to share their sentences with the rest of the class.

Vocabulary Skill
Clarify word meanings.

Grammar Link
Alternative Teaching Strategy

Examine Punctuation Tell students that a sentence with a direct quotation usually has two parts: the identification of the speaker and the actual words the speaker says. Write the following from "Amigo Brothers" on the chalkboard:

- Charlie said, "Time change. Quick knockout. This is it. We're on."

Circle the comma between *Charlie said* and the direct quote. Explain that the comma sets the speaker apart from what he said. Explain that quotation marks indicate what Charlie said. Then, change the order of the sentence and have a student underline the speaker and circle the comma and quotation marks.

- "Time change," Charlie said. "Quick knockout. This is it. We're on."

Point out to students that, even though the speaker is identified in the middle of the quote, commas still separate him from what he said. Write:

- "Time change. Quick knockout. This is it. We're on," said Charlie.

Point out that the punctuation between the dialogue and *said Charlie* is a comma followed by quotation marks, not a period; the period is placed at the end of the sentence.

(Especially for ELL)
You might ask students to read dialogue aloud from the story. Have them look for the quotation marks before reading so that they can identify dialogue.

Reading Skills Development

Use a Venn Diagram to Compare and Contrast In order to help students compare and contrast the two characters in the story, use a Venn diagram. Draw the Venn diagram on the chalkboard, eliciting from students personality characteristics for Antonio and Felix. Use these characteristics to have students verbalize the conflicts they find in "Amigo Brothers." Guide them to see that although the two friends are very different in physical appearance and fighting style, they are similar in their attitude toward their friendship. And this is precisely what sets up their internal conflict: They don't want to hurt each other and imperil their friendship.

(Core Skill)
Use the resources in the Reading Skills and Strategies section of this book to help students having difficulty comparing and contrasting. Use "Amigo Brothers" or a selection from the list that begins on page 383 of this book for the application portion of the lesson.

Literary Skills
- Understand forms of prose: the short story.
- Understand internal and external conflict.

Reading Skill
Understand comparison and contrast.

(Resources)

In this book:
- Adapted Readings
- Vocabulary and Comprehension, p. 183
- Additional Vocabulary Practice, p. 186 (includes the next selection)

Other Resources:
- *The Holt Reader*
- *Holt Adapted Reader*
- *Audio CD Library*
- *Audio CD Library, Selections and Summaries in Spanish*
- *Supporting Instruction in Spanish*

(Teacher Tip)

Have students who are reluctant to speak out in class draw Antonio and Felix.

(Teacher Tip)

As an alternative to class discussion, read the story aloud or play the audio recording. Pause to write relevant information about the two characters on the chalkboard. When you're done, review the action with students.

TARGETED STRATEGIES FOR SPECIAL EDUCATION STUDENTS

Prereading
Reteach the Key Idea

Discuss the Conflict Remind students that a short story has less than twenty pages (roughly speaking), and includes characters, conflict, complications, a climax, and a resolution. Have them count the pages in "Amigo Brothers." *(eight)* Tell them that the main characters are two friends, and the conflict is that they want the same prize. Only one can win the prize, by beating the other. Ask: How would you behave if you and your best friend wanted the same thing but only one of you could have it? Has that ever happened to you? What did you do? What did your best friend do?

Reading
Alternative Teaching Strategies

Connect with the Characters Have students make a chart with two headings: ANTONIO and FELIX. As students read, have them list what they learn about each character. Ask them what each character's words and actions tell us about that character's personality. Then have them answer the following questions:

- Why would you want to be friends with Antonio and Felix?
- Why would you *not* want to be friends with Antonio and Felix?
- Would Antonio and Felix want to be friends with you? Explain.

Use a Plot Diagram On the chalkboard, draw a plot diagram. Play the audio recording of the story. Have students raise their hands when they hear a new complication. Stop the recording, discuss the complication, and add it to the chart. Do the same for the climax and resolution.

Postreading
Alternative Assessment

Check for Comprehension Ask students to answer these questions orally or in writing:

- Why did Antonio and Felix fight?
- Why did they fight so ferociously that the people watching thought they were fighting to the death?
- Why, after hurting each other so much, did the two boxers leave the ring together, arm in arm?

Vocabulary and Comprehension

"Amigo Brothers"

A. Complete each sentence with a word from the Word Bank.

1. Both Antonio and Felix fought many

_____ with other young boxers.

2. Antonio gazed _____ at his best friend, whom he was about to face in the boxing ring.

3. Felix hit Antonio in the stomach with a

_____ of blows.

4. The _____ screams of the fans filled the air.

5. Any doubts Antonio had about his friendship were

_____.

Word Bank
pensively
bouts
torrent
frenzied
dispelled

B. Use two of the words in the Word Bank in a sentence.

1. _____

_____

2. _____

_____

C. Write T or F next to each statement to tell if it is true or false.

_____ **1.** Antonio and Felix were best friends.

_____ **2.** They lived in the same apartment building.

_____ **3.** Antonio did not want to represent the Boys' Club in the Golden Gloves Championship Tournament.

_____ **4.** The boys agreed they would not hurt each other in the ring.

_____ **5.** The fight was held in Tompkins Square Park because it was bigger than the Boys' Club.

_____ **6.** Felix dropped out of the match.

Elements of Literature
pages 496–498

"Right Hook–Left Hook:
The Boxing Controversy" by Joan Burditt

SKILLS FOCUS

Reading Skill
Understand comparison-and-contrast text structure.

Resources

In this book:
• Vocabulary and Comprehension, p. 185
• Additional Vocabulary Practice, p. 186 (includes the previous selection)

Other Resources:
• *Audio CD Library*
• *Audio CD Library, Selections and Summaries in Spanish*
• *Supporting Instruction in Spanish*

Especially for ELL

Take quick notes on each student's presentation: syntax, grammar, word use. Use that information to assign individual homework practice to reinforce needed skills.

Special Education Students

Make a comparison-contrast chart for the Reading activity to see if every point on one side is matched by a counterpoint on the other. Students can also be divided into teams to debate the controversy.

Prereading

Background

Reinforce the Main Idea Explain that the short story "Amigo Brothers" is fiction, while the essay "Right Hook–Left Hook: The Boxing Controversy" is nonfiction. Ask students how an essay is different from a short story. (*An essay expresses facts and opinions, while a short story presents a plot with characters, conflict, action, complications, climax, and resolution.*)

Reading

Alternative Teaching Strategy

Use Structure to Organize Information Point out that the essay presents both sides of the boxing controversy. On one hand (a metaphorical right hook), it reports the arguments against boxing. On the other (left hook), it gives a counterargument in favor of boxing. Have the class read the whole article. Then, have half the class identify statements against boxing while the other half of the class identifies statements in favor of boxing. Ask them to read with these questions in mind: What is the message? What information supports this message? Do you agree or disagree? Explain.

Postreading

Fluency Practice

Review Organization With the class, re-read the essay, stopping at the end of each paragraph to talk about the information in that paragraph. As the class discusses the organization of each paragraph, make notes on the chalkboard. Elicit from students that:

• the *first paragraph* introduces a theme: Violence is pervasive in our society
• the *second paragraph* gives reasons for banning boxing
• the *third paragraph* gives reasons for supporting boxing
• the *final paragraph* concludes that the controversy goes on; there has been no resolution

Vocabulary and Comprehension

"Right Hook–Left Hook: The Boxing Controversy"

A. Match words and definitions. Write the letter of the correct definition next to each word.

_____ **1.** hook

_____ **2.** ban

_____ **3.** controversy

_____ **4.** slurred

_____ **5.** instills

a. a disagreement over a serious matter that goes on for a long time

b. spoken in an unclear way

c. in boxing, a sharp blow made with the arm bent at the elbow

d. an official order forbidding something

e. puts an idea into someone's mind in a slow but sure way

B. Choose four words from above. Use each in a sentence.

1. _____

_____

2. _____

_____

3. _____

_____

4. _____

_____

C. Match words and synonyms. Write the letter of the correct synonym next to each word.

_____ **1.** tremendous

_____ **2.** concern

_____ **3.** benefits

_____ **4.** debate

a. advantages

b. formal argument

c. large

d. anxiety

Additional Vocabulary Practice

"Amigo Brothers"; "Right Hook–Left Hook: The Boxing Controversy"

A. Match words and synonyms. Write the letter of the correct synonym next to each word.

_____ **1.** bouts   **a.** matches   **b.** boxes   **c.** colds

_____ **2.** pensively   **a.** heavily   **b.** quietly   **c.** thoughtfully

_____ **3.** frenzied   **a.** silly   **b.** wild   **c.** brief

_____ **4.** torrent   **a.** flood   **b.** creek   **c.** gate

_____ **5.** controversy   **a.** money   **b.** argument   **c.** sport

B. Choose three words from above. Use each word in a sentence.

1. _____

_____

2. _____

_____

3. _____

_____

C. Complete each sentence with a word from the Word Bank.

1. The debate and _____ about boxing has been going on for years.

2. Blows to the head can cause

_____ speech.

3. Many doctors support a complete

_____ on the sport of boxing.

4. Other people say that boxing _____ self-control in young people.

Word Bank
controversy
ban
slurred
instills

from *Barrio Boy* by Ernesto Galarza

Prereading

Additional Background

Reteach the Key Idea Explain to students that the reading is taken from the autobiography *Barrio Boy*, written by Ernesto Galarza. Remind students that an autobiography is the story of a person's life written by that person, and that a biography is the story of someone's life written by another person. Explain that in either case they can expect to read about someone's life as well as opinions about the events of that life.

Vocabulary Practice

(**Especially for ELL**) **Preview Vocabulary** To help students understand the story, define the following words:

- *enrolling (p. 501):* registering
- *rehearsed (p. 501):* practiced
- *swivel chair (p. 501):* a chair whose seat turns freely around
- *flanked (p. 501):* having something on both sides
- *maneuvered (p. 501):* moved carefully

Alternative Activity

Read the Adaptation Distribute copies of the adapted reading of the excerpt from *Barrio Boy* (available in this book and, with marginal questions, in *Holt Adapted Reader*). To prepare for reading the original version and to practice fluency, students should read the adaptation silently. Encourage students to write notes, questions, predictions, reactions, and comments on the worksheets as they read.

Reading

Alternative Teaching Strategy

(**Core Skill**) **Separate Fact from Opinion** Students may need help differentiating between fact and opinion in nonfiction forms such as autobiography. Remind students that a *fact* is a statement that can be proved. An *opinion,* on the other hand, is a personal, subjective idea or preference; it cannot be proved or disproved. Draw a two-column chart on the chalkboard. Label one column FACT and the other OPINION. Read a passage from the text. A good one is on page 503 and begins "The main reason I was graduated with honors . . ."

SKILLS FOCUS

Literary Skills
Understand forms of prose: autobiography and biography.

Reading Skill
Distinguish fact from opinion.

(**Resources**)

In this book:
- Adapted Readings
- Vocabulary and Comprehension, p. 191
- Additional Vocabulary Practice, p. 192

Other Resources:
- *Holt Adapted Reader*
- *Audio CD Library*
- *Audio CD Library, Selections and Summaries in Spanish*
- *Supporting Instruction in Spanish*
- *Videocassette, Segment 5*

(**Teacher Tip**)

Divide the class into groups to practice identifying facts and opinions. Have them read the paragraph on page 501 that begins "What Miss Hopley said to us we did not know," and separate the facts in the paragraph from the opinions. When they've finished, ask a student from each group to share the group's conclusions.

Teacher Tip

Explain to students that *barrio* is a Spanish word that refers to a neighborhood or community. Also point out Mazatlán, the town in Mexico where Ernesto comes from, on a map for students.

Ask students to identify what is fact in the passage and what is opinion. Write each response in the FACT or OPINION column. Then, ask students to make their own Fact/Opinion charts and list at least three additional examples of facts and of opinions as they read.

Additional Practice

Identify and Explain Metaphors Ask a student to define *metaphor* (direct comparison of dissimilar things that does not use the word *like* or *as*). Then, have students find the following in the selection and discuss with them: "The school was not so much a melting pot as a griddle where Miss Hopley and her helpers warmed knowledge into us and roasted racial hatreds out of us." *(p. 503, col. 2)* Explain that the metaphor *melting pot* refers to America as a place where people from all over the world have come together and influence each other with their food, customs, culture, and way of life. Each country or culture is like another ingredient thrown into the pot to make up the country known as the United States. The author has taken this famous "melting pot" metaphor and changed it to a griddle for his story. Ask students why the author would think of the school as a griddle. Ask them what qualities a griddle has *(hot, gets things cooked, or done)* and why the school might be a griddle for him *(because he didn't see everything melting in the pot together as much he saw things retaining their original "flavor")*. The teachers called students by their "original" names and made them feel that their original cultures were all right, that "becoming a proud American did not mean being ashamed of being a Mexican."

Postreading
Additional Activity

Especially for ELL **Write Your Story** Ask students to write a short autobiographical paragraph. Begin by having students make a list of facts and opinions about themselves. Then, have them write about themselves, using the information they listed. As part of their autobiography, they also may want to discuss learning English. They may consider what or who has been most helpful in improving their English. Are they learning English from movies, television, friends?

Alternative Assessment

Check Comprehension Present students with questions like the following to check their comprehension:

1. Is the principal in the story male or female? *(female)*
2. How did Miss Hopley get the information she needed from Ernesto's mother? *(translator)*
3. When Ernesto was in third grade, what experience did he share with his class? *(told the story of his travels on a stagecoach)*
4. Why were children "marched up" to the principal's office? *(because they had insulted someone on the playground)*

Vocabulary Development

Reteach the Key Idea

Additional Practice Have students use the vocabulary words shown on page 499 to write sentences using examples to clarify the meaning of each word. For example:

> I had no idea what the *contraption* was, but with all its dials, lights, gears, and knobs, I thought it either would never work or would blow up before our eyes.

Have students share their sentences with the rest of the class.

Grammar Link

Alternative Teaching Strategy

Compare Adjectives Tell students that in writing and speaking we often compare people and things. Explain that it's important to use the correct ending for adjectives comparing people and things. On the chalkboard, write

-er for two people or things

-est for three or more people or things

Explain that using *-er* means using the *comparative degree* of the adjective and that using *-est* means using the *superlative degree*. Write additional examples on the chalkboard to help illustrate the lesson.

- Seiji is *taller* than Raul. *(compares two; comparative degree)*
- That is the *largest* book on the shelf. *(compares more than two; superlative degree)*

Remind students that since *-er* means "more" and *-est* means "most," they should not use those words together with the endings. Provide sentences using both comparative and superlative forms of the same adjective. Have students underline the correct form. For example:

- Who runs <u>faster</u>/fastest, Paolo or Jason?
- Of all the puppies, she was the smaller/<u>smallest</u>.

Reading Skills Development

(**Mixed Ability Group**) **Use Facts and Opinions** Students having difficulty distinguishing between facts and opinions may find it helpful to work in small groups to write their own examples of each. Arrange students in mixed ability groups to write ten sentences on a topic of their choice. Each group should work together to write the numbered list of sentences and to construct a "key" that tells whether each sentence is a fact or opinion and how they reached this conclusion. Groups can then exchange lists and identify the facts and opinions in the sentences given them. Have groups compare their answers, and share any difficult examples with the class.

SKILLS FOCUS

Vocabulary Skill
Clarify word meanings by using examples.

(**Core Skill**)

Use the resources in the Reading Skills and Strategies section of this book to help students having difficulty distinguishing fact from opinion. Use the excerpt from *Barrio Boy* for the application portion of the lesson.

SKILLS FOCUS

Literary Skills
Understand forms of prose:
autobiography and
biography.

Reading Skill
Distinguish fact from
opinion.

Resources

In this book:
• Adapted Readings
• Vocabulary and
Comprehension, p. 191
• Additional Vocabulary
Practice, p. 192

Other Resources:
• *Holt Adapted Reader*
• *Audio CD Library*
• *Audio CD Library,
Selections and Summaries
in Spanish*
• *Supporting Instruction
in Spanish*
• Videocassette, Segment 5

Teacher Tip

Ask the school librarian
to help you gather some
autobiographies and
biographies of people who
came to live in the United
States from other countries.
Encourage students to look
at the pictures and to read
the books.

TARGETED STRATEGIES FOR SPECIAL EDUCATION STUDENTS

Prereading
Additional Background

Locate Countries Explain to students that the United States is a land that includes many people who have moved here from different countries around the world. Ernesto, the main character in *Barrio Boy*, came from Mexico, where Spanish is spoken. Locate Mexico on a large map. Highlight the country with a sticky note. Ask students if they know of people who have come from other countries to live in the United States. Explain that in this story, the author is telling his own story about moving to the United States. An author's account of his or her own life experiences is called an *autobiography*. Tell students that an autobiography contains both facts and opinions about the author's experiences. If necessary, define the terms *fact* and *opinion*.

Reading
Alternative Teaching Strategy

Reinforce the Main Idea Read the selection aloud with students or play the audio recording. To help students understand the characteristics of an autobiography, pause at the end of the first sentence, and ask: Whom is this story about? Who is the narrator? Who is Ernesto? When the author says "the two of us," whom is he talking about? Elicit that the author is Ernesto and that Ernesto is telling a story about himself. Pause the recording periodically to have students identify facts and opinions about Ernesto's experiences.

Postreading
Alternative Activity

Tell About Yourself To assess students' comprehension of autobiography, have them write an autobiographical paragraph. Ask them to write about their first day at school, as Ernesto did. Was it fun? Were they scared? Did they like their teacher? What was the most important thing they learned on that day or in that school year? If some students are more comfortable speaking, ask them to tape-record their story or to talk directly to the class.

Vocabulary and Comprehension

from *Barrio Boy*

A. Match words and definitions. Write the letter of the correct definition next to each word.

_____ **1.** reassuring

_____ **2.** contraption

_____ **3.** assured

_____ **4.** formidable

_____ **5.** menace

a. guaranteed; promised confidently

b. threat or danger

c. comforting

d. awe-inspiring; impressive

e. strange machine or gadget

B. Use each word above in a sentence.

1. _____

_____

2. _____

_____

3. _____

_____

4. _____

_____

5. _____

_____

C. Answer each question below.

1. What made Miss Ryan such a good teacher?

_____

_____

2. How did Ernesto and his friends show they were proud of their culture?

_____

_____

Additional Vocabulary Practice

from *Barrio Boy*

A. Complete each sentence with a word from the Word Bank.

> | **Word Bank** |
> | --- |
> | assured |
> | formidable |
> | reassuring |
> | contraption |
> | wholeheartedly |
> | persistently |

1. The teacher gave me a _____ pat on the back that made me feel better.

2. Whenever I was unsure, she _____ me that I was doing well.

3. My parents thanked her _____ for all her interest and support.

4. The students worked hard and _____, never giving up.

5. We did a _____ amount of work in a very short amount of time.

6. One day we built a strange and unusual _____ from wire, wood, and a battery.

B. Choose two words from the Word Bank. Use each word in a sentence.

1. _____

_____

2. _____

_____

C. Match words and synonyms. Write the letter of the correct synonym next to each word.

_____ **1.** persistently   **a.** easily   **b.** steadily   **c.** quietly

_____ **2.** reassuring   **a.** comforting   **b.** friendly   **c.** wise

_____ **3.** assured   **a.** marked   **b.** guaranteed   **c.** hoped

_____ **4.** formidable   **a.** impressive   **b.** happy   **c.** silent

_____ **5.** contraption   **a.** boat   **b.** machine   **c.** cage

_____ **6.** menace   **a.** friend   **b.** enemy   **c.** threaten

Elements of Literature
pages 508–526

Song of the Trees by Mildred D. Taylor

Prereading

Additional Background

Understand Setting Explain to students that the Great Depression in the United States began in 1929 with the crash of the stock market. By 1932, one quarter of the American work force was unemployed. The Depression lasted more than a decade—hundreds of thousands of Americans lost jobs, businesses failed, and financial institutions collapsed. Students should also be aware that African Americans did not enjoy the same civil rights as white people until the 1960s. In some areas, African Americans were not allowed to attend the same schools. In parts of the country, they were not allowed to eat in "white" restaurants, stay in the same hotels, or use the same bathrooms or drinking fountains. This policy of keeping black people separate was called segregation.

Vocabulary Practice

(Especially for ELL) Introduce New Words Students may not know the following story words. Define each word, and use it in a sentence. Then, ask students to use each word in a sentence of their own.

- *billowed (p. 516):* moved with a wavelike motion
- *canister (p. 510):* container, usually metal, with a lid
- *dashed (p. 510):* moved quickly
- *kerosene (p. 510):* oil used for light and heat
- *meddlesome (p. 521):* busy with something that is not yours
- *muggy (p. 512):* hot and damp
- *reluctantly (p. 518):* unwillingly
- *shins (p. 520):* front part of the leg, between the knee and ankle

Alternative Activity

(Especially for ELL) Use Spanish Resources Spanish-speaking English-language learners may benefit from reading or listening to the selection summary in Spanish in preparation to reading the selection in English.

SKILLS FOCUS

Literary Skills
Understand forms of prose: short story, novel, and novella.

Reading Skill
Make generalizations.

(Resources)

In this book:
- Vocabulary and Comprehension, p. 197
- Additional Vocabulary Practice, p. 198

Other Resources:
- *Audio CD Library*
- *Audio CD Library, Selections and Summaries in Spanish*
- *Supporting Instruction in Spanish*

(Especially for ELL)

In many Spanish-speaking countries, *novella* refers to romance fiction.

Reading
Alternative Activity

Play the Audio Recording Struggling readers may benefit from listening to the audio recording of the selection as they follow along in their books. You may want to stop and replay any confusing sections for students.

Alternative Teaching Strategy

Examine Characteristics of a Novella Help students understand that a novella is shorter and less complex than a novel but longer and more complex than a short story. Have students count the number of characters in *Song of the Trees*. *(ten: Big Ma Logan, Mary and David Logan, Stacey, Cassie, Christopher-John, Little Man, Mr. Andersen, Tom, Claude)* Elicit from students that the main plot of this story involves two groups that are in conflict: Andersen, who has a lumber contract he plans to fulfill by logging Big Ma Logan's property, and the Logans, who do not want to sell their trees. Copy the story map from page 524 of the student book onto the chalkboard. Fill in the character names that students listed. Have students fill in the story map as they read.

Postreading
Alternative Teaching Strategy

Reteach Personification Ask students why the author chose *Song of the Trees* for the title of her novella. Why not title the novella *David Logan, a Man Who Would Not Back Down,* or *The Logan Family and the Lumberman*? Ask students to go back into the story and read aloud each section where the trees are described. For example, on page 510: "Only the trees of the forest were not gray. They stood dark, almost black, across the dusty road, still holding the night. A soft breeze stirred, and their voices whispered down to me in a song of morning greeting." If necessary, guide students in noting the personification of the trees. *(stood, holding, whispered)* Ask students what this passage tells them about Cassie's feelings for the trees. *(she tells us they gave her a song of morning greeting)* Ask students how Cassie's description of the trees changes from the beginning to page 517: "But now they would sing no more. They lay forever silent upon the ground. Those trees that remained standing were like defeated warriors mourning their fallen dead." *(they are personified— lay forever silent; defeated warriors, mourning—and their personification is of a sad, mourning people)* Tell students that Cassie uses the trees to communicate her own feelings. In the beginning, she feels happy that the trees are in the forest and tells of their "singing," but, by the end, she mourns the destruction of the trees and speaks of their mourning.

Vocabulary Development
Reteach the Key Idea

(Mixed Ability Group) **Review Denotation and Connotation**
Help students understand that choosing a special word when writing can form a strong and memorable mental image and maintain a reader's interest. Explain that different words with the same basic meaning may create different feelings and associations for the people who read or hear them. Write the following sentences on the chalkboard:

- Carlos *went* to get a sweater because it was *cold* outside.
- Carlos *rushed* to get a sweater because it was *freezing* outside.

Lead students to understand that *went* and *rushed* have the same basic meaning, as do *cold* and *freezing*. The meaning that the words share is their denotation. However, we react to the two sentences in different ways. In the second sentence, the need for the sweater seems more urgent and important.

Have students work in small groups to look through the story and locate the vocabulary words listed on page 509 of their books. Have them substitute another word with the same meaning, or denotation, in the sentence.

Grammar Link
Alternative Practice

Correct Misplaced Modifiers Explain that *to modify* means "to change or add." In grammar, a modifier can be a group of words, or phrase, that changes or adds to the meaning of another word. The phrase can appear before or after the word it describes. The phrase should be placed as close as possible to the word it modifies; otherwise, the meaning of the sentence may be unclear. The sentence may even be funny. Write the following example on the chalkboard: *Ali saw a dog driving down the road.* Ask students: Was the dog driving down the road, or was Ali driving down the road? Help them move the modifier to the correct position: *Driving down the road, Ali saw a dog.*

Reading Skills Development

Make Generalizations Remind students that they must combine information in the selection with what they already know in order to make generalizations about a selection. Have students work with partners to re-read the novella. Partners should list as many generalizations as they can based on the selection. (Items 1 and 3 in the Quickwrite on page 508 are examples of generalizations students could make from the story.) Then, have students go back and list two or three details that support their generalizations. Ask partners to share their generalizations and supporting details with the class.

Vocabulary Skills
Understand connotation and denotation.

(Especially for ELL)
Some language groups place the modifier after the noun. For example, in Spanish, *a red book* is *un libro rojo*, or *a book red*. Be aware of linguistic differences. English-language learners may need oral and written practice to be comfortable with the placement of modifiers in English.

Literary Skills
Understand forms of prose: short story, novel, and novella.

Reading Skill
Make generalizations.

Resources
In this book:
• Vocabulary and Comprehension, p. 197
• Additional Vocabulary Practice, p. 198

Other Resources:
• *Audio CD Library*
• *Audio CD Library, Selections and Summaries in Spanish*
• *Supporting Instruction in Spanish*

Teacher Tip
After reading the selection with the class, play the audio recording for students.

Pronunciation Tip
Ask each student to read a sentence from the story. If a student stumbles on a word, model the pronunciation of the word, and ask what its meaning is. If necessary, define the word, and use it in a sentence. When you're satisfied that the meaning is clear, ask the student to re-read the sentence.

TARGETED STRATEGIES FOR SPECIAL EDUCATION STUDENTS

Prereading
Additional Background

Set the Stage Tell students that the period of the Great Depression in the United States was from 1929 to 1939, when many people had no work or money. *Song of the Trees* is about a family that lived in the Mississippi woods. It's told from the point of view of a young girl named Cassie Logan. Cassie and her family learn that the forest surrounding their home, which is filled with wonderful trees they love, is in danger of being cut down. Cassie's father is away from home, trying to make enough money to support the family, and the children feel they must do something to try to stop the lumbermen. As the story progresses, we see that it is about more than protecting trees; it's about self-respect as well. Remind students that they are reading a novella, so it is longer than a short story.

Reading
Alternative Teaching Strategy

Study Personification Have students note how Cassie personifies the trees. As they listen to the audio recording of the story, pause at particular points to emphasize this personification. For example:

• Only the trees of the forest were not gray. They stood dark, almost black, across the dusty road, still holding the night. A soft breeze stirred, and their voices whispered down to me in a song of morning greeting. (*p. 510*)

• "Good morning, Mr. Trees," I shouted. They answered me with a soft, swooshing sound. "Hear 'em, Stacey? Hear 'em singing?" (*p. 512*)

• But the old pine only tapped me gently with one of its long, low branches. (*p. 513*)

• But now they would sing no more. They lay forever silent upon the ground. Those trees that remained standing were like defeated warriors mourning their fallen dead. (*p. 517*)

Postreading
Alternative Activity

Write a Book Jacket Explain to students that because *Song of the Trees* is a novella, it would be printed in book form and so would require a book jacket. Go over the generalization list on page 508 with students. Guide them toward developing a theme for the selection. Have them work collaboratively to create a book jacket that reflects the theme of *Song of the Trees*. If necessary, help them identify the theme: self-respect.

Vocabulary and Comprehension

Song of the Trees

A. Complete each sentence with a word from the
Word Bank.

> **Word Bank**
> dispute
> ambled
> curtly
> skirting
> elude
> incredulously

1. "Don't bother me, I'm busy!" he said

   _____.

2. Mr. Andersen looked at Papa _____.
   He didn't believe he would blow up the forest.

3. Little Man and Stacey argued a lot. One

   _____ was about who was going to carry the basket.

4. Stacey managed to _____ the clutches of the lumbermen.

5. The boys _____ into the forest, leading the cows and
   their calves down the narrow path.

6. Mr. Andersen dodged him as easily as if he were _____
   around mud puddles.

B. Write T or F next to each statement to tell if it is true or false.

_____ **1.** Little Man was known as a finicky dresser.

_____ **2.** Papa set sticks of dynamite in the forest.

_____ **3.** When Mr. Andersen looked at the black box, his face
became ashen.

_____ **4.** Cassie imagined that the trees were sentries guarding
the forest.

_____ **5.** Stacey was the youngest child in the Logan family.

_____ **6.** Papa allows Mr. Andersen to take all the trees he cut
down.

_____ **7.** When the lumbermen left the forest, Cassie and her dad
could hear the trees singing again.

_____ **8.** The story takes place during the Great Depression.

Additional Vocabulary Practice

Song of the Trees

A. Match words and definitions. Write the letter of the correct definition next to each word.

_____ **1.** finicky

_____ **2.** curtly

_____ **3.** ashen

_____ **4.** elude

_____ **5.** dispute

_____ **6.** delved

_____ **7.** skirting

_____ **8.** ambled

_____ **9.** sentries

_____ **10.** incredulously

a. fussy and extremely careful

b. argument

c. walked without hurrying

d. searched

e. rudely, using few words

f. escape cleverly

g. unbelievingly

h. pale

i. guards

j. avoiding

B. Choose two words from above. Use each word in a sentence.

1. _____

_____

2. _____

_____

C. Complete each sentence with a word from the list in Part A.

1. Mr. Andersen was angry and spoke _____ to the women.

2. They could not agree on a fair solution to their _____ about the trees.

3. The children ran, trying to _____ the hands of the lumbermen.

4. His face paled and became _____.

5. The tall trees stood like _____ guarding the forest.

"Fish Cheeks" by Amy Tan

Prereading

Background

(**Especially for ELL**) **Connect to Personal Experience** Tell students that "Fish Cheeks" is about the problems a teenager faces when she's caught between her family's Chinese traditions and American values. Explain that "Fish Cheeks" refers to a traditional Chinese dish, steamed fish. In the selection, the girl feels ashamed of her family's traditions, which are so different from those of the American family invited to dinner. Ask students whether they have ever felt torn between the values of their native customs and their new American culture.

Vocabulary Practice

Find the Imagery Students may not be familiar with many of the words used to create the mental images in "Fish Cheeks" and, as a result, may miss some of the humor and imagery in the essay. Introduce the vocabulary words below to students. Write them on the chalkboard, model the pronunciation for each word, and have students repeat the word. Then, read the definition, and give two or three examples of how the word may be used in a sentence. Finally, ask individual students to use the word in a sentence of their own.

- *cod (p. 529):* a type of fish
- *manger (p. 529):* low box from which horses or cows eat
- *shabby (p. 529):* old and worn out
- *lacked (p. 529):* did not have
- *outdone (p. 529):* done better than expected
- *prawns (p. 529):* large shrimp
- *bulging (p. 529):* sticking out
- *tofu (p. 529):* cheeselike food made from soybeans
- *fungus (p. 529):* a plant without leaves, flowers, or green color
- *grimaced (p. 529):* twisted the face to a look of pain or disgust
- *squid (p. 529):* a long, slender sea animal with eight arms

Alternative Activity

(**Especially for ELL**) **Use Spanish Resources** Spanish-speaking English-language learners may benefit from listening to the audio recording of the selection in Spanish in preparation for reading it in English.

SKILLS FOCUS

Literary Skill
Understand forms of prose: the essay.

Reading Skill
Understand images.

(**Resources**)

In this book:
- Vocabulary and Comprehension, p. 203
- Additional Vocabulary Practice, p. 204

Other Resources:
- *Audio CD Library*
- *Audio CD Library, Selections and Summaries in Spanish*
- *Supporting Instruction in Spanish*

Reading
Alternative Teaching Strategy

Mixed Ability Group Develop Reading Skill "Fish Cheeks" is a humorous essay, but it is also an essay written with a good deal of imagery. On the chalkboard, write the following headings: SIGHT, HEARING, SMELL, TASTE, and TOUCH. Tell students to copy these headings into their notebooks. Play the audio recording of "Fish Cheeks," and pause to bring students' attention to certain phrases, such as "Tofu, which looked like stacked wedges of rubbery white sponges" and "The minister managed to muster up a quiet burp." Ask students to tell which column these examples fit into, guiding them to understand how the first quote offers an appeal to the sense of sight while the second example offers an appeal to the sense of hearing. Have students listen to the entire essay, and then assign them to groups to finish filling in the chart with other examples. When they compare their findings, remind them that the writer has used these descriptive phrases to accomplish her goal of writing an essay that brings the reader into her experience.

Postreading
Alternative Teaching Strategy

Choose the Right Word Tell students that a writer engages the reader's senses by using words that appeal to sight, hearing, smell, taste, and touch. A good writer chooses words that both excite the reader and help the reader form the mental images the writer wants to create. Review with students the following phrases and sentences from the story.

- She was pulling black veins out of the backs of fleshy prawns. *(par. 3)*
- a slimy rock cod with bulging eyes that pleaded not to be thrown in a pan of hot oil *(par. 3)*
- Tofu, which looked like stacked wedges of rubbery white sponges. *(par. 3)*
- And then they arrived—the minister's family and all my relatives in a clamor of doorbells and rumpled Christmas packages. *(par. 4)*
- Robert was looking down at his plate with a reddened face. *(par. 6)*
- Then my father poked his chopsticks just below the fish eye and plucked out the soft meat. *(par. 5)*

Ask students what would happen to the essay if Tan said, "She deveined the shrimp, " "He looked at his plate," "She threw a rock cod into the pan," "Robert was embarrassed," and "My father used his chopsticks to help himself to the fish." Elicit from them that the sentences would be less interesting and effective.

Vocabulary Development

Vocabulary Practice

Vocabulary Skill
Complete word analogies.

(**Especially for ELL**) **Reinforce Targeted Vocabulary** To help students master the words in the selection, pair fluent students with less-fluent partners. Ask each pair to take turns reading aloud from the Vocabulary Development list on page 527 of the text. Have one student read a word and the other read its definition. Then, have each student write a sentence using the word. Tell students to repeat the exercise with all the words.

Additional Practice

Reinforce Definitions Have students provide examples from their own experience that could reinforce the meaning of the Vocabulary words. Use these or other questions to elicit responses and promote discussion.

- Can you think of anything you have heard or seen that you thought was appalling?
- The story speaks of wedges of tofu. What other food comes in wedges? Can you think of other wedge-shaped things?
- Name some places you might be where there would be a clamor.
- Packages were rumpled in the story. What things do you see every day that are rumpled or could be rumpled?

Reteach the Key Idea

Understand Analogies To help students with analogies, provide them with these examples. Point out that the best way to figure out the relationships is to analyze the first pair of words in the analogy. Write *sweet is to sour as tall is to short* on the chalkboard. Explain that in the first pair of words *sweet* is a taste and *sour* is a taste. The two tastes are opposites. Therefore, the next pair of words should be opposites. *Tall* is the opposite of *short*.

Provide students with these and other analogies. Have them define the words in each pair and explain the relationships between the words.

- *father* is to *son* as *mother* is *daughter* (*similar relationship*)
- *jump* is to *leap* as *happy* is to *glad* (*synonyms*)
- *deep* is to *shallow* as *messy* is to *neat* (*antonyms*)
- *carpenter* is to *hammer* as *cook* is to *knife* (*worker and tool*)

Reading Skills Development

Create Images Students having difficulty identifying and analyzing images may find creating their own helpful. Assign students to create three images that would add sensory detail to the essay "Fish Cheeks." Have students strive to address at least two senses with their three images. Ask volunteers to share their creations with the class, making sure they note where their images would fit in the essay.

(**Core Skill**)

Use the resources in the Reading Skills and Strategies section of this book to teach a core literary skill in which your struggling readers need remediation. Use "Fish Cheeks" for the application portion of the lesson.

Literary Skill
Understand forms of prose:
the essay.

Reading Skill
Understand images.

Resources

In this book:
• Vocabulary and
Comprehension, p. 203
• Additional Vocabulary
Practice, p. 204

Other Resources:
• *Audio CD Library*
• *Audio CD Library,
Selections and Summaries
in Spanish*
• *Supporting Instruction
in Spanish*

TARGETED STRATEGIES FOR SPECIAL EDUCATION STUDENTS

Prereading
Alternative Teaching Strategy

Preview the Selection Tell students that "Fish Cheeks" is a humorous, informal essay. While funny, it also makes us look at things in a new way.

In the essay, Amy Tan recalls a time when a non-Chinese family comes to dinner. Amy, then a teenager, imagines how the guests must be interpreting her family's Chinese traditions, and feels embarrassed. Later, her mother tells her, "You must be proud you are different. Your only shame is to have shame."

Write her mother's words on the board. Ask students if they have ever been misunderstood or felt embarrassed because they thought someone did not understand their customs. Share anecdotes. Then, ask if what Amy Tan's mother said fits with their experience.

Reading
Listening and Speaking Opportunity

Listen to the Story and Retell It Have students listen to the entire audio recording. Next, have volunteers read it aloud, paragraph by paragraph. Note difficult vocabulary, model correct pronunciation, and have a volunteer paraphrase each paragraph. After each paraphrase, ask students if there is anything they would add or change. Clear up misunderstandings. Write problem vocabulary on the board, and have students practice pronunciation orally.

Postreading
Alternative Assessment

Check Comprehension Have students answer the following questions:

1. Why did the squid remind Amy of bicycle tires? *(Their backs "were crisscrossed with knife markings…" par. 3)*

2. Why did Amy's father belch? *("'It's a polite Chinese custom to show you are satisfied,' explained my father…" par. 6)*

3. Did Robert and his father respond to this belch in the same way? *(No. Robert looked down with a red face, embarrassed. His father burped quietly to show Amy's mother that he liked the food. par. 6)*

4. Amy didn't agree with her mother that night. Did she think her mother understood her feelings at all? *(Yes. "I knew she understood how much I had suffered during the evening's dinner." par. 8)*

Vocabulary and Comprehension

"Fish Cheeks"

A. Match words and definitions. Write the letter of the correct definition next to each word.

_____ **1.** appalling

_____ **2.** wedges

_____ **3.** clamor

_____ **4.** rumpled

_____ **5.** muster

_____ **6.** stunned

a. wrinkled and untidy

b. call forth

c. horrifying

d. loud, confused noise

e. shocked or astonished

f. pie-shaped slices

B. Choose three words from above. Use each word in a sentence.

1. _____

_____

2. _____

_____

3. _____

_____

C. Answer each question below.

1. What kind of food does Amy want her mother to serve to the American guests?

_____

_____

2. Why does Amy's mother serve fish and other Chinese food at the Christmas Eve dinner?

_____

_____

NAME _____   DATE _____

Additional Vocabulary Practice   **Elements of Literature**
pages 527–532

"Fish Cheeks"

A. Complete each sentence with a word from the Word Bank.

1. I quickly ironed out the wrinkles in the

_____ tablecloth.

2. My young cousins made a noisy _____
as they sat down to eat.

3. Robin thought that the squid looked too horrible and

_____ to eat.

4. My uncle was able to _____ the courage to eat a small
bite.

5. Instead of apple pie, my mother served _____ of tofu
cheesecake for dessert.

> **Word Bank**
> rumpled
> muster
> clamor
> appalling
> wedges

B. Finish each sentence with a description that fits the underlined word.

1. If you are *appalled*, you are shocked and upset. An <u>appalling</u> amount

of food would look _____

_____

2. A *moist* cod with glistening scales might look appetizing and good

to eat. A <u>slimy</u> cod would look _____

_____

3. A carefully wrapped package would look neat and tidy. A <u>rumpled</u>

package would look _____

_____

4. *Clamor* means "loud and confused." A <u>clamorous</u> crowd would sound

_____

_____

"A Mason-Dixon Memory" by Clifton Davis

Prereading

Background

(Especially for ELL) **Explain the Title** Newcomers to this country may miss the significance of the title, "A Mason-Dixon Memory." Explain that Mason-Dixon is the name of an invisible line surveyed in 1767 that marks the border between Pennsylvania and Maryland. During and soon after the Revolutionary War, the states north of the Mason-Dixon line abolished slavery, but those to the south retained the slave system. In time, the line came to symbolize the division of the country between the Union and the Confederacy during the American Civil War.

Vocabulary Practice

Preview Additional Vocabulary Work with students as they learn to understand and use the following words in sentences.

- *banquet (p. 535):* fancy meal, usually with a lot of people
- *caper (p. 538):* small adventure
- *cement a friendship (p. 536):* make a friendship strong (like cement)
- *discrimination (p. 537):* treating certain groups of people unfairly
- *facility (p. 538):* building intended for a certain activity
- *ominous (p. 537):* threatening
- *on the double (p. 536):* very fast
- *outraged (p. 538):* very angry
- *provoked (p. 535):* caused some action or feeling
- *reserved (p. 536):* set apart for special use

If time permits, have students use each word in a sentence of their own. Suggest that students write the words in their journals.

Alternative Activity

Read the Adaptation Distribute copies of the adapted reading of "A Mason-Dixon Memory" (available in this book and, with marginal questions, in *Holt Adapted Reader*). To prepare for reading the original version and to practice fluency, students should read the adaptation silently. Encourage students to write notes, questions, predictions, reactions, and comments on the worksheets as they read.

SKILLS FOCUS

Literary Skill
Understand forms of prose: the essay.

Reading Skill
Recognize text structures: flashback.

(Resources)

In this book:
- Adapted Readings
- Vocabulary and Comprehension, p. 209
- Additional Vocabulary Practice, p. 212 (includes the next selection)

Other Resources:
- *Holt Adapted Reader*
- *Audio CD Library*
- *Audio CD Library, Selections and Summaries in Spanish*
- *Supporting Instruction in Spanish*
- Videocassette, Segment 6

(Teacher Tip)

Ask students to locate on a map of Washington, D.C., the landmarks mentioned in the essay: the White House, Arlington National Cemetery (in Virginia), the Potomac River, the Lincoln Memorial. Then, ask them to look at a map of the United States. Have them locate the Mason-Dixon line; Monroe, Louisiana; and Maryland. Call attention to the states north and south of the Mason-Dixon line.

Reading

Alternative Activity

Play the Audio Recording Struggling readers may benefit from listening to the audio recording of the selection as they follow along in their books.

Reteach the Key Idea

Examine Structure In this essay, the writer uses the literary device of flashback by telling a story set in 1991 and adding depth to the first story by telling a second story set in 1959, inviting parallels between the two. As the students read, have them note how the author uses the flashback to stress that racial prejudice is central to both stories. Ask students to mark the flashbacks with sticky notes.

Alternative Teaching Strategy

Build Background Have students locate Louisiana on a map. Point out that this state is located in the Deep South, a region that also encompasses Georgia, Alabama, and Mississippi. Explain that "Whites Only" was a sign commonly posted when segregation was prevalent in the South. Many public facilities and gathering places had such signs posted near water fountains, restrooms, and beaches. Tell students that the expression "American Dream" refers to the notion that in the United States any individual, regardless of background, can find success and make his or her dream come true through hard work.

Postreading

Fluency Practice

Discuss Literary Devices Discuss what point was made through the use of flashback. Prompt students by asking whether they feel the essay would have had the same effect if the story had been only about Dondré's experience or only about Clifton's. Also discuss the use of symbol, and remind students that here the Lincoln Memorial symbolizes the end of slavery and the promise of equality.

Alternative Assessment

Monitor Comprehension Have students make a time line on which they list chronologically the most important events in the selection. Then, as a class activity, ask students to name these events, one at a time, as you record them on the chalkboard. Because the story actually comprises two separate sequences of events, students should try to keep the time lines separate and then indicate the points at which the two different stories intersect.

Vocabulary Development

Reteach the Key Idea

Explore Synonyms: Shades of Meaning Lead students to understand that an author uses synonyms to make sure his or her readers understand the meaning of the story or essay to the fullest degree. Making the right word choice is very important. To illustrate this point, point out that the author of this essay wrote that he and his friends were *drenching* people with water balloons. Explain that he could have used synonyms such as *wetting* or *watering*. Lead students in a discussion of the different images we think of when we read the various synonyms. Explain that this difference is called *shade of meaning* or *connotation*. Have students choose several words from the essay, find synonyms in a dictionary or thesaurus, and substitute the synonyms in the original sentences. Have them share their work with the class.

Grammar Link

Alternative Activity

Sort Out Series with Commas Demonstrate for students that a series of words written without commas will become confusing. For example:

> After school I stopped by the store and bought some ice cream soda cookies and chips. Then I went to watch some videos with Billy Joe Bob and Tito.

Ask students: What did this student buy? Ice cream soda? Cream soda cookies? Who watched the videos with him? Billy Joe? Joe Bob? Then, place the commas in the sentence in the correct places.

> After school I stopped by the store and bought some ice cream, soda, cookies, and chips. Then I went to watch some videos with Billy, Joe, Bob, and Tito.

Reading Skills Development

(**Mixed Ability Group**) **Understand Sequence of Events**
Students having difficulty understanding flashback will benefit from rearranging the order of events in a different, chronologically told story. Arrange students in small, mixed ability groups to re-read together the short story "Amigo Brothers," found on student book page 485 (or, in adapted form, on page 515 of this book). After groups have re-read the selection, have them brainstorm how some of the events in the story could be told as flashbacks. Since this will likely be a difficult exercise for students, you may want to write the story events on the chalkboard for the groups to consider. You may also want to lead a brainstorming session as a whole-class activity. Ask for students' ideas of how flashbacks can add interest and suspense to a story.

SKILLS FOCUS

Literary Skill
Understand forms of prose: the essay.

Reading Skill
Recognize text structures: flashback.

(Resources)

In this book:
• Adapted Readings
• Vocabulary and Comprehension, p. 209
• Additional Vocabulary Practice, p. 212 (includes the next selection)

Other Resources:
• *Holt Adapted Reader*
• *Audio CD Library*
• *Audio CD Library, Selections and Summaries in Spanish*
• *Supporting Instruction in Spanish*
• Videocassette, Segment 6

(Teacher Tip)

Tell students that the Mason-Dixon line is an imaginary boundary between Pennsylvania and Maryland. It was used to divide the United States into free states (which did not allow slavery) and slave states (which did). Then, explain that after the Civil War, slavery was against the law in all states.

(Teacher Tip)

Write *1959* and *1991* on the chalkboard. Tell students that Clifton Davis's story happened in 1959 and that Dondré Green's story happened in 1991. Each time you stop the recording, point to the years on the board, and ask students in which of those years the flashback is taking place.

TARGETED STRATEGIES FOR SPECIAL EDUCATION STUDENTS

Prereading
Alternative Teaching Strategy

Preview the Essay Tell students that in this selection, Clifton Davis writes of an experience that reminds him of an upsetting event in his childhood. On an eighth-grade trip to Washington, D.C., in 1959, he experienced segregation firsthand when he was not allowed to visit an amusement park with the rest of his class. Explain to students that a flashback occurs when a writer uses more than one time and place in a work. In this essay, the writer tells one story set in 1991 and a second story set in 1959, inviting parallels between the two. As the students read, have them note how the author uses the flashback to let us know racial prejudice is central to both stories.

Reading
Listening and Speaking Opportunity

Flashback For students who have difficulty reading, play the audio recording of "A Mason-Dixon Memory." Stop the recording at the start of each flashback, and ask students where and when the story is now taking place. Stop at the end of each flashback, and ask students to tell you what happened in the story during the flashback and whom it's about.

Postreading
Alternative Assessment

Play a Tough-Questions Game Assess students' comprehension and oral fluency. Write questions about the essay on separate index cards, and place the cards in a box. Have a student take a card from the box and read the question. Ask a student to answer it. Here are some sample questions:

• How did Clifton Davis meet Dondré Green?
• How did Clifton raise money for his trip to Washington?
• Why couldn't Clifton go to the amusement park?
• What did the Caldwell Parish Country Club tell Dondré and his team?
• What decision did Dondré's teammates make when they were told he wasn't allowed to play?
• What decision did Clifton's schoolmates make when they were told he could not go with them to the amusement park?
• What did Dondré Green learn about love and hate?
• How are Clifton's and Dondré's stories similar?

Vocabulary and Comprehension

"A Mason-Dixon Memory"

A. Match words and definitions. Write the letter of the correct definition next to each word.

_____ **1.** erupted

_____ **2.** predominately

_____ **3.** forfeit

_____ **4.** resolve

_____ **5.** ominous

a. lose the right to compete

b. threatening

c. mainly

d. decide

e. burst forth

B. Choose two words from above. Use each word in a sentence.

1. _____

_____

2. _____

_____

C. Answer each question below.

1. Why was Clifton so upset when he wasn't allowed in the amusement park?

_____

_____

2. What do Clifton's friends do when they learn he is not allowed in the amusement park?

_____

_____

3. What did Dondré Green's teammates decide to do when the Caldwell Parish Country Club would not let Dondré play?

_____

_____

"Buddies Bare Their Affection for Ill Classmate" from the *Austin American-Statesman*

SKILLS FOCUS

Reading Skills
• Understand how to summarize.
• Understand main idea.

(Resources)

In this book:
• Adapted Readings
• Vocabulary and Comprehension, p. 211
• Additional Vocabulary Practice, p. 212 (includes the previous selection)

Other Resources:
• *Holt Adapted Reader*
• *Audio CD Library*
• *Audio CD Library, Selections and Summaries in Spanish*
• *Supporting Instruction in Spanish*

(Core Skill)

Use page 406 of this book to help students having difficulty summarizing. Use "Buddies Bare Their Affection for Ill Classmate" for the application portion of the lesson.

(Special Education Students)

Struggling readers may increase their comprehension of the selection by listening to the audio recording. Doing so may also help students summarize the article.

Prereading

Background

(**Especially for ELL**) **Preview Selection Information** English-language learners may not have heard the medical term *chemotherapy*. Explain that this is the use of powerful chemicals to treat some types of cancer. The treatment can have many side effects, including hair loss.

Vocabulary Practice

Learn Scientific Vocabulary Write the words below on the chalkboard, and ask students to find the words in the dictionary:

• *chemotherapy (p. 544):* use of drugs to treat certain diseases
• *lymphoma (p. 544):* disease of the lymph system
• *malignant (p. 544):* cancerous
• *tumor (p. 544):* extra growth on some part of the body

Alternative Activity

Read the Adaptation Distribute copies of the adapted reading of "Buddies Bare Their Affection for Ill Classmate" (available in this book and, with marginal questions, in *Holt Adapted Reader*). To prepare for reading the original version and to practice fluency, students should read the adaptation silently.

Reading

Alternative Teaching Strategy

(**Core Skill**) **Summarize the Article** As students read the article, ask them to jot down on a piece of paper the most important points of the article. Then, have them re-read the article to make sure the information they noted is essential to the story. Ask them to transfer the information to a graphic organizer as shown on page 543 of the student book.

Postreading

Listening and Speaking Opportunity

Practice Summarizing Bring in short articles that will interest students. Have volunteers read the articles aloud. Ask the listeners to identify key information and to summarize it.

Vocabulary and Comprehension

"Buddies Bare Their Affection for Ill Classmate"

A. Number these events in the order in which they occurr in "Buddies Bare Their Affection for Ill Classmate."

_____ The boys went to the barbershop together.

_____ Ian lost twenty pounds, but is eager to get back to school.

_____ Classmates found out that Ian O'Gorman was sick.

_____ The teacher was so inspired by his class that he also shaved his head.

_____ Ian decided to shave his head before all his hair fell out in clumps.

_____ "We wanted to make him feel better and not left out," said Kyle.

B. Complete each sentence with a word from the Word Bank.

1. A good _____
includes the main ideas and main events of a
text.

2. Support the main idea with the most important

_____ of the text.

> **Word Bank**
> summary
> details

C. Answer each question below.

1. Why did Kyle and the other boys decide to shave their heads?

_____

_____

2. What inspired the teacher, Mr. Alter, to shave his head?

_____

_____

3. Why do you think that Ian is eager to get back to school?

_____

_____

Additional Vocabulary Practice

"A Mason-Dixon Memory"; "Buddies Bare Their Affection for Ill Classmate"

A. Complete each sentence with a word from the Word Bank.

1. Dondré Green was a black student who went to a

_____ white Southern school.

2. The golf team decided to _____ the
tournament rather than play without Dondré.

3. His teammates showed a strong

_____ to do the right thing.

4. The entire roomful of people broke out, or

_____, in cheers at this story.

5. Clifton Davis became very _____ when he heard
Dondré's speech.

6. He too had once lived through a threatening and _____
situation.

Word Bank
erupted
predominantly
forfeit
resolve
ominous
emotional

B. Choose the correct word in parentheses to complete each sentence.

1. *(treat, treatment)* Ian started chemotherapy to _____

his disease. The _____ caused his hair to fall out.

2. *(resolve, resolution)* Kyle Hanslik made an unusual

_____. How did he _____ to support Ian?

3. *(emotion, emotional)* Ian's father became very _____
when he found out that all the boys had shaved their heads. He spoke

with deep _____ and thanked the boys.

4. *(inspired, inspiration)* The teacher found _____ in the

actions of his students. He felt so _____ that he shaved
his head too.

Elements of Literature:
Painting with Words

Alternative Teaching Strategy

Explore What a Poet Does Explain that poets may help us see things anew by using unexpected comparisons. We can understand the work of writing poetry by comparing it to other art forms:

- Like a painter, a poet uses images to share a personal vision of the world. The poet's figures of speech (personification, metaphor, simile) can help us see connections between things that we thought were unrelated.
- Like musicians, poets work with sound. They choose rhythms, rhymes, and other sounds that help express the content.
- Like sculptors, poets work with form. They may use a traditional form in which the number of lines, the rhythm pattern, and the rhyme pattern are set in advance. Most songwriters do this. Poets may also create new, freer forms that reflect the content of a poem.

Ask students to think of a line or verse of a song that they especially like. Have them first write out the lyric and then paraphrase it in different ways. Which version do they like best? Why? Does it contain a vivid image? Does it make a fresh comparison? Does rhyme make the lyric more memorable? Making these choices is part of the poet's work.

Make a Simile Point out that people often make comparisons with animals. Have students list animals and attribute characteristics to them. They may want to use the form: (<u>modifier</u>) as a (<u>noun</u>), as in these expressions: *busy as a bee, strong as a horse, quiet as a mouse.* Ask students to come up with new, unexpected comparisons.

Academic Vocabulary

(**Especially for ELL**) **Discuss Terms Related to Poetry** Explain and show examples of the following:

- *images (p. 546):* mental pictures a poet creates through words
- *figures of speech (p. 546):* language that makes startling connections between dissimilar things
- *stanza (p. 546):* group of lines that forms one section or unit of a poem
- *rhyme (p. 547):* two or more words with the same end sound
- *rhythm (p. 547):* musical beat or pattern in language

SKILLS FOCUS

Literary Skills
- Understand images, sounds, and forms in poetry.
- Understand how to read poetry.

(**Teacher Tip**)

On a large piece of poster board, write *Poet's Toolbox*. With the help of students, list all the tools a poet needs to write poetry. Tack the poster on a wall or on the bulletin board. As the class reads the poems in the chapter, add more tools to the toolbox.

Literary Skills
- Understand images, sounds, and forms in poetry.
- Understand how to read poetry.

TARGETED STRATEGIES FOR SPECIAL EDUCATION STUDENTS

Elements of Literature: Painting with Words

Alternative Activity

Sing a Poem Ask students if they know any poems. If they say no, ask if they know any songs. Explain that songs are poems set to music. Then, ask what songs they know. Write the titles on the chalkboard. When there is a selection of songs listed, choose an appropriate one, and ask students to provide the words. Write on the board the words to one or two stanzas. Should none of the listed songs be appropriate for a class discussion, write the words to "The Star-Spangled Banner." Read the lyrics as one would read a poem. Make the point that students do indeed know poetry.

Academic Vocabulary

Learn Literary Terms Explain to students that when they know the language of poetry, it will be more comprehensible because they will know what to expect from a poem.

- *images (p. 546):* pictures a poet creates in the mind through words
- *figures of speech (p. 546):* language that makes startling connections between dissimilar things
- *stanza (p. 546):* group of lines forming one section or unit of a poem
- *rhyme (p. 547):* two or more words with the same end sound
- *rhythm (p. 547):* beat or pattern in language

Alternative Teaching Strategy

Practice Alliteration Review the definition of alliteration with students. Tell them that entire sentences can be done in this style. For example, *Bats barely blink when baking bagels and breadsticks.* Ask a student to read the sentence aloud. How does it sound? Funny? Silly? How would it sound if we spoke like this all the time?

Alternative Assessment

Respond to Poetry Ask students to think about the images, feelings, and ideas in poems they have studied—"Annabel Lee" *(p. 261),* "The Highwayman" *(p. 247).* Have them illustrate a poem and share their artwork with the class.

Elements of Literature
pages 548–554

"I'm Nobody!" and "I Like to See It Lap the Miles" by Emily Dickinson

Prereading

Vocabulary Practice

(Especially for ELL) **Preview Additional Vocabulary** Help students understand the words in the two poems.

- *banish (p. 549):* to force a person to leave his or her country as a punishment; exile
- *dreary (p. 549):* without happiness or cheer; dull
- *bog (p. 549):* wet, spongy ground; a small marsh or swamp
- *neigh (p. 552):* make a sound like a horse
- *docile (p. 552):* easily taught or managed
- *omnipotent (p. 552):* having limitless authority or influence

Reading

Alternative Activity

Use *The Holt Reader* For "I'm Nobody!" you may want to have students read the poem in *The Holt Reader* and use the margins in that book to make notes and respond to the instruction.

Reteach the Key Idea

Identify Metaphors and Similes Tell students that "I'm Nobody!" includes one simile and one metaphor and then ask them to find the two *(simile: "like a frog"; metaphor: "to an admiring bog")*. Ask students whom Dickinson is comparing to a frog *(a person who is somebody, or a well-known person)* and whom she is comparing to a bog *(the fans and admirers of famous people)*. Discuss with students as well the figurative language in "I Like to See It Lap the Miles."

Postreading

Alternative Activity

Discuss the Simile and Metaphor Have students discuss what could have caused the poet to think of famous people as frogs and their audiences as admiring bogs. What would it be like to be famous? And how is a train like and unlike a horse? How do you think Dickinson feels about trains?

SKILLS FOCUS

Literary Skills
Understand figures of speech, such as simile, metaphor, and extended metaphor.

(**Resources**)

In this book:
- Vocabulary and Comprehension, p. 216
- Additional Vocabulary Practice, p. 222 (includes selections from the next two lesson plans)

Other Resources:
- *The Holt Reader* (for "I'm Nobody!")
- *Audio CD Library*
- *Audio CD Library, Selections and Summaries in Spanish*
- *Supporting Instruction in Spanish*

(**Special Education Students**)

Students may be put off by the first line of "I'm Nobody!" in which the speaker bluntly announces herself as a "nobody." Tell students that the poet is counting on their surprise, and she is using the word in a very special way. Discuss the poet's use of the word *nobody,* and ask students to think about why a poet might want to surprise her readers in this way.

Vocabulary and Comprehension

"I'm Nobody!" and "I Like to See It Lap the Miles"

A. Match words and definitions. Write the letter of the correct definition next to each word.

_____ **1.** supercilious

_____ **2.** banish

_____ **3.** dreary

_____ **4.** bog

_____ **5.** prodigious

a. small marsh or swamp

b. enormous

c. haughty

d. without happiness or cheer

e. to force a person to leave

B. Choose two words from above. Use each word in a sentence.

1. _____

_____

2. _____

_____

C. Answer each question below.

1. To what does Emily Dickinson compare a famous person?

_____

_____

2. To what does she compare the train?

_____

_____

3. Does the poet make fame sound like a positive or a negative thing to have?

_____

_____

"I Am of the Earth" by Anna Lee Walters

Prereading

Background

Know the Author Explain to students that the author of "I Am of the Earth" is a Native American. This poem reflects the respect for nature that is a part of many Native American cultures.

Vocabulary Practice

Preview Vocabulary Help students understand the poem by first previewing the vocabulary on page 556 of the student book.

> *reared (line 4):* raised; brought up *(reared children)*
>
> *cradled (line 5):* held or rocked, as does a baby's bed with rockers
>
> *embrace (line 12):* to hold closely, showing fondness or love; hug
>
> *eternity (line 12):* all time without end

Reading

Reteach the Key Idea

Explore Personification As students read "I Am of the Earth" explain how tone and meaning are conveyed by exploring personification. Remind students that personification occurs when a writer attributes human qualities or behaviors to something nonhuman. Point out that calling the earth "Mother Earth" or "Mother Nature" is a common example of personification. Explain that the author extends the metaphor by listing the things a mother does for her child. Discuss the meaning of several lines of the poem:

- She pushed the wind to make it sing *(the wind blew)*
- She built me a house of harmonious colors *(the earth itself with its many colors)*
- She punished me with the passing of time *(the aging process)*

Postreading

Alternative Activity

(Mixed Ability Group) **Use Personification** To help students understand personification, ask them to write a short poem using personification. Group students into threes or fours and allow them to brainstorm what they will personify and then how they will personify their choices. When finished, have them present their short poems to the class.

SKILLS FOCUS

Literary Skill
Understand personification.

(Resources)

In this book:
- Vocabulary and Comprehension, p. 219
- Additional Vocabulary Practice, p. 222 (includes selections from the previous and the next lesson plan)

Other Resources:
- *Audio CD Library*
- *Audio CD Library, Selections and Summaries in Spanish*
- *Supporting Instruction in Spanish*

(Especially for ELL)

Before teaching this poem, list on the chalkboard words (and short definitions) students may not know. Have students copy the words and definitions into their journals.

(Language Tip)

Explain and define *tone* (how writers show feelings to their readers) and *meaning* (what readers should come away with from a poem or other piece of writing).

(Resources)

In this book:
• Vocabulary and Comprehension, p. 219
• Additional Vocabulary Practice, p. 222 (includes selections from the previous and the next lesson plan)

Other Resources:
• *Audio CD Library*
• *Audio CD Library, Selections and Summaries in Spanish*
• *Supporting Instruction in Spanish*

TARGETED STRATEGIES FOR SPECIAL EDUCATION STUDENTS

Prereading
Reteach the Key Idea

Explain Personification Remind students that writers sometimes attribute human thoughts, behaviors, and qualities to animals and inanimate objects. This technique is called personification. Many Native American religions and traditions, like those of other cultures, teach that the earth is an actual spiritual being and that natural things such as rocks, rivers, air, and earth are alive. In the poem "I Am of the Earth," the poet expresses her appreciation of the earth and refers to the earth as "my mother." The expression "Mother Earth" refers to the earth being thought of as the source of all animate and inanimate things.

Reading
Listening and Speaking Opportunity

Play the Audio Recording Play the audio recording for students. Then, read the poem aloud while students follow in their books. Pair students, and ask each pair to take turns reading the poem to each other, one at a time. Walk among the pairs, helping where needed. Pay close attention to pronunciation. If students are having trouble reading, be sure they understand what each line means. After you've listened to all of the pairs, lead a discussion about the meaning of the poem. Write the word *earth* on the chalkboard and ask students to brainstorm actions of the earth, such as turning, quaking, and providing. Write students' suggestions on the chalkboard, and determine with them which actions are like human actions. Point out that these are examples of personification.

Postreading
Alternative Activity

Write or Draw Ask students to work collaboratively in groups of three or four to paraphrase the poem in order to make sure they understand it well. Offer students the option of illustrating a line of this poem, such as "She built me a house of harmonious colors" or "She fed me fruits of her fields." Have the groups share their work with the rest of the class.

(Teacher Tip)

To assess students' comprehension of personification, ask them to draw a picture of a *happy heart* and a *sad sack*.

Vocabulary and Comprehension

"I Am of the Earth"

A. Replace the words in parentheses with a word from the Word Bank.

1. The mother *(gave birth to)* _____ many children.

2. She *(rocked)* _____ them in her arms.

3. The earth is filled with *(pleasing or blending well together)* _____ colors.

4. Will the earth last for all *(time that has no end)* _____?

5. We harvest the *(products of many plants)* _____ of the fields.

> **Word Bank**
> bore
> cradled
> eternity
> fruits
> harmonious

B. Use three words from the Word Bank in a sentence.

1. _____

_____

2. _____

_____

3. _____

_____

C. Write T or F next to each statement to tell if it is true or false.

_____ **1.** The author thinks that she came from another planet.

_____ **2.** "She" means Mother Earth.

_____ **3.** Mother Earth has been very good to this person.

_____ **4.** The poet says that when she dies, Mother Earth will not take care of her anymore.

"Early Song" by Gogisgi/Carroll Arnett

SKILLS FOCUS

Literary Skill
Understand personification.

(Resources)

In this book:
• Vocabulary and Comprehension, p. 221
• Additional Vocabulary Practice, p. 222 (includes selections from the previous two lesson plans)

Other Resources:
• *Audio CD Library*
• *Audio CD Library, Selections and Summaries in Spanish*
• *Supporting Instruction in Spanish*

(Special Education Students)

To reinforce the connection between the words a poet chooses and a poem's tone, have students work in small groups to revise "Early Song," substituting words to change the tone. For example, ask them how the tone of the poem changes if they substitute *burn* for *warm* in line 3. When they've finished, have a volunteer from each group read its revisions to the class. Then, lead the class in a discussion about words and tone.

Prereading

Background

Introduce the Work Point out to students that the poem may appear to have two authors but Gogisgi is actually Carroll Arnett's Cherokee name. Like Anna Lee Walters, Arnett writes about his love and respect for the earth in "Early Song." Unlike Walters, however, he does not use personification in "Early Song."

Reading

Listening and Speaking Opportunity

(Mixed Ability Group) **Read in Groups/Practice Fluency** Play the audio recording for the class. Instruct them to listen carefully to the phrasing and how the words are pronounced and where the reader pauses. Then, have students work in small groups to take turns reading aloud to each other, stanza by stanza. Ask them to pay attention to pronunciation and pauses and recall the reading as they heard it. Move among the groups to assist.

Postreading

Alternative Teaching Strategy

Examine Tone Remind students that tone conveys the author's feelings about the subject. Ask them to find evidence in the poem that tells them how Arnett feels about the earth. Guide them to phrases such as "good brown earth," "four prayers of thanksgiving," "fine clear day," and "for all brothers and sisters." Have them explain what they think the author's attitude toward his subject is.

Alternative Activity

(Especially for ELL) **Capture the Meaning** Ask students to scan the poem once more to identify the four things for which the poet is giving thanks. Ask them to state the four things in plain language. Students should recognize that the poet is grateful for the new day, the land, his family and community, and his own life.

• *this fine clear day (line 8)*
• *this good brown/earth (lines 9–10)*
• *all/brothers and sisters (lines 10–11)*
• *the dark blood/that runs through me (lines 12–13)*

Vocabulary and Comprehension

"Early Song"

A. Match words and definitions. Write the letter of the correct definition next to each word.

_____ **1.** frost

_____ **2.** thanksgiving

_____ **3.** warm

a. frozen dew or vapor in the form of white crystals

b. show of gratitude or appreciation

c. heat up; make less cold

B. Use each word above in a sentence.

1. _____

_____

2. _____

_____

3. _____

_____

C. Answer each question below.

1. What part of the day does the poet refer to in the first stanza?

_____

_____

2. Name the four things that the poet offers thanks for in the morning prayers.

_____

_____

_____

_____

Additional Vocabulary Practice

"I'm Nobody!"; "I Like to See It Lap the Miles"; "I Am of the Earth"; "Early Song"

A. Complete each sentence with a word from the Word Bank.

1. Cranberries grow very well in a wet

_____.

Word Bank
banish
dreary
bog
bore
harmonious
pride
thanksgiving

2. The apple trees _____ lots of apples last year.

3. The apple growers take great _____ in their crisp, tart apples.

4. After each harvest we offer a few grateful words of

_____.

5. In autumn the trees turn _____ shades of red, orange, and yellow.

6. Today the weather is wet, cloudy, and _____.

7. Tomorrow the sun will come out and _____ the clouds.

B. Match the words and phrases in the left column with the words in the right column that best describe them. Write the letter next to each word.

_____ **1.** cradled me

_____ **2.** reared me

_____ **3.** harmonious

_____ **4.** pair

_____ **5.** the earth is my mother

a. likely to blend well together

b. example of personification

c. held me in her arms

d. two of the same kind

e. helped me to grow up

C. Finish each sentence with a description that fits the underlined word.

1. If something is <u>omnipotent</u>, it has _____.

2. If something is <u>docile</u>, it is _____.

"Madam and the Rent Man"

by Langston Hughes

Prereading

Additional Background

Introduce the Selection "Madam and the Rent Man" tells the story of an encounter between one of Langston Hughes's characters, Madam, and the man responsible for collecting her rent money. The apartment is in poor condition, and Madam doesn't want to pay the rent since no repairs have been made. The two argue over the payment, using colorful language that vividly expresses the conflict. The only thing they can agree on is the fact that they disagree. Langston Hughes wrote the poem in black American dialect to dramatize the conversational style of the characters.

Alternative Activity

Especially for ELL **Use Spanish Resources** Spanish-speaking English-language learners may benefit from listening to the audio recording of the selection in Spanish in preparation for reading it in English.

Reading

Listening and Speaking Opportunity

Hear the Poetry As students listen to the audio recording, have them note instances of phrases or words that are unfamiliar to them. *(For example: Howdy-do, you ain't done a thing, and I ain't pleased)* Explain that this is informal dialect rather than standard English and is used to make the conversation natural sounding. Have students work in pairs to paraphrase the poem and practice reading it aloud. Circulate among the pairs to assist students.

Postreading

Alternative Activity

Recognize Tone After students have paraphrased the poem and practiced reading it, review tone with them. Play the audio recording again, and tell them to listen for clues to the poet's attitude toward his subject. What does he think of Madam? What is his attitude toward the rent man? Prompt them to see how Hughes admires Madam and her no-nonsense approach. In this poem, Hughes uses poetic elements of rhythm and rhyme to emphasize that Madam is an indomitable figure with great force of personality.

SKILLS FOCUS

Literary Skill
Understand tone.

Resources

In this book:
- Vocabulary and Comprehension, p. 224
- Additional Vocabulary Practice, p. 228 (includes selections from the next lesson plan)

Other Resources:
- *Audio CD Library*
- *Audio CD Library, Selections and Summaries in Spanish*
- *Supporting Instruction in Spanish*

Language Tip

Explain that the poem contains contractions. Ask students to find the contractions in the poem and to identify the words that make the contraction. For example: *I'd = I + would.*

Special Education Students

Students may find the poem difficult to read. Point out that the writer has not used quotation marks to set off direct speech, so they will have to watch for cues to direct speech, such as "I said" and "he said."

Vocabulary and Comprehension

"Madam and the Rent Man"

A. Replace the words in parentheses with a word or words from the Word Bank.

Word Bank
rent
due
howdy-do
pass the buck
agent

1. One way to say hello to someone is to say *(how do you do)* _____.

2. I pay *(money every month)* _____ to live in this apartment.

3. The gas bill is *(required to be paid)* _____ today.

4. I am just the *(person that acts for another person or company)* _____.

5. He wanted to *(make someone else take the blame or responsibility)* _____ for the problem.

B. Choose two words or phrases from the Word Bank. Use each word or phrase in a sentence.

1. _____

_____

2. _____

_____

C. Answer each question below.

1. Why won't the woman pay her rent?

_____

_____

2. What does the agent say to her demands?

_____

_____

"Harlem Night Song" and "Winter Moon" by Langston Hughes

Prereading

Vocabulary Practice

Preview Selection Vocabulary Review the following words and their definitions with students. Alert students that while they might not find the selection vocabulary very challenging, they will need to pay close attention to the poet's *syntax,* or the way the lines are put together. Students might particularly note the lack of articles in lines 7–9 of "Harlem Night Song."

- *roam ("Harlem Night Song"):* wander
- *great ("Harlem Night Song"):* large
- *drops ("Harlem Night Song"):* small globes of liquid
- *dew ("Harlem Night Song"):* moisture that gathers in cooling temperatures
- *crook ("Winter Moon"):* sharply curved shape

Reading

Alternative Activity

Play the Audio Recording Struggling readers may benefit from listening to the audio recording of the poems while they follow along in their books.

Listening and Speaking Opportunity

(Mixed Ability Group) **Perform the Poems/Practice Fluency**
Arrange students in small groups, and have students take turns reading the poems aloud. Encourage students to be expressive. The groups can then discuss the songlike quality of the poems, and whether the quality comes out in an oral reading.

Postreading

Alternative Activity

Draw a Picture Point out to students that poems strong in imagery leave readers with strong impressions. Have students draw a picture of the scene described in each of the poems and then compare their drawings with a partner. Partners can discuss how the details of specific lines of each poem contributed to their drawings.

SKILLS FOCUS

Literary Skill
Understand imagery.

(**Resources**)

In this book:
- Vocabulary and Comprehension, p. 227
- Additional Vocabulary Practice, p. 228 (includes the previous selection)

Other Resources:
- *Audio CD Library*
- *Audio CD Library, Selections and Summaries in Spanish*
- *Supporting Instruction in Spanish*

(**Especially for ELL**)

Spanish-speaking English-language learners may benefit from reading or listening to the selection summaries in Spanish in preparation for reading the selections in English.

(**Resources**)

In this book:
• Vocabulary and Comprehension, p. 227
• Additional Vocabulary Practice, p. 228 (includes the previous selection)

Other Resources:
• *Audio CD Library*
• *Audio CD Library, Selections and Summaries in Spanish*
• *Supporting Instruction in Spanish*

(**Teacher Tip**)

You may point out to students that the poet uses only one metaphor in the two poems, in lines 9–10 of "Harlem Night Song." Discuss with students the effect of the metaphor and the effectiveness of the plain language the poet uses to create the poems' scenes.

TARGETED STRATEGIES FOR SPECIAL EDUCATION STUDENTS

Prereading
Reteach the Key Idea

Introduce the Selections Since the poet uses free verse and ignores a more traditional rhyme scheme in both poems, students may not understand what is "poetic" about the poems, especially given the two works' simple language. Point out to students that the poet is looking for the beautiful in the simple, everyday things around him. To do that, he uses simple, everyday language. Lead students to understand that the images created by Langston Hughes make the pieces "poetic." Prepare students to concentrate on the sights, sounds, and smells of the world the poet will present to them.

Reading
Alternative Teaching Strategies

Identify the Speaker Guide students in recognizing the speaker in the two poems. In "Harlem Night Song" the speaker is someone addressing his love at night in Harlem; in "Winter Moon" the reader knows only that the speaker is someone admiring the moon. Point out to students that in both cases the speaker is someone who is trying to draw the reader's attention to something beautiful. The beauty is what is important to the speaker, not that his identity is known to the reader.

Use a Chart Have students use a chart to keep track of the images in the poems. Students can copy a chart such as the following and fill it in as they read.

Sensory Details	"Harlem Night Song"	"Winter Moon"
Sights		
Sounds		
Smells		
Textures		
Tastes		

Postreading
Reteach the Key Idea

Make the Connection Review the two poems with students, and have them identify the images they found in the poems. Write students' suggestions on the chalkboard. Discuss with students how the images allow the reader to experience something in the way the poet experiences it.

Vocabulary and Comprehension

"Harlem Night Song" and "Winter Moon"

A. Match words and definitions. Write the letter of the correct definition next to each word.

____ **1.** roam	**a.** large
____ **2.** drop	**b.** sharply curved shape
____ **3.** crook	**c.** small globe of liquid
____ **4.** great	**d.** moisture that gathers in cooling temperatures
____ **5.** dew	**e.** wander

B. Choose three words from above. Use each word in a sentence.

1. _____

_____

2. _____

_____

3. _____

_____

C. Write T or F next to each statement to tell if it is true or false.

_____ **1.** In "Harlem Night Song" the poet speaks to his love.

_____ **2.** The poet in "Harlem Night Song" wants to wander in the night.

_____ **3.** In "Harlem Night Song" the stars are compared to diamonds.

_____ **4.** In "Winter Moon" the poet describes a full moon rising above the city.

_____ **5.** In "Winter Moon" the speaker is a jazz player waiting for a big concert.

Additional Vocabulary Practice

"Madam and the Rent Man"; "Harlem Night Song"; "Winter Moon"

A. Write the word from the Word Bank that rhymes with the underlined word.

1. Don't pass the _____ or you'll have bad <u>luck</u>.

2. I know where my money <u>went</u>; I used it all to

pay the _____.

3. Across the <u>loam</u> we did _____.

4. On our tent <u>tops</u> fell the rain

_____.

5. I already <u>ate</u> ; besides, my appetite is not

_____.

6. When you awake, you will <u>too</u> see the glistening morning

_____.

7. <u>Look</u>! That chattering squirrel is sitting in the _____ of a tree branch.

Word Bank
roam
buck
great
crook
dew
rent
drops

B. Choose four words from the Word Bank. Use each word in a sentence.

1. _____

_____

2. _____

_____

3. _____

_____

4. _____

_____

"I Ask My Mother to Sing" by Li-Young Lee

Prereading
Vocabulary Practice

(Especially for ELL) Preview Selection Vocabulary Students may be unfamiliar with a few of the items and places mentioned in the poem on student book page 569. Discuss the following with students.

- *accordion (line 4):* musical instrument with keys like a piano that is squeezed to make air pass through it to produce sound
- *Peking (line 5):* Chinese capital
- *Summer Palace (line 5):* traditional summer home of Chinese emperors
- *waterlilies (line 10):* water plants whose broad, flat leaves lie on the water's surface

Background

Preview Selection Geography Point out to students the location of Peking (now called Beijing) on a map, and have students judge the distance between it and the United States. The great distance should give students a better understanding of the two women's homesickness in the poem.

Reading
Fluency Practice

Improve Pronunciation and Phrasing Play the audio recording of the poem while students follow along in their books. Then, ask students to listen while you read the poem. Students should read the poem aloud with you, line by line, so they can remember phrasing and pronunciation. The simple, beautiful language of this poem makes it a good candidate for paired reading. Have students practice in pairs. Circulate from group to group to help with pronunciation.

Postreading
Alternative Activity

Write a Sonnet Have students write their own sonnets about their neighborhoods or hometowns and how they would feel to leave them. Encourage students to focus on evoking a strong emotion for the reader. Students should also make good use of images and figurative language in their poems. Ask volunteers to share their sonnets in a small-group setting.

SKILLS FOCUS

Literary Skills
- Understand lyric poems.
- Understand sonnets.

(Resources)

In this book:
- Vocabulary and Comprehension, p. 231 (includes the next selection)
- Additional Vocabulary Practice, p. 232 (includes the next selection)

Other Resources:
- *Audio CD Library*
- *Audio CD Library, Selections and Summaries in Spanish*
- *Supporting Instruction in Spanish*

(Special Education Students)

Have students identify the sonnet structure by numbering each quatrain and on a separate sheet of paper telling what each quatrain's main idea about the subject is. Reviewing the main ideas of each quatrain can help students better understand the importance of the image in the last two lines.

"Ode to Family Photographs" by Gary Soto

SKILLS FOCUS

Literary Skill
Understand odes.

Resources

In this book:
• Vocabulary and Comprehension, p. 231 (includes the previous selection)
• Additional Vocabulary Practice, p. 232 (includes the previous selection)

Other Resources:
• *Audio CD Library*
• *Audio CD Library, Selections and Summaries in Spanish*
• *Supporting Instruction in Spanish*

Special Education Students

Have students focus on the purpose of an ode. Ask: Why would anybody want to praise anything? (*Students might say out of gratitude or a feeling of inspiration.*) Write students' answers on the chalkboard, and alert them to look for these emotions in the poem as they read.

Prereading
Reteach the Key Idea

Discuss Odes Help students appreciate how "Ode to Family Photographs" exemplifies the purpose and form of an ode by reminding them that an ode traditionally celebrates a person or thing in an elegant way. Explain to students that this ode is special because it celebrates both things and people. As students read the ode, have them look for ways Soto praises (or fails to praise) the photographs themselves and the ways he ultimately comes to praise his family.

Reading
Listening and Speaking Opportunity

Especially for ELL **Listen to the Poem** Before the class listens to the audio recording of the poem, ask a Spanish-speaking student to read the poem aloud for the class so that students can hear how the names in the poem are correctly pronounced.

Alternative Activity

Look for Value Judgments Remind students that in an ode a poet generally praises someone or something. As students read the poem, direct them to note places in which the poet seems to be making judgments about either the photographs or his family. Are the judgments favorable or unfavorable? Students should be able to support their opinions.

Postreading
Alternative Teaching Strategy

Write an Ode To help students think of details that might describe a subject for an ode, you might try a visualization activity. Ask students to close their eyes and picture an object. Ask them to concentrate on the senses of sight, sound, smell, hearing, or touch. After a minute or so, have students open their eyes to jot down concrete, vivid details that they can use to describe their subject in an ode.

Vocabulary and Comprehension

"I Ask My Mother to Sing"; "Ode to Family Photographs"

A. Match words and definitions. Write the letter of the correct definition next to each word.

_____ 1. waterlilies

_____ 2. lyric poem

_____ 3. sonnet

_____ 4. narrative poem

_____ 5. accordion

a. musical instrument

b. poem that expresses emotion

c. poem that tells a story

d. lyric poem of fourteen lines

e. water plants

B. Choose three words from above. Use each word in a sentence.

1. _____

_____

2. _____

_____

3. _____

_____

C. Answer each question below.

1. What are the two women singing about in "I Ask My Mother to Sing"?

_____

_____

2. Where were the photographs in "Ode to Family Photographs" taken? Support your answer.

_____

_____

Additional Vocabulary Practice

"I Ask My Mother to Sing"; "Ode to Family Photographs"

A. Match words and definitions or descriptions. Write the letter of the correct definition or description next to each word.

_____ **1.** ode

_____ **2.** ancient Greece

_____ **3.** Peking

_____ **4.** Summer Palace

_____ **5.** beauty, joy, freedom

_____ **6.** waterlilies

_____ **7.** lyric poem

_____ **8.** sonnet

_____ **9.** narrative poem

_____ **10.** accordion

a. musical instrument

b. lyric poem that praises something

c. poem that tells a story

d. traditional summer home of a Chinese emperor

e. water plants

f. old name for the capital of China

g. poem that expresses emotion

h. traditional subjects of odes

i. lyric poem of fourteen lines

j. birthplace of the ode

B. Choose five words from above. Use each word in a sentence.

1. _____

_____

2. _____

_____

3. _____

_____

4. _____

_____

5. _____

_____

Elements of Literature:
The Sounds of Poetry

Academic Vocabulary

Know the Terms To help students understand the techniques that poets use, go over these terms and definitions. Tell them to look for examples of these terms as they read the poems in the chapter.

- *meter (p. 576):* regular pattern of stressed and unstressed syllables
- *rhyme scheme (p. 577):* pattern of rhymes used in a poem
- *free verse (p. 576):* poetry that does not have a regular pattern of stressed and unstressed syllables
- *alliteration (p. 577):* repetition of consonant sounds in words that are close together
- *onomatopoeia (p. 577):* use of words with sounds that echo their sense

Additional Practice

Especially for ELL **Identify Examples of Alliteration** On the chalkboard, write: *She sells seashells by the seashore.* Ask volunteers to read the sentence with increasing speed. Explain that in English, we call such expressions *tongue twisters*. To support comprehension, ask students if they know other examples, either in English or their native languages. Explain that tongue twisters play with extreme alliteration.

Identify a Pattern of Sound Ask a student to read "A Tutor" (page 577) aloud. Then, explain that to help students identify a sound pattern, you are going to read it aloud, exaggerating the stressed syllables. Have students raise their hands at each stressed syllable. What pattern do they see? Explain that this pattern is typical of a humorous poem called a limerick.

Write Tongue Twisters Have students make up their own tongue twisters. If they get stuck, start them off with an adjective or noun. For a further challenge, ask students to brainstorm words that have similar sounds and express related meanings. Write them on the chalkboard. (for example: *crunch, crack, crush*). Now, have them draw from this list to create tongue twisters that also use onomatopoeia.

SKILLS FOCUS

Literary Skills
Understand sounds of poetry, such as rhythm, rhyme, alliteration, onomatopoeia.

Background
Some say a poem is a painting made of words. The pictures words paint can be beautiful, patriotic, funny, sad, even shocking; but the words of a good poem always have an impact on the reader's thoughts and feelings. In the poet's toolbox are techniques to manage the sounds of words. Poets use sound to make ideas and feelings come alive for the reader.

Literary Skills
Understand sounds of
poetry, such as rhythm,
rhyme, alliteration,
onomatopoeia.

TARGETED STRATEGIES FOR SPECIAL EDUCATION STUDENTS

Elements of Literature: The Sounds of Poetry

Academic Vocabulary

Identify the Sound Effects of Poetry Explain that poets use words to create sound effects. Tell students that the following words relate to the sounds of poetry. Then, write the words and their definitions on the chalkboard and read them.

- *free verse (p. 576):* poetry that does not have a regular pattern of stressed and unstressed syllables

- *rhythm (p. 576):* refers to the rise and fall of our voices as we use language

- *rhyme (p. 576):* repetition of the sound of a stressed syllable and of any unstressed syllables that follow; end rhymes occur at the ends of lines; internal rhymes occur within lines

- *alliteration (p. 577):* repetition of consonant sounds in words that are close together

- *limerick (p. 577):* humorous five-line poem with a definite rhythm and rhyme scheme

- *onomatopoeia (p. 577):* use of words with sounds that echo their sense

Listening and Speaking Opportunity

Recognize Rhyme Help students recognize rhyme by having them listen to poetry. Students enjoy poetry with distinctive rhythm, lots of rhyming words, and humor. Tell students you are going to read a poem aloud, and have them listen for rhyming patterns in the poem. Ask them to raise their hands when they recognize a pair of rhyming words. Have students repeat the rhyming words.

Alternative Assessment

Reinforce Alliteration Have students work in pairs and select a letter of the alphabet and make up alliterative sentences. You might make things more interesting for the students by telling them they do not have to limit themselves to the one letter they selected if they can reproduce the same sound with another letter.

(**Teacher Tip**)
Shel Silverstein's poetry is
an excellent resource. The
poems are humorous and
include lots of rhymes and
rhythms.

"Father William" by Lewis Carroll;
"Sarah Cynthia Sylvia Stout . . ."
by Shel Silverstein

Prereading

Vocabulary Practice

(**Especially for ELL**) **Preview Additional Vocabulary** You may want to preview the following words and their definitions with students.

- *sage (p. 579):* wise person
- *ointment (p. 579):* medicinal cream
- *airs (p. 580):* pretensions; pretending to be better than one really is
- *scour (p. 582):* scrape; clean roughly
- *curdled (p. 583):* soured
- *rancid (p. 583):* bad smelling

Reading

Alternative Activities

Use *The Holt Reader* You may want to have students read "Sarah Cynthia Sylvia Stout Would Not Take the Garbage Out" in *The Holt Reader* and use the margins in that book to make notes and respond to the instruction.

Discuss Rhythm Write out a few lines of either poem on the chalkboard, and read the lines aloud, perhaps beating time by clapping the beat. Emphasize the fact that the poem is written in a very regular rhythm, and ask students to identify the pattern of the syllables in the lines. If students have trouble identifying the rhythm, write on the chalkboard the rhythm of the lines, using *da* for an unstressed syllable and *DUM* for a stressed syllable.

Postreading

Alternative Activity

(**Mixed Ability Group**) **Write a Humorous Poem** Students' skills in analyzing poems may improve through their own writing of poetry. Arrange students in very small groups, and have group members use "Father William" as a model for writing their own humorous poems with a regular, bouncy rhythm and a consistent rhyme.

SKILLS FOCUS

Literary Skills
- Understand humorous poems and exaggeration.
- Understand rhythm and meter.

(**Resources**)

In this book:
- Vocabulary and Comprehension, p. 237
- Additional Vocabulary Practice, p. 238

Other Resources:
- *The Holt Reader* (for "Sarah Cythia . . .")
- *Audio CD Library*
- *Audio CD Library, Selections and Summaries in Spanish*
- *Supporting Instruction in Spanish*

(**Especially for ELL**)

English-language learners may have difficulty appreciating the absurdity of some of the rhymes. Point out that both poets twist the logic of the situations they describe for the purpose of making their lines rhyme. A good example of this is stanza 5 in "Father William," in which the old man has eaten a goose's beak.

Literary Skills
• Understand humorous poems and exaggeration.
• Understand rhythm and meter.

Resources

In this book:
• Vocabulary and Comprehension, p. 237
• Additional Vocabulary Practice, p. 238

Other Resources:
• *The Holt Reader* (for "Sarah Cynthia . . .")
• *Audio CD Library*
• *Audio CD Library, Selections and Summaries in Spanish*
• *Supporting Instruction in Spanish*

Teacher Tip

You might want to point out to students that asking an older person for advice or wisdom is a well-established idea that is turned on its head in "Father William." In "Sarah Cynthia Sylvia Stout Would Not Take the Garbage Out," the humor follows the outrageous effects of one simple cause.

TARGETED STRATEGIES FOR SPECIAL EDUCATION STUDENTS

Prereading
Reteach the Key Idea

Introduce the Selections Remind students that the poems they are about to read use exaggeration to make the reader laugh. While they are realistic up to a point, both poems leave realism behind to go on to bigger and broader jokes. You may want to have students discuss humorous examples of exaggeration with which they are familiar, either from humorous stories or from films and TV shows. Have students be on the lookout for examples of exaggeration in the poems as they prepare to read.

Reading
Alternative Teaching Strategy

Make Connections Play the audio recording of each poem one time, pausing after every stanza or every few lines to allow students to discuss the examples of exaggeration found in the lines. Ask students: *Where does the exaggeration come from? What is the effect of the exaggeration?* After the recording is over, have students share their favorite examples.

Then, play each audio recording a second time to allow students to concentrate on the rhythm and meter of the lines. Pause the readings periodically to have students read as a group lines from the poems while clapping the beat. Lead students to see that there is a very predictable regularity to the rhythm of both poems. Ask them if they think this regularity adds to the humor of the pieces.

Postreading
Alternative Assessment

Discuss the Actions in the Poems Point out to students that both poems feature outrageous actions by their characters that are linked to the humorous exaggeration in the poems. Ask students what outrageous actions occur in "Father William," and what silly reasons are given for the actions. *(An example is the old man's standing on his head because he is convinced he has no brain to damage.)* Ask the same question of students for "Sarah Cynthia Sylvia Stout Would Not Take the Garbage Out." *(The main character refuses to take out the garbage, and as a result the pile bursts out of the house.)*

Vocabulary and Comprehension

"Father William"; "Sarah Cynthia Sylvia Stout Would Not Take the Garbage Out"

A. Match words and definitions. Write the letter of the correct definition next to each word.

_____ **1.** incessantly

_____ **2.** supple

_____ **3.** scour

_____ **4.** curdled

_____ **5.** suet

a. kind of fat

b. scrape

c. without stopping

d. flexible

e. soured

B. Choose three words from above. Use each word in a sentence.

1. _____

_____

2. _____

_____

3. _____

_____

C. Answer each question below.

1. Who is speaking in the poem "Father William," and what are they talking about?

_____

_____

2. "Sarah Cynthia Sylvia Stout Would Not Take the Garbage Out" offers what lesson for readers? Support your answer.

_____

_____

Additional Vocabulary Practice

"Father William"; "Sarah Cynthia Sylvia Stout Would Not Take the Garbage Out"

A. Match words and definitions or descriptions. Write the letter of the correct definition or description next to each word.

____	**1.** rancid	**a.**	wise person
____	**2.** airs	**b.**	scrape
____	**3.** scour	**c.**	pretensions; attitude of being better than others
____	**4.** curdled	**d.**	bad smelling
____	**5.** sage	**e.**	soured
____	**6.** exaggeration	**f.**	kind of fat
____	**7.** ointment	**g.**	saying something is bigger, better, or worse than it is
____	**8.** rhythm	**h.**	musical quality produced in a poem
____	**9.** meter	**i.**	pattern of syllables in a poem
____	**10.** suet	**j.**	medicinal cream

B. Choose five words from above. Use each word in a sentence.

1. _____

   _____

2. _____

   _____

3. _____

   _____

4. _____

   _____

5. _____

   _____

"The Runaway" by Robert Frost

Prereading
Vocabulary Practice

Define Some Terms Review with students the following words and definitions from student book page 587.

- *bin (line 20):* an enclosed space for storing things
- *clatter (line 15):* series of sharp, clashing sounds
- *colt (line 2):* young male horse
- *miniature (line 6):* small copy or model of something
- *pasture (line 2):* land where animals graze
- *shudders (line 18):* shakes in a sudden, violent way
- *stall (line 20):* section for one animal in a stable

Reading
Listening and Speaking Opportunity

Especially for ELL **Listen to the Audio Recording** Play the audio recording for students all the way through. Then play several lines at a time and stop and ask students to paraphrase what they heard. Have them keep their books open in front of them so they can read along as well. Guide them toward noting the changing tone of the poem; at the beginning, the narrator is casual about the horse; as the poem continues, he becomes more involved and more upset that no one is taking care of this horse. Spanish-speaking English-language learners may benefit from listening to the audio recording of the selection in Spanish.

Postreading
Alternative Activity

Understand Tone Through Rhyme Hand out copies of "The Runaway" to students. Ask them to work in small groups and mark up the copies, working out the rhyme scheme. (*ab ac bc* and then *abc a abc,* and finally *aa bc bc dd*) After marking the rhyme scheme, ask students to read the poem to each other in their groups and listen to how the rhyme scheme contributes to the tone. Guide them to see how the rhyme scheme becomes more complicated and shows the change in the poet's attitude.

SKILLS FOCUS

Literary Skills
Understand rhyme and rhyme scheme.

Resources

In this book:
- Vocabulary and Comprehension, p. 240
- Additional Vocabulary Practice, p. 244 (includes selections from the next lesson plan)

Other Resources:
- *Audio CD Library*
- *Audio CD Library, Selections and Summaries in Spanish*
- *Supporting Instruction in Spanish*

Special Education Students

Tell students "The Runaway" is a poem in which the narrator observes a young horse alone in a mountain pasture. The horse is behaving strangely and appears to be afraid of the snow.

Teacher Tip

To help students recognize the lines they are assigned to read, make photocopies of the poem before class and highlight the dialogue.

Vocabulary and Comprehension

"The Runaway"

A. Match words and definitions. Write the letter of the correct definition next to each word.

_____ **1.** pasture

_____ **2.** colt

_____ **3.** snorted

_____ **4.** bolt

_____ **5.** stall

_____ **6.** shudders

a. to run away suddenly

b. section for one animal in a stable

c. land where animals graze

d. young male horse

e. forced breath through the nose in a noisy way

f. shakes in a sudden, violent way

B. Match words and antonyms. Write the letter of the correct antonym next to each word.

_____ **1.** curled

_____ **2.** afraid

_____ **3.** dim

_____ **4.** late

a. straight

b. early

c. fearless

d. bright

C. Answer each question below.

1. Why did the speaker and a friend stop by the pasture?

_____

_____

2. Why is the fact that it is evening important in this poem?

_____

_____

3. What words does the poet use to show that the colt is afraid?

_____

_____

Elements of Literature
pages 589–592

"The Pasture" and "A Minor Bird"
by Robert Frost

SKILLS FOCUS

Literary Skills
- Understand stanzas.
- Understand couplets.

Reading Skill
Read a poem.

Prereading
Vocabulary Practice
Preview Vocabulary Preview with students the following words and their definitions.

- *pasture:* land where animals graze
- *shan't:* contraction of *shall not*
- *totters:* stands unsteadily
- *key:* musical scale used in a song

Alternative Activity
(**Especially for ELL**) **Use Spanish Resources** Spanish-speaking English-language learners may benefit from reading or listening to the selection summaries in Spanish in preparation for reading them in English.

Reading
Listening and Speaking Opportunity
(**Mixed Ability Group**) **Read Aloud/Practice Fluency** Arrange students in small groups, and have group members take turns reading aloud lines or line pairs from each poem, in a relay fashion. Encourage students to discuss their difficulties and any strategies they have for reading the poems, particularly in using pauses to separate stanzas and to end sentences. Then, have groups present their readings to the class, with group members again taking the relay approach.

Postreading
Alternative Activity
Rearrange the Poems Students may better understand the stanza structure of the poems if they try to rearrange the lines of each poem in another way. Ask students to keep the same word order of the poems but to move line breaks and create new stanzas. Ask students how their rearrangements compare to the originals. What was gained by the new arrangement? What was lost?

(Resources)

In this book:
- Vocabulary and Comprehension, p. 243
- Additional Vocabulary Practice, p. 244 (includes the previous selection)

Other Resources:
- *Audio CD Library*
- *Audio CD Library, Selections and Summaries in Spanish*
- *Supporting Instruction in Spanish*

(Especially for ELL)

English-language learners may not understand why the sentences in some poems end in the middle of lines rather than at the end of the lines. Point out to students that this strategy might make interesting rhymes or help shape the poem. Remind students as well that poems are designed to challenge the reader to see things—even everyday language—in a new light.

Literary Skills
- Understand stanzas.
- Understand couplets.

Reading Skill
Read a poem.

(**Resources**)

In this book:
- Vocabulary and Comprehension, p. 243
- Additional Vocabulary Practice, p. 244 (includes the previous selection)

Other Resources:
- *Audio CD Library*
- *Audio CD Library, Selections and Summaries in Spanish*
- *Supporting Instruction in Spanish*

(**Teacher Tip**)

Have students compare Frost's simple, direct language to Hughes's (student book pages 563–567). Ask students why poets would choose to use such language in their work.

TARGETED STRATEGIES FOR SPECIAL EDUCATION STUDENTS

Prereading
Reteach the Key Idea

Introduce the Selections Explain to students that the poems they are about to read concern very simple things in nature. The poet's message is that there is more in nature than meets the eye. Students can think of themselves as detectives while reading the poems. Ask: What important ideas does the poet find in these simple nature scenes?

Reading
Listening and Speaking Opportunity

Read Aloud/Practice Fluency Pair students, and allow each pair time to take turns reading aloud the poems to each other. Students can help each other with difficult words or phrases and offer feedback for their partner's performance.

Alternative Teaching Strategy

Examine the Stanzas and Couplets Play the audio recording of each poem one time, pausing after every stanza or couplet to allow students to discuss the main idea of each. Write students' suggestions on the chalkboard. After students have finished listening to the poems, review with them the main ideas of the stanzas and couplets. What progression or repetition of thought can students detect in the poems' organization? How do the ideas in the stanzas or couplets contribute to the main idea of the whole?

Postreading
Additional Practice

Discuss the Imagery in the Poems Give students the opportunity to review the concept of imagery by having them identify the different images in the two poems. Students should be able to name the senses appealed to by the images they mention. Ask students to evaluate the poems' images: Do they bring the reader into the world of the poems? Why or why not?

Vocabulary and Comprehension

"The Pasture" and "A Minor Bird"

A. Match words and definitions. Write the letter of the correct definition next to each word.

_____ **1.** totters

_____ **2.** minor

_____ **3.** couplet

_____ **4.** pasture

_____ **5.** stanza

a. land where animals graze

b. stands unsteadily

c. two consecutive, usually rhyming lines in a poem

d. group of lines in a poem that form a unit

e. less important or lesser in rank

B. Choose three words from above. Use each word in a sentence.

1. _____

_____

2. _____

_____

3. _____

_____

C. Write T or F next to each statement to tell if it is true or false.

_____ **1.** In "The Pasture," the speaker hurries to do his chores.

_____ **2.** The speaker in "The Pasture" wants to be left alone.

_____ **3.** In "The Pasture," the calf is compared to a human baby.

_____ **4.** In "A Minor Bird," the speaker wishes an annoying bird would go away.

_____ **5.** In "A Minor Bird," the speaker claps his hands to the beat of the bird's song.

Additional Vocabulary Practice

"The Runaway"; "The Pasture"; "A Minor Bird"

A. Match words and definitions. Write the letter of the correct definition next to each word.

_____ **1.** bin

_____ **2.** stall

_____ **3.** couplet

_____ **4.** pasture

_____ **5.** stanza

_____ **6.** totters

_____ **7.** miniature

_____ **8.** clatter

_____ **9.** shudders

_____ **10.** colt

a. a section for one animal in a stable

b. stands unsteadily

c. two consecutive, unified rhyming lines in a poem

d. an enclosed space for storing things

e. a young male horse

f. series of sharp, clashing sounds

g. shakes in a sudden, violent way

h. land where animals graze

i. a group of lines in a poem that form a unit

j. small copy or model of something

B. Choose five words from above. Use each word in a sentence.

1. _____

_____

2. _____

_____

3. _____

_____

4. _____

_____

5. _____

_____

"Names of Horses" by Donald Hall

Prereading

Vocabulary Practice

Preview Vocabulary Go over the following words and their definitions with students. Ask for volunteers to use each in a sentence.

- *brute (p. 594):* strong, unthinking
- *sledges (p. 594):* trailers designed to be dragged
- *buggy (p. 594):* small vehicle drawn by a horse
- *stall (p. 594):* section for one animal in a stable
- *slug (p. 595):* bullet

Alternative Activity

(**Especially for ELL**) **Use Spanish Resources** Spanish-speaking English-language learners may benefit from reading or listening to the selection summary in Spanish in preparation for reading the selection in English.

Reading

Alternative Activities

(**Especially for ELL**) **Play the Audio Recording** Increase comprehension of the selection by having students listen to the audio recording of the poem as they follow along in their books.

Note the Literary Elements Have students re-read the poem with pen or pencil in hand, noting examples of the literary elements in the poem on a separate sheet of paper. On their papers, students can circle the examples of imagery, underline any alliteration, and draw a box around any onomatopoeia. Remind students that they will probably need to read the poem more than once to catch all the elements used.

Postreading

Alternative Assessment

Check Students' Notes Check over students' notes of the literary elements in the poem to assess their understanding of the poem and the key ideas. Discuss with students the rhythm of the poem, and ask a volunteer to read aloud while the rest of the class taps the beat of the words.

SKILLS FOCUS

Literary Skills
- Understand free verse.
- Understand elegy.

Resources

In this book:
- Vocabulary and Comprehension, p. 246
- Additional Vocabulary Practice, p. 251 (includes the next two selections)

Other Resources:
- *Audio CD Library*
- *Audio CD Library, Selections and Summaries in Spanish*
- *Supporting Instruction in Spanish*

Special Education Students

Students may be overwhelmed by the list of literary elements on student book page 593. Help students by pointing out specific examples of each in this poem and in other poems they have read in this collection.

Vocabulary and Comprehension

"Names of Horses"

A. Match words and definitions. Write the letter of the correct definition next to each word.

_____ **1.** chaffy

_____ **2.** hames

_____ **3.** brute

_____ **4.** buggy

_____ **5.** slug

a. strong, unthinking

b. full of hay or straw

c. small vehicle drawn by a horse

d. bullet

e. pieces along a horse's collar

B. Choose three words from above. Use each word in a sentence.

1. _____

_____

2. _____

_____

3. _____

_____

C. Write T or F next to each statement to tell if it is true or false.

_____ **1.** "Names of Horses" begins with the names of the poet's favorite horses.

_____ **2.** The poet refers to the horses in the third person.

_____ **3.** The poem talks about working horses rather than racing ones.

_____ **4.** The poet describes at length the horse giving birth to a foal.

_____ **5.** At the end of the poem, the horse is set free to wander the prairie.

"maggie and milly and molly and may" by E. E. Cummings

Prereading
Additional Background

Recognize a Poet's Tone E. E. Cummings was a poet, a painter, and a playwright. He believed that art should be a living experience for the reader, viewer, and audience, as well as for the artist. Quirks of style are a trademark of his poetry. Discuss with students the meaning of "quirks of style." Point out that Cummings did not like to use capitalization in his poetry, and that this particular quirk was not limited to "maggie and milly and molly and may."

Reading
Reteach the Key Idea

(Especially for ELL) **Find Meaning in Rhyme** To help English-language learners find meaning through rhyme, read the poem aloud or play the audio recording. Ask students what they notice about the first line of the poem. Model reading the line, stressing its rhythmic ebb and flow. Have students, reading together, mimic your reading several times. Ask if they can hear the waves in the rhythm.

Ask students why the poet chose the alliterative names *maggie, milly, molly,* and *may.* Why not *douglas, donald, dennis,* and *dave?* Elicit that the *m* sound is a softer, more flowing sound, like the continuous flow of the waves.

Ask students to find the exact rhymes in the poem. Point out that the first couplet and the last two couplets are exact rhymes, and that the parentheses in the first couplet stack two words, *play* and *day,* that rhyme with *may.*

Postreading
Additional Practice

Present the Correct Sequence Prepare eight strips of paper and write the following on them: the six couplets on six of the strips, the poet's name on one strip, the title of the poem on one strip. Mix the strips up, and turn them face down. Have eight students in turn choose a strip and then read their strip aloud. After the strips have been read, have students arrange the poem in the correct order. Then ask them to read their strips again—in the correct sequence.

SKILLS FOCUS

Literary Skills
Understand exact and slant rhymes.

Resources

In this book:
- Vocabulary and Comprehension, p. 250 (includes the next selection)
- Additional Vocabulary Practice, p. 251 (includes the previous and the next selection)

Other Resources:
- *Audio CD Library*
- *Audio CD Library, Selections and Summaries in Spanish*
- *Supporting Instruction in Spanish*

Core Skill

Use the resources in the Reading Skills and Strategies section of this book to teach a core literary skill in which your struggling readers need remediation, such as recognizing theme. Use "maggie and milly and molly and may" for the application portion of the lesson.

Literary Skills
Understand exact and slant rhymes.

Resources
In this book:
• Vocabulary and Comprehension, p. 250 (includes the next selection)
• Additional Vocabulary Practice, p. 251 (includes the previous and the next selection)

Other Resources:
• *Audio CD Library*
• *Audio CD Library, Selections and Summaries in Spanish*
• *Supporting Instruction in Spanish*

TARGETED STRATEGIES FOR SPECIAL EDUCATION STUDENTS

Prereading
Additional Background

Understand the Poet's Way Introduce students to E. E. Cummings by explaining that he is a famous poet who is known for his unusual style (way) of writing poetry. Ask students to tell you if they notice anything different about the way the poem looks. Point out that he does not use capital letters.

Reading
Alternative Activity

Examine Rhyme and Rhythm Help students understand that in "maggie and milly and molly and may," the poet uses rhyme and rhythm to create the feeling of young girls playing in the sand and waves at the beach. Have students read aloud the first two lines. Point out the rhyming words, and ask students to tell which words are accented. Have them find another pair of lines that ends with a rhyme and follows the same rhythm. (*may came home with a smooth round stone/as small as a world and as large as alone*) Continue the discussion of rhythm. Point out that the poet alternates between accenting the first word and the second word at the beginning of each couplet.

Postreading
Additional Activity

Extend the Theme Help students understand that Cummings wanted his readers to live the moment he was writing about. He wanted the readers of "maggie and milly and molly and may" to experience through his words how it would be to be a child playing on the beach on a beautiful day. Have students think of a favorite place they have been. Ask them to remember what that place was like. Have them recall the smells that surrounded them. What were the sounds they heard? Were they soft and gentle or loud and distracting? Ask them to think about the things they may have touched. Were they tender and inviting or hard or prickly? Have students recall their special place as vividly as they can. Then, have them think of how they could describe spending a day at their place to a friend. Have them write a poem to share the moment, as Cummings did. Invite students to read their poems to the class.

"All in green went my love riding"
by E. E. Cummings

Prereading
Vocabulary Practice

(Especially for ELL) **Preview Vocabulary** Go over the following words and their definitions with students (found on student book page 602).

- *lean (line 4):* thin
- *merry (line 5):* happy
- *fleeter (line 6):* faster
- *dappled (line 6):* spotted; patched with color
- *lithe (line 17):* gracefully thin, flexible
- *sheer (line 25):* steep
- *daunting (line 26):* inspiring fear; dreadful

Reading
Fluency Practice

(Mixed Ability Group) **Practice Oral Reading** Play the audio recording of the poem while students follow along in their books. Next, ask students to listen while you read. Then, have them read with you, line by line, so they can remember phrasing and pronunciation. The simple, beautiful language of this poem also makes it a good candidate for oral reading in groups. Have students practice in small groups; you may have them read in Popcorn fashion (see page xxix of this book). Circulate among groups to help with pronunciation.

Postreading
Alternative Assessment

Name That Literary Element Divide the class into two teams to play "Name That Literary Element." Make a three-column chart on the chalkboard, titling the columns *Rhyme*, *Repetition*, and *Alliteration*. Call on a student from the first team to name an example of rhyme in the poem and to write the example in the correct column. Then, ask a member of the second team to name an example of repetition in the poem and to write that example in the correct column. Continue to alternate between the two teams, filling in their answers in the columns in order. The team that gives the most correct answers wins.

SKILLS FOCUS

Literary Skills
Understand the sounds of poetry, such as rhyme, repetition, and alliteration.

(Resources)

In this book:
- Vocabulary and Comprehension, p. 250 (includes the previous selection)
- Additional Vocabulary Practice, p. 251 (includes the previous two selections)

Other Resources:
- *Audio CD Library*
- *Audio CD Library, Selections and Summaries in Spanish*
- *Supporting Instruction in Spanish*

(Special Education Students)

Students may have trouble with the inverted word order in many of the lines of the poem. You may have students work in small groups to rewrite the poem in their own words.

Vocabulary and Comprehension

"maggie and milly and molly and may"; "All in green went my love riding"

A. Complete each sentence with a word from the Word Bank.

1. Someone who is sleepy or exhausted might have a

_____ air.

2. Never throw a rock off a _____ cliff
because you never know what might be below.

3. Carrie prefers to cook with _____ meat
because it has less fat in it.

4. The dancers performed the piece with a _____ grace.

5. Which is _____, a galloping horse or a sprinting human?

Word Bank
languid
lithe
fleeter
lean
sheer

B. Choose two words from above. Use each word in a sentence.

1. _____

_____

2. _____

_____

C. Write T or F next to each statement to tell if it is true or false.

_____ **1.** The poem "maggie and milly and molly and may" is
about a trip to the beach.

_____ **2.** Each character in "maggie and milly and molly and
may" finds something interesting.

_____ **3.** In "All in green went my love riding," the speaker's love
is hunting deer.

_____ **4.** The speaker's love in "All in green went my love riding"
is accompanied by four dogs.

Additional Vocabulary Practice

"Names of Horses"; "maggie and milly and molly and may"; "All in green went my love riding"

A. Complete each sentence with a word from the Word Bank.

1. If cleverness doesn't work to open that jam jar, try

   _____ strength.

2. Pedro found the idea of completing all of the algebra

   homework very _____.

3. The sunlight _____ the lush meadow
   with spangles of gold.

4. The rescuers had to make a homemade _____ with which
   they could drag the injured man to safety.

5. The _____ reeds along the riverbanks bent in the evening
   breeze.

> **Word Bank**
> brute
> sledge
> daunting
> dappled
> lithe

B. Choose two words from above. Use each word in a sentence.

1. _____

   _____

2. _____

   _____

C. Give a definition for each of the following terms.

1. imagery:

   _____

2. alliteration:

   _____

3. onomatopoeia:

   _____

"Arithmetic" by Carl Sandburg

SKILLS FOCUS

Literary Skill
Understand catalog poems.

(**Resources**)

In this book:
• Vocabulary and Comprehension, p. 254 (includes the next selection)
• Additional Vocabulary Practice, p. 255 (includes the next selection)

Other Resources:
• *Audio CD Library*
• *Audio CD Library, Selections and Summaries in Spanish*
• *Supporting Instruction in Spanish*

(**Special Education Students**)

Alert students to the highly figurative use of language in the poem. You may want to review the definition of *metaphor* with students and ask them to provide examples.

Prereading
Reteach the Key Idea

Introduce the Selection Ask students for their ideas on how a list could possibly be poetic. Lead them to see that a poet often describes a series of beautiful things in a poem, and that a catalog poem might merely be a more direct and efficient way of getting at that beauty. Then, ask: *What could be beautiful about arithmetic?* After students have shared their opinions and predictions, have them read the poem.

Alternative Activity

(**Especially for ELL**) **Use Spanish Resources** Spanish-speaking English-language learners may benefit from reading or listening to the selection summary in Spanish in preparation for reading the selection in English.

Reading
Alternative Activities

Play the Audio Recording To increase comprehension and help students hear the irregular meter of the poem, have students listen to the audio recording of the poem as they follow along in their books.

Restate in Your Own Words Because so many of the items in Sandburg's list are highly metaphorical, it may be helpful for students to restate the "main idea" of each item in the list. Emphasize to students that they are not trying to find a set answer for each item, but only to come up with their own personal interpretation of the poet's wordplay. Students may record their ideas in a chart to keep each item organized and separate from the others.

Postreading
Alternative Activity

(**Mixed Ability Group**) **Write a Catalog Poem** Have students meet in pairs to use "Arithmetic" as a model for writing their own catalog poems. Remind groups that their lists should contain items that fall under one subject or overall theme. Ask volunteers to share their groups' results with the class.

"For Poets" by Al Young

Prereading

Reteach the Key Idea

Introduce the Selection Ask students if they think writing poetry is an art—like painting, for example. Why or why not? Discuss with students how any art involves hard work and practice. Ask: *Is it possible to work too hard in perfecting one's art?*

Alternative Activity

(**Especially for ELL**) **Use Spanish Resources** Spanish-speaking English-language learners may benefit from reading or listening to the selection summary in Spanish in preparation for reading the selection in English.

Reading

Alternative Activity

Play the Audio Recording Have struggling readers listen to the audio recording of the poem as they follow along in their books. Invite them to listen for examples of metaphors and similes and jot them down as they listen.

Fluency Practice

Practice Oral Reading After you play the audio recording of the poem, read the poem aloud yourself. Then, ask students to read aloud with you, line by line, so they can concentrate on the phrasing. Discuss the different ways one might read the poem aloud, using different pauses and emphases. What choices of phrasing, pausing, and emphasis do students prefer, and why?

Postreading

Alternative Assessment

Paraphrase the Poem Point out to students that as a poem about writing poetry, "For Poets" has a main idea and might even include supporting details. Have students paraphrase the poem. Then, have students circle the main ideas in their paraphrases and underline any supporting details. Have partners check each other's main ideas and details for validity.

SKILLS FOCUS

Literary Skills
• Understand ars poetica.
• Understand figures of speech.

Reading Skill
Read a poem.

(**Resources**)

In this book:
• Vocabulary and Comprehension, p. 254 (includes the previous selection)
• Additional Vocabulary Practice, p. 255 (includes the previous selection)

Other Resources:
• *Audio CD Library*
• *Audio CD Library, Selections and Summaries in Spanish*
• *Supporting Instruction in Spanish*

(**Special Education Students**)

Prepare students for reading the poem by asking them what they have learned by writing their own poetry. What would they not have realized about poetry if they had not written their own poems? Discuss with students how poets might talk to one another about the craft of writing poetry.

Vocabulary and Comprehension

"Arithmetic"; "For Poets"

A. Complete each sentence with a word or phrase from the Word Bank.

1. "The diving hawk was a ray of sun" is an example of

a(n) _____.

2. Language that is not literal is called

_____.

3. "As silent as the night" is an example of a

_____.

4. A poem written about poetry is called an _____.

5. A _____ poem is simply made up of a list.

Word Bank
metaphor
simile
catalog
ars poetica
figurative
language

B. Choose three words from above. Use each word in a sentence.

1. _____

_____

2. _____

_____

3. _____

_____

C. Write T or F next to each statement to tell if it is true or false.

_____ **1.** The poem "Arithmetic" is about a boy's first day at a new school.

_____ **2.** "Arithmetic" is a list of practical, everyday ways to use mathematics.

_____ **3.** "For Poets" advises poets to write four hours every day.

_____ **4.** In "For Poets," the poet advises other poets not to forget to use proper punctuation.

_____ **5.** One piece of advice the poet gives in "For Poets" is to "stay beautiful."

Additional Vocabulary Practice

"Arithmetic"; "For Poets"

A. Match words and definitions. Write the letter of the correct definition next to each word.

_____ **1.** simile

_____ **2.** figurative

_____ **3.** *ars poetica*

_____ **4.** catalog poem

_____ **5.** metaphor

a. poem in the form of a list

b. poem about poetry

c. not literal

d. comparison using *like* or *as*

e. direct comparison

B. Choose three words from above. Use each word in a sentence.

1. _____

_____

2. _____

_____

3. _____

_____

C. Give an example of each.

1. metaphor:

_____

2. simile:

_____

Author Study: Sandra Cisneros

Literary Skill
Interpret a writer's message.

Reading Skill
Make generalizations.

Resources {icon}
In this book:
• Vocabulary and
Comprehension, p. 258
• Additional Vocabulary
Practice, p. 259

(Especially for ELL)

Students may find much of the material Cisneros writes about to be very familiar to them, or they may have experienced similar emotions about being a bilingual speaker in the United States. Have students channel this natural interest by allowing them time to quickwrite about Cisneros's work. They can use their notes when examining the author's messages.

Prereading
Vocabulary Practice

Preview Additional Vocabulary The vocabulary of the selections should not be too much trouble for students, but you may want to preview the following words and their definitions.

• *raw (p. 616):* unfinished; unpolished
• *nub (p. 616):* small end: leftover bit
• *fashion (p. 622):* custom
• *fan (p. 620):* make air blow over a surface
• *scuffed (p. 621):* dirtied by dragging

Reading
Alternative Activity

Use a Chart You may consider reading the selection aloud to students, stopping from time to time to discuss the images, metaphors, and messages of the text and to fill in a chart like the following.

	Images	Metaphors	Messages
"Salvador Late or Early"			
"Chanclas"			
"Abuelito Who"			
"The Place Where Dreams Come From"			

Postreading
Alternative Assessment

(Mixed Ability Group) **Interview the Author** Arrange students in small groups, and have each group member write a question he or she would like to ask Sandra Cisneros. Then, have group members take turns playing the writer and answering their fellow group members' questions. Students should be able to point to specific places in the works that support their answers.

TARGETED STRATEGIES FOR SPECIAL EDUCATION STUDENTS

Literary Skill
Interpret a writer's message.

Reading Skill
Make generalizations.

Resources
In this book:
- Vocabulary and Comprehension, p. 258
- Additional Vocabulary Practice, p. 259

Prereading
Reteach the Key Idea

Review Images and Metaphors Ask students to think of examples of images that involve different senses, and lead students to discuss how imagery helps a writer share an experience with a reader. You may want to have students think of images related to their immediate surroundings—the classroom or the school. Then, ask students for similar examples of metaphors. Remind them that a metaphor is a direct comparison. Discuss with students how both elements can make a text rich and alive to a reader.

Reading
Alternative Teaching Strategy

Read the Works Aloud Students will benefit from hearing the stories, poem, and essay read aloud. To help students focus on the message of each piece, encourage them to draw a picture as they listen to the work. In the case of the poem, you may want to have several volunteers take turns reading it. Emphasize to students that they should try to express in their drawings the feelings stirred in them by the texts and then relate those feelings to what they think are the main ideas of the selections. Students should label each drawing with the text's title and then try to put the feelings into words, writing on the back of each drawing a list of words that describe the text's message.

Postreading
Alternative Activity

Make Generalizations Ask students to think of times when they make generalizations in their everyday lives. Point out that generalizations help people predict and understand things. Move the discussion next to the subject of the selections students have just read. What generalizations did they make based on the selections, and how did the generalizations help them understand the selections? Remind students to give examples to support their statements.

Vocabulary and Comprehension

Author Study: Sandra Cisneros

A. Match words and definitions. Write the letter of the correct definition next to each word.

_____ **1.** fan

_____ **2.** scuffed

_____ **3.** fashion

_____ **4.** nub

_____ **5.** raw

a. dirtied by dragging

b. custom

c. small end; leftover bit

d. unfinished; unpolished

e. make air blow over a surface

B. Choose three words from above. Use each word in a sentence.

1. _____

_____

2. _____

_____

3. _____

_____

C. Write T or F next to each statement to tell if it is true or false.

_____ **1.** In "Chanclas," a young girl is eager to show off her new dance moves.

_____ **2.** Cisneros states that "Salvador Late or Early" is based on a real boy.

_____ **3.** In "Abuelito Who," Cisneros draws on fond memories of her grandfather.

_____ **4.** In "The Place Where Dreams Come From," Cisneros discusses the inspiration for "Abuelito Who."

_____ **5.** Cisneros does not approve of writing in more than one language at a time.

Additional Vocabulary Practice

Author Study: Sandra Cisneros

A. Complete each sentence with a word or phrase from the Word Bank.

1. If you are hot, you should _____ yourself with this leaflet.

2. After dragging his heels in the dirt, Alex found his

brand-new boots were _____.

3. Yolanda wanted to write the answer on the board but

could find only a _____ of chalk.

4. Timothy works on a ranch and likes to dress in cowboy

_____.

5. The _____ recruit did not know how to do anything except state his name and stare.

Word Bank
raw
nub
fashion
fan
scuffed

B. Choose three words from above. Use each word in a sentence.

1. _____

_____

2. _____

_____

3. _____

_____

C. Define each of the following literary terms.

1. author's message:

_____

2. generalization:

_____

Collection 6
Our Literary Heritage:
Greek Myths and World Folk Tales

Elements of Literature: The Myths of Greece and Rome

Alternative Teaching Strategies

Imagine a Classical Conflict Tell students that the Greek and Roman gods were often in conflict with humans and with one another. The gods were at times described as being motivated by such familiar human characteristics as selfishness, jealousy, love, hate, and generosity. Sometimes, the realms of the gods overlapped, which caused friction among them. Have students review the list of the Greek and Roman gods and goddesses on page 647 of their books, and ask them to imagine ways in which the concerns of those listed might have conflicted. Write students' conflict suggestions on the chalkboard, and encourage them to keep their ideas in mind as they read the selections in the first part of this collection.

(Mixed Ability Group) Create a Modern Myth Remind students that Greek and Roman myths were designed to explain things around the ancient Greeks and Romans. Ask students to imagine how the Greeks and Romans might explain things students see around them in their own lives, such as weather events, disasters, or technological devices such as cell phones and television sets. Challenge small groups of students to pick one distinctly modern element—a microwave oven, for example, or tornadoes—and create a god for that element. What characteristics would the goddess of tennis shoes have, and why? With what problems or conflicts would such a goddess find herself involved? Ask groups to share their brief tales with the class.

Academic Vocabulary

(Especially for ELL) Build Vocabulary Help students develop their academic vocabulary by reinforcing these words and their definitions.

- *civilization (p. 646):* an organized, structured society with shared traditions, laws, and values
- *ancient (p. 646):* old; from long ago
- *classical (p. 646):* of or relating to the periods of ancient Greek and Roman civilization
- *originated (p. 646):* began
- *divinities (p. 647):* gods

SKILLS FOCUS

Literary Skills
Understand Greek and Roman myths.

(Cultural Tip)

Emphasize to students that the Greeks and Romans were not the only civilizations to draw on mythology to explain the world around them. You may want to bring to class articles or books on other world mythological systems for students to peruse and discuss.

(Teacher Tip)

To engage students' interest, turn discussion sessions into a game with ball tosses. The person making a statement or asking a question tosses the ball, and the person catching it comments on the statement or attempts to answer the question.

(**Teacher Tip**)

The names of the Greek and
Roman gods will be new to
most students. Allow for
frequent review of the
names, their pronunciation,
and the main characteristics
or areas of power of
each god.

TARGETED STRATEGIES FOR SPECIAL EDUCATION STUDENTS

Elements of Literature: The Myths of Greece and Rome

Background

Greek and Roman Gods' Names in the World Today Students
may recognize the names of some of the Greek and Roman gods. Ask
students to identify familiar names and to give the context in which
they have heard the names used. Students may note, for example,
that many of the gods' names have been given to planets in the solar
system. Discuss with students why the planets might be given such
names and what the use of the gods' names tells us about how we
view these classical deities today.

Reteach the Key Idea

View Classical Art Students will have an easier time identifying
and understanding the different classical gods if they have viewed
representations of them. Bring to class books that contain photographs
of classical statues and paintings of the gods and goddesses. Discuss
with students what they can tell about the gods' characteristics from
the representations of them.

Alternative Activity

Reinforce the Concept: The Uses of Mythology Ask students if
they have read a story that teaches a moral. Discuss with students
how the moral comes through in the stories they mention. Ask: Why
are stories useful in presenting a lesson or explanation? Point out to
students that myths offer lessons about life and often concentrate on
why something in life is the way it is.

Alternative Assessment

(**Mixed Ability Group**) **Play a Matching Game** Have students
work in small groups to prepare two sets of note cards, one set that
includes the name of a god or goddess on each card and one set that
gives a description of a god or goddess. (Use the chart on student
book page 647.) Group members can take turns shuffling the cards
and then matching each god or goddess to his or her correct
description.

"The Origin of the Seasons"

retold by Olivia Coolidge

Prereading

Alternative Activities

Use *The Holt Reader* You may consider having students use the Before You Read page in *The Holt Reader,* either instead of or in addition to the Before You Read page in the student book.

Read the Adaptation Distribute copies of the adapted reading of "The Origin of the Seasons" (available in this book and, with marginal questions, in *Holt Adapted Reader*). To prepare for reading the original version and to practice fluency, students should read the adaptation silently. Encourage students to write notes, questions, predictions, reactions, and comments on the worksheets as they read.

Vocabulary Practice

Preview Selection Vocabulary Preview with students the following words and their definitions. Have students use each word in an original sentence.

- *majestic (p. 655):* impressive; royal in appearance
- *ears (p. 655):* spikes bearing the grain
- *garlands (p. 655):* decorative chains or lengths of harvested plants or fruit
- *cascaded (p. 656):* fell in a rush
- *turf (p. 656):* ground
- *tidings (p. 656):* information
- *chariot (p. 656):* a vehicle pulled by horses
- *consent (p. 656):* agreement
- *immortal (p. 658):* one who will not die
- *anoint (p. 658):* ritually apply a sacred substance
- *embers (p. 658):* fire coals
- *stoop (p. 658):* bend down
- *crooning (p. 658):* singing
- *sower (p. 660):* planter
- *crafty (p. 661):* clever; resourceful
- *gloomier (p. 661):* sadder
- *decreed (p. 661):* stated officially

SKILLS FOCUS

Literary Skill
Understand origin myths.

Reading Skill
Understand cause and effect.

Resources

In this book:
- Adapted Readings
- Vocabulary and Comprehension, p. 267
- Additional Vocabulary Practice, p. 273 (includes the next two selections)

Other Resources:
- *The Holt Reader*
- *Holt Adapted Reader*
- *Audio CD Library*
- *Audio CD Library, Selections and Summaries in Spanish*
- *Supporting Instruction in Spanish*

Especially for ELL

You may want to have students share any origin myths that they know from their own or other cultures. After students share their examples, ask the class what each myth explains.

Teacher Tip

Students may not
understand the significance
of the harvest failures as
described in the story.
Remind students that when
this tale was told, people
were highly dependent
upon good weather to
provide them with food.
One crop failure could
mean disaster for many
people.

Reading
Alternative Activities

Use *The Holt Reader* You may consider having students read the
selection in *The Holt Reader* and use the margins in that book to
make notes and respond to the instruction.

Especially for ELL **Play the Audio Recording** Struggling
readers will benefit from listening to the audio recording of the
selection while they follow along in their books. Encourage students
to make notes of the causes and effects in the story.

Additional Practice

Mixed Ability Group Use a Flowchart/Practice Fluency
Arrange students in small groups to read the story aloud together. As
the groups read, the members should pause periodically to identify
causes and effects in the section of the story they have just read. Have
groups record their causes and effects in a flowchart such as the one
below. Emphasize to students that causes and effects form a chain in
a story, with the effect of one cause becoming the cause itself of the
next effect. After groups have finished reading, allow them time to
share their results with the class. Draw a collective cause-and-effect
chain flowchart on the chalkboard after the groups have shared their
work.

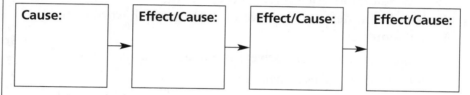

| Cause: | Effect/Cause: | Effect/Cause: | Effect/Cause: |

Postreading
Alternative Activity

Use *The Holt Reader* You may consider having students use the
After You Read page in *The Holt Reader,* either instead of or in
addition to the After You Read page in the student book.

Listening and Speaking Opportunity

Mixed Ability Group **Perform a Scene from the Myth** Arrange
students in small groups, and have each group choose an important
scene from the myth. Tell groups that they should be prepared to
identify and explain the important causes and effects of the scene
they choose. Group members can assign roles for the speaking parts
and enlist any additional members to act as props, such as trees or
chairs. Give students time to rehearse. Then, have each group
perform its scene for the class. Encourage students to be very
expressive in their reading of their roles.

Vocabulary Development

Reteach the Key Idea

Understand Prefixes To underscore what a prefix adds to a word, have students review the words they listed in their charts for the Practice activity on page 663 of their books. Students should look up the root of each of the words in a dictionary and add the root's meaning to each row in their charts. Then, ask students to compare the meaning of the root to the meaning of the word that results with the addition of the prefix. What, if anything, does the prefix add to the root? Does it alter the root's meaning?

Additional Practice

Use Descriptive Words Have each student write a one-paragraph description of a room at their school, using as many descriptive words as possible and appealing to as many senses as possible. Ask volunteers to read their descriptions aloud to the class.

Reading Skills Development

Identifying Causes and Effects Point out to students having difficulty identifying causes and effects in the story that causes answer the question "Why?" Causes tell why events happen. Effects answer the question "What happened?" Effects tell how characters react to events. Have students read the myth "The Flight of Icarus" that begins on student book page 676. As they read the myth, students should stop from time to time to ask, "Why?" or "What happened?" Students can record the answers to their questions and then, after reading, arrange their notes in the form of a cause-and-effect flowchart like the one below. Have students compare their charts with those of partners.

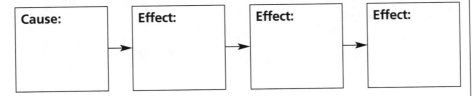

Vocabulary Skills
- Understand Greek prefixes.
- Use descriptive words.

TARGETED STRATEGIES FOR SPECIAL EDUCATION STUDENTS

Prereading
Reteach the Key Idea

Introduce the Selection Explain to students that "The Origin of the Seasons" attempts to make a different world seem realistic. One way the story succeeds in making that world real is by using many vivid words to describe the setting and events of the story. Prepare students for the descriptive language in the story by having them brainstorm vivid words or phrases that describe their own world— for example, the place where they live and the people they meet every day.

Reading
Alternative Teaching Strategy

Identify the Main Idea of the Story Guide students in recognizing that the title of the story tells them what the myth will explain: the origin of the seasons, or how the different seasons came into existence. Discuss briefly the differences between spring and summer on the one hand and fall and winter on the other, describing not only how the natural world appears but also how humans react to the seasonal changes. Have students record their ideas in a simple chart such as the one below. As they read, students should look for specific details that explain the differences among the seasons and note those details in their charts as well.

Spring and Summer	Fall and Winter

Postreading
Reteach the Key Idea

Make the Connection After students have finished reading the story, have them each write in their own words an answer to this question: *Why are the seasons different according to the Greeks?* Have students give the myth's reasons for the differences among the seasons, including details that support the main idea of the story.

Vocabulary and Comprehension

"The Origin of the Seasons"

A. Match words and definitions. Write the letter of the correct definition next to each word.

_____ **1.** narcissus

_____ **2.** pomegranate

_____ **3.** plowshare

_____ **4.** ambrosia

_____ **5.** reaping

a. cutting and gathering grain

b. a type of flower

c. food of the gods

d. cutting blade of a plow

e. a type of fruit

B. Choose three words from above. Use each word in a sentence.

1. _____

_____

2. _____

_____

3. _____

_____

C. Write T or F next to each statement to tell if it is true or false.

_____ **1.** Demeter was the goddess of the underworld.

_____ **2.** Persephone was always a very sad little girl.

_____ **3.** Persephone was taken by Zeus to Mount Olympus.

_____ **4.** Persephone agreed to marry Hades.

_____ **5.** While in the underworld, Persephone ate seven pomegranate seeds.

"Orpheus, the Great Musician"

retold by Olivia Coolidge;

"The Power of Music"

from Nadja on My Way, by Nadja Salerno-Sonnenberg

SKILLS FOCUS

Literary Skill
Identify elements of myth: the underworld.

Reading Skills
• Summarize.
• Distinguish fact from opinion.
• Understand anecdote.

Resources

In this book:
• Vocabulary and Comprehension, p. 272
• Additional Vocabulary Practice, p. 273 (includes the previous selection)

Other Resources:
• Audio CD Library
• Audio CD Library, Selections and Summaries in Spanish
• Supporting Instruction in Spanish

Teacher Tip

Explain to students that the word *retold* in the byline of "Orpheus, the Great Musician" means the writer is giving her version of an old tale that originally existed in an oral form and that other written versions exist.

Prereading

Alternative Activity

Especially for ELL **Use Spanish Resources** Spanish-speaking English-language learners may benefit from reading or listening to the summaries of "Orpheus, the Great Musician" and "The Power of Music" in Spanish in preparation for reading the selections in English.

Vocabulary Practice

Preview Additional Vocabulary Preview with students these words and definitions from the selection "Orpheus, the Great Musician." Have students use each word in an original sentence.

• *legend (p. 666):* a traditional story about a hero from long ago
• *sorrowed (p. 666):* mourned
• *ferryman (p. 667):* a man who handles a boat that ferries people from one place to another, usually across a river or bay
• *ranks (p. 667):* lines or organized groups
• *ebony (p. 667):* made of the dark wood of a tropical tree
• *shade (p. 668):* ghost
• *hastened (p. 668):* hurried
• *flitting (p. 668):* moving about quickly

Reading

Alternative Activity

Play the Audio Recording Play the audio recording of "Orpheus, the Great Musician," and ask pairs of students to follow along in their books. Pause every few paragraphs for partners to identify the elements of myth (main characters, conflict, main events, and resolution) in what they have just read.

Reteach the Key Idea

Core Skill Identify Fact and Opinion in "The Power of Music"

Remind students that a fact is a piece of information that can be proved true or false, while an opinion is someone's viewpoint on a subject, which cannot be proved true or false. Review the examples of fact and opinion found on student book page 672. On the chalkboard, make a two-column chart, like the one below, labeled "Fact" and "Opinion." Pause at appropriate points in the reading to have students identify facts and opinions. Record their responses in the chart.

Fact	Opinion

Fluency Opportunity

Especially for ELL **Practice Shadow Reading** To help students practice fluency in reading and speaking, ask them to shadow-read "The Power of Music" with you. When students shadow-read, they listen to the teacher's voice and speak immediately after, trying to imitate the teacher as closely as possible. This encourages students to focus on pronunciation and intonation.

Postreading

Alternative Activities

Core Skill **Compare Myths** Students having difficulty comparing "Orpheus, the Great Musician" with "The Origin of the Seasons" may benefit from using a Venn diagram instead of the chart on student book page 670. Draw on the chalkboard the diagram below and ask pairs of students to fill it in using the questions from the chart on page 670 of their texts.

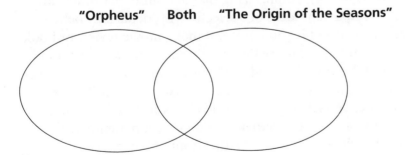

"Orpheus"   Both   "The Origin of the Seasons"

Write a Letter of Advice Remind students that myths explain the origins of things but also serve as lessons on how people should behave. Discuss with students their ideas about how the story of Orpheus gives a lesson in human behavior. What mistakes does Orpheus make, and why? Have each student write a brief, informal letter Orpheus might send back from the underworld to offer friendly advice on ways others might learn from his own mistakes.

> **Especially for ELL**
> Students may have difficulty keeping track of the names of the characters in the myth. Have students make a list on a separate sheet of paper of the characters' names and their descriptions. The glossary will aid them in comprehending the reading and in summarizing the selection.

Vocabulary Skills
- Clarify word meanings.
- Understand figurative language.

Vocabulary Development

Additional Practice

Clarify Word Meanings   Have students make up reasonable answers to the following questions. Each of the items includes an underlined word from the selection "Orpheus, the Great Musician."

1. The prince <u>sorrowed</u>. What just happened to the prince?
2. The poet told of an interesting <u>legend</u>. What kind of story did the poet tell?
3. The soldiers stood in <u>ranks</u>. What might be the event the soldiers are attending?
4. The prince <u>hastened</u> to the meadow. What was in the meadow?
5. The princess <u>flitted</u> to her window. What was at the princess's window?

Reteach the Key Idea

More Examples of Similes   Students will benefit from examining examples of similes that use words other than *like*. Provide students with the following examples. Have students identify the word of comparison and the two words being compared.

1. The sky at sunset resembled a glowing coal from a dying fire. (<u>resembled</u>; *sky* and *coal*)
2. He was angrier than a rattlesnake tied up in a granny knot. (<u>than</u>; *he* and *rattlesnake*)
3. The dancer moved as gracefully as a swan across the stage. (<u>as</u>; *dancer* and *swan*)

(Core Skill)

Use the resources in the Reading Skills and Strategies section of this book to help students having difficulty distinguishing fact from opinion. Use "The Power of Music" for the application portion of the lesson.

Reading Skills Development

(Mixed Ability Group) **Summarize**   Briefly review with students what to include in a summary (see the Before You Read page on student book page 664), emphasizing that in a summary one relates only the most important ideas of a selection. Students may better understand the concept if you point out that a movie review or book review is sometimes little more than a summary plus a statement of whether or not the work is "good" or "worthwhile." Arrange students in small, mixed ability groups to take turns reading from "Orpheus, the Great Musician" (see page xxix of this book for the Break-in reading activity) and note together with their group members the main ideas of each section of the myth. Group members can use these notes after they have finished reading to put together a summary of the myth.

TARGETED STRATEGIES FOR SPECIAL EDUCATION STUDENTS

Prereading
Alternative Teaching Strategy

Preview Autobiographical Anecdote Before reading the selection "The Power of Music," review the terms *autobiography* and *anecdote* with students. Ask them to give their opinions on why a writer might feel compelled to tell a personal story to make a point. What kinds of important lessons can one learn from one's own experiences? Encourage students to think about important points they could make with their own experiences, and allow students to freewrite on the subject, telling them beforehand that they will not have to share their responses with anyone.

Reading
Alternative Teaching Strategy

Make a Comic Strip To help students summarize "Orpheus, the Great Musician," ask them to make a comic-strip version of the myth as they read. Tell students that the panels for their comics should cover no more than a page and should number no more than about a dozen panels. Students should choose what they think are the most important scenes from the story to reproduce in their strips. Encourage students to use captions to tell the important parts of the story and to use "word bubbles" in the panels to relate the characters' dialogue and thoughts. Ask volunteers to share their comic strips with the class.

Postreading
Alternative Assessment

Check Comprehension To assess students' comprehension of "Orpheus, the Great Musician" and "The Power of Music," ask them either to meet with a partner to retell the myth briefly as if they were an oral storyteller or to work on their own to write a poem that expresses their feelings on the power of music with references to either or both of the selections.

Literary Skill
Identify elements of myth: the underworld.

Reading Skills
- Summarize.
- Distinguish fact from opinion.
- Understand anecdote.

Resources
In this book:
- Vocabulary and Comprehension, p. 272
- Additional Vocabulary Practice, p. 273 (includes the previous selection)

Other Resources:
- *Audio CD Library*
- *Audio CD Library, Selections and Summaries in Spanish*
- *Supporting Instruction in Spanish*

Vocabulary and Comprehension

"Orpheus, the Great Musician"; "The Power of Music"

A. Match words and definitions. Write the letter of the correct definition next to each word.

_____ **1.** ascended

_____ **2.** ghastly

_____ **3.** inconsolable

_____ **4.** reluctance

_____ **5.** minstrel

a. singer

b. moved up

c. horrible; ghostlike

d. unable to be comforted

e. unwillingness

B. Choose three words from above. Use each word in a sentence.

1. _____

_____

2. _____

_____

3. _____

_____

C. Answer each question below.

1. In "Orpheus, the Great Musician," is Orpheus successful in rescuing Eurydice? Why, or why not?

_____

_____

2. What are some of the claims Salerno-Sonnenberg makes about the power of music?

_____

_____

Additional Vocabulary Practice

"The Origin of the Seasons"; "Orpheus, the Great Musician"; "The Power of Music"

A. Match words and definitions or descriptions. Write the letter of the correct definition or description next to each word.

_____ **1.** croon

_____ **2.** anoint

_____ **3.** stoop

_____ **4.** immortal

_____ **5.** decree

_____ **6.** shade

_____ **7.** flit

_____ **8.** hasten

_____ **9.** rank

_____ **10.** legend

a. ritually apply a sacred substance

b. organized group; line

c. hurry

d. move about quickly

e. traditional story about a hero from long ago

f. sing

g. bend down

h. ghost

i. undying

j. make an official statement

B. Choose five words from above. Use each word in a sentence.

1. _____

_____

2. _____

_____

3. _____

_____

4. _____

_____

5. _____

_____

"The Flight of Icarus" retold by Sally Benson

SKILLS FOCUS

Literary Skill
Understand morals in myths.

Reading Skill
Make generalizations.

Resources
In this book:
• Adapted Readings
• Vocabulary and Comprehension, p. 278
• Additional Vocabulary Practice, p. 284 (includes the next two selections)

Other Resources:
• *Holt Adapted Reader*
• *Audio CD Library*
• *Audio CD Library, Selections and Summaries in Spanish*
• *Supporting Instruction in Spanish*

Teacher Tip

To help students use the additional vocabulary words in sentences, suggest that they create sentences that describe characters from previous stories they have read.

Prereading
Reteach the Key Idea

Identify Morals Invite students to demonstrate understanding of morals by having them volunteer examples from familiar folk tales or children's stories. Remind students that a moral is a lesson about the right way to behave. Then, ask students: *Why do writers use stories to tell readers the right way to behave? Would it be more effective for a writer simply to tell readers how to behave? Why, or why not?*

Alternative Activities

Read the Adaptation Distribute copies of the adapted reading of "The Flight of Icarus" (available in this book and, with marginal questions, in *Holt Adapted Reader*). To prepare for reading the original version and to practice fluency, students should read the adaptation silently. Encourage students to write notes, questions, predictions, reactions, and comments on the worksheets as they read.

Especially for ELL **Use Spanish Resources** Spanish-speaking English-language learners will benefit from listening to or reading the summary of "The Flight of Icarus" in Spanish in preparation for reading the selection in English.

Vocabulary Practice

Preview Additional Vocabulary Preview with students the following words and their definitions. Have students use each word in an original sentence.

- *labyrinth (p. 677):* a large maze, usually constructed with walls or hedges
- *bribery (p. 677):* the offer of money for a (usually illegal) benefit or service
- *stow away (p. 677):* secretly take passage on a ship, without paying
- *ingenious (p. 677):* clever
- *bewitched (p. 678):* full of rapt attention, as if through magic
- *enchanted (p. 678):* delighted
- *submerged (p. 679):* overwhelmed; sunk
- *exaltation (p. 679):* joy and celebration

Reading

Alternative Activity

(Especially for ELL) **Play the Audio Recording** To increase students' comprehension of the selection, you may have struggling readers listen to the audio recording of "The Flight of Icarus" as they follow along in their books.

Alternative Teaching Strategies

(Core Skill) **Make Predictions** Alert students to make predictions as they read the story. How do they think the characters will act next? Have students read the myth, pausing from time to time to jot down their predictions and their ideas on how the characters *should* act. At the end of the story, students can evaluate how accurate their predictions and advice were.

Use a Diagram to Identify Conflict Ask students to put to the test the generalization on the Before You Read page (student book page 675) that every story has a conflict. Have students read the story and then use a Venn diagram to identify the story's conflict. Students should label one circle "What Daedalus Wants" and the other circle "What Icarus Wants." Students should then label the overlap of the circles "Conflict" and write in that space how the two characters, because of the conflict between them, get something that neither one of them wants. Ask volunteers to identify the main conflict of the story by using the diagram as a guide. Ask students to explain how the conflict is resolved.

What Daedalus Wants   Conflict   What Icarus Wants

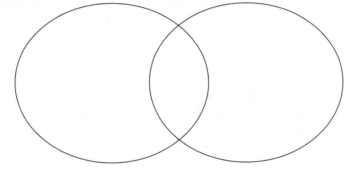

Postreading

Alternative Activity

(Mixed Ability Group) **Interview a Main Character** Pair students, and have partners take turns role-playing the part of the character of Icarus, with the other partner acting as an interviewer. Partners should ask each other what lessons Icarus may have learned from the experience, answering the questions in character. Have students share their answers, and use students' suggestions as a springboard to get them to talk about the moral the myth teaches.

Copyright © by Holt, Rinehart and Winston. All rights reserved.

(Teacher Tip)
Students may have difficulty making predictions or judgments about the characters' actions in the story. Encourage students to put themselves in the characters' places. What would they do if they were stranded on an island with no way off? Could they resist the urge to fly higher, if given the chance Icarus had? Students may benefit from pausing to do brief quickwrites on these questions as they read the myth.

Vocabulary Development
Reinforce the Key Idea

See the Connection Remind students that it is common for one language to borrow words or ideas from another. Tell them that the myths of the ancient Greeks and Romans have provided the English language with many additions through the names of gods and people who appear in the stories.

On the chalkboard, write the following names:

Apollo	Cupid	Mars
Hercules	Mercury	Echo
Vulcan	Siren	Nike
Pluto	Calliope	Jupiter
Titan	Amazon	
Midas	Venus	

Have students identify how some of the names are used today. (*planets, elements, clothing, automobiles, personal characteristics*) Ask if they can provide additional examples of how names from mythology are used today.

Reading Skills Development

(**Mixed Ability Group**) **Make Generalizations** Students may be aware only of the negative connotations of the word *generalization*. Point out to students that while making a broad statement with little support is a dangerous thing to do, people make well-founded generalizations all the time in their daily lives. Tell students they can avoid making *over*generalizations by using words like *often* and *usually* rather then *always* or *never*. You might have students practice making generalizations on nonliterary topics before moving on to making generalizations about myths. Arrange students in small groups, and have each group make at least one well-supported generalization about each of the following topics: school, weather, and sports. Students should attempt to support each generalization with at least two pieces of evidence. Have volunteers from each group share their group's work with the class.

TARGETED STRATEGIES FOR SPECIAL EDUCATION STUDENTS

Prereading
Reteach the Key Idea

Introduce the Selection Tell students the story they are about to read teaches an important lesson about life. Ask students to think of other stories they have read that taught lessons. What kinds of stories and lessons were they? Point out that most such stories warn against a failing common to humans, usually a character trait or desire. Alert students to be on the lookout for a dangerous desire in the myth.

Reading
Listening and Speaking Opportunity

Read Aloud/Practice Fluency Pair students of comparable reading abilities, and allow each pair time to take turns reading aloud to each other from the myth. Students can help each other with difficult words or phrases and offer feedback for their partner's performance.

Alternative Teaching Strategy

Connect to a Real-Life Lesson As students read the myth, challenge them to think of people they know, either personally or through the news, who have characteristics or personalities similar to those of the characters in the story. When students have read what happens to Icarus, have them try to relate the event to an Icarus-like person from their own lives or experience. Discuss with students their comparisons. Could these real-life people learn from the same lesson that Icarus did? What exactly is that lesson?

Postreading
Additional Practice

Questioning a Generalization Tell students that a good generalization must be able to withstand scrutiny; that is, it must be well supported. One way students can make sure their generalizations are well supported is to question them by asking, "What reasons can I give to support this statement?" If students have difficulty finding such reasons, they may need to go back to work on their generalizations.

Literary Skill
Understand morals in myths.

Reading Skill
Make generalizations.

Resources

In this book:
- Adapted Readings
- Vocabulary and Comprehension, p. 278
- Additional Vocabulary Practice, p. 284 (includes the next two selections)

Other Resources:
- *Holt Adapted Reader*
- *Audio CD Library*
- *Audio CD Library, Selections and Summaries in Spanish*
- *Supporting Instruction in Spanish*

Teacher Tip

Invite students to visualize how this myth might look if it were a movie. Ask: *How would the characters look in the opening scene? What would the last scene show?*

Vocabulary and Comprehension

"The Flight of Icarus"

A. Match words or phrases and definitions. Write the letter of the correct definition next to each word or phrase.

_____ **1.** labyrinth

_____ **2.** bribery

_____ **3.** bewitched

_____ **4.** exaltation

_____ **5.** stow away

a. the offer of money for an illegal service

b. made attentive, as if through magic

c. a large maze

d. secretly take passage on a ship, without paying

e. joy and celebration

B. Choose three words from above. Use each word in a sentence.

1. _____

_____

2. _____

_____

3. _____

_____

C. Answer each question below.

1. Who is Daedalus, and why is he imprisoned on the island of Crete?

_____

_____

2. What mistake does Icarus make?

_____

_____

Elements of Literature
pages 682–695

"King Midas and the Golden Touch"

retold by Pamela Oldfield;

"The Funeral Banquet of King Midas" from *Muse* magazine, by John Fleischman

Prereading

Background

Review Genre Tell students that the two selections they are going to read have a common character but different purposes. One is an ancient myth, and one is an informational magazine article from contemporary times. The purpose of the myth is to entertain and instruct the audience with a tale about the dangers of a common human failing. The purpose of the article is to inform the audience about a real historical figure. Have students discuss these different purposes and what they expect from each selection.

Alternative Activity

(**Especially for ELL**) **Read the Summaries in Spanish** Spanish-speaking English-language learners will benefit from reading or listening to the selection summaries in Spanish in preparation for reading the selections in English.

Vocabulary Practice

Preview Additional Vocabulary Preview with students these words and definitions from "King Midas and the Golden Touch." Have students use each word in an original sentence.

- *discontented (p. 684):* unhappy
- *roamed (p. 684):* wandered
- *unrepentant (p. 684):* without apology or shame
- *quick-tempered (p. 684):* easily moved to anger
- *jubilant (p. 685):* overjoyed
- *console (p. 685):* reassure

Reading

Listening and Speaking Opportunity

(**Especially for ELL**) **Play the Audio Recording/Build Fluency**
Make the audio recording of the selections available to students. Encourage students to listen to a selection as they follow along in

SKILLS FOCUS

Literary Skill
Understand irony.

Reading Skills
- Use prior knowledge.
- Summarize a text.

(**Resources**)

In this book:
- Vocabulary and Comprehension, p. 283
- Additional Vocabulary Practice, p. 284 (includes the previous selection)

Other Resources:
- *Audio CD Library*
- *Audio CD Library, Selections and Summaries in Spanish*
- *Supporting Instruction in Spanish*

Students may benefit from classifying the different types of irony. Tell students there are three types: *verbal,* in which one thing is said but another meant; *situational,* in which something happens that is the opposite of what is expected; and *dramatic,* in which a character is unaware of something important that the audience knows. Students can use the three classifications as they identify irony in "King Midas and the Golden Touch."

their books. Ask students to pay attention to the rhythm and flow of the language. Suggest that students choose a paragraph or two to read along with the recording.

Alternative Teaching Strategies

Mixed Ability Group **Form and Answer Questions** Pair students to read together "King Midas and the Golden Touch," pausing at important points to add questions and answers to the prior knowledge activity they completed on student book page 682. Pairs should add to their maps every time Midas makes an important decision, especially at his forgiving of Silenus, his choice of wish, and his decision of whether or not to keep his power. Do they approve or disapprove of Midas's choice? Group members should be able to support their opinions.

Core Skill **Identify the Main Idea** If students are struggling with their summaries of "The Funeral Banquet of King Midas," they may need additional practice in identifying the main idea of an informational article. As students read the article, have them make lists of key words and phrases, using a chart like this:

Key Words/Phrases in Article	Possible Main Ideas for Article

After they finish reading, assign students to small groups to have them compare their notes to identify common ideas and details that will point to the main idea. Students should then complete their summaries of the selection, making sure to include these main ideas and important details.

Postreading

Alternative Activity

Use a Diagram to Identify Irony After students have read "King Midas and the Golden Touch," have them make note of the difference between what Midas wants in the story and what he receives. Encourage students to include in their notes the specific details of the consequences of the king's wish. Students record their notes in a simple chart such as the one below.

What Midas Wants	What Midas Gets

Vocabulary Development

Additional Practice

Using Allusion After completing the "Using Allusion" activity on student book page 687, have students create their own sentences containing allusions to the myths they have read. Remind students that their allusions should draw a comparison between one of the mythological figures, settings, or plots and a similar instance in the world today. Ask volunteers to share their results with the class.

Using Context Clues After students have completed the Practice activity on page 695 of their books, have them return to the additional vocabulary they studied prior to reading the myth (page 279 of this book). Ask students to choose three words from the list and to use each of the words in a very brief passage in which clues to the word's meaning are given in context. Students can then exchange passages with a partner and identify the context clues that helped them define each word.

Reading Skills Development

Use Prior Knowledge Help struggling readers practice using prior knowledge by introducing the KWL chart. Draw on the chalkboard a KWL chart like the one below. Practice the activity on the informational selection "The Search Goes On" on student book page 740. Begin by choosing a volunteer to read the title of the selection aloud. Then, ask what the title suggests about the selection. Allow students a moment to flip through the selection, paying special attention to the pictures and their subtitles or captions. Continue by asking students to discuss what they know about the ancient Maya. Place student responses in the "K" column of the chart. Explain to students that they have just used their prior knowledge, or what they already know about a subject, to understand a piece of writing. Finally, ask the class what they would like to know about the ancient Maya, placing their suggestions in the "W" column of the KWL chart. Remind students to complete the final "L" column after they finish reading the selection and to go back and correct any incorrect information in the "K" column.

K What I Know	W What I Want to Know	L What I Learned

Vocabulary Skills
- Understand word origins.
- Understand allusions.
- Clarify word meanings by context.

(Core Skill)

Use the resources in the Reading Skills and Strategies section of this book to teach a core literary or informational skill in which your struggling readers need remediation. Use "King Midas and the Golden Touch" or "The Funeral Banquet of King Midas" for the application portion of the lesson.

SKILLS FOCUS

Literary Skill
Understand irony.

Reading Skills
• Use prior knowledge.
• Summarize a text.

(**Resources**)

In this book:
• Vocabulary and Comprehension, p. 283
• Additional Vocabulary Practice, p. 284 (includes the previous selection)

Other Resources:
• *Audio CD Library*
• *Audio CD Library, Selections and Summaries in Spanish*
• *Supporting Instruction in Spanish*

(**Teacher Tip**)

After reading so many myths, students may have difficulty shifting gears to read the informational magazine article. You may want to introduce the selection with a discussion on how myths are created, telling students that often a myth or legend is based partly on a real historical figure.

TARGETED STRATEGIES FOR SPECIAL EDUCATION STUDENTS

Prereading
Reteach the Key Idea

Introduce the Selection Students will probably have read stories or seen movies or TV shows that follow greedy characters. Ask students how the characters fared in these other works: Did they get what they wanted? If not, why not? Then, prepare them for the story of King Midas by telling them that in this myth, a king wishes for the power to turn anything into gold with his touch. Ask if students foresee any problems with the king's wish.

Reading
Alternative Activity

(**Core Skill**) **Use a Diagram to Analyze Character** As students read the myth, have them create a cluster diagram to examine the character of King Midas. The king's name should be written in the central circle of the diagram, and the individual characteristics of the king's personality should be listed in the next group of circles. Connected to these secondary circles should be more circles in which examples and effects of the king's characteristics are given. Understanding character will help students better understand the moral of the myth.

Postreading
Alternative Assessment

Write a Paragraph The irony in the myth stems from the fact that what happens is not at all what Midas expects to happen when his wish is granted. To assess whether students understand the irony of the story, ask them to write a paragraph telling how the story would have been different if King Midas had made a wise decision with his wish. Would irony have played as large a role in the story? Why, or why not?

Additional Activity

Write a Modern-Day Myth Ask students if people still act from greedy impulses today, and have students give either general or specific examples from the news or the world around them. Then, have students write a brief tale based on a character they mention, using as a model the myth of King Midas. Challenge students to include irony in their stories (for example, instead of ending up with priceless bracelets, a thief could end up in handcuffs). Ask for volunteers to share their modern-day myths with the class.

Vocabulary and Comprehension

"King Midas and the Golden Touch"; "The Funeral Banquet of King Midas"

A. Match words and definitions. Write the letter of the correct definition next to each word.

____ **1.** interior

____ **2.** archaeologist

____ **3.** excavate

____ **4.** avalanche

____ **5.** jubilant

a. overjoyed

b. mass of loosened snow, earth, rocks, and so on, suddenly and swiftly sliding down a mountain

c. scientist who studies the culture of the past

d. uncover or expose by digging

e. inner part of anything

B. Choose three words from above. Use each word in a sentence.

1. _____

_____

2. _____

_____

3. _____

_____

C. Write T or F next to each statement to tell if it is true or false.

_____ **1.** In "King Midas and the Golden Touch," Midas is cursed from birth with the ability to turn anything he touches into gold.

_____ **2.** King Midas receives his wish for being kind to a follower of Dionysus.

_____ **3.** One day, King Midas finds a satyr asleep in his garden.

_____ **4.** King Midas was a real historical figure.

_____ **5.** The airtight walls of wood and clay helped preserve the contents of the tomb.

Additional Vocabulary Practice

"The Flight of Icarus"; "King Midas and the Golden Touch"; "The Funeral Banquet of King Midas"

A. Match words and definitions. Write the letter of the correct definition next to each word.

____ **1.** labyrinth	**a.** without apology or shame
____ **2.** submerge	**b.** delight
____ **3.** ingenious	**c.** unhappy
____ **4.** enchant	**d.** wander
____ **5.** console	**e.** overjoyed
____ **6.** jubilant	**f.** reassure
____ **7.** unrepentant	**g.** easily moved to anger
____ **8.** roam	**h.** sink
____ **9.** discontented	**i.** a large maze
____ **10.** quick-tempered	**j.** clever

B. Choose five words from above. Use each word in a sentence.

1. _____

_____

2. _____

_____

3. _____

_____

4. _____

_____

5. _____

_____

Elements of Literature:
Folk Tales

Reinforce the Key Idea

Discuss Folk Tales Share with students these additional points about folk tales:

- In many folk tales the animals have human characteristics.
- The use of animals to represent human behavior makes it easier to examine human imperfections and learn moral lessons.
- Folk tales reflect the values and beliefs of a culture. As the tales are told and retold, they serve as tools for passing beliefs and values from one generation to the next.

Then, ask students to name a few folk tales that they have heard, such as "He Lion, Bruh Bear, and Bruh Rabbit."

Additional Activity

Record a Folk Tale Prepare students for reading the folk tales by having them each collect a folk tale from a parent or other adult. Students can prompt the storyteller by asking him or her to remember a story from his or her childhood that was told by a family member or friend. Ask students to write down the story they are told in wording as close to the original as possible. Give volunteers time to share their stories in class, and ask students if they have heard of similar stories. Point out that since they are passed on by word of mouth, folk tales survive in many versions until a written version becomes popular and widespread.

Academic Vocabulary

(**Especially for ELL**) **Build Vocabulary** Help students develop their academic vocabulary by reinforcing these terms and their definitions.

- *motifs (p. 696):* common features in stories
- *animal tale (p. 697):* folk tale in which the characters are all animals
- *escape story (p. 697):* a folk tale about escaping slavery

Literary Skill
Understand folk tales.

(**Cultural Tip**)

Emphasize to students that folk tales will differ from culture to culture but that most stories will be about common human desires, dreams, and fears. You may want to illustrate the point by asking students with different cultural backgrounds to share stories on a common theme, such as a fear of the dark or the desire to fly.

Literary Skill
Understand folk tales.

TARGETED STRATEGIES FOR SPECIAL EDUCATION STUDENTS

Elements of Literature: Folk Tales

Background

Folk Tales Students may not understand how folk tales relate to their student book's example of the parent or other family member telling a story from his or her past. Point out to students that many stories are born out of a desire to explain or share something about the world. The difference between a folk tale and a personal story is that the folk tale has survived several retellings and does not tell about a person directly known to the listener. Ask students to brainstorm the types of experiences that would be likely told as folk tales, and lead students to see common threads among their suggestions.

Academic Vocabulary

Teach New Vocabulary Help students understand the following terminology from the student book. You may need to give examples of each to aid understanding.

- *motifs (p. 696):* common features in stories
- *animal tale (p. 697):* folk tale in which the characters are all animals
- *escape story (p. 697):* a folk tale about escaping slavery

Reteach the Key Idea

Aspects of the Folk Tale Challenge students to name specific examples of the different motifs listed in their books. You may want to bring to class a book of fairy tales and read one of the stories to students for them to discuss its elements—not only its characters, plot, and setting but also its motifs, formulas, and repetitions.

Alternative Activity

Reinforce the Concept Ask students if they have ever read or heard a story that involves animals acting like humans. How are such stories "realistic," and how are they fantastic? Lead students to see that although such stories involve animals, they really are about human traits.

"Oni and the Great Bird"

retold by Abayomi Fuja

Prereading

Alternative Activities

Use *The Holt Reader* You may consider having students use the Before You Read page in *The Holt Reader*, either instead of or in addition to the Before You Read page in the student book.

(**Especially for ELL**) **Use Spanish Resources** To increase students' comprehension, you may have Spanish-speaking English-language learners read or listen to the summary of "Oni and the Great Bird" in Spanish in preparation for reading the selection in English.

Vocabulary Practice

Preview Additional Vocabulary Preview with students the following words and their definitions. Have students use each word in an original sentence.

- *slain (p. 700):* killed
- *banish (p. 700):* force out of the country
- *perished (p. 701):* died
- *talons (p. 702):* a bird's claws
- *discharged (p. 702):* fired; shot
- *bedraggled (p. 703):* unkempt; disheveled
- *accord (p. 704):* willingness; agreement
- *marveled (p. 704):* wondered
- *curfew (p. 704):* prohibited time to be outside one's house

Reading

Fluency Opportunity

(**Especially for ELL**) **Use Echo Reading** To help students with pronunciation, pair English-language learners with native English speakers. First, have the native English speaker read a paragraph aloud. Then, have the ELL student re-read the same paragraph aloud.

SKILLS FOCUS

Literary Skill
Understand motifs.

Reading Skill
Summarize.

(**Resources**)

In this book:
- Vocabulary and Comprehension, p. 291
- Additional Vocabulary Practice, p. 302 (includes the next two selections)

Other Resources:
- *The Holt Reader*
- *Audio CD Library*
- *Audio CD Library, Selections and Summaries in Spanish*
- *Supporting Instruction in Spanish*

(**Especially for ELL**)

You may want to have students share any hero tales that they know from other cultures. After students share their examples, ask the class what each tale has in common.

Alternative Activities

Use *The Holt Reader* You may consider having students read the selection in *The Holt Reader* and use the margins in that book to make notes and respond to the instruction.

Play the Audio Recording To help struggling readers identify the main ideas of the folk tale, you may have them listen to the audio recording of the folk tale while they follow along in their books.

Mixed Ability Group **Chart the Main Points** Have students work in small groups to read the folk tale aloud together. As the groups read, the members should pause periodically to identify the main points of the story. Have groups record their notes in a chart such as the following. After groups have finished reading, allow them time to organize their notes to make a summary of the story. Emphasize to the groups that they should include only the most important points from the story for their summaries. Have spokespersons from each group share with the class the group's summary, and discuss any differences among the summaries presented.

Main Characters	Time and Place	Magical Elements	Conflict	Main Events	Resolution

Postreading

Alternative Activity

Use *The Holt Reader* You may consider having students use the postreading activities in *The Holt Reader,* either instead of or in addition to the postreading activities in the student book.

Alternative Assessments

Name the Motifs Have students name the motifs in the story and, if possible, they should give examples of other stories with such an introductory first sentence, a use of song, a voyage by boat, a slaying of a magical creature, and the fitting of a special shoe.

Use a Time Line Have students fill in a time line, using the one below as a starting point, to organize the many events of the story. Point out to students that the tale covers a great deal of time, from the hero's birth, but picks out only the most significant events to relate in detail. Students can use their time lines to make sure their summaries follow chronological order and do not include extraneous details.

SKILLS FOCUS

Vocabulary Skill
Clarify word meanings.

Oni receives half
of the kingdom.

Oni is born.

Vocabulary Development

Additional Practice

Clarify Word Meanings To give students more practice in clarifying word meanings, have them use five of the additional vocabulary words to expand the summaries they write about the superheroes.

Reading Skills Development

(**Core Skill**)
Use the resources in the Reading Skills and Strategies section of this book to teach a core literary skill in which your struggling readers need remediation. Use "Oni and the Great Bird" for the application portion of the lesson.

(**Mixed Ability Group**) **Practice Summarizing** Students may have difficulty paring down the events they include in a plot summary, which can make their understanding of the reading unfocused. Arrange students in mixed ability groups to re-read "Oni and the Great Bird." Have group members take turns reading small sections of the story. Group members should ask each reader what important events happened in the section just read. Encourage students to use as their definition of an "important event" any occurrence, decision, or revelation of information that promises to affect the story's course. Students may find the chart below useful in helping them to identify important events. After the groups have finished reading, ask volunteers to share their group's findings and discuss as a class whether any of the information included is extraneous.

Who	What	When	Where	Why	How

SKILLS FOCUS

Literary Skill
Understand motifs.

Reading Skill
Summarize.

(**Resources**)
In this book:
• Vocabulary and Comprehension, p. 291
• Additional Vocabulary Practice, p. 302 (includes the next two selections)

Other Resources:
• *The Holt Reader*
• *Audio CD Library*
• *Audio CD Library, Selections and Summaries in Spanish*
• *Supporting Instruction in Spanish*

(**Teacher Tip**)

Students may become confused by the many different events in the story. Point out to students that the title of the folk tale lets them know that the main plot tells of the conflict between Oni and the great bird. That is the part of the story on which students should concentrate.

TARGETED STRATEGIES FOR SPECIAL EDUCATION STUDENTS

Prereading
Reteach the Key Idea

Discuss Summarizing and Literary Elements Students will have trouble summarizing the story if they do not keep in mind the different literary elements that answer the *5W-How?* questions. On the chalkboard, draw a chart such as the one below. Point out to students that the question *Who?* is answered by the names of the main characters; *When?* and *Where?* are answered by the story's setting; and *What? Why?* and *How?* are answered by the story's plot. Students should copy the chart on their own paper and use it to keep track of the story's elements in order to write their summaries.

Who	What	When	Where	Why	How

Reading
Alternative Teaching Strategy

Identify the Beginning, Middle, and End of the Tale Guide students to identify the different parts of the plot of the story between Oni and the great bird. Using charts created in Prereading, students will be able to determine the *What? Why?* and *How?* of the story as they read. They can use the additional chart below to divide the story into three parts: the beginning, in which the problem the hero must face is given; the middle, in which the hero comes up with a plan to solve the problem; and the end, in which the audience sees the result of the hero's plan. Have students share their results with the class after they have completed their charts.

Beginning	Middle	End

Postreading
Alternative Assessment

(**Mixed Ability Group**) **Retell the Story** Have students work in small groups to build a time line of the story. Make sure there is at least one student in each group who can lead while students work together to make a time line of what happened when. Then, have students summarize the story using the time line as a guide.

Vocabulary and Comprehension

"Oni and the Great Bird"

A. Match words and definitions. Write the letter of the correct definition next to each word.

_____ **1.** hovered

_____ **2.** impostor

_____ **3.** implored

_____ **4.** invincible

_____ **5.** commenced

a. person who pretends to be someone or something that he or she is not

b. hung in the air

c. unbeatable

d. began

e. asked or begged

B. Choose three words from above. Use each word in a sentence.

1. _____

_____

2. _____

_____

3. _____

_____

C. Write T or F next to each statement to tell if it is true or false.

_____ **1.** Oni was born with a magic bow and arrow.

_____ **2.** Oni decided to leave home and see the world.

_____ **3.** The small village of Ajo is being plagued by a giant bird.

_____ **4.** When the villagers look under the body of the bird, they find Oni.

_____ **5.** Oni is given half the kingdom for killing the bird.

"Master Frog" retold by Lynette Dyer Vuong

SKILLS FOCUS

Literary Skill
Understand metamorphosis.

Reading Skill
Make predictions.

(Resources)

In this book:
• Vocabulary and Comprehension, p. 296
• Additional Vocabulary Practice, p. 302 (includes the previous selection and the next selection)

Other Resources:
• *Audio CD Library*
• *Audio CD Library, Selections and Summaries in Spanish*
• *Supporting Instruction in Spanish*

(Especially for ELL)

Students may have difficulty pronouncing the names of the characters in the story. Alert students to the phonetic spellings that are given at the bottom of the page for each name, and have students practice saying the names aloud before they begin reading the tale. If you have a student who speaks Vietnamese, ask the student to model the pronunciation of each name for the class.

Prereading

Reteach the Key Idea

Discuss Metamorphosis Explain to students that they have read about metamorphoses in myths and fairy tales. For example, in a version of the Cinderella story, a pumpkin is magically transformed into a fabulous carriage. Then, ask students to think of and discuss metamorphoses they remember from other stories they have read.

Alternative Activity

(Especially for ELL) Use Spanish Resources Spanish-speaking English-language learners may benefit from reading or listening to the selection summary in Spanish in preparation for reading the selection in English.

Vocabulary Practice

Preview Additional Vocabulary Preview with students the following words and their definitions. Have students use each word in an original sentence.

- *resigned (p. 708):* gave in
- *mischievous (p. 709):* trouble making
- *perched (p. 709):* sat
- *apprentice (p. 709):* student worker; trainee
- *stammered (p. 709):* stuttered
- *beckoned (p. 710):* called to come over
- *lumbered (p. 711):* walked slowly and heavily
- *filed (p. 711):* moved in a column, one after the other
- *pomp (p. 711):* grand display
- *deception (p. 712):* trickery; lying
- *endearments (p. 713):* fond words of praise
- *writhing (p. 713):* twisting
- *agony (p. 713):* horrible pain
- *prostrated (p. 714):* bowed in submission
- *reining (p. 715):* pulling back on the cords attached to a horse's bit to slow the horse
- *prosperity (p. 715):* wealth

Reading
Reteach the Key Idea

Mixed Ability Group Make Predictions/Practice Fluency

Briefly review with students the strategy of making predictions, reminding students that the idea is not necessarily to be correct in one's predictions but to pay close attention to the plot twists of the story in order to adjust predictions. Before students read the folk tale, arrange them in small groups and have them make a few initial predictions. Group members can then take turns reading the tale aloud, pausing whenever something surprising happens in order to guess what might happen next or to revise an earlier prediction. Students should note their predictions and review them whenever they pause in their reading. A chart like the one below may help students keep track of their predictions. After reading, they can discuss their predictions and what they learned through the process of making predictions while reading the story.

What I Think Will Happen	What Actually Happens

Alternative Activity

Play the Audio Recording To help struggling readers make and revise predictions, have them listen to the audio recording of the selection as they follow along in their books. Pause the recording frequently to allow them time to revise predictions and make new ones.

Alternative Teaching Strategy

Core Skill Reviewing Predictions Some students may become frustrated with making predictions because their predictions are consistently off the mark. Remind students that the idea is to remain engaged with the selection. Direct students to look for clues they might have missed in their first reading of the selection. Students should re-read the tale silently to themselves, pausing at the points at which they paused in their first reading to make predictions. Have students ask themselves the following questions: What clues are in the story that hint at what will happen next? What do these clues tell me about the characters, plot, setting, or other elements of the story? In this way, students will gain a greater understanding of the story, regardless of the accuracy of their predictions.

Teacher Tip

Have students discuss other stories they know that involve metamorphoses.

Core Skill

Use the resources in the Reading Skills and Strategies section of this book to help students having difficulty making predictions. Use "Master Frog" for the application portion of the lesson.

Vocabulary Skills
- Clarify word meanings.
- Use specific words.

Postreading
Alternative Assessments

(**Mixed Ability Group**) **Act Out a Scene** Arrange students in small groups to choose a scene to act out for the class. A good group size is four, which would allow the group members to play all three sisters and Master Frog. Have each group introduce the scene with what they think is most entertaining about this part of the story and add more dialogue to the scene as they see fit.

Create a Family Portrait Ask students to draw a picture of Master Frog with his new extended family, including his mother, wife, sisters-in-law, and father-in-law, as well as his father, the Jade Emperor. Challenge students to make the subjects' personalities come through in their appearances, props, or poses. Students may also wish to add to their portraits some of the royal frog's faithful subjects.

Vocabulary Development
Additional Practice

Use Specific Words Have students write a descriptive paragraph about themselves and their favorite sport or hobby. Encourage students to use specific words and active verbs. Then, have students exchange paragraphs with a partner. Each partner should select five words, either verbs or nouns, and replace them with more specific, vivid, and evocative choices. If students feel their partners' work is already quite descriptive, suggest that they replace five words with similar ones that change the tone of the passage.

Reading Skills Development

(**Mixed Ability Group**) **Make Predictions/Practice Fluency**
Students will benefit from more practice in making predictions. Choose a selection from the "Making Predictions" section of the list that begins on page 383 of this book. Ask students to take turns reading the selection aloud with a partner (See Partner Reading on page xxx of this book). Remind students to pause frequently to make and revise their predictions and to be sure to note their predictions when they make them. You may want to have the groups share their results with the rest of the class.

Targeted Strategies for Special Education Students

Literary Skill
Understand metamorphosis.

Reading Skill
Make predictions.

(**Resources**)

In this book:
- Vocabulary and Comprehension, p. 296
- Additional Vocabulary Practice, p. 302 (includes the previous selection and the next selection)

Other Resources:
- *Audio CD Library*
- *Audio CD Library, Selections and Summaries in Spanish*
- *Supporting Instruction in Spanish*

(**Teacher Tip**)

To make sure students understand the events in the story, have them re-read with a partner any scenes they find confusing. Students may have the most trouble with the details of the tale's magic and metamorphosis.

Prereading
Reteaching the Key Ideas

(**Core Skill**) **Review Making Predictions** Ask students if they have ever found themselves trying to read a story more quickly in order to find out what happens next. Point out to students that stories encourage a reader's curiosity by withholding some details at the beginning and giving the reader clues as the plot progresses. Tell students that each time they feel themselves drawn forward by a story, they should stop for a moment to think about what may happen next. Students can practice making predictions by looking at the title of this folk tale. What do they think a story called "Master Frog" will be about, and why?

Introduce Metamorphosis Point out to students that a metamorphosis in a story usually involves the transformation from one thing into something opposite. The example given, that of the change from an ugly frog to a handsome prince, fits this pattern. Ask students to discuss why a metamorphosis usually involves the change from one opposite to another. One way to begin is by asking students if the transformation of a frog into a snake would be as interesting. Why, or why not?

Reading
Alternative Teaching Strategy

Make a Story Map Students may have difficulty keeping track of all the events in the story, especially if they pause frequently to make predictions. As students stop to make predictions, have them also make a brief note of the major events that have taken place in the tale since the last time they paused. Students can review these notes after they have finished reading the tale.

Postreading
Alternative Assessment

Check Comprehension To assess students' comprehension of the tale, ask them to express in their own words the moral the story teaches. Tell students to provide support for their choice of the moral the story teaches.

Vocabulary and Comprehension

"Master Frog"

A. Match words and definitions. Write the letter of the correct definition next to each word.

_____ **1.** cowered   **a.** crouched and trembled in fear

_____ **2.** entreaties   **b.** warned or urged

_____ **3.** admonished   **c.** earnest requests

_____ **4.** presumptuous   **d.** obvious pretense or act

_____ **5.** charade   **e.** too bold; arrogant

B. Choose three words from above. Use each word in a sentence.

1. _____

_____

2. _____

_____

3. _____

C. Answer each question below.

1. What is a metamorphosis? What example of metamorphosis is found in "Master Frog"?

_____

_____

2. What moral does the story teach?

_____

_____

Elements of Literature
pages 718–725

"The Crane Wife"
told by Sumiko Yagawa, translated by Katherine Paterson

Prereading

Reteach the Key Idea

Review Taboo Review with students the example of taboo in "Orpheus, the Great Musician," which is discussed in the Before You Read section of their books (page 718). Ask students what problem the taboo presented Orpheus and what his failure to abide by the taboo revealed about his character. If students have difficulty with the second part of the question, ask them what they might have done differently than Orpheus. If so, how or why?

Alternative Activity

(**Especially for ELL**) **Use Spanish Resources** Spanish-speaking English-language learners may benefit from reading or listening to the summary of "The Crane Wife" in Spanish in preparation for reading the selection in English.

Vocabulary Practice

(**Especially for ELL**) **Preview Additional Vocabulary** Preview with students the following words and their definitions. Have students use each word in an original sentence.

- *swooped (p. 719):* descended quickly
- *tended (p. 719):* treated in a helpful manner; looked after
- *refined (p. 719):* of high quality or purity; cultured
- *dreary (p. 720):* uninviting; sad or depressing
- *loom (p. 720):* machine for making fabric
- *pathetic (p. 721):* pitiful; evoking sympathy
- *relent (p. 721):* give in
- *entreaty (p. 722):* request
- *tarry (p. 722):* stay for a short time
- *discern (p. 722):* distinguish

SKILLS FOCUS

Literary Skills
- Understand taboo.
- Recognize onomatopo

Reading Skill
Draw conclusions.

(**Resources**)

In this book:
- Vocabulary and Comprehension, p. 301
- Additional Vocabulary Practice, p. 302 (includes the previous two selections)

Other Resources:
- *Audio CD Library*
- *Audio CD Library, Selections and Summaries in Spanish*
- *Supporting Instruction in Spanish*

Teacher Tip

Students may have difficulty drawing conclusions about the story because the narration of the tale does not itself offer much in the way of judgment about the characters or events. Tell students they will have to rely on their own knowledge to draw conclusions. Remind them that they should be able to provide support for the judgments they make.

Reading
Alternative Activities

Mixed Ability Group **Understand Taboo** Alert students that a taboo in a story is usually not an arbitrary or "added" feature but is most often central to the story's conflict and revealing of the main character's personality. As students read the story together in small groups, have them be on the lookout for the story's taboo. When they find it, they should pause to note two things: how the taboo creates a conflict in the story, and what the conflict says about the main character's personality.

Use a Diagram to Draw Conclusions Ask groups formed for the "Understand Taboo" activity above to use a diagram to keep track of the conclusions they draw while reading the story. Group members should pause their reading whenever they have a question about the story or feel like sharing a personal response with the others. Tell students that most of their conclusions will probably fall under the headings of "Characters" and "Plot," but that they should also try to draw conclusions about the vividly described setting of the story and the story's overall meaning, or theme. Ask groups to share their conclusions after they have finished reading.

Characters	Plot	Setting	Theme

Postreading
Alternative Activity

Discuss Onomatopoeia Students can review the examples of onomatopoeia in the story after they have read it through once. Conduct a whole-class discussion to have students decide if the examples succeed as sound effects in the story. Ask students to discuss the benefits of having such sound effects in the story, leading them to consider their use in an oral reading. Remind students that folk tales are often told orally.

Alternative Assessment

Present a Story Review Have students use the conclusions they made about the story to create a story review that they can present to a small group. Students should give the story a "grade" and support their conclusions and evaluations with details from the text. Circulate among the groups to make sure each student provides adequate evidence.

Vocabulary Development

Additional Practice

Create a Sound Word Challenge students to think of a common, everyday sound or action that could benefit from having an onomatopoetic word people could use to refer to it. You may want to suggest possibilities, such as a word for the "ringing" of a cellular phone (since cellular phones rarely actually "ring") or the sound elevator doors make when they close.

Grammar Link

Additional Practice

Use *Good* and *Well* Correctly Have each student write three sentences that include a choice between *good* and *well* to complete the sentence. Students should exchange sentences with a partner and circle the correct choices in their partners' sentences. Partners can check the results together. Be ready to settle any disagreements and to write any particularly challenging choices on the chalkboard for the class to discuss.

Reading Skills Development

Mixed Ability Group Draw Conclusions To give students additional practice with drawing conclusions, have them work with partners to re-read "Oni and the Great Bird." Direct students to take turns reading aloud. Students should pause at the end of their reading turn to discuss with their partner how they feel about the characters and setting and what they think will happen next in the plot. (You might try the Think Aloud activity found on page xxix of this book.) Then, students should fill in a chart like the one below with conclusions that can be made from the story. Point out to students that they can base their conclusions not only on the story but also on their prior knowledge and experience. Ask volunteers to share with the class some of the conclusions they came to while reading the story.

Conclusions	Reasons for My Conclusions

Vocabulary Skill
Use onomatopoeia.

Core Skill

Use the resources in the Reading Skills and Strategies section of this book to teach a core literary skill in which your struggling readers need remediation. Use "The Crane Wife" for the application portion of the lesson.

Literary Skills
• Understand taboo.
• Recognize onomatopoeia.

Reading Skill
Draw conclusions.

(**Resources**)
In this book:
• Vocabulary and Comprehension, p. 301
• Additional Vocabulary Practice, p. 302 (includes the previous two selections)

Other Resources:
• *Audio CD Library*
• *Audio CD Library, Selections and Summaries in Spanish*
• *Supporting Instruction in Spanish*

TARGETED STRATEGIES FOR SPECIAL EDUCATION STUDENTS

Prereading

Additional Background

Recall Metamorphosis Discuss the title of the story with students. Ask them what they expect from a tale titled "The Crane Wife." How can a crane, which is a bird, be a person's wife? Lead students to recall the motif of metamorphosis and to be on the lookout for the motif in the story.

Alternative Teaching Strategy

Connect to a Real-Life Lesson Ask students what prohibitions they find around them in their own daily lives. What are the reasons for the prohibitions? What bad things might happen if the rules are broken? Encourage students to apply their understanding of life's rules to the taboo broken by the main character in the folk tale they are about to read.

Reading

Listening and Speaking Opportunity

Use the Audio Recording Play the audio recording of the tale for students, pausing briefly at key points to allow students to draw conclusions about the tale. If students are hesitant to make judgments, prompt them by asking how they feel about the story so far and what they think of the main characters. Write students' suggestions on the chalkboard so that students can keep track of their conclusions and revise them as they read.

Postreading

Reteach the Key Idea

Reading Aloud Onomatopoeia After reading the tale, lead students in reviewing the examples of onomatopoeia found in the tale. Have students read the examples out loud together and discuss what the sounds add to the story. Do the words help students better imagine the events and setting of the tale?

Vocabulary and Comprehension

"The Crane Wife"

A. Match words and definitions. Write the letter of the correct definition next to each word.

_____ **1.** discern   **a.** of high quality; cultured

_____ **2.** relent   **b.** distinguish

_____ **3.** dreary   **c.** treated in a helpful manner

_____ **4.** refined   **d.** sad or depressing

_____ **5.** tended   **e.** give in

B. Choose three words from above. Use each word in a sentence.

1. _____

_____

2. _____

_____

3. _____

_____

C. Answer each question below.

1. What taboo is central to this folk tale?

_____

_____

2. What does Yohei discover from breaking the taboo?

_____

_____

Additional Vocabulary Practice

"Oni and the Great Bird"; "Master Frog"; "The Crane Wife"

A. Match words and definitions or descriptions. Write the letter of the correct definition or description next to each word.

_____ **1.** tarry

_____ **2.** slain

_____ **3.** perished

_____ **4.** curfew

_____ **5.** prosperity

_____ **6.** pathetic

_____ **7.** prostrated

_____ **8.** agony

_____ **9.** swooped

_____ **10.** entreaty

a. prohibited time to be outside one's house

b. died

c. killed

d. request

e. descended quickly

f. wealth

g. horrible pain

h. bowed in submission

i. stay for a short time

j. pitiful; evoking sympathy

B. Choose five words from above. Use each word in a sentence.

1. _____

_____

2. _____

_____

3. _____

_____

4. _____

_____

5. _____

_____

"Aunty Misery" By Judith Ortiz Cofer

Prereading

Reinforce the Concept

Discuss Wishes Motif Students will have read other stories in which someone's wishes have unintended adverse effects. Have students name the stories, and write the details they recall on the chalkboard. Ask students why the wishes had the effects they did. What do the effects say about humans? Students may conclude that it is difficult to see every possible effect of a cause.

Vocabulary Practice

(**Especially for ELL**) **Preview Additional Vocabulary** Preview with students the following words and their definitions. Have students use each word in an original sentence.

- *bid (p. 727):* asked
- *taunt (p. 728):* tease or torment
- *shimmied (p. 728):* moved in short, shaking bursts
- *gnarled (p. 728):* disfigured; misshapen
- *miseries (p. 728):* hardships

Reading

Alternative Activity

Play the Audio Recording Struggling readers will benefit from listening to the audio recording of "Aunty Misery" as they follow along in their books. Pause the recording to allow students to discuss the possible effects of Aunty Misery's wish and her tricking of Death. Students can record their answers in a cause-and-effect chain, such as the one on student book page 726.

Postreading

Alternative Assessment

(**Mixed Ability Group**) **Paraphrase Key Ideas** Students having difficulty identifying the causes and effects in the tale may also have difficulty identifying the major events in the story. Pair students, and together have them re-read the folk tale aloud, alternating paragraph by paragraph. Students should take turns paraphrasing each paragraph. For example: *The first paragraph describes a woman who lives alone and cares for a pear tree. People steal fruit from the tree and insult the woman.*

SKILLS FOCUS

Literary Skill
Understand the motif of wishes.

Reading Skill
Follow a cause-and-effect chain.

(**Resources**)

In this book:
- Vocabulary and Comprehension, p. 305
- Additional Vocabulary Practice, p. 310 (includes the next two selections)

Other Resources:
- *Audio CD Library*
- *Audio CD Library, Selections and Summaries in Spanish*
- *Supporting Instruction in Spanish*

(**Core Skill**)

Use the resources in the Reading Skills and Strategies section of this book to teach a core literary skill in which your struggling readers need remediation. Use "Aunty Misery" for the application portion of the lesson.

SKILLS FOCUS

Literary Skill
Understand the motif of wishes.

Reading Skill
Follow a cause-and-effect chain.

Resources

In this book:
• Vocabulary and Comprehension, p. 305
• Additional Vocabulary Practice, p. 310 (includes the next two selections)

Other Resources:
• *Audio CD Library*
• *Audio CD Library, Selections and Summaries in Spanish*
• *Supporting Instruction in Spanish*

Teacher Tip

Students may have difficulty seeing possible problems with the disappearance of death from the world. You may want to have students role-play that they are members of the professions mentioned in the story that are affected by Death's imprisonment. Ask students to add to their Quickwrites from this new perspective.

TARGETED STRATEGIES FOR SPECIAL EDUCATION STUDENTS

Prereading
Reteach the Key Idea

Causes and Effects Point out to students that big effects can come from small causes. To illustrate the point, play a game with students in which you provide an initial cause and they each take turns adding effects, in a chain. For example, you might say, "Because I woke up late, I missed the bus," to which students could add, "Because I missed the bus, I was late to school," and "Because I was late to school, I missed an important test," and so on.

Reading
Listening and Speaking Opportunity

Listen to Identify Causes and Effects Play the audio recording of the tale for students, and pause frequently to encourage students to identify the causes and effects in the story. One way to prompt students is to ask them what is happening in the story and, after they answer, to ask them why these events are occurring. Write their answers on the chalkboard in the form of a cause-and-effect chain, showing how the effect of one cause becomes the cause of the next effect.

Postreading
Alternative Assessment

Review and Assess To help students restate the main causes and effects throughout the tale, have them complete a *Somebody . . . Wants . . . But . . . So . . .* plot chart, in which each row is about a character *(Somebody)* and each cell in that row relates to that character's actions or desires *(Wants . . . But . . . So . . .)*. Ask students to write the four words in a column on a piece of paper and to fill in the blanks, looking back at the tale when necessary. Have students share their responses with the class. Record students' responses on the chalkboard.

Vocabulary and Comprehension

"Aunty Misery"

A. Match words and definitions. Write the letter of the correct definition next to each word.

_____ **1.** bid

_____ **2.** miseries

_____ **3.** gnarled

_____ **4.** taunt

_____ **5.** shimmied

a. moved in short, shaking bursts

b. asked

c. tease or torment

d. disfigured; misshapen

e. hardships

B. Choose three words from above. Use each word in a sentence.

1. _____

_____

2. _____

_____

3. _____

_____

C. Write T or F next to each statement to tell if it is true or false.

_____ **1.** Aunty Misery has a favorite apple tree in her backyard.

_____ **2.** Aunty Misery puts a spell on the tree with her magic wand.

_____ **3.** When Death comes for her, Aunty Misery tricks him into climbing the tree.

_____ **4.** People complain about the lack of death.

_____ **5.** Aunty Misery lets Death go if he promises not to let her tree die.

"The Hummingbird King"

retold by Argentina Palacios

SKILLS FOCUS

Literary Skill
Understand the origin motif.

Reading Skill
Retell a story.

Resources

In this book:
- Vocabulary and Comprehension, p. 309 (includes the next selection)
- Additional Vocabulary Practice, p. 310 (includes the previous selection and the next selection)

Other Resources:
- *Audio CD Library*
- *Audio CD Library, Selections and Summaries in Spanish*
- *Supporting Instruction in Spanish*

Core Skill

Use the resources in the Reading Skills and Strategies section of this book to help students having difficulty understanding plot. Use "The Hummingbird King" for the application portion of the lesson.

Prereading

Alternative Activity

Especially for ELL **Use Spanish Resources** Spanish-speaking English-language learners may benefit from reading or listening to the summary of "The Hummingbird King" in Spanish in preparation for reading the selection in English.

Vocabulary Practice

Preview Additional Vocabulary Preview with students the following words and their definitions. Have students use each word in an original sentence.

- *stately (p. 733):* elegant; dignified
- *plaza (p. 733):* town square
- *excelled (p. 734):* did very well
- *reckless (p. 735):* taking unwise risks
- *merits (p. 736):* values; benefits
- *crest (p. 737):* a group of feathers at the top of a bird's head

Reading

Alternative Activity

Use a Retelling Summary Sheet to Track Events Filling out a Retelling Summary Sheet, such as the one on page 12 of their books, will help students complete the Reading Check activity on student book page 738. You may want to copy the summary sheet on the chalkboard, reviewing each item with students: Introduction, Characters, Conflict, Complication, Climax, Resolution, and Personal Response. Review the beginning of the sample retelling of "Duffy's Jacket" with students to help get them started.

Postreading

Alternative Assessment

Create Story Panels Have students each create three to five sketches showing important scenes from the folk tale. Students can refer to the drawings when taking turns retelling the story in small groups.

TARGETED STRATEGIES FOR SPECIAL EDUCATION STUDENTS

Prereading
Reteach the Key Idea

The Origin Tale Discuss with students why someone might want to know how something came to be or why something is the way it is; for example, how the stars came to light up the night sky or why the daytime sky is blue. Point out that one way to answer the question is to create a story. Alert students that the story they are about to read does not merely explain the origin of something; it also reveals something about the ways humans act and interact.

Additional Background

Origin Motif Students will have read other stories in which the origins of something are explained. Ask students to name such stories with which they are familiar, including the Greek myth of Demeter and Persephone mentioned in their books. What do students think a story called "The Hummingbird King" will explain?

Reading
Listening and Speaking Opportunity

Listen to Identify Key Points Play the audio recording of the tale for students, and direct students to raise their hands when they hear a key idea or detail in the text. Pause the recording then, and discuss the point with students. Write on the chalkboard the points students all agree are important so that students can use the notes to retell the story afterward.

Postreading
Alternative Assessment

Review and Assess After students have read the tale, review with students the comments they made before reading about the origin motif. Have them compare "The Hummingbird King" to other origin stories they have read. How are the stories similar? How are they different?

SKILLS FOCUS

Literary Skill
Understand the origin motif.

Reading Skill
Retell a story.

Resources

In this book:
- Vocabulary and Comprehension, p. 309 (includes the next selection)
- Additional Vocabulary Practice, p. 310 (includes the previous selection and the next selection)

Other Resources:
- *Audio CD Library*
- *Audio CD Library, Selections and Summaries in Spanish*
- *Supporting Instruction in Spanish*

"The Search Goes On"

from *The Mystery of the Ancient Maya,*
by Carolyn Meyer and Charles Gallenkamp

SKILLS FOCUS

Reading Skill
Summarize the main ideas.

Resources

In this book:
• Vocabulary and Comprehension, p. 309 (includes the previous selection)
• Additional Vocabulary Practice, p. 310 (includes the previous two selections)

Other Resources:
• *Audio CD Library*
• *Audio CD Library, Selections and Summaries in Spanish*
• *Supporting Instruction in Spanish*

Special Education Students

You may need to direct students to limit the number of main ideas they record for each paragraph to only one or two short sentences. After reading, students can review their sentences and delete any that are not absolutely necessary to make their summaries complete and clear.

Prereading
Vocabulary Practice

(**Especially for ELL**) **Preview Additional Vocabulary** Preview with students the following words and their definitions. Have students use each word in an original sentence.

• *revelations (p. 740):* important releases of information
• *legacy (p. 740):* tradition, knowledge, or gift from ancestors
• *relief (p. 741):* a raised design
• *dignitary (p. 741):* important citizen or official
• *plunder (p. 742):* rob; strip of value

Reading
Alternative Activity

(**Core Skill**) **Chart the Main Idea** Play the audio recording of the selection as students follow along in their books. Pause the recording after each paragraph to allow students time to write down the main idea and supporting details. Students may find it helpful to use an outline, such as the one below, for each paragraph. Students can then use their notes when writing their summaries afterward.

    I. Paragraph 1
        A. Main Idea
            1. Supporting Detail
            2. Supporting Detail

Postreading
Listening and Speaking Opportunity

Write and Deliver a News Story Have students fashion their summaries as news stories about the search to discover ancient Mayan artifacts in Guatemala. Students can take turns reading aloud their news stories in small groups. Remind students that news stories aim to give as quickly as possible the answers to the *5W-How?* questions.

Vocabulary and Comprehension

"The Hummingbird King";
"The Search Goes On"

A. Match words and definitions. Write the letter of the correct definition next to each word.

_____ **1.** decipher

_____ **2.** ransacked

_____ **3.** unscrupulous

_____ **4.** connoisseurs

_____ **5.** artifacts

a. searched thoroughly for goods to steal

b. interpret

c. objects made by people

d. dishonest

e. people who are experts on something

B. Choose three words from above. Use each word in a sentence.

1. _____

_____

2. _____

_____

3. _____

_____

C. Write T or F next to each statement to tell if it is true or false.

_____ **1.** The number thirteen is a lucky number for the Maya.

_____ **2.** When Kukul was born, a giant hummingbird appeared to the people.

_____ **3.** Chirumá helped Kukul in whatever way he could.

_____ **4.** The Maya were an ancient people living in present-day Guatemala.

_____ **5.** Many important Mayan ruins have been robbed by looters.

Additional Vocabulary Practice

"Aunty Misery"; "The Hummingbird King"; "The Search Goes On"

A. Match words and definitions. Write the letter of the correct definition next to each word.

_____ **1.** stately

_____ **2.** reckless

_____ **3.** merits

_____ **4.** plaza

_____ **5.** plunder

_____ **6.** miseries

_____ **7.** excelled

_____ **8.** crest

_____ **9.** dignitary

_____ **10.** relief

a. values; benefits

b. taking unwise risks

c. a group of feathers at the top of a bird's head

d. rob; strip of value

e. did very well

f. town square

g. elegant; dignified

h. hardships

i. a raised design

j. important person

B. Choose five words from above. Use each word in a sentence.

1. _____

_____

2. _____

_____

3. _____

_____

4. _____

_____

5. _____

_____

Comparing Literature:
The Cinderella Story

Prereading
Vocabulary Practice

(**Especially for ELL**) **Preview Additional Vocabulary** Preview with students the following words and their definitions.

- *pious (p. 748):* strictly following a religion
- *obliged (p. 748):* expected; forced
- *utmost (p. 748):* greatest extent
- *flourished (p. 749):* thrived and grew
- *bidden (p. 749):* asked (past participle of *bid*)
- *fast (p. 749):* securely tightened
- *alighted (p. 750):* landed
- *dainty (p. 758):* graceful and light
- *dashing (p. 759):* elegant and handsome
- *drab (p. 759):* plain

Reading
Alternative Teaching Strategy

(**Mixed Ability Group**) **Check for Motifs/Practice Fluency** Pair students, and ask partners to keep track of the motifs found in the three selections as they read them aloud together. Point out to students that some story motifs are mentioned on page 696 of their books.

Postreading
Alternative Assessment

Compare and Contrast To assess students' understanding of the characters, plot, tone, and theme of the three selections, complete this whole-class activity. Reproduce the chart found on student book page 757. Call on students, one at a time, to go to the chalkboard, and have them fill in the blanks on the chart. Once the chart is complete, discuss the answers with the class, making any corrections or additions as necessary.

SKILLS FOCUS

Literary Skill
Analyze the Cinderella story.

Reading Skill
Compare and contrast texts.

(**Resources**)

In this book:
- Vocabulary and Comprehension, p. 313
- Additional Vocabulary Practice, p. 314

(**Core Skill**)

Use the resources in the Reading Skills and Strategies section of this book to help students having difficulty comparing and contrasting. Use "Aschenputtel," "Dinorella," or "Interview" (any two) for the application portion of the lesson.

Literary Skill
Analyze the Cinderella
story.

Reading Skill
Compare and contrast texts.

Resources

In this book:
• Vocabulary and
Comprehension, p. 313
• Additional Vocabulary
Practice, p. 314

Teacher Tip

Students may have difficulty
comparing and contrasting
such different selections.
You can help them by
asking them to name from
the selections each specific
feature in the list on page
746 of their books.

TARGETED STRATEGIES FOR SPECIAL EDUCATION STUDENTS

Prereading
Additional Background

Cinderella Students will probably have read or seen other versions
of the Cinderella story. Briefly discuss with students the main
elements they remember from the other versions.

Reteach the Key Idea

Compare and Contrast Remind students that when they compare
and contrast, they point out both the similarities and differences
between things. Students will benefit from practicing comparing
and contrasting with two familiar things, such as two objects in the
room or the classroom and the cafeteria. Write a simple chart on
the chalkboard with the column headings "Similarities" and
"Differences" to help students organize their suggestions.

Reading
Listening and Speaking Opportunity

Listen to Identify Story Elements You may want to read the
selections aloud to students or have volunteers read aloud, pausing
frequently to encourage students to identify the elements in the
selections: main characters, plot, tone, and theme. Write students'
responses on the chalkboard, and after the last selection, review the
notes to help students begin to compare and contrast the selections.

Postreading
Alternative Assessment

Make Evaluations Have students make comparative and evaluative
statements about the selections on each of the main literary
elements. The kinds of statements students make will be up to them,
but you may want to prompt them with the following questions:
Which Cinderella character did you find most appealing? Which plot
was the most interesting? Which of the selections' tones fit the story
the best? Which selection did you find most meaningful? Students
should support their statements with reasons.

Vocabulary and Comprehension

Comparing Literature:
The Cinderella Story

A. Match words and definitions. Write the letter of the correct definition next to each word.

_____ **1.** biddable

_____ **2.** stunted

_____ **3.** curry favor

_____ **4.** pitch

_____ **5.** ordained

a. black, sticky tar

b. ordered or decreed

c. obedient

d. try to win approval by flattering and fawning

e. not properly grown

B. Choose three words from above. Use each word in a sentence.

1. _____

_____

2. _____

_____

3. _____

_____

C. Answer each question below.

1. What main character do all three selections have in common? Describe this character.

_____

_____

2. How is the main character treated by her family in each selection?

_____

_____

Comparing Literature:
The Cinderella Story

A. Match words and definitions or descriptions. Write the letter of the correct definition or description next to each word.

_____ **1.** utmost

_____ **2.** dainty

_____ **3.** alighted

_____ **4.** bidden

_____ **5.** drab

_____ **6.** pious

_____ **7.** obliged

_____ **8.** dashing

_____ **9.** flourished

_____ **10.** fast

a. expected; forced

b. strictly following a religion

c. elegant and handsome

d. thrived and grew

e. graceful and light

f. asked

g. greatest extent

h. landed

i. securely tightened

j. plain

B. Choose five words from above. Use each word in a sentence.

1. _____

_____

2. _____

_____

3. _____

_____

4. _____

_____

5. _____

_____

Collection 7
Literary Criticism: Where I Stand

Elements of Literature: Literary Criticism

SKILLS FOCUS

Literary Skill
Understand literary criticism.

Background

Learn the Language of Literature Some students may come from cultures where it is impolite to disagree or be controversial in any way. Explain that literary criticism requires that they express their opinions about what they are reading. Remind students that they have been learning the vocabulary of literary criticism since Collection One. Tell them that as they read the selections in this chapter, they should think about whether they enjoy them and identify what literary elements make them enjoyable.

(Teacher Tip)

In many cultures it is considered rude to challenge the teacher or a person in authority.

Alternative Teaching Strategy

(Especially for ELL) Make a Checklist Asking students to analyze a piece of literature may seem too abstract. Work with them to make the task more concrete by compiling a checklist. (See pp. 786–787 of the text.) Write the checklist on the board and ask students to copy it into their notebooks for reference. Title it: "Checklist for Literary Criticism." Tell students to have this checklist at hand as they read.

Characters	Plot	Theme	Language	Nonfiction
Are they believable?	Did it hold your attention?	Was the message clear?	Did the writer use figurative language?	Is it objective?
Are their motivations clear?	Is it believable?	Did it make you think?	Did the writer use imagery?	Is it accurate?
Do you like them?	Are the causes and effects clearly connected?	Was the message fresh or had you heard it all before?		Are the primary sources credible?
Do you identify with any of them?				Do the biographical characters come to life?
What connections can you make?				

SKILLS FOCUS

Literary Skill
Understand literary criticism.

TARGETED STRATEGIES FOR SPECIAL EDUCATION STUDENTS

Elements of Literature: Literary Criticism

Background

Do You Like It? Some students may find the idea of analyzing literature too difficult to think about.

- Ask: Did you like the books you read?
- Ask: Why did you like some books and not others?

Tell students that determining why they like or dislike a piece of literature is the beginning of literary criticism. To be a literary critic, they have to be able to use the language of criticism—academic terms they have been learning all year.

Alternative Teaching Strategy

Born Literary Critics To help students analyze a literary work and determine the extent to which the literary elements in the work shaped their response, ask them how they might feel if they read a story about space aliens and astronauts from earth meeting in a distant galaxy. They might respond, "That would be exciting." When you probe to find out what would be exciting about such a story, lead them to identify:

- *plot*—the events in the story probably happen quickly, and the reader wants to find out what happens.
- *characters*—the people and other beings that motivate or respond to the events of the plot.

As homework, ask students to read a story and then report whether they liked it. Ask them to tell if the plot was exciting and if they liked the characters. Have them explain what made the plot exciting, and why they liked the characters. They should be able to support their viewpoints with details.

Academic Vocabulary

Learn the Language There are some standard academic terms used in literary criticism. Tell students to look at the boldface terms on pages 786–787. Review these terms and their definitions with students. Help students use the terms by writing sentences describing books they have read.

Elements of Literature
pages 792–809

King Arthur: The Sword in the Stone retold by Hudson Talbott

Prereading
Additional Background

Explore a Legend Why do some stories spark the imaginations of people from generation to generation? The Arthurian legend has been told and retold for 1,500 years. People respond to the goodness of the character, his idealistic goals, and the promise that he will return to lead his countrymen to victory against the enemy in England's darkest hour. Children identify with the young Arthur astounding everyone by pulling the sword from the stone, adults identify with the wise, mature Arthur, and readers of all ages would welcome having Merlin, the wily sorcerer, as an ally.

Alternative Activity

Use *The Holt Reader* You may consider having students use the Before You Read page in *The Holt Reader*, either instead of or in addition to the Before You Read page in the student book.

Reading
Alternative Activities

Use *The Holt Reader* You may have students read the selection in *The Holt Reader* and use the margins in that book to make notes and respond to the instruction.

Feel the Magic Point out that this legend shares elements of the fairy tale, a genre familiar to many cultures. Help students list some standard elements of the fairy tale that appear in *King Arthur: The Sword in the Stone.*

- Its setting is long ago and in a faraway land: "in ancient times, when Britain was still a wild and restless place."
- Its characters are kings, queens, sorcerers, and a beautiful child.
- It involves a contest that the main character must win to prove his worthiness.

Identify the Hero's Tale Define the elements of the hero's tale and point out to students that *King Arthur: The Sword in the Stone* incorporates them. On the chalkboard, draw the chart that appears on page 808 of the student book. Have students copy the chart and fill it

SKILLS FOCUS

Literary Skill
Understand legends.

Resources

In this book:
- Vocabulary and Comprehension, p. 321
- Additional Vocabulary Practice, p. 322

Other Resources:
- *The Holt Reader*
- *Audio CD Library*
- *Audio CD Library, Selections and Summaries in Spanish*
- *Supporting Instruction in Spanish*

Especially for ELL

Ask students to share with the class any legends of their native cultures that are similar to the Arthurian legend.

in as they read. Ask them how they feel when they read that Arthur is able to pass the trial of kingship by pulling the sword from the stone. Do students feel a sense of justice, of good prevailing over evil? Elicit from them that it is Arthur's goodness, as well as his parentage, that makes him fit to pass the trial. Ask students to name some ways that the writer shows Arthur to be a good person. (Students may note that Arthur is humble, loyal, and loving to his family and to animals.)

Alternative Teaching Strategy

Explore Emotional Response Help students respond to *King Arthur: The Sword in the Stone*. Tell them to prepare for a class discussion by noting which points of the story they enjoy most. Have them copy the following elements into their notebooks:

- believable plot and characters
- enchanting magic
- significant relationships
- meaningful themes

Tell them that you will discuss the story later, using these elements as discussion points.

Postreading

Alternative Activity

Use *The Holt Reader* You may consider having students use the postreading activities in *The Holt Reader*, either instead of or in addition to the postreading activities in the student book.

Alternative Teaching Strategy

(**Mixed Ability Group**) **Analyze Responses** To help students respond to a literary work and determine the extent to which the literary elements in the work shape the response, have students work in groups to discuss the story. Have students use the chart on page 315 of this book as a guide.

- Ask students if they think the characters are believable. Ask: Do you like the characters? Which ones? Why? Would you like to meet them? Do you identify with any of them?

- Ask students if they think the plot is believable in the context of the story. Did it hold their interest? Did they like it?

- Ask about theme. What message is the author sending to his readers? Does that message apply today? Do you think that good always triumphs over evil? While reading the story, did you want Arthur to triumph?

Vocabulary Development

Reteach the Key Idea

Trace Word Roots The language spoken during the time of King Arthur was a form of Old English. One of the early influences on English was Latin, which was introduced to England by the ancient Romans during their period of exploration and conquest. The following vocabulary words are from *King Arthur: The Sword in the Stone*. Have students use the information in their books to guess which words come from Old English and which come from Latin.

wild *(OE)*   position *(L)*

order *(L)*   wisdom *(OE)*

patiently *(L)*   duke *(OE)*

quickly *(OE)*   anvil *(OE)*

devoted *(L)*   confessed *(L)*

stone *(OE)*   future *(L)*

restless *(OE)*   child *(OE)*

ominously *(L)*   candidate *(L)*

credentials *(L)*   month *(OE)*

greatness *(OE)*   register *(L)*

After students have completed their guesses, have them check their answers in a dictionary.

Vocabulary Practice

Use the Dictionary Give students further practice using the Word Bank words on page 809. Have students look up their meanings in the dictionary and write the root word and origin of each in a chart like the one below.

Word	Root Word	Definition
turbulent *(p. 794)*	turbulentus (L)	wild, disorderly
tournament *(p. 796)*	torneiement (OF)	series of contests
integrity *(p. 798)*	integritas (L)	honesty, uprightness
congregation *(p. 799)*	ongregatio (L)	gathering

For example, for *turbulent* they should write *turbulentus* and *L* for "Latin." Ask students to read the definition and to write a definition in their own words. Work with students to explore other words that are close to the target word to see if the words are related. Ask them to add the related words to the chart. For example, words close to *turbulent* might include *turboprop*, *turbojet*, and *turbine*. Ask volunteers to list the words that they have found that are related to the target vocabulary and explain what they mean and how that meaning relates to the meaning of their roots.

Vocabulary Skills
Understand Latin and Anglo-Saxon word origins.

Especially for ELL

Spanish-speaking students and other ELLs may find it difficult to identify words with an Old English origin. Spanish and English do share Latin as the basis for much of their vocabularies, but Spanish does not derive from Old English.

Core Skill

Use the resources in the Reading Skills and Strategies section of this book to teach a core literary skill in which your struggling readers need remediation. Use *King Arthur: The Sword in the Stone* for the application portion of the lesson.

Literary Skill
Understand legends.

In this book:
• Vocabulary and
Comprehension, p. 321
• Additional Vocabulary
Practice, p. 322

Other Resources:
• *The Holt Reader*
• *Audio CD Library*
• *Audio CD Library,*
Selections and Summaries
in Spanish
• *Supporting Instruction*
in Spanish

Teacher Tip

The points of the hero's
story are: (1) born in an
obscure place, (2) unknown
parentage, (3) threatened as
a child, (4) passes a test, and
(5) unlikely person to be
king. Explain that only
Merlin truly knows when
Arthur was born and who
his parents are.

TARGETED STRATEGIES FOR SPECIAL EDUCATION STUDENTS

Prereading
Additional Background

Grow a Legend Prepare students for reading *King Arthur: The Sword in the Stone* by explaining that it is a legend. Explain that a legend is a very old story about a hero and his or her great deeds that has been told by storytellers for many years. As each story was told and retold, it was changed and embellished until its heroes or events bear little resemblance to the people or events that inspired the original story.

Explain that King Arthur was famous for ruling his kingdom with the help of a council of knights that met around a great round table in his castle. The knights chosen by King Arthur to be his round table advisors had proven themselves to be particularly honest, good-hearted, valiant in battle, and wise.

Reading
Additional Activity

Introduce the Hero To help students identify the King Arthur story as a legend, draw the chart on page 808 of the student book on the chalkboard. Play the audio recording and ask students to raise their hands when they hear something about Arthur that matches a point on the chart. Discuss the points on the chart until the story is completed and students are convinced that King Arthur's story fits the pattern of a legend.

Postreading
Additional Activity

Analyze the Response Help students understand that specific literary elements make this story enjoyable. Ask: Did you like the characters? Why or why not? Ask if the plot held their interest. As they read, did they want to know what would happen next? Finally, ask what they learned from the story.

After the class discussion, have students work in small groups. Have one student in each group act as moderator, leading others to focus the discussion on whether they responded positively to the story because of the style of the writing, the subject, the plot, the characters, or other elements. Ask the groups to write down their findings to present to the class.

Vocabulary and Comprehension

King Arthur: The Sword in the Stone

A. Complete each sentence with a word from the Word Bank.

1. The years after King Uther's death were wild and

_____ ones.

2. Knights compete in the _____.

3. A _____ of lords and ladies from all over England came to watch the celebration.

4. Knights acted with fairness and _____.

> **Word Bank**
> turbulent
> tournament
> integrity
> congregation

B. Write T or F next to each statement to tell if it is true or false.

_____ **1.** King Uther had no son.

_____ **2.** Merlin was a sorcerer.

_____ **3.** Arthur was raised as Sir Kay's younger brother.

_____ **4.** Arthur was raised by Merlin.

_____ **5.** King Lot and King Urien do not want to accept Arthur as the heir to the throne.

C. Answer each question below.

1. Why did Merlin take Arthur away from his father?

_____

_____

2. According to Merlin, what is Arthur's destiny?

_____

_____

3. How does Arthur react when he learns that he is the heir to the throne?

_____

_____

Additional Vocabulary Practice

King Arthur: *The Sword in the Stone*

A. Match words and definitions. Write the letter of the correct definition next to each word.

_____ **1.** integrity   **a.** wild; disorderly

_____ **2.** tournament   **b.** series of contests

_____ **3.** congregation   **c.** honesty; uprightness

_____ **4.** turbulent   **d.** gathering

B. Choose three words from above. Use each word in a sentence.

1. _____

_____

2. _____

_____

3. _____

_____

C. Use context clues to determine the meaning of the underlined word.

1. During the *joust*, knights fought each other on horseback with

long lances. <u>Joust</u> means _____

_____

_____

2. The knight used his *lance*, or long, pointed pole, to knock his enemy off

his horse. <u>Lance</u> means _____

_____

_____

Three Responses to Literature

Prereading

Background

(**Especially for ELL**) **Respond to Literature** Help students understand that they are to analyze the three essays on pages 811–813 of their book and then judge which essay best answers the question: Does Arthur have potential for greatness? Tell students to look at the notes on the right side of the first article for clues about analyzing essays.

Reading

Alternative Teaching Strategy

Use a Chart to Compare To help students compare and contrast these essays, draw a chart on the board with three headings: ESSAY 1, ESSAY 2, ESSAY 3. Down the left side write:

- Answers the question directly
- States the main idea
- Supports the main idea with quotes and examples from the text
- Compares/contrasts Arthur with other characters to show his potential for greatness
- Summarizes the main idea

Have students copy the chart on a piece of blank paper. Then, have them write under the proper heading their responses to the five statements above. Guide students to the realization that Essay 1 has the best organization and presentation. It stays focused on the question and draws evidence directly from the story. While Essay 2 answers the question, its presentation is not as thorough and convincing. It uses direct quotations, but does not compare and contrast Arthur with other characters. Essay 3 merely summarizes the story without addressing the question and lacks analysis and evidence.

Postreading

Additional Activity

Write a Response Have students write a paragraph on the question, "Is the sorcerer Merlin a good or bad character?" Support for their answers should include direct quotations from the text.

SKILLS FOCUS

Reading Skill
Analyze responses to a literary work.

(**Resources**)
In this book:
- Vocabulary and Comprehension, p. 324
- Additional Vocabulary Practice, p. 325

(**Core Skill**)
Use the resources in the Reading Skills and Strategies section of this book to help students having difficulty comparing and contrasting. Use two of the Three Responses to Literature covered in this lesson plan for the application portion of the lesson.

Vocabulary and Comprehension

Three Responses to Literature

A. Complete each sentence with a word from the Word Bank.

1. The stars form a dragon and _____
Arthur's great future.

2. Arthur's fate, or _____, is to become
England's greatest king.

3. Arthur has faith in the strength and

_____ of his people.

> **Word Bank**
> courage
> destiny
> foreshadow

B. Write the letter of the phrases in the right column that best describe the
word, phrases, or sentence in the left column.

_____ **1.** "Greatness surrounds
you," said Merlin.

_____ **2.** Merlin told Arthur that
greatness surrounded him.

_____ **3.** essay

_____ **4.** details and examples

_____ **5.** summarize

a. an indirect quotation

b. a direct quotation

c. a short piece of writing,
giving the writer's personal
ideas

d. to tell the main points
in a few words

e. support for a main idea

C. Answer each question below.

1. How does Essay 1 compare and contrast Kay and Arthur?

_____   _____

_____

2. What are four qualities that Essay 2 says Arthur possesses?

_____

_____

3. What is the main problem with Essay 3?

_____

_____

Additional Vocabulary Practice

Three Responses to Literature

A. Write the word in the Word Bank that fits each group of related words.

_____ **1.** courageous, courageously, courageousness

_____ **2.** destined, destination, predestined

_____ **3.** wise, wisely, wiser, unwise

_____ **4.** honorable, dishonor, honorary, honorarium

_____ **5.** glorious, glorify, glorification

_____ **6.** rightful, rightly, righteous, rights

_____ **7.** quotation, quotable, misquote, quoted

> **Word Bank**
> courage
> destiny
> glory
> honor
> quote
> right
> wisdom

B. Choose two words from above. Use each word in a sentence.

1. _____

_____

2. _____

_____

C. Choose the correct word in parentheses to complete each sentence.

1. *(summary, summarize)*   A _____ restates the main ideas. Don't use details to _____ the main ideas.

2. *(quote, quotations)*   When you repeat the exact words of a person, you _____ him or her. Many newspaper articles include _____ by the people who were interviewed.

3. *(direct, indirect)*   When you report someone's exact words, you are using _____ quotations. When you rephrase something that someone said, you are using _____ quotations.

"He's No King"

SKILLS FOCUS

Reading Skills
Understand stereotype and bias.

Vocabulary Skill
Understand Greek roots.

(Resources)

In this book:
• Vocabulary and Comprehension, p. 327
• Additional Vocabulary Practice, p. 328

Other Resources:
• *Audio CD Library*
• *Audio CD Library, Selections and Summaries in Spanish*
• *Supporting Instruction in Spanish*

(Special Education Students)

Students who have difficulty reading may learn more by listening to the audio recording of the selection. Listening to the selection may also help struggling readers identify bias and stereotype.

Prereading
Vocabulary Practice

(Especially for ELL) **Define Terms** Be sure that English-language learners understand the terms *stereotype, bias,* and *prejudice.*

• *Stereotype* is an unfair, fixed idea about a group of people.
• *Bias* is an attitude or belief that shapes thinking in spite of the facts.
• *Prejudice* is extreme bias.

Ask students to generate their own examples of these terms. Then, have students predict how the terms might apply to King Arthur's story. Remind them to check their predictions as they read.

Reading
Alternative Teaching Strategy

Use a Chart to Identify Bias and Stereotype Make a chart on the board with two headings: BIASES and STEREOTYPES. Have students identify examples of bias and stereotypes in the letter. Write their responses on the chart and discuss why each belongs in its category.

Postreading
Alternative Assessment

(Mixed Ability Group) **Write a Response** Divide the students into groups of three or four, and ask them to write a response to Kings Lot and Urien that addresses the bias in the kings' letter and explains why Arthur should be the rightful king.

Vocabulary Development
Vocabulary Practice

(Especially for ELL) **Identify Greek Roots** English-language learners may find it challenging to complete the Practice exercise on page 819 in the student edition. Copy the sentences on the board, and guide students in completing them correctly. Then, ask students to underline the Greek root in each answer and discuss how the meaning of the root relates to the meaning of the word.

Vocabulary and Comprehension

"He's No King"

A. Write a sentence for each word, using the definitions given. Your sentences should be about "He's No King."

1. *bias:* prejudice; a leaning in favor of or against someone or something

_____

_____

2. *stereotype:* a fixed way of thinking about a person or group, allowing for no individuality

_____

_____

B. Use each word above in a sentence.

1. _____

_____

2. _____

_____

C. Answer each question below.

1. What are King Lot and King Urien protesting?

_____

_____

2. What reason do they give to support their claim that they should rule?

_____

_____

3. Give two reasons they use to show that Arthur is too weak to rule.

_____

_____

Additional Vocabulary Practice

"He's No King"

A. Complete each sentence with a word from the Word Bank.

1. A person who has an important job but is controlled

by others is called a _____ .

2. The play was about a poor and _____
shepherd.

3. He loved a young lady, but she thought he was a

_____ without strong character.

4. What was the ending, or _____, of his sad story?

Word Bank
lowly
puppet
outcome
weakling

B. Choose two words from the Word Bank. Use each word in a sentence.

1. _____

_____

2. _____

_____

C. Finish each sentence with a description that fits the underlined word.

1. If you are a <u>puppet on a string</u>, you _____

_____

2. A person who is <u>lowly</u> is _____

_____

"Merlin and the Dragons"
retold by Jane Yolen

Prereading

Background

Discuss Historical Figures Tell students that just as there really was a man named Arthur who was a king, there really was a man named Merlin who acted as Arthur's advisor.

Vocabulary Practice

Reinforce Targeted Vocabulary Help students learn these four words from "Merlin and the Dragons."

- *ruthless (p. 823):* without pity. Vortigern is a man without pity; he is *ruthless.*
- *bedraggled (p. 823):* hanging limp and wet; dirty. The *bedraggled* banners hung, dirty and limp, from broken windows.
- *insolence (p. 828):* disrespect. Emrys hurled insults at the approaching king, unconcerned that the warrior was furious at his *insolence.*
- *recognition (p. 829):* knowing; awareness. It was Arthur's *recognition* of the dragon's tooth that made him aware of Merlin's identity.

Reading

Alternative Teaching Strategy

Mixed Ability Group **Analyze the Structure** Help students analyze how the structure of "Merlin and the Dragons" shapes the reader's response. Ask groups of students to use the chart on student book page 808 to determine whether Merlin's story fits the pattern of the hero's story. For example: Birth—Merlin was the son of a princess, so people probably knew where he was born; Parentage—no one knew who his father was; Threat—after he predicted an eclipse, everyone was sure he was a demon; Test—Merlin passed a test that proved he was a prophet; Unlikeliness—he, as a fatherless boy about to be sacrificed, was an unlikely hero.

Remind students that a hero often gathers a band of followers and embarks on a quest to save his people from some threat. Discuss whether saving Arthur and preparing him for kingship fulfills the same function. Lead students to realize that the Merlin story, with slight variations, fulfills the pattern of the hero's story. He will never be king, but he will be a powerful figure during King Arthur's reign.

SKILLS FOCUS

Literary Skill
Understand heroes.

Resources

In this book:
- Vocabulary and Comprehension, p. 332
- Additional Vocabulary Practice, p. 333

Other Resources:
- *Audio CD Library*
- *Audio CD Library, Selections and Summaries in Spanish*
- *Supporting Instruction in Spanish*

Especially for ELL

English-language learners may benefit from listening to the audio recording of the selection as they follow along in their books. You may want to stop and replay any confusing sections for students.

Vocabulary Skills
• Understand prefixes and suffixes.
• Clarify word meanings by using examples.

Postreading
Additional Activity

Hold a Focus Group To help students analyze their responses to Merlin's hero story, tell them that they are going to be part of a focus group. The purpose of the focus group is to find out what students think of the story form they have been studying, the hero story. Ask questions like: Since you were already familiar with the pattern of the hero's story when you read "Merlin and the Dragons," did you know what to expect? Did the plot hold any surprises? Did you think that the character of young Merlin, or Emrys, is as likeable as the young Arthur? Why? Was Merlin's story more or less exciting than Arthur's? Why? How did you feel when you found out that young Emrys was really Merlin? Guide students to identify the literary elements that made them like or dislike "Merlin and the Dragons."

Vocabulary Development
Vocabulary Practice

Recognize Prefixes and Suffixes Show students how they can use knowledge of Anglo-Saxon and Latin affixes to break down and figure out the meanings of unfamiliar words and increase their vocabularies. List on the chalkboard the affixes listed in Practice One on page 832 of the student book, and help students make word maps for each of the affixes. Sample sentences for *un-*, *ex-*, *in-*, and *-less* are listed below.

un- is a common prefix from Middle English, meaning "not." It is ultimately derived from the Latin prefix *in-*.

• *un-* used with *able* forms *unable,* meaning "lacking the ability." The dog was *unable* to run freely in the city.

ex- is a prefix meaning "out from" and is derived from Latin via Greek.

• *ex-* used with *press* forms *express,* meaning "to say, to put into words." The shy person found it difficult to get his ideas out, or to *express* his ideas.

in- is a prefix meaning "lack of" from Latin, usually giving a negative meaning.

• *in-* used with *correct* means "not right." The question on the test was *incorrect*.

The suffix *-less* means "without or lacking." It comes from Old English *leas* meaning "free or loose."

• *-less* used with *rest* is *restless,* meaning "fidgety, unable to sit still." The children were *restless* on this rainy day.

TARGETED STRATEGIES FOR SPECIAL EDUCATION STUDENTS

Prereading
Background

Clarify Important Information Tell students that they have read one hero story and are about to read another. Explain that "Merlin and the Dragons" is a story about the sorcerer who saved, taught, and advised Arthur. In this story, Arthur lives with Merlin and has pulled the sword from the stone but doesn't yet know who his father was. Merlin tells Arthur a story that comforts and encourages Arthur because through that story Arthur learns that he is the son of King Uther and thus the true heir to the throne.

Reading
Alternative Teaching Strategy

Analyze the Story Within a Story Help students understand that many times a story character will spin a story within the story in order to tell the listener something important. Ask them to identify the important information Merlin gives Arthur. Explain that the story begins with dreams; Arthur can't sleep because of bad dreams. Point out that dreaming will appear again and is important to this story. After students reach the end of the story, ask them what was important about Arthur's and Emrys's dreams. *(They always come true in some way.)* Then, ask students to tell how the dreams in the story change from beginning to end. Help students recognize that the story starts with scary dreams and ends with promising dreams.

Postreading
Alternative Assessment

Analyze the Story To monitor how well students understand the literary elements in "Merlin and the Dragons," ask them to write a brief review of the story for a friend. Have them answer these questions:

- Is the plot exciting?
- Why or why not?
- Are the characters believable?
- Do you like them?
- What did you learn from the story?
- What is the story's theme?

Literary Skill
Understand heroes.

Resources
In this book:
- Vocabulary and Comprehension, p. 332
- Additional Vocabulary Practice, p. 333

Other Resources:
- *Audio CD Library*
- *Audio CD Library, Selections and Summaries in Spanish*
- *Supporting Instruction in Spanish*

Vocabulary and Comprehension

"Merlin and the Dragons"

A. Match words and definitions. Write the letter of the correct definition next to each word.

_____ **1.** recognition

_____ **2.** bedraggled

_____ **3.** ruthless

_____ **4.** insolence

a. without pity

b. knowing; awareness

c. hanging limp and wet; dirty

d. disrespect

B. Answer each question below.

1. What kinds of dreams does Emrys have? How does he use them?

_____

_____

2. Where are the white and red dragons found?

_____

_____

3. Whom does the white dragon symbolize? What relationship does this knight have with Arthur?

_____

_____

4. Who is Emrys?

_____

_____

5. What is the main reason that Merlin tells Arthur the story of Emrys and the dragons?

_____

_____

Additional Vocabulary Practice

"Merlin and the Dragons"

A. Complete each sentence with a word from the Word Bank.

1. The horse and rider were dirty and

_____ after their long ride.

2. The cruel and _____ man showed no
mercy.

3. The boy gave no sign of _____ as he
passed his uncle.

4. The other children gasped at the disrespect and _____
of the boy.

Word Bank
recognition
ruthless
bedraggled
insolence

B. Choose two words from above. Use each word in a sentence.

1. _____

_____

2. _____

_____

C. Finish each sentence with a description that fits the underlined word.

1. A *prophet* claims to tell what will happen in the future. A <u>prophecy</u> is

_____

2. An *estimate* is a guess about the quality or value of something. When
Merlin told Arthur not to <u>underestimate</u> his real strength in pulling out

the sword, he meant _____

_____

_____

3. If *worthless* means "having no value," then <u>worthy</u> means

_____

_____

Elements of Literature
pages 833–844

"Sir Gawain and the Loathly Lady" retold by Betsy Hearne

SKILLS FOCUS

Literary Skill
Understand the quest.

Resources

In this book:
• Adapted Readings
• Vocabulary and Comprehension, p. 338
• Additional Vocabulary Practice, p. 339

Other Resources:
• *The Holt Reader*
• *Holt Adapted Reader*
• *Audio CD Library*
• *Audio CD Library, Selections and Summaries in Spanish*
• *Supporting Instruction in Spanish*

Especially for ELL

Spanish-speaking English-language learners may benefit from reading or listening to the selection summary in Spanish in preparation for reading the selection in English.

Teacher Tip

Have students add several words from the story to their journals. Tell them to look up the words in a dictionary and then share their information with the class.

Prereading

Background

Introduce Characters and Setting King Arthur and the Knights of the Round Table appeared in tales spanning several centuries and many countries. King Arthur is the best-known king in English literature. The Round Table, the meeting place of Arthur and his knights, was round so that no one member was favored over others. From the beginning, Gawain played an important part in King Arthur's court because of his loyalty, honor, courtesy, and bravery.

Vocabulary Practice

Especially for ELL **Introduce Additional Vocabulary** Preview with students the following words and definitions.

• *betray (p. 835):* fail to keep a promise, be unfaithful
• *bower (p. 839):* old-fashioned word for a private room
• *enchantment (p. 840):* effect of a magic spell
• *foresworn (p. 836):* untrue to one's word; shown to be a liar
• *sorrow (p. 836):* deep distress, sadness, or regret
• *tarry (p. 838):* linger; delay
• *troth (p. 839):* engage to marry

Alternative Activities

Read the Adaptation Distribute copies of the adapted reading of "Sir Gawain and the Loathly Lady" (available in this book and, with marginal questions, in *Holt Adapted Reader*). To prepare for reading the original version and to practice fluency, students should read the adaptation silently.

Use *The Holt Reader* You may consider having students use the Before You Read page in *The Holt Reader,* either instead of or in addition to the Before You Read page in the student book.

Alternative Teaching Strategy

Introduce the Ideas In order to analyze the selection based on the literary elements as well as personal taste, ask students to make a chart with the headings shown on page 335 in this book. Have them think of questions they could ask themselves as they listen to and read the story.

You may want to suggest these or other questions:

Characters	Motivation	Situation	Plot
Who are they? Do they seem real? Do I like them? Why?	What motivates the characters? What do they want? Do you know? Is motivation believable?	Is the situation believable? Is it supposed to be realistic? Is it fun?	Does the plot seem possible? Is the plot interesting or exciting? Is the plot (story) more important than character?

Teacher Tip

The first Arthurian stories, written in Latin, appeared in about A.D. 600. By the 13th and 14th centuries, the Arthurian legend was a popular subject. The best-known Arthurian book of the 14th century was an anonymous work titled *Sir Gawain and the Green Knight.*

Reading
Alternative Activities

Use *The Holt Reader* You may have students read the selection in *The Holt Reader* and use the margins in that book to make notes and respond to the instruction.

(**Especially for ELL**) **Use Audio** For students who have great difficulty reading the story, play the audio recording. Pause frequently to discuss what is happening. Give students a chance to jot down notes in their charts so they can discuss the story in detail.

Additional Activity

(**Core Skill**) **Make Predictions** Invite students to make predictions about the story. Do students believe that King Arthur will be able to come up with an answer to save his life? Why? Do they think that Sir Gawain will marry the loathly lady? What leads them to make this prediction? What do students think will happen to Dame Ragnell after Gawain marries her? Be sure students can support their predictions, and have them check their predictions as they continue reading.

Postreading
Alternative Activity

Use *The Holt Reader* You may consider having students use the postreading activities in *The Holt Reader,* either instead of or in addition to the postreading activities in the student book.

Additional Practice

(**Mixed Ability Group**) **Create a Modern Legend** Have students brainstorm the elements of a modern-day Arthurian legend. Where would it be set? What would the king be like? What qualities would the knights have to have? What would their code of chivalry be? What situation or complication would set the plot into motion? Ask small groups of students to create a modern-day Arthurian legend inspired by "Sir Gawain and the Loathly Lady."

(**Teacher Tip**)

Although 1066 marks the
last time England was
invaded by foreign troops,
the Norman Invasion was an
unusual victory. William the
Conqueror could not speak
English and, in fact, spent
about half his reign in
France. At the age of 43,
he tried to learn English
but soon gave it up. The
Norman French decided
that their language was to
be reserved for the nobles
and court and that ordinary
people were not to speak it.
So although many French
words found their way to
the British Isles, the English
still speak English.

(**Core Skill**)

Use the resources in the
Reading Skills and
Strategies section of this
book to teach a core literary
skill in which your
struggling readers need
remediation. Use "Sir
Gawain and the Loathly
Lady" for the application
portion of the lesson.

Vocabulary Development
Additional Practice

Use Targeted Vocabulary Words in Context Ask students to
choose the correct word to complete each of the following sentences.
(Words: *chivalry, countenance, loathsome, sovereignty*)

1. Sir Gawain, the knight, knew the code of ___ very well, and
   that's why his behavior was so special. *(chivalry)*
2. The sad look that crossed his ___ told us he was unhappy with
   the situation. *(countenance)*
3. King Arthur didn't want Sir Gawain to have to marry the ___
   creature. *(loathsome)*
4. The all-powerful king has ___ over his subjects. *(sovereignty)*

Alternative Teaching Strategy

Learn the Background of the Language Many English words
come from other languages because there were periods of heavy
immigration to England as there were to the United States. Every
new wave of immigration brought new people with their customs,
traditions, and language. Not surprisingly, new words came into the
language as the cultures intermingled. Ask students to select three
words from the list shown on page 833 of their books and to research
their origins in the dictionary. Allow time for students to report back
to class with their findings.

Grammar Link
Additional Practice

Watch Your Language Review the correct uses of *its* and *it's* and
your and *you're* on page 844 of the student book. Copy the following
sentences onto the chalkboard. Ask volunteers to come to the
chalkboard and choose the correct word to complete the sentence.

1. (Your/<u>You're</u>) ___ going to like this story very much.
2. (Its/<u>It's</u>) ___ about a very famous knight.
3. (<u>It's</u>/Its) ___ (<u>your</u>/you're) ___ book, so you can read it
   whenever you want.
4. "When (your/<u>you're</u>) ___ a knight, (its/<u>it's</u>) ___ all in the line of
   duty."
5. (Its/<u>It's</u>) ___ unfortunate that we no longer have knights with a
   code of chivalry.
6. I regret the passing of this fine tradition, but (<u>its</u>/it's) ___ days
   of glory are in the past.

TARGETED STRATEGIES FOR SPECIAL EDUCATION STUDENTS

SKILLS FOCUS

Literary Skill
Understand the quest.

Prereading

Background

Introduce the Story Briefly explain to students that the legendary figure of King Arthur has appeared in literature for hundreds of years. Ask if anyone knows what a *knight* is. Explain the term if necessary. Then, introduce a knight's code of behavior, or *chivalry*. As a class, brainstorm what that code of behavior might include. Then, confirm whether or not they were correct about the code of chivalry.

Reading

Listening and Speaking Opportunity

Use Audio Play the audio recording of the story for students. Pause frequently to ask comprehension questions to be sure students are following the story. Have them pay particular attention to the characters and their actions. Ask students to identify each character's motivation for doing what he or she does. Keep prompting students to think about motivation as they listen.

Postreading

Alternative Activity

Responding to Literature Discuss the literary elements of the story with students, focusing especially on the characters. Ask which character students liked best. Why? Have them explain a favorite character's motivation. Allow enough time to discuss whether or not they liked the story. Ask them to explain their reasons.

Alternative Assessment

Check Comprehension Ask students to tell if the following statements are true or false. If they are false, have students rewrite them to make them true.

_____ 1. King Arthur knew Sir Gromer from his childhood, when they played together. *(F)*

_____ 2. Sir Gromer met King Arthur in the forest to ask him for advice about women. *(F)*

_____ 3. Arthur has to discover what women most desire. *(T)*

_____ 4. Sir Gawain saves Arthur from being killed by Gromer. *(F)*

_____ 5. Sir Gawain falls in love with Dame Ragnell. *(T)*

> **Resources**
>
> **In this book:**
> • Adapted Readings
> • Vocabulary and Comprehension, p. 338
> • Additional Vocabulary Practice, p. 339
>
> **Other Resources:**
> • *The Holt Reader*
> • *Holt Adapted Reader*
> • *Audio CD Library*
> • *Audio CD Library, Selections and Summaries in Spanish*
> • *Supporting Instruction in Spanish*
>
> **Teacher Tip**
>
> Ask students to illustrate the story. Tell them to select a scene or two that appeals to them and that they'd like to illustrate for the rest of the class.

Vocabulary and Comprehension

"Sir Gawain and the Loathly Lady"

A. Match words and definitions. Write the letter of the correct definition next to each word.

_____ **1.** loathsome   **a.** a code of knightly behavior

_____ **2.** chivalry   **b.** disgusting

_____ **3.** countenance   **c.** control; authority

_____ **4.** sovereignty   **d.** face; appearence

B. Number the following events in the correct sequence.

_____ King Arthur asks Sir Gromer to spare his life.

_____ Dame Ragnell tells King Arthur what women desire most.

_____ Arthur agrees to meet Sir Gromer in a year with an answer to a riddle.

_____ King Arthur chases after a deer in the forest.

_____ Dame Ragnell turns into a beautiful woman.

_____ Sir Gawain marries Dame Ragnell.

C. Answer each question below.

1. What deal did King Arthur make with Sir Gromer?

_____

_____

2. In your own words, explain the answer to the riddle.

_____

_____

3. Tell why Dame Ragnell's appearance changes on her wedding night.

_____

_____

Additional Vocabulary Practice

"Sir Gawain and the Loathly Lady"

A. Choose the correct word in parentheses to complete each sentence.

  1. *(chivalry, chivalrously)*   Knights of the Middle Ages followed a code of

  _____. They helped the weak and behaved courteously

  and _____ toward women.

  2. *(sovereign, sovereignty)*   The ruler who reigns over a country is called a

  _____. The person who has control, or

  _____, over people has great authority.

  3. *(loathe, loathsome)*   Some people _____ lizards and

  snakes. They think reptiles are disgusting and _____.

  4. *(countenance, countenanced)*   The anger that showed on his

  _____ was obvious to everyone. However, no one

  supported, or _____, his anger.

B. Match words and definitions. Write the letter of the correct definition
next to each word.

  _____ **1.** loathly   **a.** horrible; disgusting

  _____ **2.** beautiful   **b.** an agreement to do or not to do
                                 something

  _____ **3.** foul   **c.** repulsive

  _____ **4.** promise   **d.** fair; lovely

C. Choose two words from above. Use each word in a sentence.

  1. _____

     _____

  2. _____

     _____

Comparing Literature: Real Heroes

SKILLS FOCUS

Literary Skill
Understand heroes.

Reading Skill
Compare and contrast heroes.

Resources

In this book:
• Vocabulary and Comprehension, p. 342
• Additional Vocabulary Practice, p. 343

Core Skill

Use the resources in the Reading Skills and Strategies section of this book to help students having difficulty comparing and contrasting heroes. Use "Rosa Parks" and the excerpt from *Long Walk to Freedom* for the application portion of the lesson.

Prereading
Vocabulary Practice

Especially for ELL **Preview Additional Vocabulary** Preview with students the following words and their definitions.

• *oppression (p. 847):* authority or power that is unjust
• *transformation (p. 847):* a process of change
• *extinguished (p. 848):* put out
• *obligations (p. 848):* duties; responsibilities
• *indivisible (p. 850):* unable to be separated or divided
• *eavesdrop (p. 854):* to listen secretly; to overhear
• *humiliations (p. 854):* injuries to one's pride or dignity
• *scrutiny (p. 856):* thorough study or inspection
• *mimeographed (p. 857):* made stenciled copies on a machine
• *inconsequential (p. 858):* unimportant

Reading
Alternative Activity

Make a Chart Ask students to use a chart like the one below to analyze the heroic characteristics of Nelson Mandela and Rosa Parks as they read the two selections. Remind students to note important thoughts, words, actions, or descriptions that reveal something about each person. After students have finished reading, make a master chart together on the chalkboard.

Hero	Words/ Thoughts	Actions	Descriptions
Nelson Mandela			
Rosa Parks			

Postreading
Additional Activity

Make an Outline Students who choose to write a comparison-contrast essay should outline their essays using the Comparing and Contrasting Real Heroes charts from student book pages 852 and 860. You may want to check that students have cited details from the selections to support their responses.

TARGETED STRATEGIES FOR SPECIAL EDUCATION STUDENTS

Prereading

Reteach the Key Idea

Freewrite on Apartheid To activate students' prior knowledge before reading the selections, you may want to have them freewrite on what they know about apartheid. Explain to students that apartheid is racial segregation, or the practice of separating racial groups in schools, social buildings, buses, or living quarters.

Reading

Alternative Activity

Listen for Characteristics of a Hero Read the two selections aloud. As you read, pause often to allow students to discuss what they can tell so far about Nelson Mandela and Rosa Parks. Ask students to think of adjectives that describe these two people, and write students' suggestions on the chalkboard. After finishing the two selections, review the adjectives on the chalkboard and ask students what traits the two people have in common. Then, ask how the two differ.

Fluency Practice

Read the Selections/Practice Fluency To increase students' comprehension of the selections and to give them practice reading aloud, have them participate in an oral reading of the selections. You may want to try Popcorn Reading or Break-in Reading (see page xxix of this book).

Postreading

Alternative Activity

Use a Venn Diagram If students have difficulty using the chart in the After You Read activities to compare and contrast the heroic characteristics of Nelson Mandela and Rosa Parks, you may have them use a Venn diagram instead. Draw a Venn diagram on the chalkboard, labeling the first circle "Nelson Mandela," the second circle "Rosa Parks," and the overlapping area "Both." Have students work with partners to compare and contrast these two heroes by filling in this graphic organizer.

SKILLS FOCUS

Literary Skill
Understand heroes.

Reading Skill
Compare and contrast heroes.

Resources

In this book:
- Vocabulary and Comprehension, p. 342
- Additional Vocabulary Practice, p. 343

Teacher Tip

To help students think about the heroic characteristics of Nelson Mandela and Rosa Parks, ask them to think of questions that they would like to ask either person after reading the selections. Then, have student volunteers take turns answering these questions. Students should be able to point to specific places in the works that support their answers.

Vocabulary and Comprehension

Comparing Literature: Real Heroes

A. Match words and definitions. Write the letter of the correct definition next to each word.

_____ **1.** transitory

_____ **2.** curtailed

_____ **3.** disintegration

_____ **4.** template

_____ **5.** serendipity

_____ **6.** mealies

_____ **7.** retribution

_____ **8.** plaintiff

_____ **9.** N.A.A.C.P.

_____ **10.** cloche

a. cut short

b. passing; temporary

c. accident, usually accidental luck

d. the breaking up of something

e. pattern

f. punishment for evil or reward for good

g. National Association for the Advancement of Colored People

h. in South Africa, ears of corn

i. person who brings a suit, or complaint, into a court of law

j. tight-fitting women's hat

B. Choose five words from above. Use each word in a sentence.

1. _____

_____

2. _____

_____

3. _____

_____

4. _____

_____

5. _____

_____

Additional Vocabulary Practice

Comparing Literature: Real Heroes

A. Match the words in the left column with the clues in the right column. Write the correct letter in the blanks.

_____ **1.** oppression

_____ **2.** indivisible

_____ **3.** humiliations

_____ **4.** mimeographed

_____ **5.** inconsequential

a. copied

b. not able to be separated or divided

c. the opposite of *important*

d. injuries to one's pride or dignity

e. unjust authority or power

B. Choose two words from above. Use each word in a sentence.

1. _____

_____

2. _____

_____

C. Replace the word or phrase in parentheses with the correct word from the Word Bank.

1. After all the candles were *(put out)*

_____, the room became very dark.

2. Micah did not mean to *(listen secretly)*

_____, but he was seated right next to the talking passengers.

3. The lump of clay underwent a *(process of change)*

_____ as the art student molded it into a sculpture.

4. Juan's mother gave his report card much *(thorough study or inspection)*

_____ before happily exclaiming, "You got all A's!"

5. June enjoyed a restful afternoon after fulfilling her Saturday morning

(duties; responsibilities) _____.

Word Bank
transformation
extinguished
obligations
eavesdrop
scrutiny

Collection 8
Reading for Life

Reading Informational Texts: Reading for Life

Background

Identify Documents To begin to familiarize students with various kinds of informational documents, describe the common kinds of consumer, workplace, and public documents: for example, instructions on how to fill out job applications and tax forms; how to assemble toys and furniture; how to use such appliances as stoves, VCRs, and telephones with special features. Ask volunteers to identify which of the documents they have seen and which ones they or their families have used.

Alternative Teaching Strategy

Classify Documents Draw a three-column chart on the board. Label the columns CONSUMER DOCUMENTS, WORKPLACE DOCUMENTS, and PUBLIC DOCUMENTS. Tell students that you will be working together to classify the different types of documents.

Vocabulary Practice

(**Especially for ELL**) **Reinforce Targeted Vocabulary** Help students develop their English vocabularies by reviewing these words and their definitions.

Ask students to take turns identifying the category of documents to which each of the words belongs. Enter each in the appropriate column on the chart.

- *advertisement (p. 880):* a public announcement that tells about or praises a product or service
- *schedule (p. 880):* a list of the times at which certain things are to happen
- *warranty (p. 880):* a guarantee of repair or replacement of a product if something goes wrong within a certain time
- *contract (p. 880):* a binding, legal agreement between two or more parties
- *application (p. 880):* a form to be filled out when requesting something
- *tax form (p. 880):* a form to be filled out with information used to calculate tax withholding or to file a tax return
- *memorandums (p. 881):* short, informal notes written to give information to a person in your office

SKILLS FOCUS

Reading Skills
Understand consumer, workplace, and public documents.

(**Core Skill**)

Use the resources in the Reading Skills and Strategies section of this book to teach a core informational skill in which your struggling readers need remediation. Use the selections in the following lesson plans for the application portion of the lesson.

TARGETED STRATEGIES FOR SPECIAL EDUCATION STUDENTS

Reading Informational Texts: Reading for Life

Reteach the Key Idea

Make a Chart Discuss with students how reading is necessary to get information. On the chalkboard, make a chart like the one below. Tell students that you will fill in the chart together.

Consumer Documents	Workplace Documents	Public Documents
Advertisements	Employment applications	Newspaper articles
Travel schedules	Tax forms	Internet information
Labels on packages	Insurance forms	Government publications and pamphlets

Alternative Teaching Strategy

Read for Comprehension Read the essay, paragraph by paragraph. After each paragraph, pause and ask students to summarize. Ask students simple comprehension questions to make sure they are following the presentation. Let students suggest documents that are not listed in the reading.

Reteach the Key Idea

Fill in the Chart Work with students to fill in the chart above. Use guided questions to help them name the main types of consumer documents: for example, advertisements, schedules, and package labels. Write each of these names under CONSUMER DOCUMENTS. Then, select one of the types of documents, for example, *advertisements*. Encourage students to brainstorm all the different types of advertisements they know. Write each of these types of informational materials in the space under the word *advertisements*. Repeat the process for the other types of consumer documents, and then for workplace and public documents.

Analyzing Information in Public Documents: Casting Call

Prereading

Background

Make a Web Explain that a public announcement is a type of public document that provides information. Write ANNOUNCEMENTS within a circle on the board. Draw spokes radiating from the circle and write CASTING CALL on one spoke. Ask: What other kinds of announcements can you find in magazines or newspapers?

Reading

Alternative Activity

Use *The Holt Reader* You may have students read the selection in *The Holt Reader* and use the margins in that book to make notes and respond to the instruction.

Alternative Teaching Strategy

Understand Structure Understanding the structure, or format, of an announcement will make it easier for students to focus on the important information. Point out that Casting Call has a headline, a lead paragraph that explains what the people making the announcement are looking for, a bulleted list that describes the type of person they are looking for, and the time and place—when and where—the action or event will take place.

Postreading

Alternative Assessment

Mixed Ability Group **Make a Casting Call** Divide students into small groups to create their own casting call. Select a play or story with which students are familiar. Help each group choose a character from that play or story they would like to cast. Then have them work together to write a description of the characteristics they think the person trying out for the part should have. After they have finished, give each group an opportunity to read their casting call to classmates.

SKILLS FOCUS

Reading Skill
Analyze information in public documents.

Resources

In this book:
- Vocabulary and Comprehension, p. 351 (includes the next two selections)
- Additional Vocabulary Practice, p. 356 (includes the next six selections)

Other Resources:
- *The Holt Reader*
- *Audio CD Library, Selections and Summaries in Spanish*
- *Supporting Instruction in Spanish*

Especially for ELL

Many students may be familiar with dates and times when they see them written, but may not have had an opportunity to read them aloud. Point to the date: Saturday, May 25, 2004, and the times: 10:00 A.M. to 5:00 P.M., and model how to read them. Give students an opportunity to practice saying these and other dates and times.

SKILLS FOCUS

Reading Skill
Analyze information in public documents.

Teacher Tip

Tell students that long ago in this country, and still today in some countries, it was common for a "town crier" to deliver announcements orally. This person walked through the streets of the town or stood in the public square and shouted out the news and announcements. Give students an opportunity to play the role of the town crier and read their announcements aloud to the class.

TARGETED STRATEGIES FOR SPECIAL EDUCATION STUDENTS

Prereading
Alternative Activity

Use a Graphic Organizer to View Structure To help students understand what kinds of information an announcement will contain, draw a four-column chart on the board with columns headed WHAT, WHO, WHEN, and WHERE. Choose an event that is scheduled to take place at school, and help students identify what the event is, who is invited, and when and where it will take place.

Reading
Alternative Teaching Strategy

Fill In the Chart To help students keep track of the information they read in the announcement, pause in the reading each time you come to information that answers one of the questions above. Help students identify the information. Write it in the chart. Encourage students to look for other information that appears in the announcement. For example: *Bring your bike* and *See you in the movies*. Explain that they give additional information and add appeal to the announcement.

Postreading
Alternative Activity

Create Announcements Divide students into small groups and invite them to make their own announcements. Explain that first they need to choose an event to announce. Then they need to identify for *whom* or for *what* purpose the event is being held and *when* and *where* it will take place. Encourage them to write their announcements on paper. They can be based on events that are already scheduled to take place or on an imaginary event.

Alternative Assessment

Core Skill **Summarize the Information** Point out that after reading an announcement, students might find themselves repeating the important information to a friend. Encourage students, working in pairs, to take turns summarizing the information in Casting Call for each other. Ask how many students think they have enough information from their partner's summary to decide whether or not they meet the requirements for the casting call.

Analyzing Information in Public Documents: Hollywood Beat

Prereading

Background

Explain *The Hobbit* Since some students may not be familiar with *The Hobbit*, by J.R.R. Tolkien, explain that it is a fantasy story that takes place in imaginary Middle Earth. It is the story of an imaginary creature called a *hobbit*, who joins forces with dwarfs and a wizard on a quest for treasure. The treasure is guarded by a dragon. During their quest, the hobbit, dwarfs, and wizard are captured by trolls in the Middle Earth and are almost eaten. The book tells the story of their adventures and how they triumph over the Powers of Darkness.

Reading

Alternative Activity

Use *The Holt Reader* You may have students read the selection in *The Holt Reader* and use the margins in that book to make notes and respond to the instruction.

Listening and Speaking Opportunity

Read Aloud It is important for students to hear the intonation and expression used when different types of material are read aloud. Read "Shhhhhh!" aloud, and have students follow along in their books. Pause after you have read the passage that explains what the movie will be about, and have a student re-read it aloud. Pause again and do the same after you have read the information about why a character in a movie remake of *The Hobbit* would need to ride a bike.

Postreading

Alternative Teaching Strategy

Use the Web Point out that Sam searched the World Wide Web on the Internet to find more information about the movie. Ask what other types of information can be found on the Web. Write students' ideas on the board. Then, choose some information that might be interesting for students to learn more about, and demonstrate how to search for articles and Web sites with information on that topic.

SKILLS FOCUS

Reading Skill
Analyze information in public documents.

Resources

In this book:
- Vocabulary and Comprehension, p. 351 (includes the previous and the next selection)
- Additional Vocabulary Practice, p. 356 (includes the previous selection and the next five selections)

Other Resources:
- *The Holt Reader*
- *Audio CD Library, Selections and Summaries in Spanish*
- *Supporting Instruction in Spanish*

Especially for ELL

Explain that *Shhhhhh!* is an interjection that tells the listener to be quiet. Ask students to name other interjections. *(Hey!, Psst)*

Special Education Students

This may be a good opportunity to show students how to search online for information for a science project or a social studies report. This will help them get started on learning or reviewing how to search for information on the World Wide Web.

Analyzing Information in Public Documents: Application for Permission to Work

SKILLS FOCUS

Reading Skill
Analyze information in public documents.

(**Resources**)

In this book:
• Vocabulary and Comprehension, p. 351 (includes the previous two selections)
• Additional Vocabulary Practice, p. 356 (includes the previous two selections and the next four selections)

Other Resources:
• *The Holt Reader*
• *Audio CD Library, Selections and Summaries in Spanish*
• Supporting Instruction in Spanish

(**Special Education Students**)

Explain to students that in the first section of the application they will be asked to give personal information. The second section requires information from the school. The last section is a health record, and needs to be completed by a doctor.

Prereading

Alternative Activity

(**Especially for ELL**) **Preview the Application** Ask students to imagine that they have just been given this application to complete. Show them how to skim the application to determine what type of information they will need to supply to complete the form. Help them outline what is in each section.

Reading

Alternative Activity

Use *The Holt Reader* You may have students read the selection in *The Holt Reader* and use the margins in that book to make notes and respond to the instruction.

Alternative Teaching Strategy

Follow the Steps Explain that the best way to complete an application is to begin at the beginning and fill in each piece of information as you go along. Guide students in reading what the application is for and then proceeding to the section labeled Procedures for Obtaining Work Permit. One by one, choose volunteers to read the steps. At the end of the first section, point out that a parent's or guardian's signature is required. Have them examine the second section to determine who should fill in the information. Ask them to re-read the second procedure at the top of the page that tells them that school authorities must complete the second section. Repeat this with the third section, and guide students in understanding that this section must be completed by a doctor.

Postreading

Alternative Assessment

Practice Filling Out Forms If possible, provide students with a variety of application forms or let them search for application forms on the World Wide Web. Have them practice filling in application forms by entering their personal information on the forms. Encourage students to share their applications with classmates and explain what the applications are for.

Vocabulary and Comprehension

Casting Call; Hollywood Beat; Application for Permission to Work

A. Write a sentence for each word below, using the definition given.

1. *audition:* try out for a part in a performance

_____

2. *application:* a form to be filled in with information needed to apply for something such as a job

_____

3. *permit:* a document granting permission

_____

B. Write T or F next to each statement to tell if it is true or false.

_____ **1.** You can audition if you are eighteen but look as if you were fifteen.

_____ **2.** Auditions will be held in San Francisco in July.

_____ **3.** You don't need a bike to audition.

_____ **4.** Only people who meet requirements should audition.

_____ **5.** Sam saw the casting call in a biking magazine.

C. Answer each question below.

1. What is Sam like? Describe her interests and personality.

_____

_____

2. What requirements for the audition does Sam meet?

_____

_____

Analyzing Information in Workplace Documents:
A Business Letter and Talent Instructions

SKILLS FOCUS

Reading Skill
Analyze information in workplace documents.

(**Resources**)
In this book:
• Adapted Readings
• Vocabulary and Comprehension, p. 355 (includes the next two selections)
• Additional Vocabulary Practice, p. 356 (includes the previous three selections and the next two selections)

Other Resources:
• *Holt Adapted Reader* (for A Business Letter)
• *Audio CD Library, Selections and Summaries in Spanish*
• *Supporting Instruction in Spanish*

(**Especially for ELL**)
Write the expression 24/7. Choose a volunteer to read aloud the sentence in which it appears *(p. 895, second bulleted item)*. Help students use the context clue, *anytime,* to determine that this is a short way of writing twenty-four hours a day, seven days a week.

Prereading
Vocabulary Practice

Understand Business Vocabulary Business correspondence often uses vocabulary that may be unfamiliar to people who do not work in an office. Write these words from the letter on page 895 and their definitions on the board. Preview the vocabulary with students.

- *on behalf of:* speaking or acting for
- *responsible:* expected to take care of something
- *authorize:* to give someone the right or power to do something
- *bonus:* something given in addition to what is due or expected
- *fulfill:* to satisfy or meet
- *punctuality:* the fact, condition, or practice of being on time

Reading
Alternative Activity

Read the Adaptation You may want to have struggling readers read the adapted version of A Business Letter (available in this book and, with marginal questions, in *Holt Adapted Reader*).

Alternative Teaching Strategy

Identify Parts of a Letter If possible, copy the letter on page 895 onto an overhead transparency and project it so the whole class can see it. As students read, pause and help them identify the different sections of the letter. Label each on the transparency.

Postreading
Alternative Activity

(**Mixed Ability Group**) **Write Instructions** Give students an opportunity to practice writing lists of instructions, using the numbered list from Talent Instructions as a guide. In small groups, have them choose an event or activity that takes place at school and write a list of instructions for it.

TARGETED STRATEGIES FOR SPECIAL EDUCATION STUDENTS

Prereading
Alternative Activity

Preview the Letter Ask students to open their books to the business letter on page 895. Explain that the notes along the right-hand column of the letter are used to identify what each section is about. Check to see that they understand all the vocabulary, and explain any words that are unfamiliar. Write the title "Responsibilities" on the board, and list the responsibilities in a column under it as students read them.

Reading
Alternative Teaching Strategy

Make a Chart As students read the letter, encourage them to refer to the list of responsibilities on the board. Have them pause after reading each bullet to determine the responsibility stated in that bullet. Help them summarize it and write it in the appropriate column on the chart.

Listening and Speaking Opportunity

Increase Fluency The Talent Instructions include a numbered list of the items that outline correct behavior on the movie set. This list will provide an excellent opportunity for students to develop fluency. Read the information in the first item aloud. Invite students to re-read it in chorus after you. Then, have students read each of the remaining bullets after you.

Postreading
Alternative Activity

Write a List Divide students into small groups. Assign each group two or three responsibilities from the chart created earlier. Using the margin notes as guides, ask them to work together to write their own instructions to Sam outlining her responsibilities. Encourage them to use italics to emphasize words that they think are very important.

Alternative Assessment

Retell the Instructions To assess students' comprehension of the workplace documents, ask them to retell what happened to Sam. Prompt them to talk about Sam's interview. Then, prompt them to summarize the talent instructions.

Reading Skill
Analyze information in workplace documents.

Resources

In this book:
- Adapted Readings
- Vocabulary and Comprehension, p. 355 (includes the next two selections)
- Additional Vocabulary Practice, p. 356 (includes the previous three selections and the next two selections)

Other Resources:
- *Holt Adapted Reader* (for A Business Letter)
- *Audio CD Library, Selections and Summaries in Spanish*
- *Supporting Instruction in Spanish*

Language Tip

Help students identify the words that are written in italics in the "Talent Instructions." Point out that these words are written in a different style to emphasize them visually. Explain that when reading the list aloud, the reader should also emphasize these words.

Analyzing Information in Workplace Documents: E-mail Memos and Directory

SKILLS FOCUS

Reading Skill
Analyze information in workplace documents.

Resources
In this book:
• Vocabulary and Comprehension, p. 355 (includes the previous two selections)
• Additional Vocabulary Practice, p. 356 (includes the previous five selections)

Other Resources:
• *Audio CD Library, Selections and Summaries in Spanish*
• *Supporting Instruction in Spanish*

Teacher Tip

Point to the *cc* at the top of the e-mail memo. Explain that *cc* was originally an abbreviation for *carbon copy*. This expression comes from the time when memos were typed on the typewriter and a sheet of carbon paper was used to make a copy. Today *cc* means *courtesy copy* or simply *copy*. Tell students that the name of the person or persons to receive the copy should be written after the colon.

Prereading

Background

Put E-mail in Perspective Tell students that e-mail has become readily available and popular only in the past few years. Ask them to name other forms of communication that people used prior to e-mail. Help them determine the benefits and disadvantages of these different forms of communication.

Reading

Listening and Speaking Opportunity

Especially for ELL **Read Aloud** Let students take turns reading aloud the information on the e-mail memo. Explain that when reading informative text, like a memo, it is not necessary to use as much expression as when reading a story or stating a list of demands. Model the tone you would like students to use.

Alternative Activity

Use Date Sequence for Reference Point out that to determine the order in which e-mail memos are received, the reader has to check the dates in the directory. The dates may be listed chronologically, with the most recently received memo at the top or at the bottom. Help students locate the first memo that was sent regarding the schedule. *(Tentative Schedule, Group C)* Have them read down the list to find the date of the next update of the schedule. *(June 17, 2004)* Then ask them when the most recent e-mail about the schedule was sent. *(July 15, 2004)*

Postreading

Alternative Activity

Identify Icons Explain that e-mail uses icons together with words to make it easier for people to use e-mail. Print out some of the icons and paste them on separate index cards. Write what the icons represent on another set of index cards. Place the index cards face down on the table. Let students take turns turning over two cards at a time. If they match, students can hold on to the pair of cards. If they don't match, have the student turn them back over, and let another take a turn at matching. Repeat until all icons and words they represent have been paired.

Vocabulary and Comprehension

A Business Letter; Talent Instructions; E-mail Memos; Directory

A. Match words and definitions. Write the letter of the correct definition next to each word.

_____ **1.** responsible

_____ **2.** bonus

_____ **3.** authorize

_____ **4.** fulfill

a. something given in addition

b. satisfy

c. expected to take care of

d. give the right to do something

B. Use one or more words from the list above to complete each sentence.

1. Sam's parents must _____ her grandfather to act as her guardian.

2. She and her grandfather are _____ for their own transportation.

3. To earn an extra _____ when filming is completed, Sam has to _____ all aspects of her contract.

C. Answer each question below.

1. What are actors allowed to do when they are waiting to film their scenes?

_____

_____

2. Why does Sam need to check her e-mail every morning and night?

_____

_____

3. What kind of information is found in an e-mail directory?

_____

_____

Additional Vocabulary Practice

Casting Call; Hollywood Beat;
Application for Permission to Work;
A Business Letter; Talent Instructions;
E-mail Memos; Directory

A. Match words and definitions. Write the letter of the correct definition next to each word.

_____ **1.** work permit

_____ **2.** fulfill

_____ **3.** audition

_____ **4.** talent

a. short performance in which actors or musicians who want a job show their skills

b. unusual natural skill

c. paper that gives official permission for someone to work

d. satisfy

B. Choose the correct word in parentheses to complete each sentence.

1. *(punctual, punctuality)* Sam was always on time and very

_____. Her _____ was important to the film director.

2. *(direct, directory)* To locate a list of names and addresses, look in a

_____. This will _____ you to what you want to find.

C. Finish each sentence with a description that fits the underlined word.

1. *Charisma* means "a special quality that fascinates people."

If you are <u>charismatic</u>, you _____

_____

2. If *individuality* makes a person different from others, an <u>individualist</u>

would be _____

_____

Analyzing Information in Consumer Documents: BART System Map

Prereading

Background

Discuss Types of Maps Ask students what kind of maps they've seen. List them on the chalkboard. Explain that maps may be of the world, the country, the state, the town, or even bus or train routes. Ask how many students know how to read maps.

Reading

Alternative Teaching Strategy

Clarify Process Steps Introduce a step-by-step process to help students read the BART map. As they read the selection, they will learn that Sam needs to take the train from Walnut Creek to the Embarcadero Station. Encourage them to run their eyes or their fingers along the lines from the one location to the other. Model how to look at the key on the right side of the map to determine which line they will need to take. *(the Pittsburg/Bay Point–Colma line, so named because it starts in Pittsburg/Bay Point and ends in Colma)*

Postreading

Additional Practice

(**Mixed Ability Group**) **Work with the Map** Have students work in pairs. One student names two points on the BART System Map; the other locates the points and tells what line(s) to take to get from one point to the other. Then, have partners change roles. Allow students to repeat the activity several times to develop their skills in giving directions.

Alternative Activity

(**Mixed Ability Group**) **Draw Maps** Divide students into small groups. Let each group pick a point in town with which they are all familiar. Then, have them work together to draw a map from that point in town to school. After students have completed their maps, invite them to take turns sharing them with the class while they give oral instructions on how to get from their point in town to school. When necessary, provide students with appropriate language. For example: "Turn left at the light, go straight down Elm Street, go past the blue house, and then turn right."

SKILLS FOCUS

Reading Skill
Analyze information in consumer documents.

(**Resources**)

In this book:
- Vocabulary and Comprehension, p. 361 (includes the next three selections)
- Additional Vocabulary Practice, p. 364 (includes the next four selections)

Other Resources:
- *Audio CD Library, Selections and Summaries in Spanish*
- *Supporting Instruction in Spanish*

(**Especially for ELL**)

Write *BART* on the board and ask students if they know what the letters stand for. Write the words *Bay/Area/Rapid/Transit* under each of the letters. Explain that *BART* is an acronym—a word formed from the initial letters of a name. Encourage students to name other acronyms they have seen or used.

Reading Skill
Analyze information in consumer documents.

Resources

In this book:
• Vocabulary and Comprehension, p. 361 (includes the next three selections)
• Additional Vocabulary Practice, p. 364 (includes the next four selections)

Other Resources:
• *Audio CD Library, Selections and Summaries in Spanish*
• *Supporting Instruction in Spanish*

TARGETED STRATEGIES FOR SPECIAL EDUCATION STUDENTS

Prereading

Background

Use a Web Tell students that they will be reading several consumer documents in this lesson. Write "Consumer Documents" on the chalkboard. Guide students in naming consumer documents, such as packaged-food ingredients, movie listings, and train schedules. Write each type of document on a spoke radiating from the term.

Vocabulary Practice

Discuss Multiple-Meaning Words Words with more than one meaning may be confusing to students. Write several words from page 899 on the board. Explain that each word has more than one meaning. Write the meanings beside the words, for example:

• *treated*	paid for someone	cared for medically
• *bay*	inlet of the sea	a long bark
• *trains*	type of transportation	instructs

Encourage students to suggest other words they know that have multiple meanings.

Reading

Alternative Teaching Strategy

Use a Color Code Use color to help students follow the different lines of the BART system. If possible, reproduce the BART System Map on a transparency. Use colored markers to highlight the different lines listed in the key. Then, choose volunteers to run their fingers along each line tracing the color assigned it in the key. Encourage students to refer to the color-coded map as they read to help them see how to get from one place to another.

Postreading

Alternative Assessment

Summarize Sam's Route To assess students' comprehension, encourage them to summarize how Sam will get to work. Ask: Why do Sam and her grandfather decide to take the train? Under what conditions is it permissible for Sam to travel with her bike on BART?

Analyzing Information in Consumer Documents: Riding BART: Bicycle Rules, Ticket Guide, and Schedule

Prereading

Background

Learn Acronyms Write the acronym *BART* on the board. Explain that an acronym is a word formed from the initial letters of a series of words. Point to the acronym *BART (Bay Area Rapid Transit)*. Write each word underneath the corresponding letter.

Reading

Listening and Speaking Opportunity

(**Especially for ELL**) **Read Difficult Terms** The ticket guide contains a lot of numbers, percentages, and dollar values that may be challenging for students to read. Model reading the information about red tickets, explaining what each number-related term means. Then, choose a volunteer to repeat it after you.

Alternative Teaching Strategy

Scan Informative Text Tell students that, generally, people do not read an entire ticket guide or schedule, but scan the documents for the information they need. As students scan the ticket guide, help them identify the information that would be useful for Sam. Then, have them turn to the timetable. Since her call is for 8:00 A.M., Sam will need to be at the van by 6:00 A.M. Help students scan the schedule to determine which is the latest train that Sam can take to arrive at the Embarcadero station by 6:00 A.M. Once they have identified the train, have them check to see if there are any bicycle restrictions.

Postreading

Alternative Activity

Role-play Reading schedules and buying transit tickets is or will be a real part of many students' lives. To help them understand what this interchange involves and to be sure they have the language they need to accomplish it, have them role-play selling and buying tickets. Encourage buyers to ask questions about times of departure and fares. Have ticket sellers use the train schedule and list of fares to answer the questions.

SKILLS FOCUS

Reading Skill
Analyze information in consumer documents.

(**Resources**)

In this book:
- Vocabulary and Comprehension, p. 361 (includes the previous selection)
- Additional Vocabulary Practice, p. 364 (includes the previous selection and the next selection)

Other Resources:
- *Audio CD Library, Selections and Summaries in Spanish*
- *Supporting Instruction in Spanish*

(**Teacher Tip**)

Encourage students to ask questions about the BART schedule and rules. Remind them that at some train stations they can purchase a ticket at a machine. Explain that if they choose to do that, they must read the directions and follow the instructions very carefully.

Teacher Tip

As students read the ticket
guide, help them calculate
the percentage discounts to
confirm that the amounts
stated are correct. Model
how to determine a 75%
discount on a $16 ticket.
Then, give students an
opportunity to calculate
how much other percentage
discounts would amount to.

TARGETED STRATEGIES FOR SPECIAL EDUCATION STUDENTS

Prereading

Background

Review Schedules Tell students that they will be reading a train
schedule. Ask them to talk about other schedules that they have seen.
Show them your schedule for the school day, a movie schedule, and
any other schedules that you have available. Ask them to talk about
how a schedule helps them organize their time.

Reading

Alternative Teaching Strategy

Separate Information Visually Students may be overwhelmed by
the amount of information in a timetable. In order to make the
timetable more usable for them, model how to use a sheet of paper to
underline each separate line in the table. If some students are still
distracted by the uncovered lines, show them how to create a stencil
with a narrow box cut out. When placed on the timetable, the box
should allow them to see a single row at a time.

Postreading

Alternative Activity

Make Schedules Ask students to make schedules of their own
activities in school and after school for a week. Encourage them to
add information on homework assignments and tests so they can
allow time for study on their weekly plan as well. Have them begin by
drawing a chart with one column for each day of the week. Then,
have them write in their school and after-school activities, except
bedtime, by hour or half-hour segments.

Alternative Assessment

Read Consumer Documents To assess students' comprehension of
how to use a timetable and ticket guide, provide them with scenarios
like those listed below. Ask them to determine what train the person
would have to take and how much his or her ticket would cost.

• A mother has to take her four-month-old baby from Walnut
Creek to the doctor in Embarcadero. Their appointment is at
9:00 A.M.

• A man in a wheelchair has to travel from Walnut Creek to
Embarcadero for a meeting at 8:30 A.M.

Vocabulary and Comprehension

BART System Map;
Riding BART: Bicycle Rules,
Ticket Guide, and Schedule

A. Write a sentence for each word below, using the definition given.

1. *commute:* travel daily to and from work

_____

_____

2. *discount:* amount taken off the full price

_____

_____

B. Number the following events in the correct sequence.

_____ Sam and her grandfather ride to the Embarcadero station.

_____ The movie company van brings them to the shooting site.

_____ Sam checks online to see which trains allow bikes.

_____ Sam and her grandfather go to the Walnut Creek station.

C. Answer each question below.

1. What information about BART does Sam find on the Internet?

_____

_____

2. Why does Sam need to know the rules for bringing bikes on the trains?

_____

_____

3. When can Sam take her bike to Embarcadero on BART?

_____

_____

Following Technical Directions:
"How to Change a Flat Tire"

SKILLS FOCUS

Reading Skill
Follow technical directions.

(Resources)

In this book:
• Vocabulary and Comprehension, p. 363
• Additional Vocabulary Practice, p. 364 (includes the previous four selections)

Other Resources:
• *Audio CD Library, Selections and Summaries in Spanish*
• *Supporting Instruction in Spanish*

(Especially for ELL)

ELLs sometimes need to get crucial information from people whom they might have trouble understanding. Have them practice these polite questions: *Could you repeat that, please? Excuse me. What does ___ mean?*

(Especially for ELL)

Spanish-speaking English-language learners may benefit from reading or listening to the selection summaries in Spanish in preparation for reading the selections in English.

Prereading
Vocabulary Practice

Define Technical Terms Following directions requires the understanding of technical vocabulary. Write the following words from page 906 of the student edition on the board: *wheel rim, automatic transmission, manual transmission, emergency triangles, flares, spare tire, jack, lug wrench, counterclockwise.* Divide students into small groups, and have them define these words. Tell them to begin with the words they can define from their own knowledge base. Next, suggest that they look up unknown terms in a dictionary. Tell them that if they are unsure about a word's meaning, they should look it up. Remind them to use context clues in determining the definitions. When the groups have finished the task, elicit definitions that all students agree on.

Reading
Alternative Teaching Strategy

Do It Safely Explain to students that "How to Change a Flat Tire" not only describes a procedure, but also the safety precautions for particular steps. Work with them to set up a two-column chart. Write the column heads STEPS and SAFETY on the chalkboard. Have them summarize each step, and then write any related precautions beside it.

Postreading
Listening and Speaking Opportunity

(Mixed Ability Group) **Check Comprehension** Divide students into pairs. Have Student A in each pair explain how to change a flat without referring to the book. Tell Student B to listen carefully, without making any comments until A has finished. After A has finished, B reminds A of anything that was left out. Next, B describes the safety precautions, relating them to particular steps and explaining their purpose. B does this without referring to the textbook. Student A listens carefully, without comment until the end, and then reminds B of anything that was left out. Next, both students check their answers against the book.

Vocabulary and Comprehension

"How to Change a Flat Tire"

A. Complete each sentence with a word from the Word Bank.

1. To complete a mechanical task, follow the

step-by-step _____
directions.

2. The directions in a manual tell you how to

_____ a mechanical
device.

3. When you get a flat tire, replace it with the

_____ tire in your car trunk.

4. A lug _____ is used to loosen or tighten the
lug nuts that hold the tire onto the car.

5. To loosen the lug nuts, turn the lug wrench to the left, or

_____.

6. Follow the illustrations in the manual to set up the

_____, which raises the car off the ground.

> **Word Bank**
> technical
> counterclockwise
> jack
> operate
> spare
> wrench

B. Answer each question below.

1. What safety precautions should you take when you get a flat tire?

_____

_____

2. What is the purpose of a lug wrench?

_____

_____

3. How high should you raise the car with the jack?

_____

_____

Additional Vocabulary Practice

BART System Map; Riding BART:
Bicycle Rules, Ticket Guide, and Schedule;
"How to Change a Flat Tire"

A. Complete each sentence with a word from the Word Bank.

1. Sam takes the train every day to

   _____ to her job at the studio.

2. She pays for the cost of the ride, or

   _____, with a ticket.

3. Instead of paying full price, she purchased a ticket

   at a _____.

4. To find out how often the trains run, she looked up the

   _____ on the Internet.

5. The Web pages contained a great deal of useful _____
   information.

> **Word Bank**
> schedule
> consumer
> fare
> commute
> discount

B. Use two of the words in the Word Bank in a sentence.

1. _____

   _____

2. _____

   _____

C. Match words and definitions. Write the letter of the correct definition
next to each word.

____ **1.** jack

____ **2.** wrench

____ **3.** counterclockwise

____ **4.** spare

a. an extra tire

b. a tool for turning nuts and bolts

c. a tool used to lift a car

d. the direction opposite to the direction that
clock hands move

Answer Key

Collection 1
Facing Danger

Vocabulary and Comprehension
Rikki-tikki-tavi, p. 37

A. 1. d   4. b
    2. c   5. a
    3. e

B. Sentences will vary.

C. Sample answers given.
    1. When a flood washed Rikki-tikki out of his burrow, the family rescued him and decided to keep him as a pet.
    2. When Nag falls asleep in the bathroom, Rikki-tikki attacks him. They struggle and the man wakes up and shoots Nag.
    3. He distracts Nagaina until Teddy's father can get Teddy out of Nagaina's reach.

Vocabulary and Comprehension
India's History, p. 39

A. 1. inset
    2. boldface type
    3. table of contents
    4. index
    5. captions

B. Sample answers given.
    1. Maps and illustrations help convey the message of the text visually.
    2. Questions at the end of a section help the reader review the key points that were covered.
    3. Reading checks help the reader review what was learned.
      Summary or focus statements at the beginning of a chapter alert the reader to the main points that will be covered.
      Headings and subheads help break the content into small sections and also point out the topic of each section.
      Boldface words alert the reader to key terms.
      Questions help the reader assess whether the information was understood.

Additional Vocabulary Practice
Rikki-tikki-tavi;
India's History, p. 40

A. 1. a   4. b
    2. c   5. e
    3. d

B. 1. a   3. c
    2. b   4. d

C. Sample answers given.
    1. A bungalow is a house.
    2. A veranda is an open porch with a roof.
    3. A garden is where flowers or vegetables are grown.
    4. A burrow is a hole in the ground made by an animal.
    5. A nest is a home that birds build for themselves.

Vocabulary and Comprehension
Three Skeleton Key, p. 45

A. 1. c   4. a
    2. e   5. d
    3. b

B. Sentences will vary.

C. Sample answers given.
    1. Three convicts had escaped there, but they died of hunger and thirst. All that was left was their skeletons.
    2. When the ship crashes, the rats swim to shore and attack the lighthouse.
    3. Another ship tows a barge filled with meat close to the island, and when the rats swim to the barge, the sailors on the ship set the barge on fire. Any rats that survive are eaten by sharks.

Vocabulary and Comprehension
Eeking Out a Life, p. 47

A. 1. d   4. e
    2. f   5. b
    3. a   6. c

B. Sample answers given.
    1. An interesting lead will make the reader want to continue reading the article.
    2. The first two or three paragraphs contain answers to the questions *who? what? when? where? why?* and *how?*
    3. Putting the most important information first ensures that readers will get the facts of the story if they don't read the entire article.
    4. It's a humorous story, because not too many people keep a rat as a pet. The people are happy to offer the rat safety, "disregarding one little incident with a curious cat," which is a humorous way of saying the cat nearly killed the rat.

Additional Vocabulary Practice
Three Skeleton Key;
Eeking Out a Life, p. 48

A. 1. edible, inedible
   2. wild, wilderness
   3. deride, derisive

B. 1. vermin
   2. fathom
   3. hordes
   4. receding

C. Sentences will vary.

Vocabulary and Comprehension
The Monsters Are Due on Maple Street, p. 53

A. 1. transfixed
   2. assent
   3. menace
   4. intimidated
   5. converging
   6. idiosyncrasy

B. Sample answers given.
   1. When strange things happen, people become upset and look for a enemy. They start to attack each other, looking for a scapegoat, until eventually they destroy themselves.
   2. Les Goodman can't sleep at night and often goes outside to look at the stars.

Vocabulary and Comprehension
Cellular Telephone Owner's Manual, p. 55

A. 1. b   3. c
   2. a   4. d

B. 1. instructions, instruct
   2. replace, replacement
   3. remove, removal

C. Sample answers given.
   1. An instruction manual explains how to operate and care for a device. It includes instructions, diagrams, a glossary of terms, and a telephone number to call if the user needs help from the manufacturer.
   2. By reading all the instructions first, the user has a better understanding of how the device works.

Additional Vocabulary Practice
The Monsters Are Due on Maple Street;
Cellular Telephone Owner's Manual, p. 56

A. 1. c   4. b
   2. e   5. d
   3. a

B. 1. diagram
   2. directions
   3. glossary
   4. manual

C. 1. explicit
   2. intelligible
   3. defiant
   4. transfixed

Vocabulary and Comprehension
Comparing Literature:
Science Fiction, p. 59

A. 1. b   3. e   5. d
   2. a   4. c

B. Sentences will vary.

C. 1. F   3. F   5. T
   2. T   4. F

Additional Vocabulary Practice
Comparing Literature:
Science Fiction, p. 60

A. 1. b   3. d   5. a
   2. c   4. e

B. Sentences will vary.

C. 1. implacable
   2. respite
   3. frenetic
   4. tableau
   5. foray

Collection 2
Characters: Living
Many Lives

Vocabulary and Comprehension
Mother and Daughter, p. 67

A. 1. meager
   2. sophisticated
   3. tirade
   4. matinees
   5. antics

B. 1. F   4. F   7. T
   2. T   5. F
   3. T   6. F

Additional Vocabulary Practice
Mother and Daughter, p. 68

A. 1. c   3. e   5. d
   2. b   4. a

B. 1. gobbled up
   2. throbbing
   3. riot
   4. stashed away
   5. slammed

C.
1. c		3. f		5. d
2. b		4. e		6. a

Vocabulary and Comprehension
The Smallest Dragonboy, p. 73

A.
1. c	3. e	5. b
2. d	4. a	

B. Sample answers given.
1. A dragonrider helps protect the planet, so it is an honor to be one.
2. Dragons are fed a special rock called firestone that makes them breathe fire.
3. Dragons choose their dragonriders when they hatch out of their shells.
4. Keevan is hit hard and loses consciousness. The leaders of the Weyr realize what a bully Beterli is.
5. Keevan is chosen by a bronze dragon, the most powerful kind of dragon.

Vocabulary and Comprehension
Here Be Dragons, p. 75

A.
1. b	3. a
2. d	4. c

B. Sentences will vary.

C.
1. c	2. c

Additional Vocabulary Practice
The Smallest Dragonboy;
Here Be Dragons, p. 76

A. Across
2. evasion
3. transparent
7. obscured
8. console

Down
1. fleetingly
4. punctual
5. enviable
6. aspire

Vocabulary and Comprehension
A Rice Sandwich, p. 81

A. Across
3. suffering
4. canteen
Down
1. triangles
2. anemic
3. Spartan

B. Sample answers given.
1. Esperanza nags her mother to let her eat lunch in the school canteen instead of coming home for lunch.

2. Esperanza does not enjoy lunch in the canteen, because she feels humiliated when the nun yells at her and makes her point out her house.

Additional Vocabulary Practice
A Rice Sandwich, p. 82

A.
1. f	4. b
2. a	5. c
3. e	6. d

B. Physical Characteristics
anemic
tired
skinny

Emotional Characteristics
shy
sad
joyous

C. Sentences will vary.

Vocabulary and Comprehension
Antaeus, p. 87

A.
1. d	3. a	5. c
2. b	4. e	

B. Sentences will vary.

C.
1. F	3. F	5. F
2. T	4. T	

Vocabulary and Comprehension
In a Mix of Cultures, an Olio of Plantings, p. 89

A.
1. b	3. c	5. d
2. e	4. a	

B. Sentences will vary.

C. Sample answer: The city gardens are a good idea because they reclaim cluttered lots from drug dealers and debris and provide a place in which people can grow their own food.

Additional Vocabulary Practice
Antaeus; In a Mix of Cultures, an Olio of Plantings, p. 90

A.
1. d	3. b	5. e
2. c	4. a	

B. Sentences will vary.

C.
1. husk
2. herb
3. debris
4. till
5. pungent

Vocabulary and Comprehension
Comparing Literature:
Characters and Character Traits, p. 93

A. 1. e   3. a   5. b
    2. d   4. c

B. Sentences will vary.

C. 1. T   3. F   5. F
    2. F   4. T

Additional Vocabulary Practice
Comparing Literature:
Characters and Character Traits, p. 94

A. 1. a   3. b
    2. c   4. d

B. Sentences will vary.

C. 1. epidemic
    2. pitch
    3. sore at
    4. solemn

Collection 3
Living in the Heart

Vocabulary and Comprehension
The Highwayman, p. 101

A. 1. b   3. d
    2. a   4. c

B. 1. T   3. F   5. T
    2. F   4. F   6. T

C. Sample answers given.
    1. The highwayman hopes to return to her by dawn but knows that soldiers may delay him.
    2. The soldiers are waiting to shoot the highwayman.
    3. The soldiers tie Bess up so that she cannot call out a warning.
    4. Bess is able to pull the trigger on the gun the soldiers bound against her chest.

Vocabulary and Comprehension
Gentlemen of the Road, p. 103

A. 1. countryside
    2. jewels
    3. gentlemen
    4. aristocrats
    5. steeds

B. 1. F   4. F   7. T
    2. F   5. F   8. F
    3. F   6. T   9. T

Additional Vocabulary Practice
The Highwayman;
Gentlemen of the Road, p. 104

A. 1. moonlight
    2. lace
    3. bonny
    4. gallop
    5. musket

B. Sentences will vary.

C. Sentences will vary.

Vocabulary and Comprehension
Annabel Lee, p. 109

A. 1. sepulcher
    2. kingdom
    3. beams
    4. maiden

B. Sentences will vary.

C. Sample answers given.
    1. The poem is named after the narrator's wife.
    2. Annabel Lee dies and is buried in a tomb by the sea.
    3. The speaker says that the angels were jealous of their love and, for that reason, they took Annabel Lee away from him.

Vocabulary and Comprehension
The Fall of the House of Poe? p. 111

A. 1. spokesman
    2. petitions
    3. landmark
    4. floorboards
    5. boardinghouse

B. 1. T   4. T   7. F
    2. F   5. F   8. F
    3. F   6. T   9. T

Additional Vocabulary Practice
Annabel Lee;
The Fall of the House of Poe? p. 112

A. 1. c   3. b
    2. d   4. a

B. Sentences will vary.

C. Sentences will vary.

Vocabulary and Comprehension
User Friendly, p. 117

A. 1. screen
    2. computer table
    3. diskette
    4. keyboard

B. 1. F   4. T   7. T
    2. F   5. F   8. F
    3. F   6. T

C. **1.** d   **3.** a
    2. c   **4.** b

Vocabulary and Comprehension
It Just Keeps Going and Going . . ., p. 119

A. **1.** corruption
    2. chaos
    3. pesky
    4. motives
    5. villains

B. **1.** T   **5.** T   **9.** F
    2. T   **6.** T   **10.** T
    3. F   **7.** T
    4. F   **8.** T

Additional Vocabulary Practice
User Friendly
It Just Keeps Going and Going . . ., p. 120

A. **1.** d   **3.** a   **5.** b
    2. e   **4.** c

B. Sentences will vary.

C. **1.** brain
    2. real ticked off
    3. pull the plug on

Vocabulary and Comprehension
Echo and Narcissus, p. 125

A. **1.** Echo
    2. Mount Olympus
    3. detain
    4. Narcissus
    5. Aphrodite
    6. Zeus
    7. unrequited

B. **1.** F   **5.** F   **9.** T
    2. T   **6.** T   **10.** T
    3. F   **7.** F
    4. T   **8.** T

Additional Vocabulary Practice
Echo and Narcissus, p. 126

A. **1.** d   **3.** a   **5.** e
    2. c   **4.** b

B. Sentences will vary.

C. **1.** detain
    2. unrequited
    3. vainly
    4. parched
    5. intently

Vocabulary and Comprehension
Comparing Literature: Characters, Settings, Themes, p. 129

A. **1.** c   **3.** e   **5.** d
    2. b   **4.** a

B. Sentences will vary.

C. **1.** T   **3.** F   **5.** T
    2. F   **4.** T

Additional Vocabulary Practice
Comparing Literature: Characters, Settings, Themes, p. 130

A. **1.** e   **3.** d   **5.** b
    2. a   **4.** c

B. Sentences will vary.

C. **1.** consoled
    2. reign
    3. jostling
    4. agape
    5. swaggering

Collection 4
Point of View:
Can You See It My Way?

Vocabulary and Comprehension
After Twenty Years, p. 137

A. **1.** c   **3.** a   **5.** b
    2. d   **4.** e

B. Sentences will vary.

C. **1.** T   **3.** T   **5.** T
    2. F   **4.** T   **6.** F

Vocabulary and Comprehension
What's Really in a Name?, p. 139

A. **1.** d   **3.** a   **5.** c
    2. e   **4.** b

B. **1.** pseudonym
    2. sophistication
    3. memorable
    4. roots

C. **1.** T   **4.** F   **7.** T
    2. T   **5.** T
    3. F   **6.** F

Additional Vocabulary Practice
After Twenty Years;
What's Really in a Name?, p 140

A. **1.** c   **5.** e   **9.** b
    2. a   **6.** i   **10.** j
    3. g   **7.** f
    4. h   **8.** d

B. 1. guardian
2. spectators
3. chilly
4. gusts
5. drizzle
6. destiny
7. hustled
8. pseudonym
9. credits

Vocabulary and Comprehension
Bargain, p. 145

A. 1. c   **3.** a
   2. b   **4.** d

B. Sentences will vary.

C. Sample answers given.
  1. The narrator is a schoolboy named Al, whose parents have died.
  2. Mr. Baumer wants Slade to pay his bill for $21.50.
  3. Mr. Baumer hires Slade to take some merchandise from the railroad station to his store.
  4. Slade dies after drinking wood alcohol from a barrel. The barrel is clearly marked "Deadly Poison," but Slade can't read.

Additional Vocabulary Practice
Bargain, p. 146

A. 1. stooped
2. freighter
3. errands
4. bargain
5. string

B. 1. slouching, slouch
2. merchant, merchandise
3. mistake, mistaken
4. beat, beaten

Vocabulary and Comprehension
Yeh-Shen, p. 151

A. 1. spirit
2. desire
3. dread
4. transformed
5. timidly

B. Sample answers given.
  1. The main characters are Yeh-Shen, her stepmother, the fish, and the king.
  2. The fish bones have magic powers.
  3. The fish helps Yeh-Shen by granting her wish to go to the festival. He gives her beautiful clothes to wear and a pair of golden slippers.
  4. A villager finds the missing shoe and sells it to a merchant.

Vocabulary and Comprehension
Mirror, Mirror, on the Wall . . . ? p. 153

A. 1. d   **3.** e   **5.** b
   2. a   **4.** c

B. Sample answers given.
  1. Most girls say they are too fat.
  2. The students want to wear designer clothing that has a specific brand name or logo on it.
  3. The main idea is that students do not feel good about the way they look because they are so influenced by advertising.
  4. Students don't think they are pretty because they aren't as pretty or thin as the models in advertisements.

Additional Vocabulary Practice
Yeh-Shen;
Mirror, Mirror, on the Wall . . . ? p. 154

A. 1. b   **4.** b   **7.** a
   2. a   **5.** c
   3. c   **6.** c

B. 1. influencing
2. advertisements
3. self-esteem
4. illusion
5. insecure

Vocabulary and Comprehension
Names/Nombres, p. 159

A. 1. ethnicity
2. heritage
3. convoluted

B. 1. F   **2.** T   **3.** T

C. Sample answers given.
  1. No one can pronounce their name correctly and Alvarez becomes Elbures, Alberase, or Alburest.
  2. Other students ask Julia where she is from because she has dark coloring and an accent. She simply says she is from the Caribbean.
  3. A person's identity is reflected in a name. Julia's Spanish name reflects her cultural identity, while the Americanized name reflects her experiences in America that have also shaped who she is.

Additional Vocabulary Practice
Names/Nombres, p. 160

A. 1. c   **3.** a
   2. d   **4.** b

B. 1. pronunciation, pronounce
2. foreigner, foreign
3. ethnicity, ethnic
4. affection, affectionate

C. Sentences will vary.

Vocabulary and Comprehension
An Unforgettable Journey, p. 165

A. 1. d 3. a
2. c 4. b

B. Sentences will vary.

C. Sample answers given.
1. The story is told by Maijue Xiong, who was a child when she and her family escaped from Laos.
2. The Hmong fled Laos because they had been fighting against the Communists, who finally took over the country.
3. The father had been a soldier who had served with the CIA. They also had a stepuncle in the United States who agreed to sponsor them.

Vocabulary and Comprehension
Exile Eyes, p. 167

A. 1. c 3. e 5. b
2. d 4. f 6. a

B. Sample answers given.
1. The author is writing about people who fled other countries to find safety in the United States.
2. The story is set in a beauty parlor in Madison, Wisconsin.
3. "Exile eyes" refers to the look in the eyes of people who have seen terrible horrors and have lost everything but are determined to continue living.
4. The author is from Latvia, a country in eastern Europe.
5. The author is interested in exiles because she understands what they are going through. She too is an exile.

Additional Vocabulary Practice
An Unforgettable Journey; Exile Eyes, p. 168

A. 1. b 3. a 5. d
2. e 4. c

B. Sentences will vary.

C. 1. refuge
2. refugee
3. persecution
4. deprivation
5. transition

Vocabulary and Comprehension
Elizabeth I, p. 171

A. 1. a 3. b 5. e
2. d 4. f 6. c

B. Sentences will vary.

C. 7 Elizabeth I dies.
5 Pope Pious V excommunicates Elizabeth.
4 Elizabeth becomes queen of England.
6 Elizabeth's navy defeats the Spanish Armada.
2 Henry VIII dies.
1 Anne Boleyn, Elizabeth's mother, is executed.
3 Mary, Elizabeth's half-sister, marries the king of Spain.

Additional Vocabulary Practice
Elizabeth I, p. 172

A. 1. reign
2. monarch
3. tutors
4. staff
5. revival

B. Sentences will vary.

Vocabulary and Comprehension
Comparing Literature:
Mood and Theme, p. 175

A. 1. d 3. a 5. c
2. e 4. b

B. Sentences will vary.

C. 1. F 3. F 5. F
2. F 4. F

Additional Vocabulary Practice
Comparing Literature:
Mood and Theme, p. 176

A. 1. a 3. b 5. e
2. c 4. d

B. Sentences will vary.

C. 1. warily
2. spillway
3. frond
4. pageant

Collection 5
Worlds of Words:
Prose and Poetry

Vocabulary and Comprehension
Amigo Brothers, p. 183

A. 1. bouts
2. pensively
3. torrent
4. frenzied
5. dispelled

B. Sentences will vary.

C. 1. T   3. F   5. T
     2. T   4. F   6. F

Vocabulary and Comprehension
Right Hook–Left Hook:
The Boxing Controversy, p. 185

A. 1. c   3. a   5. e
     2. d   4. b

B. Sentences will vary.

C. 1. c   3. a
     2. d   4. b

Additional Vocabulary Practice
Amigo Brothers;
Right Hook–Left Hook:
The Boxing Controversy, p. 186

A. 1. a   3. b   5. b
     2. c   4. a

B. Sentences will vary.

C. 1. controversy
     2. slurred
     3. ban
     4. instills

Vocabulary and Comprehension
from Barrio Boy, p. 191

A. 1. c   3. a   5. b
     2. e   4. d

B. Sentences will vary.

C. Sample answers given.
     1. She encouraged her students to speak out loud and praised them when they learned to say something correctly in English.
     2. They spoke in their native languages on the playground without feeling ashamed and told about life in their homelands.

Additional Vocabulary Practice
from Barrio Boy, p. 192

A. 1. reassuring
     2. assured
     3. wholeheartedly
     4. persistently
     5. formidable
     6. contraption

B. Sentences will vary.

C. 1. b   3. b   5. b
     2. a   4. a   6. c

Vocabulary and Comprehension
Song of the Trees, p. 197

A. 1. curtly
     2. incredulously
     3. dispute
     4. elude
     5. ambled
     6. skirting

B. 1. T   4. T   7. F
     2. T   5. F   8. T
     3. T   6. F

Additional Vocabulary Practice
Song of the Trees, p. 198

A. 1. a   5. b   9. i
     2. e   6. d   10. g
     3. h   7. j
     4. f   8. c

B. Sentences will vary.

C. 1. curtly
     2. dispute
     3. elude
     4. ashen
     5. sentries

Vocabulary and Comprehension
Fish Cheeks, p. 203

A. 1. c   3. d   5. b
     2. f   4. a   6. e

B. Sentences will vary.

C. Sample answers given.
     1. She knew that the American guests would expect traditional food like turkey.
     2. She served all of Amy's favorite foods as a way of trying to make her happy and proud of being Chinese.

Additional Vocabulary Practice
Fish Cheeks, p. 204

A. 1. rumpled
     2. clamor
     3. appalling
     4. muster
     5. wedges

B. Sentences will vary.

Vocabulary and Comprehension
A Mason-Dixon Memory, p. 209

A. 1. e   3. a   5. b
     2. c   4. d

B. Sentences will vary.

C. Sample answers given.
1. This is the first experience he has had with racial segregation.
2. When Clifton's friends learn that he is not allowed in the amusement park, they say that they will not go either.
3. Dondré's teammates decide that they would rather forfeit the tournament than play without him.

Vocabulary and Comprehension
Buddies Bare Their Affection for Ill Classmate, p. 211

A.
- 4 The boys went to the barbershop together.
- 6 Ian lost twenty pounds, but is eager to get back to school.
- 2 Classmates found out that Ian O'Gorman was sick.
- 5 The teacher was so inspired by his class that he also shaved his head.
- 1 Ian decided to shave his head before all his hair fell out in clumps.
- 3 "We wanted to make him feel better and not left out," said Kyle.

B. 1. summary
2. details

C. Sample answers given.
1. They cared about Ian's feeling and knew that he did not want to feel different from the other boys. If all the boys were bald, Ian would not stand out.
2. The teacher was inspired by his students.
3. Ian wants to continue living the normal life of an eleven-year-old.

Additional Vocabulary Practice
A Mason-Dixon Memory;
Buddies Bare Their Affection for Ill Classmate, p. 212

A. 1. predominately
2. forfeit
3. resolve
4. erupted
5. emotional
6. ominous

B. 1. treat, treatment
2. resolution, resolve
3. emotional, emotion
4. inspiration, inspired

Vocabulary and Comprehension
I'm Nobody!; I Like to See It Lap the Miles, p. 216

A. 1. c   3. d   5. b
2. e   4. a

B. Sentences will vary.

C. Sample answers given.
1. Emily compares a famous person to a frog.
2. She compares the train to a horse.
3. She makes being famous seem negative. She says that it would be boring to have to constantly impress people.

Vocabulary and Comprehension
I Am of the Earth, p. 219

A. 1. bore
2. cradled
3. harmonious
4. eternity
5. fruits

B. Sentences will vary.

C. 1. F   3. T
2. T   4. F

Vocabulary and Comprehension
Early Song, p. 221

A. 1. a   3. c
2. b

B. Sentences will vary.

C. Sample answers given.
1. The poet refers to early morning, just as the sun is rising.
2. He offers thanks for the fine day, the good earth, his brothers and sisters, and the blood that runs through him and back into the earth.

Additional Vocabulary Practice
I'm Nobody!; I Like to See It Lap the Miles;
I Am of the Earth;
Early Song, p. 222

A. 1. bog
2. bore
3. pride
4. thanksgiving
5. harmonious
6. dreary
7. banish

B. 1. c   3. a   5. b
2. e   4. d

C. 1. authority or influence
2. peaceful

Vocabulary and Comprehension
Madam and the Rent Man, p. 224

A. 1. howdy-do
2. rent
3. due
4. agent
5. pass the buck

B. Sentences will vary.

C. Sample answers given.
   1. She refuses to pay the rent because the apartment has so many problems that the landlord has refused to fix.
   2. The agent says that he is only the rent collector, not the one responsible for making the repairs.

Vocabulary and Comprehension
Harlem Night Song;
Winter Moon, p. 227

A. 1. e   3. b   5. d
   2. c   4. a

B. Sentences will vary.

C. 1. T   3. F   5. F
   2. T   4. F

Additional Vocabulary Practice
Madam and the Rent Man;
Harlem Night Song; Winter Moon, p. 228

A. 1. buck
   2. rent
   3. roam
   4. drops
   5. great
   6. dew
   7. crook

B. Sentences will vary.

Vocabulary and Comprehension
I Ask My Mother to Sing;
Ode to Family Photographs, p. 231

A. 1. e   3. d   5. a
   2. b   4. c

B. Sentences will vary.

C. Sample answers are given.
   1. They are singing about waterlilies in their distant homeland.
   2. At least one is taken at a zoo, where there is a giraffe.

Additional Vocabulary Practice
I Ask My Mother to Sing;
Ode to Family Photographs, p. 232

A. 1. b   5. h   9. c
   2. j   6. e   10. a
   3. f   7. g
   4. d   8. i

B. Sentences will vary.

Vocabulary and Comprehension
Father William; Sarah Cynthia Sylvia Stout Would
Not Take the Garbage Out, p. 237

A. 1. c   3. b   5. a
   2. d   4. e

B. Sentences will vary.

C. Sample answers are given.
   1. Father William is being asked by his son why he engages in various silly activities.
   2. The poem warns against failing to take out the garbage, lest it pile up enormously.

Additional Vocabulary Practice
Father William; Sarah Cynthia Sylvia Stout Would
Not Take the Garbage Out, p. 238

A. 1. d   5. a   9. i
   2. c   6. g   10. f
   3. b   7. j
   4. e   8. h

B. Sentences will vary.

Vocabulary and Comprehension
The Runaway, p. 240

A. 1. c   3. e   5. b
   2. d   4. a   6. f

B. 1. a   3. d
   2. c   4. b

C. Sample answers given.
   1. They saw the colt and were concerned because it seemed that something was wrong.
   2. Yes. It was getting late and the colt should have been brought back to its stall by now.
   3. The words "fled," "afraid of the snow," "running away," "whited eyes," and "shudders" show that the colt is afraid.

Vocabulary and Comprehension
The Pasture; A Minor Bird, p. 243

A. 1. b   3. c   5. d
   2. e   4. a

B. Sentences will vary.

C. 1. F   3. F   5. F
   2. F   4. T

Additional Vocabulary Practice
The Runaway; The Pasture;
A Minor Bird, p. 244

A. 1. d   5. i   9. g
   2. a   6. b   10. e
   3. c   7. j
   4. h   8. f

B. Sentences will vary.

Vocabulary and Comprehension
Names of Horses, p. 246

A. 1. b 3. a 5. d
2. e 4. c

B. Sentences will vary.

C. 1. F 3. T 5. F
2. F 4. F

Vocabulary and Comprehension
maggie and milly and molly and may; All in green went my love riding, p. 250

A. 1. languid
2. sheer
3. lean
4. lithe
5. fleeter

B. Sentences will vary.

C. 1. T 3. T
2. T 4. T

Additional Vocabulary Practice
Names of Horses; maggie and milly and molly and may; All in green went my love riding, p. 251

A. 1. brute
2. daunting
3. dappled
4. sledge
5. lithe

B. Sentences will vary.

C. 1. a detailed description that appeals to the senses
2. the repetition of consonant sounds
3. the use of words that sound like what they mean

Vocabulary and Comprehension
Arithmetic; For Poets, p. 254

A. 1. metaphor
2. figurative language
3. simile
4. *ars poetica*
5. catalog

B. Sentences will vary.

C. 1. F 3. F 5. T
2. F 4. F

Additional Vocabulary Practice
Arithmetic; For Poets, p. 255

A. 1. d 3. b 5. e
2. c 4. a

B. Sentences will vary.

C. Examples will vary.

Vocabulary and Comprehension
Author Study: Sandra Cisneros, p. 258

A. 1. e 3. b 5. d
2. a 4. c

B. Sentences will vary.

C. 1. F 3. T 5. F
2. T 4. T

Additional Vocabulary Practice
Author Study: Sandra Cisneros, p. 259

A. 1. fan
2. scuffed
3. nub
4. fashion
5. raw

B. Sentences will vary.

C. 1. main themes of an author's work
2. a broad statement about something

Collection 6
Our Literary Heritage:
Greek Myths and World Folk Tales

Vocabulary and Comprehension
The Origin of the Seasons, p. 267

A. 1. b 3. d 5. a
2. e 4. c

B. Sentences will vary.

C. 1. F 3. F 5. T
2. F 4. F

Vocabulary and Comprehension
Orpheus, the Great Musician; The Power of Music, p. 272

A. 1. b 3. d 5. a
2. c 4. e

B. Sentences will vary.

C. Sample answers are given.
1. Orpheus is unsuccessful because at the last moment he looks back over his shoulder, breaking the one rule he must follow to rescue Eurydice.
2. The musician claims that music has a power to move and delight people.

Additional Vocabulary Practice
The Origin of the Seasons; Orpheus, the Great Musician; The Power of Music, p. 273

A. 1. f   5. j   9. b
    2. a   6. h   10. e
    3. g   7. d
    4. i   8. c

B. Sentences will vary.

Vocabulary and Comprehension
The Flight of Icarus, p. 278

A. 1. c   3. b   5. d
    2. a   4. e

B. Sentences will vary.

C. Sample answers are given.
    1. Daedalus is the famous inventor of the labyrinth from which Theseus escaped. King Minos was angry that Theseus escaped and so punished its builder by imprisoning him on Crete.
    2. Icarus flew too high, where the strong sunlight melted the wax from his wings and made him fall.

Vocabulary and Comprehension
King Midas and the Golden Touch; The Funeral Banquet of King Midas, p. 283

A. 1. e   3. d   5. a
    2. c   4. b

B. Sentences will vary.

C. 1. F   3. T   5. T
    2. T   4. T

Additional Vocabulary Practice
The Flight of Icarus; King Midas and the Golden Touch; The Funeral Banquet of King Midas, p. 284

A. 1. i   5. f   9. c
    2. h   6. e   10. g
    3. j   7. a
    4. b   8. d

B. Sentences will vary.

Vocabulary and Comprehension
Oni and the Great Bird, p. 291

A. 1. b   3. e   5. d
    2. a   4. c

B. Sentences will vary.

C. 1. F   3. T   5. T
    2. F   4. F

Vocabulary and Comprehension
Master Frog, p. 296

A. 1. a   3. b   5. d
    2. c   4. e

B. Sentences will vary.

C. Sample answers are given.
    1. A metamorphis is a change in shape. In "Master Frog," the frog changes into a handsome young man.
    2. The story teaches that there is more to people than meets the eye.

Vocabulary and Comprehension
The Crane Wife, p. 301

A. 1. b   3. d   5. c
    2. e   4. a

B. Sentences will vary.

C. Sample answers are given.
    1. Yohei's wife tells him not to peek at her while she is busy weaving.
    2. Yohei discovers his wife is actually a crane.

Additional Vocabulary Practice
Oni and the Great Bird; Master Frog; The Crane Wife, p. 302

A. 1. i   5. f   9. e
    2. c   6. j   10. d
    3. b   7. h
    4. a   8. g

B. Sentences will vary.

Vocabulary and Comprehension
Aunty Misery, p. 305

A. 1. b   3. d   5. a
    2. e   4. c

B. Sentences will vary.

C. 1. F   3. T   5. F
    2. F   4. T

Vocabulary and Comprehension
The Hummingbird King; The Search Goes On, p. 309

A. 1. b   3. d   5. c
    2. a   4. e

B. Sentences will vary.

C. 1. T   3. F   5. T
    2. T   4. T

Additional Vocabulary Practice
Aunty Misery; The Hummingbird King; The Search Goes On, p. 310

A. 1. g   5. d   9. j
    2. b   6. h   10. i
    3. a   7. e
    4. f   8. c

B. Sentences will vary.

Vocabulary and Comprehension
Comparing Literature:
The Cinderella Story, p. 313

A. 1. c   3. d   5. b
    2. e   4. a

B. Sentences will vary.

C. Sample answers are given.
    1. All three selections focus on a young female who must do the most menial chores.
    2. The main character is treated poorly by her family. She is insulted and forced to do hard work.

Additional Vocabulary Practice
Comparing Literature:
The Cinderella Story, p. 314

A. 1. g   5. j   9. d
    2. e   6. b   10. i
    3. h   7. a
    4. f   8. c

B. Sentences will vary.

Collection 7
Literary Criticism:
Where I Stand

Vocabulary and Comprehension
King Arthur: The Sword in the Stone, p. 321

A. 1. turbulent   3. congregation
    2. tournament   4. integrity

B. 1. F   3. T   5. T
    2. T   4. F

C. Sample answers given.
    1. Merlin saw trouble ahead for Uther and felt that he alone could protect the child.
    2. Merlin saw that Arthur could become the greatest king of England.
    3. Arthur is saddened that he must leave Sir Ector and his home, but he agrees to take his place as the heir to the throne.

Additional Vocabulary Practice
King Arthur: The Sword in the Stone, p. 322

A. 1. c   3. d
    2. b   4. a

B. Sentences will vary.

C. Sample answers given.
    1. A joust is a contest between knights on horseback in which they fight with lances.
    2. A lance is a long, pointed pole used in a joust to knock the opponent off his horse.

Vocabulary and Comprehension
Three Responses to Literature, p. 324

A. 1. foreshadow
    2. destiny
    3. courage

B. 1. b   3. c   5. d
    2. a   4. e

C. Sample answers given.
    1. The writer uses details from the story to describe each boy and then to show how each boy is different from the other.
    2. Essay 2 opens with the four qualities: kindness, honesty, a good heart, and courage. Then the writer supports each quality with details from the story.
    3. Essay 3 relates the story events in the order in which they happened. It is a summary, not an analysis of Arthur's character.

Additional Vocabulary Practice
Three Responses to Literature, p. 325

A. 1. courage
    2. destiny
    3. wisdom
    4. honor
    5. glory
    6. right
    7. quote

B. Sentences will vary.

C. 1. summary, summarize
    2. quote, quotations
    3. direct, indirect

Vocabulary and Comprehension
He's No King, p. 327

A. Sentences will vary.

B. Sentences will vary.

C. Sample answers given.
    1. The kings do not want Arthur to become the next ruler of Britain.
    2. They claim that because they are married to the daughters of King Uther, they are part of the royal family.
    3. They say that Arthur is a nobody and a lowly squire; that he has no ability to rule. They also say that Merlin will really be the king and Arthur just his puppet.

Additional Vocabulary Practice
He's No King, p. 328

A. 1. puppet
    2. lowly
    3. weakling
    4. outcome

B. Sentences will vary.

C. Sample answers given.
1. You act, talk, and think according to what someone else tells you.
2. A lowly person is of low social status, or humble and meek.

Vocabulary and Comprehension
Merlin and the Dragons, p. 332

A. 1. b   3. a
2. c   4. d

B. Sample answers given.
1. Emrys dreamed about dragons and stones, and a tower. He uses these dreams to tell Vortigen how to release the two dragons.
2. The dragons are found in a pool of water under the tower.
3. The white dragon symbolizes King Uther Pendragon, who is Arthur's father.
4. Emrys is Merlin.
5. Merlin tells the story as a way of letting Arthur understand why he always dreams about a boy who pulls a sword out of stone.

Additional Vocabulary Practice
Merlin and the Dragons, p. 333

A. 1. bedraggled
2. ruthless
3. recognition
4. insolence

B. Sentences will vary.

C. Sample answers given.
1. A prophecy is a prediction about the future.
2. Merlin meant that Arthur should not undervalue his strength and character.
3. *Worthy* means having real value, or being good enough for something.

Vocabulary and Comprehension
Sir Gawain and the Loathly Lady, p. 338

A. 1. b   3. d
2. a   4. c

B. 2 King Arthur asks Sir Gromer to spare his life.
4 Dame Ragnell tells King Arthur what women desire most.
3 Arthur agrees to meet Sir Gromer in a year with an answer to a riddle.
1 King Arthur chases after a deer in the forest.
6 Dame Ragnell turns into a beautiful woman.
5 Sir Gawain marries Dame Ragnell.

C. Sample answers given.
1. Arthur agrees to meet Sir Gromer with the answer to a riddle. If he does not find the answer, Sir Gromer will kill him.
2. Women want to have authority over men, to be allowed to make their own choices and not be ruled by men.

3. The stepmother's spell on her has been broken because she is truly loved by a fair knight.

Additional Vocabulary Practice
Sir Gawain and the Loathly Lady, p. 339

A. 1. chivalry, chivalrously
2. sovereign, sovereignty
3. loathe, loathsome
4. countenance, countenanced

B. 1. c   3. a
2. d   4. b

C. Sentences will vary.

Vocabulary and Comprehension
Comparing Literature:
Real Heroes, p. 342

A. 1. b   5. c   9. g
2. a   6. h   10. j
3. d   7. f
4. e   8. i

B. Sentences will vary.

Additional Vocabulary Practice
Comparing Literature:
Real Heroes, p. 343

A. 1. e   3. d   5. c
2. b   4. a

B. Sentences will vary.

C. 1. extinguished
2. eavesdrop
3. transformation
4. scrutiny
5. obligations

Collection 8
Reading for Life

Vocabulary and Comprehension
Casting Call;
Hollywood Beat;
Application for Permission to Work, p. 351

A. Sentences will vary.

B. 1. T   3. F   5. T
2. F   4. T

C. Sample answers given.
   1. Sam does very well in school and works hard at her homework. She is also very skilled at riding her bike. She likes to take dance lessons, too. She is smart, and she knew enough to go to the Internet to find out whether she would be able to apply for a work permit.
   2. Sam is an expert at riding a BMX bike; she owns her bike; she is twelve years old; and she can get a work permit.

Vocabulary and Comprehension
A Business Letter;
Talent Instructions;
E-mail Memos; Directory, p. 355

A. 1. c   3. d
   2. a   4. b

B. 1. authorize
   2. responsible
   3. bonus
   4. fulfill

C. Sample answers given.
   1. They can listen to music as long as they wear headphones or play electronic games if the sound is turned off. They can read a book. They can also watch the filming as long as they do not talk.
   2. Sam needs to check her e-mail to make sure that she is on the set whenever she is needed.
   3. An e-mail directory lists the memos she has received, as well as the names and e-mail addresses of the senders.

Additional Vocabulary Practice
Casting Call;
Hollywood Beat;
Application for Permission to Work;
A Business Letter;
Talent Instructions;
E-mail Memos; Directory, p. 356

A. 1. c   3. a
   2. d   4. b

B. 1. punctual, punctuality
   2. directory, direct

C. Sentences will vary.

Vocabulary and Comprehension
BART System Map;
Riding BART: Bicycle Rules, Ticket Guide, and Schedule, p. 361

A. Sentences will vary.

B. 3 Sam and her grandfather ride to the Embarcadero station.
   4 The movie company van brings them to the shooting site.
   1 Sam checks online to see which trains allow bikes.
   2 Sam and her grandfather go to the Walnut Creek station.

C. Sample answers given.
   1. Sam finds out the train routes, which trains allow bikes, how much the tickets cost, and the schedules of the trains.
   2. Sam will be bringing her bike to work, so she needs to know the times that she can travel on BART with her bike.
   3. Sam can bring her bike anytime other than commuter hours. Commuter hours are between 6:45 and 8:20 A.M.

Vocabulary and Comprehension
How to Change a Flat Tire, p. 363

A. 1. technical
   2. operate
   3. spare
   4. wrench
   5. counterclockwise
   6. jack

B. Sample answers given.
   1. You should move your car as far off the road as possible. Put the car in park or in neutral. Turn off the engine, and put the emergency brake on. Set up emergency triangles or flares.
   2. The lug wrench loosens or tightens the lug nuts.
   3. Use the jack to raise the car a few inches off the ground, just high enough so that you can remove the old tire and put the spare on.

Additional Vocabulary Practice
BART System Map;
Riding BART;
Bicycle Rules, Ticket Guide, and Schedule;
How to Change a Flat Tire, p. 364

A. 1. commute
   2. fare
   3. discount
   4. schedule
   5. consumer

B. Sentences will vary.

C. 1. c   3. d
   2. b   4. a

Table of Contents

Overhead transparencies for the Reading Skills and Strategies Lessons can be found in the front cover pocket of this book.

Suggested *Elements of Literature* Selections for Reading Skills Application

Each of the ten Reading Skills lessons in this section includes an application activity. The following list provides suggestions for selections from the *Elements of Literature* Student Edition (or from the Adapted Readings section of this book) appropriate for the application of a given skill. All page references refer to the *Elements of Literature* Student Edition unless otherwise noted.

Informational Comprehension Skills

Identifying Author's Purpose

Determine the author's message, intent, and attitude toward the subject and recognize the effects of these on the text.

Any short informational selection may be used to apply the skill. Below are suggested readings from each collection.

Coll. 1 *from* People, Places, and Change (p. 33)
Eeking Out a Life* (*Holt Reading Solutions*, p. 464)

Coll. 2 Here Be Dragons (p. 165)
In a Mix of Cultures, an Olio of Plantings (p. 188)

Coll. 3 Gentlemen of the Road* (*Holt Reading Solutions*, p. 493)
Mongoose on the Loose (p. 340)

Coll. 4 Canines to the Rescue (p. 351)
Names/Nombres* (*Holt Reading Solutions*, p. 511)

Coll. 5 A Mason-Dixon Memory* (*Holt Reading Solutions*, p. 522)
An Interview with Sandra Cisneros (p. 614)

Coll. 6 The Power of Music (p. 673)
The Funeral Banquet of King Midas (p. 689)

Coll. 7 He's No King (p. 817)
Looking for Heroes (p. 872)

*Adapted Reading

Determining Main Idea

Determine central ideas in informational text, and identify important details that support the central ideas.

Any short informational selection may be used to apply the skill. Below are suggested readings from each collection.

Coll. 1   *from* People, Places, and Change (p. 33)
Eeking Out a Life* (*Holt Reading Solutions,* p. 464)

Coll. 2   Here Be Dragons (p. 165)
In a Mix of Cultures, an Olio of Plantings (p. 188)

Coll. 3   Gentlemen of the Road* (*Holt Reading Solutions,* p. 493)
The Only Girl in the World for Me (p. 323)

Coll. 4   What's *Really* in a Name?* (*Holt Reading Solutions,* p. 503)
Can We Rescue the Reefs? (p. 470)

Coll. 5   *from* Barrio Boy* (*Holt Reading Solutions,* p. 519)
The Place Where Dreams Come From (p. 624)

Coll. 6   The Funeral Banquet of King Midas (p. 689)
The Search Goes On (p. 740)

Coll. 7   *from* Long Walk to Freedom (p. 847)
Rosa Parks (p. 853)

*Adapted Reading

Making Inferences

Make informed judgments based on evidence from the text, and use personal observations and prior experience to make and confirm inferences.

Any short informational selection, excluding process or how-to passages, may be used to apply the skill. Below are suggested readings from each collection.

Coll. 1   *from* People, Places, and Change (p. 33)
Eeking Out a Life* (*Holt Reading Solutions,* p. 464)

Coll. 2   Here Be Dragons (p. 165)
In a Mix of Cultures, an Olio of Plantings (p. 188)

Coll. 3   The Fall of the House of Poe* (*Holt Reading Solutions,* p. 494)
It Just Keeps Going and Going* (*Holt Reading Solutions,* p. 495)

Coll. 4   Mirror, Mirror, on the Wall, Do I See Myself as Others Do? (p. 390)
Exile Eyes (p. 411)

Coll. 5   A Good Reason to Look Up (p. 481)
Right Hook—Left Hook: The Boxing Controversy (p. 497)

Coll. 6   The Myths of Greece and Rome (p. 646)
The Search Goes On (p. 740)

Coll. 7   He's No King (p. 817)
Looking for Heroes (p. 872)

*Adapted Reading

Summarizing

Compare original text to a summary to determine whether the summary accurately captures the ideas, includes critical details, and conveys the underlying meaning; synthesize content to demonstrate comprehension.

Any short informational selection may be used to apply the skill. Below are suggested readings from each collection.

Coll. 1   *from* People, Places, and Change (p. 33)
Cellular Telephone Owner's Manual* (p. 465)

Coll. 2   Here Be Dragons (p. 165)
In a Mix of Cultures, an Olio of Plantings (p. 188)

Coll. 3   The Fall of the House of Poe* (*Holt Reading Solutions*, p. 494)
The Only Girl in the World for Me (p. 323)

Coll. 4   Canines to the Rescue (p. 351)
Can We Rescue the Reefs? (p. 470)

Coll. 5   Fish Cheeks (p. 528)
Buddies Bare Their Affection for Ill Classmate* (*Holt Reading Solutions*, p. 526)

Coll. 6   The Funeral Banquet of King Midas (p. 689)
Folk Tales: Telling Tales (p. 696)

Coll. 7   Rosa Parks (p. 853)
Themes in Arthurian Legends (p. 870)

*Adapted Reading

Distinguishing Fact from Opinion

Evaluate whether the author presents objective facts or subjective opinions; assess the adequacy, accuracy, and appropriateness of the author's evidence to support claims and assertions; distinguish between logical and illogical statements in a text; identify biases, stereotypes, and persuasive techniques in texts.

Coll. 1   Eeking Out a Life* (*Holt Reading Solutions*, p. 464)

Coll. 2   Here Be Dragons (p. 165)
In a Mix of Cultures, an Olio of Plantings (p. 188)

Coll. 3   The Fall of the House of Poe* (*Holt Reading Solutions*, p. 494)
It Just Keeps Going and Going* (*Holt Reading Solutions*, p. 495)

Coll. 4   Mirror, Mirror, on the Wall, Do I See Myself As Others Do? (p. 390)
Names/Nombres* (*Holt Reading Solutions*, p. 511)

Coll. 5   Right Hook—Left Hook: The Boxing Controversy (p. 497)
The Place Where Dreams Come From (p. 624)

Coll. 6   The Funeral Banquet of King Midas (p. 689)
Folk Tales: Telling Tales (p. 696)

Coll. 7   Letter to the Editor (p. 789)
Women Characters in the King Arthur Stories (p. 870)

*Adapted Reading

Literary Comprehension Skills

Making Predictions

Determine the most likely outcomes; predict ideas or events that may take place; give a rationale for predictions.

Any short literary selection may be used to apply the skill. Below are suggested readings from each collection.

Coll. 1 Zoo (p. 85)
Coll. 2 A Rice Sandwich (p. 169)
Coll. 3 Hearts and Hands (p. 239)
Coll. 4 Yeh-Shen* (*Holt Reading Solutions*, p. 508)
Coll. 5 Amigo Brothers* (*Holt Reading Solutions*, p. 515)

Coll. 6 The Flight of Icarus* (*Holt Reading Solutions*, p. 530)
Coll. 7 King Arthur: The Sword in the Stone* (*Holt Reading Solutions*, p. 317)

*Adapted Reading

Understanding Characters

Recognize and understand characters' traits; determine characters' motivation and feelings based on clues in the text; understand characters' relationships; analyze interactions between main and subordinate characters; make inferences based on characters' words, actions, and reactions to other characters.

Any short literary selection featuring a character or characters may be used to apply the skill. Below are suggested readings from each collection.

Coll. 1 Three Skeleton Key* (*Holt Reading Solutions*, p. 458)
Coll. 2 Stolen Day (p. 197)
Coll. 3 The Highwayman* (*Holt Reading Solutions*, p. 485)

Coll. 4 An Unforgettable Journey (p. 403)
Coll. 5 Salvador Late or Early (p. 616)
Coll. 6 Aunty Misery (p. 727)
Coll. 7 Merlin and the Dragons (p. 821)

*Adapted Reading

Recognizing Theme

Identify ideas and insights about life and human nature expressed in literature; form interpretations of narrative text by making inferences, generalizing, drawing conclusions, and analyzing.

Any short literary selection may be used to apply the skill. Below are suggested readings from each collection.

Coll. 1 The Dinner Party (p. 118)
Coll. 2 Girls (p. 131)
Coll. 3 Echo and Narcissus* (*Holt Reading Solutions*, p. 497)
Coll. 4 Names / Nombres* (*Holt Reading Solutions*, p. 511)

Coll. 5 Sarah Cynthia Sylvia Stout Would Not Take the Garbage Out (p. 582)
Coll. 6 Belling the Cat (p. 778)
Coll. 7 Sir Gawain and the Loathly Lady* (*Holt Reading Solutions*, p. 532)

*Adapted Reading

Understanding Plot

Analyze the development of plot in a narrative text; recognize the basic situation or central conflict, the events or complications related to the central conflict, the climax, and the resolution; know how cause-and-effect relationships affect the plot; understand where and when a story takes place and trace the author's development of time and sequence.

Any short literary selection may be used to apply the skill. Below are suggested readings from each collection.

Coll. 1 Rikki-Tikki-tavi* (*Holt Reading Solutions*, p. 453)

Coll. 2 A Day's Wait (p. 191)

Coll. 3 Charles (p. 297)

Coll. 4 After Twenty Years* (*Holt Reading Solutions*, p. 500)

Coll. 5 Amigo Brothers* (*Holt Reading Solutions*, p. 515)

Coll. 6 The Crane Wife (p. 719)

Coll. 7 King Arthur: The Sword in the Stone* (*Holt Reading Solutions*, p. 317)

*Adapted Reading

Comparing and Contrasting

Compare and contrast aspects of narrative texts such as characters, settings, plot elements (for example, conflict), and themes.

Coll. 1 Zoo (p. 85) / Frankenstein (p. 108) — setting, writer's attitude

Coll. 2 A Rice Sandwich (p. 169) / Stolen Day (197) — conflict

Coll. 3 The Highwayman* (*Holt Reading Solutions*, p. 485) / Annabel Lee (p. 261) — characters, theme

Coll. 4 Bargain* (*Holt Reading Solutions*, p. 504) / An Unforgettable Journey (p. 403) — point of view

Coll. 5 I Like to See It Lap the Miles (p. 552) / The Runaway (p. 587) — images

Coll. 6 King Midas and the Golden Touch (p. 683) / The Hummingbird King (p. 733) — characters

Coll. 7 Merlin and the Dragons (p. 821) / Sir Gawain and the Loathly Lady* (*Holt Reading Solutions*, p. 532) — conflict, endings

* Adapted Reading

(CORE SKILL) **Identifying Author's Purpose**   Teacher Notes

At a Glance

- Because authors do not typically state a purpose for writing, readers must infer the purpose based on details in the text.

- The following lesson presents a strategy that encourages students to check their inferences about purpose against supporting details in the text.

Direct Instruction

Pass out the Student Notes (p. 389). As an introduction, you may want to make a few statements and allow students to infer your purpose. For instance, a few negative statements about a mock proposal will likely cause students to infer that you are against the proposal and that your purpose may be to persuade them to think likewise. Then, provide students an opportunity to point to your statements as supporting details by asking a follow-up question such as "How do you know that?"

Guided Practice

Distribute copies of the MiniReads (pp. 390–91) and the MiniRead Practice (p. 392). Guide students through MiniRead Practice Exercise A by using the steps below and Transparency 1.

1. Point out that an important question to answer when reading any selection is, "Why did the author write this?"

2. Read the selection aloud, using intonation to stress important details (such details may include facts, opinions, explanations, humor, story elements, repeated ideas, and so on). Then, focusing on the three basic purposes, ask students what the author's main purpose seems to be. Encourage detail in students' statements of purpose (for example, not simply "to inform" but "to inform the reader about how volcanoes form"). List a working response on Transparency 1.

3. Go back to the selection and guide students in underlining important details. Then, discuss whether the underlined details support the statement of purpose. As needed, revise the statement of purpose for accuracy and level of detail.

Independent Practice

Have students read MiniRead B and complete MiniRead Practice Exercise B.

Assessment

To give students another opportunity to apply the skill, choose a selection from the list on page 383. Then, have students complete the Application activity (p. 393).

NAME _____ DATE _____

Identifying Author's Purpose

At a Glance

- An **author's purpose** is the main reason he or she has for writing. The three basic purposes are **to inform, to persuade,** and **to entertain.**
- The simple strategy below will help you figure out an author's purpose.

Step-by-Step Strategy

1. Read the selection. As you do, ask yourself, "Why did the author write this?"

2. At the end of the selection, complete the following statement of purpose.

   The author wrote this mostly to . . . .

   Be sure to include details from the selection in your statement.

3. Finally, check your work. First, go back to the selection and underline details that seem important. Then, study the details. Do the underlined details support or fit in with your statement of purpose? If not, you might need to change or even rewrite your statement of purpose.

Example

Wetlands are an <u>important part of our environment.</u> However, many of our wetlands are being filled in and used for farming and building. Between 1985 and 1995, we <u>lost over one million acres of wetlands.</u> I believe that <u>Congress needs to pass tougher laws</u> for using wetlands.	**Statement of Purpose:** The author wrote this mostly to persuade the reader that having tougher laws for wetlands is important.

TIP Use the short explanations below to help you identify an author's main purpose.

To Inform   mostly presents information or explains, like in a textbook or news story

To Persuade   mostly argues a point or tries to convince, like in an editorial or advertisement

To Entertain   mostly provides entertainment, like in a poem or funny essay

Identifying Author's Purpose

DIRECTIONS: Use the following MiniRead with Exercise A on page 392.

MiniRead A

A Need for Green

A   Is anything better than seeing fresh flowers or biting into a home-grown tomato? Don't our students deserve these experiences? A group of teachers and students at Brewer Middle School think so. We have come up with a plan to begin a school garden. We don't need much—just a bit of space on the school grounds and some basic gardening supplies.

B   Students in city schools like ours may not have an opportunity to garden. Living in an apartment building surrounded by pavement makes it hard to experience growing plants. As the center of our community, the school should provide this opportunity for students. The Brewer school grounds have one of the largest pieces of green land in this part of the city. Therefore, this is the ideal place to begin this "groundbreaking" program.

C   Growing plants gives students much more than just flowers and vegetables. It also teaches them patience and responsibility. It gives them a sense of pride in their efforts. Students in this program will learn to care for their plants every day. They will decide when to harvest and what to do with their bounty. In short, by giving up a little space and money, the school can provide valuable life experiences for its students.

D   Students who learn to care for plants will become more in touch with their environment. They may move from improving our campus to improving their own neighborhoods. It all starts here. Our school can plant the "seed" by providing the space and supplies we have requested. We urge administrators to help our students "grow" into well-rounded adults.

Identifying Author's Purpose

DIRECTIONS: Use the following MiniRead with Exercise B on page 392.

MiniRead B

Giving Back

A   For decades, Bill Cosby has made people laugh. He has been an author, an actor, and a stand-up comic. In his movies and TV shows, he has had many memorable roles. However, one of his most important roles is that of giver. Bill Cosby has earned millions. He has also given away millions.

B   Bill Cosby has given his time and money to many good causes. Often, Cosby does his comedy act or gives speeches at benefits. He gave twenty million dollars to Spelman College. The money went toward teacher salaries and buildings. Also, Cosby created The Future Filmmakers Program. This program helps people studying to work in film.

C   Cosby's giving comes from his belief that success starts with education. This belief might seem funny coming from someone who at first struggled in school. Cosby was a natural comic but not a natural student. At one point, he even dropped out of high school.

D   Cosby later realized that he would never really have personal success if he didn't have a good education. So, while Cosby worked as an entertainer, he also worked as a student. He earned a bachelor's degree from Temple University. He even studied education itself and eventually earned an advanced degree in that field.

E   Throughout his career, Bill Cosby has been committed to charity and education—and that's no joke.

Identifying Author's Purpose

MiniRead Practice

Exercise A

1. Write a statement of purpose for "A Need for Green." Make sure that your statement has enough details to tell what the selection is about.

   _____

2. List several important details from the selection.

   _____

3. Do all the details in Question 2 support your statement of purpose? If not, revise your statement or write a new statement.

   _____

4. Which details give the most important clue to the author's purpose? Explain your answer.

   _____

Exercise B

1. Write a statement of purpose for "Giving Back." Make sure that your statement has enough details to tell what the selection is about.

   _____

2. List several important details from the selection.

   _____

3. Do all the details in Question 2 support your statement of purpose? If not, revise your statement or write a new statement.

   _____

4. Which details give the most important clue to the author's purpose? Explain your answer.

   _____

Identifying Author's Purpose

DIRECTIONS: Read the selection your teacher assigned. Then, in the chart below, write the author's purpose. Finally, to check your work, review the reading and identify important details. Write those details in the chart below. If the details do not support your main idea, revise it or write another one.

Title of Selection: _____

Author's Purpose	
Important Supporting Details	

CORE SKILL **Determining Main Idea**   Teacher Notes

At a Glance

- Readers struggling with the concept of main idea (especially implied main idea) often need help seeing how details, taken together, signal main idea.

- The following lesson provides a simple, three-step strategy designed to help students practice identifying main idea—whether stated or implied.

Direct Instruction

After passing out the Student Notes (p. 395), review the strategy, especially focusing on the importance of inferring main idea from a group of details.

Guided Practice

Distribute copies of the MiniRead (pp. 396–97) and the MiniRead Practice (p. 398). Guide students through MiniRead Practice Exercise A by using the steps below and Transparency 2.

1. Read the selection aloud. Then, help students identify the topic of paragraph B. As a prompt, ask a question like "What is this paragraph mostly about?" To keep students from focusing on the details of the paragraph, limit descriptions of the topic to short phrases.

2. Guide students in identifying the important details that tell about the topic. For simplicity, you may want to focus on identifying one detail per sentence. Encourage the use of short phrases to describe the details.

3. Finally, ask students to identify the writer's main idea about the topic. Prompt students by asking a question like "Based on the details, what seems to be the writer's most important point about the topic?" Even if the paragraph has a stated main idea, have students rephrase the sentence as an aid to reading comprehension. Note that interpretations may vary slightly; the standard for a good statement of main idea is supportability.

Repeat the basic process for paragraph C.

Independent Practice

Have students use the MiniRead to complete MiniRead Practice Exercise B.

Assessment

To give students another opportunity to apply the skill, choose a selection from the list on page 384. Then, have students complete the Application activity (p. 399).

Determining Main Idea

At a Glance

- The **main idea** of a paragraph is the writer's most important point.
- The following strategy will help you practice identifying main ideas.

Step-by-Step Strategy

1. Identify the **topic**.
   Here's how: Read the paragraph. Then, ask yourself, "What is this paragraph mostly about?" Write down your answer in a few words.

2. Next, identify the **important details.**
   Here's how: Review the paragraph. Then, for each sentence, briefly restate what the writer is saying about the topic.

3. Finally, figure out the **main idea.**
   Here's how: Review the important details. Then, ask yourself, "What is the writer's most important point about the topic?" Write down the most important point (main idea).

Example

Many stories told in different parts of the world are surprisingly similar. No one is sure why this is so. It may be because certain real-life wishes and fears are so powerful that people the world over want to express them in story form. Whatever the reason is, we learn something from all these tales. We learn that people around the world have much in common—despite cultural differences.	**Topic:** stories around the world **Important Details:** Many of them are similar; no one knows why; maybe because the ideas are powerful to all people; cultures are different, but people are similar. **Main Idea:** Although there are many different cultures, some stories show that people around the world have a lot in common.

TIP Sometimes a sentence in the paragraph may already state the most important point. If so, rewrite that sentence in your own words.

Determining Main Idea

DIRECTIONS: Use the following MiniRead with the exercises on page 398.

Hoax Hysteria

A   "Put down that fast-food sandwich! It's made of genetically engineered Franken-chicken! Eating it will stunt your growth! Forward this message to all of your friends!" Ever found a message like this in your e-mail inbox? Chances are, if you haven't gotten a hysterical warning about some new scare, you will soon. It's also likely that the message will be a fake, or hoax.

B   Hoaxes are nothing new. Nearly a century ago, scientists in England found what looked like a human fossil. They called it Piltdown man. The skull and jaw fit scientists' ideas about what a prehistoric human head should look like. However, later, scientists found that the "fossil" was a modern human skull with an ape jaw. No one knows who planted the fake fossil. It caused scientists a great deal of embarrassment.

C   Because hoaxes can seem so real, some people mistakenly think some real events are hoaxes. Some people believe the moon landings that began in 1969 were staged by NASA, the U.S. space agency. Fortunately, strong evidence—from moon rocks to the astronauts themselves—proves that the landings happened. In a way, people who claim that the landings were staged are creating a hoax of their own.

D   These two famous hoaxes show how important it is to consider all of the evidence before accepting any surprising claim. Today, hoaxes spread faster than ever. An e-mail warning that soda cans might carry a deadly virus can race across the country in a day or two. The only way to stop such hoaxes is to consider the evidence before forwarding messages to friends.

E   A hoax e-mail often contains certain clues. It may seem very urgent and request that you forward the message to others. A hoax e-mail may have a note that the message is not a hoax. Also, it may predict negative consequences for not taking action. If you see these clues in a message, take

Determining Main Idea *continued*

the time to gather more evidence. If a warning is real, major news outlets will probably report on it.

F   Hoaxes are not going away, even if everyone becomes more careful about forwarding e-mail. Finding ways to trick each other seems to be human nature. Also, some hoaxes can be harmless fun. To paraphrase P. T. Barnum (a famous creator of hoaxes), people seem to be amused even when they know they are being tricked.

Determining Main Idea

MiniRead Practice

Exercise A Use "Hoax Hysteria" to complete the following.

1. Paragraph B

   A. topic _____

   B. important details _____

   _____

   C. main idea _____

2. Paragraph C

   A. topic _____

   B. important details _____

   _____

   C. main idea _____

Exercise B Use "Hoax Hysteria" to complete the following.

1. Paragraph D

   A. topic _____

   B. important details _____

   _____

   C. main idea _____

2. Paragraph E

   A. topic _____

   B. important details _____

   _____

   C. main idea _____

Determining Main Idea

Application

DIRECTIONS: Read the selection. For two paragraphs, apply the strategy for determining main ideas. Show your work in the graphic organizers below.

Topic	
Important Details	
Main Idea	

Topic	
Important Details	
Main Idea	

(CORE SKILL) **Making Inferences**   Teacher Notes

At a Glance

- Making inferences, including drawing conclusions and forming generalizations, can help readers better understand and remember the ideas in a text.

- The following strategy can help readers make inferences by exploring their own questions about a text.

Direct Instruction

Begin by showing students a poster or transparency of a painting. Have students work in pairs to develop and then to answer *5W-How?* questions about the painting. Note that in answering the questions, students should use details from the painting and from their own experience. Next, pass out the Student Notes (p. 401) and formally introduce the skill and strategy.

Guided Practice

Distribute copies of the MiniRead (pp. 402–403) and the MiniRead Practice (p. 404). Guide students through MiniRead Practice Exercise A by using the steps below and Transparency 3.

1. Have students read paragraphs A–C, jotting down *5W-How?* questions as they read. Help them focus on important ideas that the writer doesn't directly state or explain. When they are finished, ask students to share some of their questions with the class.

2. Choose one question requiring an inference (for example, "Why did Fleet Walker have such a hard time in the major league?"). Have students suggest details from the text and from their own experiences that will help answer the question.

3. Lead students to use the details they suggested in Step 2 to make an inference that answers the question.

4. Choose another question requiring an inference, and repeat Steps 2 and 3.

Independent Practice

Have students use the MiniRead to complete MiniRead Practice Exercise B.

Assessment

To give students another opportunity to apply the skill, choose a selection from the list on page 384. Then, have students complete the Application activity (p. 405).

NAME _____ DATE _____

Making Inferences

At a Glance

- As you read, you sometimes make an **inference,** or an educated guess, about something the writer doesn't say or explain.
- To make a good inference, combine **what you read** and **what you already know.**

Step-by-Step Strategy

1. Ask yourself a *5-W How?* question about something the writer doesn't say or explain. The *5-W How?* questions are *Who? What? When? Where? Why?* and *How?*

2. List any details, or clues, that might help you answer your question. First, list any details from **what you read.** Then, list details about **what you already know.**

3. Finally, to answer your question, combine what you read and what you know. In other words, make an inference, or a guess.

Example

Question: In "The Emperor's New Clothes," why did almost everyone agree that the emperor was wearing clothes?

What I Just Read
- They didn't want anyone thinking they couldn't do their jobs.
- They didn't want to look foolish.

What I Already Know
- People will go along with the crowd to be accepted.
- Children are usually not afraid to speak the truth.

Answer: They pretended because they were worried about what other people might think. The child, who didn't care about this, told the truth.

Making Inferences

MiniRead

DIRECTIONS: Use the following MiniRead with the exercises on page 404.

The Unknown Stars of Baseball

A   You may have heard of Jackie Robinson. He was the first African American baseball player to join a major-league team in modern times. However, he was not the first to play professional baseball with white players. Other African American players went before him. Jackie Robinson was a great player, but so were some of these less famous players.

B   Before 1900, African Americans played on white minor-league teams. The first was Bud Fowler. He played on a white team in 1872. Fowler's career was long. He played on both white and black teams. He later started his own teams.

C   Early major-league teams also included African American players. In 1884, Fleet Walker was on a major-league team. Walker was the first African American in the majors. Unfortunately, he had a hard time. Some of the fans were very rude. Like Robinson, though, Walker was a gentleman.

D   Within a few years, several African American players had joined major-league teams. However, this positive trend soon ended. In 1887, the league stopped signing new African American players. This shut out some of the game's best players.

E   Those who stayed in the league had a tough time. Frank Grant is a good example. He was the best batter on his team. However, his white teammates would not join him in the team photograph. Other African Americans had a tough time, too. Sometimes, players on other teams would slide into African Americans in order to hurt them. These slides led to the first shin guards. Bud Fowler and Frank Grant were the first to wear wooden planks around their legs.

Making Inferences *continued*

F   Fleet Walker was cut from his team in 1890. For over fifty years afterward, no African American player was in the major leagues. During that time, great players such as Satchel Paige played in a separate league. Then, in 1947, Jackie Robinson made history. He took the field as a Brooklyn Dodger. Today, fans get to see all the best players showing off their skills—together.

Making Inferences

Exercise A Use "The Unknown Stars of Baseball" to complete the following.

1. Write one *5W-How?* question about an important idea in paragraphs A–C.

   _____

2. Below, write details from what you read and from what you know that may help you answer the question.

What I Just Read	**What I Already Know**
_____	_____
_____	_____
_____	_____

3. Answer the question based on the details in both columns above.

   _____

Exercise B Use "The Unknown Stars of Baseball" to complete the following.

1. Here are two *5W-How?* questions about important ideas from the selection.

   Why were those other players not as famous as Jackie Robinson? In 1887, why did the

   major league stop signing African American players?

2. Choose one of the questions above. Then, below, write details from what you read and from what you know that may help you answer the question.

What I Just Read	**What I Already Know**
_____	_____
_____	_____
_____	_____

3. Answer the question based on the details in both columns above.

   _____

Making Inferences

Application

DIRECTIONS: Read the selection your teacher assigned. As you do, use the chart below to help you make an inference. First, write down a few *5W-How?* questions about the selection. Then, choose one question and list details that might help you answer the question. Finally, use the details to come up with your answer.

My questions about the text:

_____

_____

_____

_____

_____

_____

Details to use in answering my chosen question:

What I Just Read	**What I Already Know**
_____	_____
_____	_____
_____	_____
_____	_____

My answer (combining what I just read and what I already know):

_____

_____

(CORE SKILL) **Summarizing**   Teacher Notes

At a Glance

- The **GIST** summary strategy (**G**enerating **I**nteractions between **S**chemata and **T**ext; Cunningham, 1982) is a simple approach appropriate for all readers.

- Students using the strategy learn to summarize increasingly larger chunks of text by building on summaries of smaller chunks.

Direct Instruction

After passing out copies of the Student Notes (p. 407), guide students through the explanation of the skill. Then, review the steps of the **GIST** summary strategy, focusing on the example following the strategy.

Guided Practice

Distribute copies of the MiniReads (pp. 408–409) and the MiniRead Practice (p. 410). Guide students through MiniRead Practice Exercise A by using the steps below and Transparency 4.

1. Break the reading into sections. (The MiniRead is already broken into sections.)

2. Read aloud the first section, guiding students to identify—by underlining or circling—important words and ideas. (Additionally, you may want to have students cross out nonessential or repetitive ideas.) Record selected words and ideas in the Section Notes column of Transparency 4.

3. Focusing on the Section Notes column, have students suggest short summary sentences. The summary does not have to be a single sentence, but it should be twenty-five words or fewer. Students should use their own words as much as possible. Record a selected response.

4. Repeat the above process for the second section. This time, however, have students create a twenty-five-word summary that is a combination of the first and second sections. You may want to note that the combination summary doesn't need to contain equal amounts of information from both sections.

5. For longer selections, you would continue repeating the basic steps, with the ultimate goal of creating a single summary of the entire selection.

Independent Practice

Have students read MiniRead B and complete MiniRead Practice Exercise B.

Assessment

To give students another opportunity to apply the skill, choose a selection from the list on page 385. Then, have students complete the Application activity (p. 411).

406   Core Reading Skills and Strategies

Summarizing

At a Glance

- A **summary** is a short restatement of the most important ideas in a text.
- Using the GIST summary strategy will help you summarize long selections.

Step-by-Step Strategy

1. Divide the selection into sections.

2. Read the first section. As you do, note important words and ideas.

3. Write a short summary that includes only the most important ideas from the first section. Use your own words as much as possible. Try not to use more than twenty-five words in all.

4. Read the second section. Then, write another short summary. This time, however, include important ideas from *both* sections.

5. Repeat Step 4 as needed. You'll be done when you have a single summary for the whole selection. Remember—try not to use more than twenty-five words!

Example

When Dr. James Naismith was challenged to invent a game that could be played indoors, he had no idea his new game would become so popular. The first game of basketball was played in 1891.

In the original game, the goal was a fruit basket ten feet above the ground. Once a basket was scored, a player had to climb up and get the ball. Of the thirteen original rules for the game, some are still used today. For example, players cannot hold the ball and run; they must dribble it.

Summary of Section 1:
Dr. James Naismith came up with a new game called basketball, which could be played indoors. The game was first played in 1891.

Summary of Sections 1 and 2:
Dr. James Naismith invented the indoor game of basketball. Since it was first played in 1891, some things about the game have changed.

TIPS

- Use your own words as much as possible.
- Replace big word groups with a few words that stand for the whole group.

Summarizing

DIRECTIONS: Use the following MiniRead with Exercise A on page 410.

MiniRead A

Understanding Dyslexia

A   Albert Einstein was a genius. Surprisingly, though, he was a poor student. Einstein had dyslexia. People with dyslexia have trouble with words. Although over a tenth of Americans have dyslexia, most people don't know much about it.

       People with dyslexia have trouble learning how to read and spell. Reversing letters is one sign of dyslexia. For example, a person with dyslexia might read the word *saw* as the word *was*. Mixing up directions, such as right and left, is another sign.

       People with dyslexia have trouble with letters and sounds. The word *cat,* for example, is made up of three sounds: *kuh, aa,* and *tuh.* Readers usually sound out words quickly. However, people with dyslexia take longer. Because of this, they often read at a slower rate.

B   Because children with dyslexia have trouble learning to read, some people jump to the wrong conclusion. They think that these children are not bright. However, dyslexia is not a sign of low intelligence. Many people with dyslexia are highly creative and talented people. Remember Albert Einstein? Walt Disney, Muhammed Ali, Whoopi Goldberg, Winston Churchill, and Tom Cruise also overcame dyslexia to succeed.

       Also, some people mistakenly believe that people with dyslexia just need to work harder. However, most dyslexic students work very hard. They sometimes just need a different kind of instruction. Many dyslexics learn better through graphics, touch, and movement. Students may also need help matching sounds to letters more easily.

       Dyslexia can be a challenge, but it does not mean failure. Just ask any of the accomplished, successful people who have it.

Summarizing

DIRECTIONS: Use the following MiniRead with Exercise B on page 410.

MiniRead B

The Animal Mind: Smart and Sensitive

A   We humans are used to thinking that our minds separate us from other animals. But new studies show that animals are quite intelligent and sensitive.

     Animal intelligence isn't found only in mammals. It can be found in other animals, such as birds. Although we sometimes call people "birdbrains" as an insult, our feathered friends can be very smart. Some can solve puzzles. For example, ravens can untie knots. Some birds can use tools. Some crows, for example, use twigs as spears. Some birds can even use our language. An African Grey parrot named Alex does more than just imitate human sounds. This parrot can name dozens of objects. It also seems to understand the ideas of "same," "different," and "amount."

B   Animals are able to feel emotion, too. This ability can be as painful for them as it is for humans. For example, some baboons live in groups where the leaders control through fear. low-ranking baboons can live in a constant state of stress. This stress can cause health problems, just as it does in humans.

     Some animals feel sadness when a family member dies. Elephants show interest even in decades-old elephant bones. Like humans, they are connected to each other in many ways.

Summarizing

Exercise A

1. Read section A of "Understanding Dyslexia." Then, create a GIST statement that summarizes section A. Use no more than twenty-five words.

_____

_____

_____

2. Read section B of "Understanding Dyslexia." Then, create a GIST statement that summarizes section A *and* section B. Use no more than twenty-five words.

_____

_____

_____

Exercise B

1. Read section A of "The Animal Mind." Then, create a GIST statement that summarizes section A. Use no more than twenty-five words.

_____

_____

_____

2. Read section B of "The Animal Mind." Then, create a GIST statement that summarizes section A *and* section B. Use no more than twenty-five words.

_____

_____

_____

Summarizing

DIRECTIONS: Divide the assigned reading into three sections. Read the first section. As you do, write important ideas in the Section Notes column below. Then, use the notes to create a summary. Repeat the steps for the next two sections. Remember that each new summary should include ideas from the previous summary.

Section Notes	Summary (twenty-five words or fewer)

CORE SKILL Distinguishing Fact from Opinion

Teacher Notes

At a Glance

- Distinguishing facts from opinions can help students better understand an author's ideas and purpose for writing.

- The following simple strategy can help readers at all levels distinguish facts from opinions.

Direct Instruction

Pass out copies of the Student Notes (p. 413). Then, review and discuss the skill and the steps of the strategy, focusing on the example provided.

Guided Practice

Distribute copies of the MiniRead (pp. 414–15) and the MiniRead Practice (p. 416). Guide students through MiniRead Practice Exercise A by using the steps below and Transparency 5.

1. Read aloud paragraphs A–C, and have students select statements from the selection to analyze. Tell them to choose one statement that seems significant in making the author's case or that sounds debatable (for example ". . . not providing such a park would be unfair" or "[A public skatepark] would also be an excellent way for Springfield to encourage its youth").

2. Ask the class to discuss whether the statement can be proved true. If a student says that it can be proved, ask what type of source might provide such proof. Lead students to consider a variety of sources.

3. If students decide that the statement cannot be proved true, guide them in explaining why it is an opinion. You may want to caution students about false facts—that is, opinions stated as if they were facts.

4. Repeat the process for one or two other statements.

Independent Practice

Have students use the MiniRead to complete MiniRead Practice Exercise B.

Assessment

To give students another opportunity to apply the skill, choose a selection from the list on page 385. Then, have students complete the Application activity (p. 417).

Distinguishing Fact from Opinion

At a Glance

- A **fact** is a statement that can be proved true. You can get proof for a fact from a trusted source, such as a textbook, a dictionary, or an encyclopedia.
- An **opinion** cannot be proved true. It is a personal belief that people can disagree with or debate.

Step-by-Step Strategy

1. As you read, underline statements that seem important to the author's point.

2. For each statement, ask, "Can this statement be proved true?"

   Yes. Identify at least one source that might provide proof.

   No. Explain why it is only a personal belief that people can disagree with or debate.

Example

Statement	Can statement be proved true?
Dogs make lovable pets.	No. People could disagree. They might think dogs aren't lovable. The statement is an opinion.
A beagle is a kind of hound dog that has long, floppy ears.	Yes. You could find this in an encyclopedia. The statement is a fact.
We should donate our bake-sale money to an animal shelter.	No. People could disagree. They might think the money should be spent another way—or not at all. The statement is an opinion.

TIP Watch out for words like the following, which sometimes signal opinions.

- I believe / feel / think that . . .
- good / bad
- best / worst
- must / should

Distinguishing Fact from Opinion

MiniRead

DIRECTIONS: Use the following MiniRead with the exercises on page 416.

Springfield Needs a Skatepark

A   The youth of Springfield are in a tough position. They have skateboards and safety equipment. Yet, if they skate in public, they are fined because of a city ordinance, or law. That ordinance makes it illegal to skateboard on streets, sidewalks, and parking lots. Skateboarders report that they have no other places to skate. A public skatepark would be a safe place for this sport. It would also be an excellent way for Springfield to encourage its youth.

B   American Sports Data estimates that there are two million skateboarders who say they skate every day. It is not only the very young who skate. More skaters are staying with the sport past the age of sixteen. Surveys show that skateboarding is the third-largest sport for people between six and eighteen. There is definitely interest in the sport in our town. Over five hundred people signed the request for a public skatepark. So, not providing such a park is unfair.

C   Skateboarding has many benefits. First, it teaches balance, coordination, and muscle control. Doing tricks like a heelslip or lipslide requires a lot of skill. Second, mastering tricks gives skaters self-confidence. Third, the sport appeals to many people who are not interested in team sports.

D   Some people argue that skateboarding is dangerous and should not be supported by the city. However, skateboarding is not as dangerous as some other sports. Statistics show that emergency-room visits for skateboarding injuries are far fewer than for some other sports, such as basketball.

E   Still, skateboarders do get injured. And according to the National Safety Council, poor riding surfaces—such as cracks or rocks in the road—lead to more than half of the injuries. Lack of safety equipment also contributes. So, why not create a skatepark? According to researcher Michael Nance, M.D., "You tend to find that the kids who go to the parks wear the equipment. They're doing things in a safer setting."

Distinguishing Fact from Opinion *continued*

F   Skateboarding is a fun sport. However, skateboarders shouldn't have to put up with tickets and rough roads. Springfield must give its skateboarders a safe place to skate. A skatepark is a safe, legal alternative to public places. Young citizens of the city have shown their interest in a park. Now, the city council should act.

Distinguishing Fact from Opinion   MiniRead Practice

Exercise A Use "Springfield Needs a Skatepark" to complete the following.

1. Choose one statement to study in paragraphs A–C.

    A. Statement: _____

    B. Any source that might prove the statement true: _____

    C. The statement is a (fact, opinion) because _____

    _____

2. Choose another statement to study in paragraphs A–C.

    A. Statement: _____

    B. Any source that might prove the statement true: _____

    C. The statement is a (fact, opinion) because _____

    _____

Exercise B Use "Springfield Needs a Skatepark" to complete the following.

1. Below is one statement to study in paragraphs D–F.

    A. Statement: "However, skateboarding is not as dangerous as some other sports."

    B. Any source that might prove the statement true: _____

    C. The statement is a (fact, opinion) because _____

    _____

2. Choose another statement to study in paragraphs D–F.

    A. Statement: _____

    B. Any source that might prove the statement true: _____

    C. The statement is a (fact, opinion) because _____

    _____

Distinguishing Fact from Opinion

Application

DIRECTIONS: Choose a statement in your reading that seems important. It may be a statement that people could disagree about. Use the steps illustrated in the flowchart below to help you figure out whether the statement is a fact or an opinion.

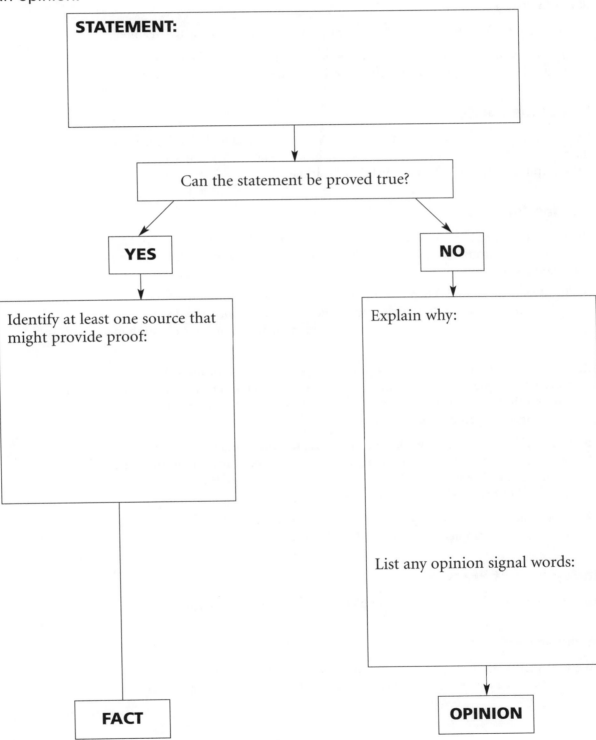

STATEMENT:

Can the statement be proved true?

YES

NO

Identify at least one source that might provide proof:

Explain why:

List any opinion signal words:

FACT

OPINION

(CORE SKILL) **Making Predictions**   Teacher Notes

At a Glance

• The **A-P-C** (Ask-Predict-Check) strategy promotes purposeful, active reading.

• Readers will pause to ask questions and predict answers based on textual details and prior knowledge. Students then continue reading to verify predictions.

Direct Instruction

Pass out copies of the Student Notes (p. 419). When introducing the skill, emphasize the role of textual details and the reader's background knowledge. Then, review the A-P-C strategy steps and the accompanying example.

Guided Practice

Distribute copies of the MiniRead (pp. 420–21) and the MiniRead Practice (p. 422). Guide students through MiniRead Practice Exercise A by using the steps below and Transparency 6.

1. Read section A aloud. Then, ask questions to elicit predictions. Questions can be specific or general ("What might happen next?"or "What did Tom do to make his younger brother, Daniel, so angry?"). For simplicity, record one question in Transparency 6.

2. Ask students to make predictions about the question. Then, prompt students to support each prediction by citing the text and by using background knowledge (for example, "I bet Tom got into a fight with Daniel, because Daniel is crying and is upset"). Record one prediction.

3. Continue reading, pausing after section B. Ask whether students can now verify, or check, the prediction. If so, record a model response, which can be broadened to include newly encountered details. Before continuing, guide students to ask questions of their own. Record one question.

4. Repeat Steps 2 and 3 until you feel students understand the basic process. Then, have students complete the Independent Practice.

Independent Practice

Have students use the MiniRead to complete the MiniRead Practice Exercise.

Assessment

To give students another opportunity to apply the skill, choose a selection from the list on page 386. Then, have students complete the Application activity (p. 423).

Making Predictions

At a Glance

- Active readers think ahead to predict, or guess, what might happen next.
- The **A-P-C** (Ask-Predict-Check) strategy will help you make good predictions.

Step-by-Step Strategy

1. Read until you find a good stopping place. You might stop at the end of a paragraph or at a break in the action. Then, **ask** a question about what might happen next.

2. **Predict** an answer to your question. Use the word *because* to explain why you made the prediction.

3. Keep reading until you find another good stopping place. **Check** your prediction. If you have enough information, tell whether your prediction was right. Then, ask another question.

4. Repeat steps 2 and 3 as needed. When you're done with the reading, be sure that you have checked all of your predictions.

Example

Tanya pushed up her ski goggles and gave an annoyed look at the crowds on the slopes. Today was a Saturday and a holiday, too, so the slopes were crowded. As all those skiers moved noisily around her, Tanya glanced at the quiet woods to her left.	**Ask:** "What will Tanya do about the crowded slopes?" **Predict:** "I bet she will decide to ski through the woods because it seems that she wants to be alone."
Tanya usually stayed on the popular slopes. Today, though, she decided to check out the less-traveled trails that led through the woods.	**Check:** "Tanya does decide to leave the crowded trails and check out the forest."

TIP Good predictions are supported by details in the reading and by your own experience. "The car will break down because there's smoke coming from under the hood." "The character will win because the underdog usually wins in stories like this."

Making Predictions

MiniRead

DIRECTIONS: Use the following MiniRead with the exercise on page 422.

The Barn

A   The side door of the barn flew open. Daniel and his older brother, Tom, rushed in and slammed the door. "I can't believe you did it again," Daniel shouted. His face was red with anger and streaked with tears. "You promised!"

"I'm sorry. It can't be helped. Now be quiet and let me think," his older brother said. Fishing a match out of his pocket, he lit a lantern and sat it on a nearby bale of hay. Then, he slumped down on one of the two mattresses to think.

B   They had worked hard to make the old barn livable. An old crate doubled as a table and a dresser drawer. Two pairs of overalls, some shirts, and socks were stacked neatly inside. Bales of hay sectioned off their "bedroom" from the rest of the barn. The harnesses and saddles that had once been carelessly piled in the corner now hung neatly from hooks. In the short time they had been there, the old barn had begun to feel like home.

"You swore we could stay here, Tom." Daniel cried out in frustration. "You promised there would be no more running."

C   "I said be quiet," his older brother hissed again. "Let me think."

Daniel sat on his makeshift bed and wrapped his arms around his legs. He reached out to touch a photograph of his mother that rested on the wooden crate. He hadn't seen her since he and his brother had been on the run, and he thought that at this rate, it would be a long time before he saw her again. He knew that Tom's crimes were serious. It was only a matter of time before the authorities found them again, and Daniel was sick of it.

D   "Look, kid," Tom said. "Mother's not here. Maybe we'll be able to see her again one of these days. But right now, I'm all you've got."

Making Predictions *continued*

"Great," Daniel said with disgust. "So I have to live with a thief *and* a liar? You promised no more stealing. You promised to get a job. But no. You had to go and steal again, and now they're after you."

Picking up a canvas bag, Tom ordered, "Put your things in here. Now! We're leaving."

"No. You leave. I'm staying." Daniel stood up and crossed his arms in defiance.

"What do you mean, no? You know they'll find this place soon enough, and I don't plan to be here when they do."

E   "Fine. I'm not going. You can run, but I'm staying. I'm not the thief."

"I said to pack!" Tom yelled. He threw the bag at his younger brother, expecting him to catch it, but Daniel wasn't prepared for the force of the throw and fell backward. As he threw his arm out to break his fall, he knocked the lantern to the floor with a crash. Instantly, the hay caught fire and flames shot high.

F   "Run!" Tom shouted as he pulled Daniel to his feet. Coughing and choking from the smoke, they ran outside. Looking across the field, Tom saw men on horses riding fast. "Come on," he yelled. "We've go to get out of here!" He ran for the cornfield, hoping to hide among the tall stalks.

G   But Daniel didn't run. He watched sadly as the smoke poured out of the barn doors. Then, he began slowly walking toward the men.

Making Predictions

Exercise

As you read "The Barn," apply the **A-P-C** prediction strategy. For each lettered section of the reading, ask one question and predict an answer to it. Then, continue reading to check out your prediction. Be sure to write all of your work in the chart below.

Ask	Predict	Check
What did Tom do to make his younger brother, Daniel, so angry?		

Making Predictions

DIRECTIONS: Read the selection your teacher chose. As you do, pause at least three times to apply the **A-P-C** prediction strategy. Each time you pause, ask one question and predict an answer to it. Then, continue reading to check out your prediction. Be sure to write all of your work in the chart below.

Title of story:_____

Ask	Predict	Check

(CORE SKILL) Understanding Characters Teacher Notes

At a Glance

- Understanding characters enriches the literary experience, helping readers to make connections to the text and to recognize its themes.

- Creating a **character web** helps students discover many facets of a character.

Direct Instruction

Ask students to name well-known characters from movies, television shows, or literature. Choose one character that all students are familiar with, and have them discuss the traits of that character. Then, hand out copies of the Student Notes (p. 425). Discuss the skill and the strategy, focusing on the example provided.

Guided Practice

Distribute copies of the MiniReads (pp. 426–27) and the MiniRead Practice (p. 428). Guide students through MiniRead Practice Exercise A by using the steps below and Transparency 7.

1. Read the selection aloud, and have students choose a character to analyze. Guide them to choose a character about whom the author provides many details. Write the chosen character's name on Transparency 7.

2. Ask students how they learn about a character. Then, have them list the types of clues authors usually provide (appearance, speech, actions, others' reactions, thoughts/feelings).

3. Have students give details about the character, and ask them to link the details to the corresponding type of clue. If a student is unsure how to categorize a detail, allow other students to help. Add student responses to the web.

4. Ask students to sum up the ideas in the character web in a sentence or two. What kind of person is the character?

Independent Practice

Have students read MiniRead B and complete MiniRead Practice Exercise B.

Assessment

To give students another opportunity to apply the skill, choose a selection from the list on page 386. Then, have students complete the Application activity (p. 429).

NAME _____ DATE _____

Understanding Characters

At a Glance

- Understanding characters will help you get more from the literature you read.
- A **character web** helps you think about the different sides of a character.

Step-by-Step Strategy

1. Begin a character web by writing the character's name in a circle.

2. What type of clues tell you about the character? Clues can include how a character looks, talks, and acts, and how others react to him or her. Write each type of clue in its own circle and connect it to the character circle.

3. Review the selection you read and look for clues about the character. Add these clues to your web. Make a new circle for each clue and connect it to the right type of clue.

4. Use the clues in your character web to sum up what kind of person the character is.

Example

Here is part of a character web and a summary statement for Keevan, a character in "The Smallest Dragonboy."

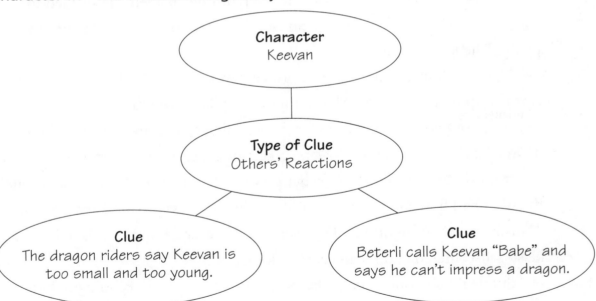

What the character is like: Even though some think he is too small, Keevan is brave and determined. He does eventually impress a dragon.

TIP In writing your summary statement, think about why the character acts or thinks as he or she does.

Understanding Characters

DIRECTIONS: Use the following MiniRead with the exercises on page 428.

MiniRead A

The Princess and the Amphibian

A   Once upon a time, there was a self-centered princess. The princess had long, dark hair. Her eyes were like shiny, black glass from cooled molten lava. Her arms were sculpted from working out. She looked good, and she knew it.

B   The princess would have been happy except for one thing: She had promised to marry an amphibian—an ugly, bug-eyed frog. She was only five years old when she made the promise. She had gotten in trouble for being mean to another kid, so she made this promise to convince her parents she really could be nice. How could she be responsible for something she had said when she was so young? Couldn't she get out of this?

C   Her father, the king, felt sorry for her, but he also felt she needed to learn a lesson. "A promise is a promise. You need to learn to live up to your pledge," he kept saying.

D   The wedding day arrived. The princess woke up when the sun was just coming up on the horizon. She clamped the pillow over her head and refused to get out of bed. So everything for the wedding ceremony was brought to the bedroom: chairs for guests, flowers, cake, punch, and the minister. She peeked out from under her pillow to see her groom. He was using his tongue to catch flies that had flown in the open window. The princess groaned and screamed, "This is the worst nightmare I've ever had! If I ever get out of this, I'll never be so self-centered and mean again as long as I live!"

E   Suddenly, she woke up, the last sentence of her dream echoing in her mind. She peered out from under the covers and breathed a long sigh. It had been a dream.

F   Her eyes focused on the faint light from the window. There on the windowsill sat a huge, ugly frog. She picked up a running shoe and flung it as hard as she could.

Understanding Characters

DIRECTIONS: Use the following MiniRead with Exercise B on page 428.

MiniRead B

Androcles

based on Aesop's fable

A   Long ago, there was a slave named Androcles, who had run away from his master. One day, he crept into the cave and found a lion lying on its side and groaning in pain. Afraid of being eaten, Androcles started to run away.

B   To Androcles' surprise, though, the lion did not chase him. Androcles turned around and approached the lion. As he did, the lion slowly put out its paw, which was bleeding. It seems that the lion had stepped on a thorn. "If I remove this thorn," Androcles thought, "the lion might feel well enough to eat me. But if I don't, the lion will continue to suffer."

C   It only took a moment for Androcles to decide what was right. So, he reached down and pulled out the thorn. At the sharp pain, the huge lion rose up and roared, but then he licked Androcles' face.

D   Androcles and the lion became great friends. But one day, Androcles was caught. As punishment for the escape, the king sentenced Androcles to be thrown to a lion—the very lion that Androcles had saved.

E   Everyone came to see the punishment carried out. Androcles was led into the stadium. As he stood there, he watched calmly as people cheered for what was about to happen. Then, the king let the lion loose.

F   The lion, which hadn't been fed for many days, swiftly ran toward Androcles. Anyone else would have run away in fear, but not Androcles. He remained still. Then, as the lion was about to pounce on Androcles, something happened. Androcles put out his hand, and the lion licked it.

G   The king asked Androcles why the lion hadn't pounced, and Androcles told the whole tale. After hearing it, the king set them both free.

H   *Thankfulness is the sign of great souls.*

NAME _____ DATE _____

Understanding Characters

MiniRead Practice

Exercise A Use "The Princess and the Amphibian" to complete the following.

1. Complete the character web below.

   A. Write the character's name.

   B. Identify another type of clue that tells what the character is like.

   C. For each type of clue, write two clues from the story.

A.

B.

Actions

C.

2. Write a statement that sums up what the character is like. _____

_____

Exercise B Use "Androcles" to complete the following.

1. Complete the character web below.

   A. Write the character's name.

   B. Identify two types of clues that tell what the character is like.

   C. For each type of clue, write two clues from the story.

A.

B.

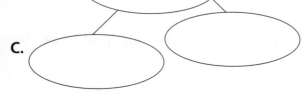
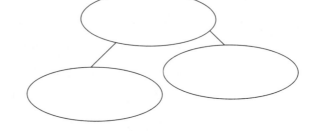

C.

2. Write a statement that sums up what the character is like. _____

_____

Understanding Characters

Application

DIRECTIONS: Read the selection your teacher chose. Then, fill out the web below to analyze the character. In the center circles, write the character's name and two types of clues the author gives. In the outside circles, write clues from the story. Finally, at the bottom of the page, write what the character is like based on the clues.

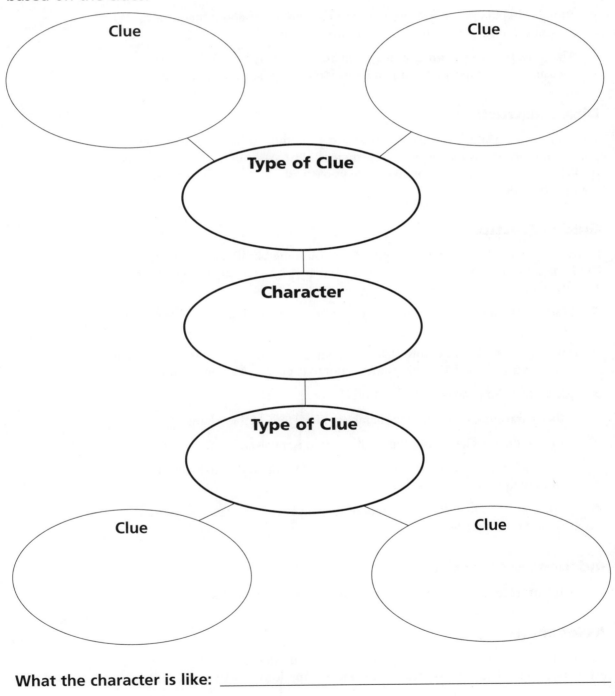

Clue

Clue

Type of Clue

Character

Type of Clue

Clue

Clue

What the character is like: _____

_____

(CORE SKILL) Recognizing Theme   Teacher Notes

At a Glance

- Recognizing theme requires students to make inferences about the author's meaning and to connect the text with their life experiences.

- The **Most Important Word** strategy will help students identify theme by focusing on an important word and how it relates to narrative elements.

Direct Instruction

Write a few universal themes on the board and have students list stories, movies, poems, or other works that express these themes. Next, pass out the Student Notes (p. 431). Review the skill and discuss the steps of the strategy, focusing on the example provided.

Guided Practice

Distribute copies of the MiniReads (pp. 432–33) and the MiniRead Practice (p. 434). Guide students through MiniRead Practice Exercise A by using the steps below and Transparency 8.

1. As students read the selection, have them note any repeating words, images, or ideas.

2. Have students select one word that they think is the most important and write it in the space provided. Caution students not to choose a character's name.

3. Ask students how the word relates to . . .

   - the characters—What are the characters like? How do they change?

   - the conflict—What causes the conflict? Who is involved in the struggle?

   - the resolution—How is the conflict resolved? What do the characters learn from their struggles?

4. Instruct students to write a statement of theme based on the most important word and how it relates to the story.

Independent Practice

Have students read MiniRead B and complete MiniRead Practice Exercise B.

Assessment

To give students another opportunity to apply the skill, choose a selection from the list on page 386. Then, have students complete the Application activity (p. 435).

Recognizing Theme

At a Glance

- **Theme** is a story's lesson or message about life. The theme usually is not stated directly. You have to figure it out yourself.
- The **Most Important Word** strategy will help you identify the theme of a story.

Step-by-Step Strategy

1. Read the story. Note any repeating word or ideas.

2. Think about the story and how it ends. Then, select one word that you think is the most important and write it down. *(Do not choose a character's name.)*

3. Next, think about why the word is important. Write down what the word has to do with

    - the characters—What are the characters like? How do they change?

    - the conflict—What causes the problem? Who is involved in the struggle?

    - the resolution—How does the conflict end? What do the characters learn from their struggles?

4. Review your ideas about the word and write a statement of theme.

Example

Here is one student's work for "Hansel and Gretel."

Most Important Word:	Clever
Characters:	The woodcutter's evil wife persuades him to leave their children, Hansel and Gretel, in the forest.
Conflict:	A witch captures the children and plans to roast and eat them.
Resolution:	Gretel tricks the witch and pushes her into the oven. Then, Hansel and Gretel find their way home.
Theme:	You can sometimes help yourself out of a tough situation by using your brain—being clever—and acting quickly.

TIP Don't worry if the theme you identified is different from someone else's. A selection usually has more than one theme.

Recognizing Theme MiniRead

DIRECTIONS: Use the following MiniRead with Exercise A on page 434.

MiniRead A

The Roar of the Jets

A   The ringing phone jarred me awake. As I answered, I wondered who would dare to call me so early on a Saturday morning. "Get up, Lea!" Raul ordered. "We're going to watch the airplanes. I'll be there in 30 minutes."

B   Before I could object, Raul hung up. He often took me to interesting events, but an air show? At that moment, I preferred to sleep in.

C   As we stood in line at the entrance of the airfield, I saw a many different airplanes scattered across the field. Raul knows a lot about aircraft. He was pointing here and there saying, "Look! There's a B-17, and over there's an F-117 Nighthawk." I just stared in amazement at all the people who had gotten up early to come to see an air show.

D   Just then, an announcer crackled over a loudspeaker. Six pilots in navy jumpsuits marched across the airplane runway and climbed into the F-16 fighter jets. With a loud BOOM, the pilots started the jet engines, waved at the crowd, and took off.

E   They flew back and forth overhead, their wings almost touching. Then, they began doing flips, rolls, and dives. Several times I found myself gasping, thinking the jets were about to crash. Then, without our noticing it, one jet peeled off from the others. Suddenly, it appeared out of nowhere, roaring over our heads. The ground shook. It sounded like a bomb exploding behind us.

F   We screamed and then laughed in relief as the single jet joined the others.

G   Too soon, the show was over. The jets landed, taxied down the runway, and parked. The crowd cheered wildly as the pilots approached. I applauded and yelled myself hoarse.

H   Raul looked over at me with a devilish twinkle in his eye. "Just think. You could have slept through all of this," he said.

Recognizing Theme

DIRECTIONS: Use the following MiniRead with Exercise B on page 434.

MiniRead B

The Frogs Who Wished for a King
based on Aesop's fable

A   The Frogs lived a carefree life in a swamp that was just perfect for them. They bothered no one, and no one bothered them. They spent their days croaking and splashing about. But some of the Frogs began to wish for a king, someone who would rule them and keep them in order. So, one day, the Frogs sent a request for a king to Jupiter.

B   Jupiter laughed at their request and threw down a huge log, which fell into the water with a great splash. The Frogs, thinking the new king to be some fearful giant, hid themselves among the reeds and grasses. Although the Frogs were afraid, a few of the braver ones moved in to get a closer look. One frog even worked up the courage to touch the log. The log didn't move, though. Seeing this, the bravest Frog of them all jumped onto the log and started dancing. Soon, all the Frogs were on the great log dancing and laughing.

C   For a long time after the arrival of King Log, the Frogs went about their days just as they had before. After a while, though, they began to complain that they were not satisfied. They wanted a real king, one who would rule over them. So, they sent Jupiter another request for a king.

D   Jupiter, who was angry at their request, decided he would send the Frogs a stork for a king. Well, shortly after arriving at the swamp, the Stork began gobbling up all the Frogs. In terrible and sad croaks, they begged Jupiter to take away the cruel King before they should all be destroyed. The Frogs had learned a lesson—but a little too late.

Recognizing Theme

MiniRead Practice

Exercise A Use "The Roar of the Jets" to complete the following.

1. Write down what you believe is the **most important word**: _____

2. Think about why the word you chose is important and how it relates to the story's characters, conflict, and resolution.

   A. Characters: _____

   _____

   B. Conflict: _____

   _____

   C. Resolution: _____

   _____

3. Write a statement of **theme** based on how the word relates to the story.

   _____

Exercise B Use "The Frogs Who Wished for a King" to complete the following.

1. Write down what you believe is the **most important word**: _____

2. Think about why the word you chose is important and how it relates to the story's characters, conflict, and resolution.

   A. Characters: _____

   _____

   B. Conflict: _____

   _____

   C. Resolution: _____

   _____

3. Write a statement of **theme** based on how the word relates to the story.

   _____

NAME _____ DATE _____

Recognizing Theme

Application

DIRECTIONS: As you read the selection, write down repeating words or ideas. Decide which word you think is most important. Write that word in the center circle below. Then, in each outside circle, write details that tell what the word has to do with that part of the story. Finally, at the bottom of the page, write the theme, or lesson, the details point to.

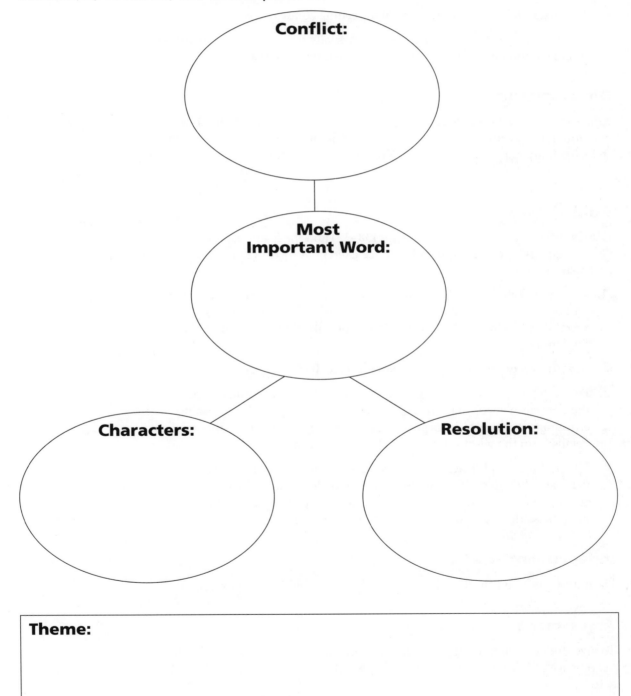

Conflict:

Most Important Word:

Characters:

Resolution:

Theme:

(CORE SKILL) Understanding Plot   Teacher Notes

At a Glance

- Understanding plot is fundamental to reading comprehension.

- The following strategy will help readers visually represent plot elements as an aid to comprehending and appreciating narrative text as a whole.

Direct Instruction

As a lead-in to the **Storyboard** strategy, you might begin with a short comic strip containing the basic elements of plot. After discussing the elements in the comic strip, hand out copies of the Student Notes (p. 437) and formally discuss the concept and strategy.

Guided Practice

Distribute copies of the MiniReads (pp. 438–39) and the MiniRead Practice (p. 440). Guide students through MiniRead Practice Exercise A by using the steps below and Transparency 9.

1. As you read aloud, pause at appropriate points to help students take notes on plot elements. As an aid to students having difficulty, you may want to add text-specific details by asking basic plot questions like those listed in Step 1 of the Student Notes (p. 437).

2. Record selected responses in the Notes box in Transparency 9.

3. For each plot element, help students brainstorm ways of visually representing the element. Representations can be literal or more symbolic. In brainstorming, encourage students to incorporate ideas from their notes and other relevant details from the selection. Then, sketch out an example.

4. Finally, for each plot element, help students create a sentence or two describing that part of the plot. If the sentence has more details than the illustration, encourage students to add to the illustration. If the illustration has more details than the sentence, encourage revision of the sentence.

Independent Practice

Have students read MiniRead B and complete MiniRead Practice Exercise B.

Assessment

To give students another opportunity to apply the skill, choose a selection from the list on page 387. Then, have students complete the Application activity (p. 441) activity.

Understanding Plot

At a Glance

- **Plot** is the chain of events that makes up a story. The three main parts of a plot are the **conflict,** the **climax,** and the **resolution.**
- Using the **Storyboard** strategy for plot can help you better understand and remember the stories you read.

Step-by-Step Strategy

1. As you read, jot down notes about what is happening in the story. Finding answers to the questions below will help you take good notes.

Conflict	Who are the main characters? What problem or trouble do they face?
Climax	When is the problem or trouble the worst? What is the highest or most exciting point?
Resolution	How does the problem get solved or the trouble end? What finally happens?

2. After you read, draw three connected boxes on a sheet of paper. These boxes will be your storyboard. Label the first box "Conflict." Label the second box "Climax." Label the third box "Resolution."

3. In each box, draw a picture that illustrates that part of the plot. For example, in the "Conflict" box, draw a picture that shows what the conflict of the story is. Use your notes and any other details that you remember about the story.

4. Finally, in each box, write a description of that part of the plot.

Example

Here is a student's "Conflict" box for "Zlateh the Goat," a story about a boy who gets stuck in a snowstorm on his way to sell the family goat.

To keep from freezing, Aaron and Zlateh the goat take shelter in a snow-covered haystack.

Understanding Plot

MiniRead

DIRECTIONS: Use the following MiniRead with Exercise A on page 440.

MiniRead A

In a Flash

A   One hour into the camping trip, a huge, dark cloud popped over the mountain. As the wind began to rise and rain began to torpedo down, Mike and Andre raced toward the shelter of a tree. Big mistake. The ferocious winds whipped the tree until a heavy limb split off from the trunk. The boys, who were huddled beneath the tree, had no chance to run. The limb crashed to the earth, pinning Mike to the ground.

B   "Andre, help me!"

C   Jumping up, Andre tried to shift the tree limb. He was able to move it a few feet, but Mike's foot was still trapped. "Can you get your foot out?"

D   Mike struggled for a minute, then gasped, "No, I think it's broken."

E   Andre tried again to move the branch, his feet sinking into the mud as the rain intensified. "It won't budge," he cried. "Oh no! Mike? What's that?" He pointed a shaking finger toward a blur on the horizon.

F   Just then a flash of lightning lit up the sky. Mike gasped. "It's a tornado!" Suddenly, hail began pelting them. Andre tried to cover them both with the tent he had pulled from his backpack. They hunkered down under the feeble shelter wishing they were home safe.

G   The hail became larger, leaving red marks where it pounded the boys through the tent. Soon they heard an unmistakable roar. Mike lifted an edge of the tent and peered out.

H   "Boys! Get in!" yelled the camp counselor over the noise of the storm and the roaring truck engine.

I   "Help me move this limb!" called Andre. Together, they lifted the branch off Mike's foot and carried him to the truck. Just as Andre slammed the truck door, a bolt of lightening struck a nearby tree. The counselor backed the truck up and raced towards the safety of the lodge.

Understanding Plot *continued*

MiniRead

DIRECTIONS: Use the following MiniRead with Exercise B on page 440.

MiniRead B

The Last Day

A   The alarm beeped, and Luisa pulled the pillow over her head. Maybe if she ignored the clock, today would never start, and Dad could stay.

B   Of course, that was impossible. All of her tears and pleading had amounted to nothing last night, when her parents had called a "family meeting" to announce that they were getting a divorce. They had explained the situation to her and her little brother as if they were kindergartners. It didn't help that Anthony didn't seem to care. He only wanted to know if he would have his own room at Dad's new apartment. Luisa wanted to know if she would still have a dad at all.

C   Her mom tapped a guarded knock on her door. "Honey? It's time to get up," she said quietly.

D   "Go away," Luisa mumbled. This couldn't be happening. This was supposed to be the best year yet, the year Luisa got her driver's license and made the varsity track team. Now none of that mattered. Everything was careening out of control, and there was nothing she could do to fix it.

E   "Sweetheart?" called her dad. "Can I come in?"

F   Luisa sat up and set the pillow aside. "I guess."

G   Her dad came in and took her hand. "Lu, I know this is hard for you. But I'm not going to disappear from your life. I'll come to all of your track meets and school events, and you can stay over any time you want. My apartment is only a mile away. Call me every five minutes if you want to."

H   "Dad," Luisa said, "that would be silly. Why don't I just keep you on the phone all day instead?"

I   He laughed. "I'm so proud of you, Honey. I know you'll do fine."

J   Luisa managed a faint smile. Yes, she thought, it would be tough, but she'd get through it.

Understanding Plot

MiniRead Practice

Exercise A Use "In a Flash" to complete the following.

1. Explain the **conflict**—the trouble the main characters face. _____

   _____

2. Identify the **climax**—the point at which the conflict is the worst. _____

   _____

3. Explain the **resolution**—how is the problem resolved? _____

   _____

4. On the back of this page, draw a picture showing the **conflict** you explained for question 1. At the bottom of your picture, write a sentence explaining the picture. Then, draw a picture and write a sentence for both the **climax** and the **resolution**.

Exercise B Use "The Last Day" to complete the following.

1. Explain the **conflict**—the trouble the main characters face. _____

   _____

2. Identify the **climax**—the point at which the conflict is the worst. _____

   _____

3. Explain the **resolution**—how is the problem resolved? _____

   _____

4. On the back of this page, draw a picture showing the **conflict** you explained for question 1. At the bottom of your picture, write a sentence explaining the picture. Then, draw a picture and write a sentence for both the **climax** and the **resolution**.

NAME _____ DATE _____

Understanding Plot

Application

DIRECTIONS: Apply the **Storyboard** strategy for plot. As you read, use the lines below to write notes about the three parts of the story: conflict, climax, and resolution. Then, in each storyboard box below, draw a picture that shows that part of the plot. Finally, at the bottom of each box, write a description of that part of the plot. If you need more room, use your own paper.

NOTES

_____

_____

_____

_____

_____

STORYBOARD

Conflict

_____

_____

Climax

_____

_____

Resolution

_____

_____

(CORE SKILL) **Comparing and Contrasting**   Teacher Notes

At a Glance

- Comparing and contrasting characters, events, or ideas from two literary works or within a single work can help students better understand literature.

- Creating a **Venn diagram** can help readers make clear and insightful connections between and within works of literature.

Direct Instruction

Hand out copies of the Student Notes (p. 443). Discuss the skill and the strategy, focusing on the example provided.

Guided Practice

Distribute copies of the MiniReads (pp. 444–45) and the MiniRead Practice (p. 446). Guide students through MiniRead Practice Exercise A by using the steps below and Transparency 10.

1. Read the selection aloud, and have students choose two characters, two settings, or two events to compare and contrast (two settings will work best for MiniRead A). Then, have students note similarities and differences about each of the subjects.

2. Ask students to label each circle of the Venn diagram (for example, "the gym before" and "the gym after"). Then, ask students to place the "similar" details in the center of the diagram and the "different" details in the separate part of the appropriate circle.

3. Have students identify the types of details included in the Venn diagram (for example, "appearance" or "personality"). If the circles do not contain the same types of details, have students look for more details. For example, if a comparison-contrast of settings notes how the gym smelled before but not after, students should add details about the gym's smell after it had been cleaned.

4. Have students summarize, in one or two sentences, the most important similarities or differences.

Independent Practice

Have students read MiniRead B and complete MiniRead Practice Exercise B.

Assessment

To give students another opportunity to apply the skill, choose a selection from the list on page 387. Then, have students complete the Application activity (p. 447).

Comparing and Contrasting

At a Glance

- Comparing and contrasting can help you understand what you read.
- A **Venn diagram** will help you note similarities and differences.

Step-by-Step Strategy

1. Choose two subjects to compare and contrast. For example, you could chose two characters, two settings, or two events. Next, re-read the selection and write down details about the two subjects.

2. Label the two circles of a Venn diagram with the subjects you chose. Then, put the details you noted in Step 1 in the circles. A detail that applies to both subjects goes in the middle area. A detail that applies to only one subject goes in the outside area under that subject.

3. Review your diagram to make sure you included the same types of details for both subjects.

4. Study the information in your diagram. Then, write a sentence or two that summarizes how the subjects are alike and different.

Example

Here is one student's work for "The Stone," a story in which the character Maibon is given one wish.

before his wish	**both**	after his wish

- focuses on how time passing makes him feel old and weak
- wishes for time to stand still, to stay young

- has a choice to make

- notices crops don't grow and chickens don't lay eggs, life grinds to a halt
- gives back his wish

Summary: Maibon chooses to makes a foolish wish. After seeing the results of his wish, he wisely chooses to give back the wish and return to his normal life.

TIP Don't just include physical details. For example, if you are comparing and contrasting two characters, describe their feelings or how they change. Also, describe their appearance or how they act.

Comparing and Contrasting

MiniRead

DIRECTIONS: Use the following MiniRead with Exercise A on page 446.

MiniRead A

The Great Cover-Up

A   The old gym was disgusting. Paint peeled off the bleachers and walls. Water stains decorated the ceiling, and the odor of sweat filled the air. No way were they going to be able to put on a nice dance here, Ani thought.

B   "So, Ani, where do we start?" asked Max. He and seven other student council members stood in the doorway.

C   "Obviously, we can't clean this up," she said. "Maybe we can cover it up, though. The principal said we can use the custodial supplies. What if we cover the walls with these black trash bags?"

D   "Yeah!" said Max. "I can bring in strings of Christmas lights. They'll look great against all those shiny trash bags."

E   "We can use air freshener for the smell," chimed Mara.

F   "We can cut out a bunch of stars and hang them from the ceiling," said Dante. "If we do that and dim the lights, nobody will notice how ugly it is."

G   Ani was relieved. They might make it a nice dance, after all. "Great ideas, everybody. Let's get started."

H   Three days later, Ani walked into the transformed gym. This time she had on a delicate blue dress instead of work clothes. As she looked up at the old water-stained ceiling, she was relieved—it was almost invisible among the suspended stars that spun and swooped in the breeze of the gym fan. Her team's work had made the place into a shimmering dreamland. It didn't smell half bad, either. They had not been able to do much with the bleachers, but no one in the crowd seemed to care.

I   "This is fantastic!" Max said with a grin.

J   "Yeah, it looks pretty nice," replied Ani. As the music for the Chicken Dance began, the two friends hurried to the dance floor.

Comparing and Contrasting

DIRECTIONS: Use the following MiniRead with Exercise B on page 446.

MiniRead B

Success Story

A **Suburban Driveway** *Two boys play basketball in the driveway of a suburban house. Rick struggles to guard his older brother, Steve, who is almost a foot taller.*

B **RICK** (*voice-over*): Steve and I were always competing. In school. In sports. In life.

   Steve fakes to his left, and Rick goes for it. Steve spins around and heads in the opposite direction. Rick tries to change directions but loses his balance and falls on the pavement. Rick jumps up and yells at Steve.

C **RICK** (*voice-over*): And when we weren't competing, we were arguing.

   Steve shows Rick the move he just made, only this time in slow motion. Rick watches closely as Steve walks through the move.

D **RICK** (*voice-over*): But no matter how many times Steve beat me, he never rubbed it in. Instead, he would try to teach me something.

   Steve dribbles the ball and then fakes left. This time, Rick doesn't budge.

E **Sports Arena** *The stands are packed with cheering fans watching a professional basketball game.*

F **RICK** (*voice-over*): Steve was always the better basketball player, but I'm the one who made it to the pros.

   A tall player fakes to his left and then tries to drive right. Rick covers the taller player tightly.

G **RICK** (*voice-over*): Steve should have made the cut. He was good enough, and he wanted it as much as I did.

   Rick snatches the ball from his taller opponent and sprints down the court.

H **RICK** (*voice-over*): But when it came right down to it, there was one thing my bigger brother wanted more than to play professional basketball.

   Rick dunks the ball. Steve, who is in the crowd, leaps to his feet.

I **RICK** (*voice-over*): He wanted his little brother to make it.

Comparing and Contrasting

MiniRead Practice

Exercise A Use "The Great Cover-Up" to complete the following.

1. Label the top lines in the Venn diagram below with two subjects to compare and contrast. In the middle area, write the details from the story that apply to both subjects. In each outside area, write the details that apply only to that subject.

_____ **both** _____

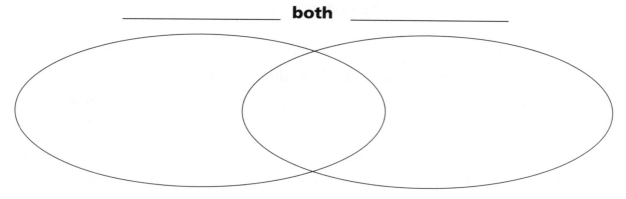

2. Write a sentence or two summarizing how the subjects are alike and different.

_____

_____

Exercise B Use "Success Story" to complete the following.

1. Complete the Venn diagram below for two characters in the selection.

Rick   **both**   **Steve**

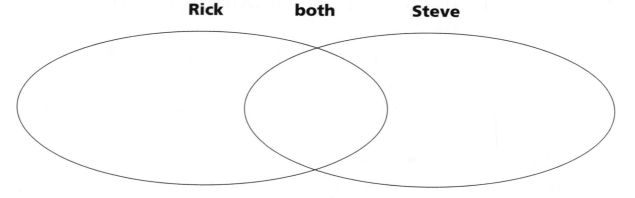

2. Write a sentence or two summarizing how the characters are alike and different.

_____

_____

NAME _____ DATE _____

Comparing and Contrasting

DIRECTIONS: Choose two subjects to compare and contrast. You may choose two characters, two settings, or two events. Then, fill out the diagram below. On the top lines, write the subjects. In the middle area, write details from the story that apply to both subjects. In each outside area, write details that apply only to that subject. Finally, at the bottom, write a sentence that summarizes how the subjects are alike and different.

_____ **both** _____

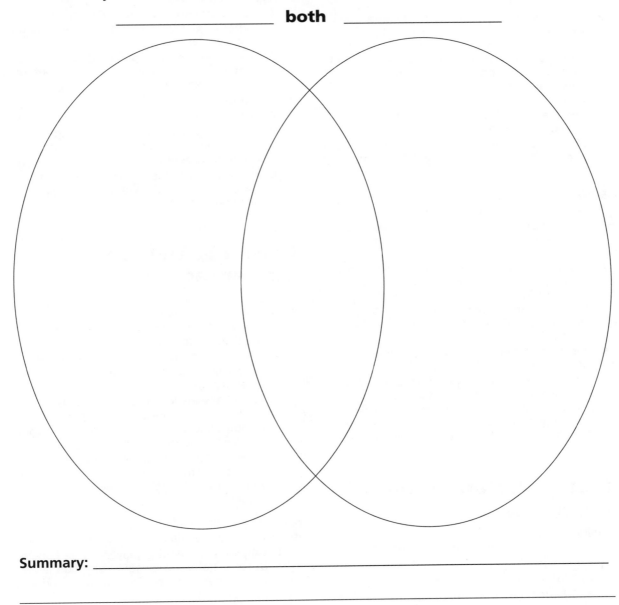

Summary: _____

_____

Answer Key

Lesson 1: Identifying Author's Purpose

MiniRead Practice Exercise A
Answers will vary. Samples are provided.

1. The author wrote this mostly to persuade administrators to provide space and supplies for a school garden.
2. The author says that students "deserve" the experiences of gardening and says that "the school should provide this opportunity"; the author also mentions benefits of the program, such as developing "patience," "responsibility," and "pride," and urges administrators to support it.
3. Yes, these details all support my statement of the author's purpose.
4. I think the last sentence gives the most important clue because it says "We urge" administrators to do something.

MiniRead Exercise B
Answers will vary. Samples are provided.

1. The author wrote this mostly to provide information about Bill Cosby's focus on charity and education.
2. "[Cosby] has given his time and money to many good causes"; "his belief that success starts with education"; "He earned a bachelor's degree . . . and an advanced degree [in education]"; "Bill Cosby has been committed to charity and education."
3. Yes, these details all support my statement of the author's purpose.
4. I think the facts about specific contributions Bill Cosby has made are the most important clues about the purpose. That information makes it clear that it isn't just the author's opinion that Bill Cosby gives a lot to educational charities.

Lesson 2: Determining Main Idea

MiniRead Exercise A
Answers will vary. Samples are provided.

1. Paragraph B
   A. Piltdown man
   B. Scientists nearly a century ago believed the hoax, which was just a human skull and an ape jaw. Their mistake was embarrassing.
   C. The Piltdown Man hoax fooled scientists nearly a century ago.

2. Paragraph C
   A. moon landings
   B. Some people think they were a hoax. Strong evidence proves they happened.
   C. In spite of strong evidence to the contrary, some people believe the moon landings were a hoax.

MiniRead Exercise B
Answers will vary. Samples are provided.

1. Paragraph D
   A. stopping hoaxes
   B. It's important to consider evidence for surprising claims. Hoaxes spread faster today than ever before.
   C. To stop hoaxes from spreading quickly, people should consider the evidence before sending messages.

2. Paragraph E
   A. evaluating messages
   B. Hoax e-mails have clues to watch out for. People can gather more evidence from major news outlets.
   C. To evaluate whether a message is a hoax, watch for certain clues and check major news outlets for more evidence.

Lesson 3: Making Inferences

MiniRead Exercise A
Answers will vary. Samples are provided.

1. Why did Fleet Walker have such a hard time in the major league?
2. **What I Just Read:** He was the first African American in the major league; he remained a gentleman.
   What I Already Know: Being the only one can be hard because sometimes people pick on you; I know Jackie Robinson faced racism when he went into the major leagues.
3. Because Walker was the only African American in the league, fans and teammates were hard on him. Walker faced a lot of racism.

MiniRead Exercise B
Answers will vary. Samples are provided.

1. Why were those other players not as famous as Jackie Robinson? In 1887, why did the major league stop signing African American players?

2. (based on first question)

What I Just Read: They are described as "less famous"; many African Americans were in other leagues; in 1887, the major league stop signing African American players; after that, no African American played in a major league until 1947.

What I Already Know: Minor-league games don't get as much attention; people didn't have TVs in the late 1800s; people sometimes remember only the most recent accomplishments.

3. Although these players were very good, some of them played a long time before Jackie Robinson and might have gotten less attention in the media. Also, Jackie Robinson was the first African American to be in the major league in the 1900s.

Lesson 4: Summarizing

MiniRead Exercise B
Answers will vary. Samples are provided.

1. Dyslexia makes reading and spelling difficult for some intelligent people. Dyslexics may confuse letters or directions and have trouble sounding out words that they see.

2. Dyslexia is a misunderstood reading problem that some intelligent, successful people have. Special instruction can help dyslexics better see the relationship between letters and sounds.

MiniRead Exercise B
Answers will vary. Samples are provided.

1. Animals possess intelligence. Some birds can use tools, solve problems, and even understand human language.

2. Animals possess intelligence and emotion. They use tools, solve problems, understand language, and suffer from stress. They also seem to feel sadness.

Lesson 5: Distinguishing Fact from Opinion

MiniRead Exercise A
Answers will vary. Samples are provided.

1. A. "[A public skatepark] would also be an excellent way for Springfield to encourage its youth."
   B. no source
   C. The statement is an opinion because no source would prove it true. It is a personal belief that people could disagree with. Also, *excellent* could be considered an opinion signal word.

2. A. "There is definitely interest in the sport in our town."
   B. Although the true level of support is unknown, the article does mention that over five hundred people signed the skatepark petition. These people seem interested.
   C. The statement is a fact. You could look at the petition and count the number of people who signed it.

MiniRead Exercise B
Answers will vary. Samples are provided.

1. A. "However, skateboarding is not as dangerous as some other sports."
   B. The article mentions statistics ("emergency room visits for skateboarding injuries are far fewer than for some other sports") that could be confirmed by studies or articles found in magazines or on the Internet.
   C. The statement is fact.

2. A. "However, skateboarders shouldn't have to put up with tickets and rough roads."
   B. no source
   C. The statement is an opinion because no source would prove it true. What a person should "put up with" is debatable.

Lesson 6: Making Predictions

MiniRead Exercise
Answers will vary. Samples, which are grouped by section, are provided.

In section A

Question 1: What did Tom do to make his younger brother, Daniel, so angry?

Prediction 1: I bet Tom got into a fight with Daniel because Daniel is crying and is upset.

In section B

Question 2: Why are they living in the barn?

Prediction 2: I think they have run away from home, because they seem to be on their own.

In section C

Verification 1 and 2: No, Daniel isn't angry with Tom because they got into a fight. He's angry because Tom had committed several crimes and the law was after them. They have run away from home, but because of Tom's crimes, they have to stay on the run.

Question 3: What crimes did Tom commit?

Prediction 3: I bet he robbed a bank or stole something.

In section D

Verification 3: I was right. Tom did steal something, and in doing so, he also broke his promise to Daniel that he wouldn't steal.

Question 4: Will Tom convince Daniel to go with him?

Prediction 4: I bet they will both run away again because Tom is the only family Daniel has.

In section E

Question 5: What will happen to the barn?

Prediction 5: I bet they will be able to put out the fire, gather their belongings, and leave.

In section F

Verification 5: They didn't even try to put out the fire. They just rescued themselves, and when Tom saw the men riding toward them, he bolted.

In section G

Verification 4: No, I was wrong. Daniel decides not to run away this time.

Lesson 7: Understanding Characters

MiniRead Exercise A
Answers will vary.

1. **A.** the princess
   B. actions, speech
   C. **actions:** She was mean to another kid and got into trouble; she threw the shoe at the frog even after she discovered she had only dreamed about having to marry a frog.
   speech: While she was still dreaming, she said, "If I ever get out of this, I'll never be so self-centered and mean again as long as I live!"

2. The princess is a self-centered person who could have learned a lesson about not being mean. However, once she figured out that she had only dreamed the episode with the frog, she went back to her old ways.

MiniRead Exercise B
Answers will vary.

1. **A.** Androcles
   B. actions, speech
   C. **actions:** He pulled the thorn from the lion's paw; he was calm when the lion was charging; he put out his hand to the lion.
   speech: Androcles said, "If I remove this thorn, . . . the lion might feel well enough to eat me. But if I don't, the lion will continue to suffer."

2. Androcles is a brave and kind character who risked his life to help the lion. He also showed great faith by trusting in his friendship with the lion.

Lesson 8: Recognizing Theme

MiniRead Exercise A
Answers will vary. Samples are provided.

1. Rewarding
2. **A.** Raul wakes Lea up one Saturday morning and insists that she go to an air show with him.
   B. Lea doesn't really want to go, but since Raul doesn't give her much choice, she goes anyway.
   C. Lea ends up thoroughly enjoying herself.
3. You never know whether something is worth the effort until you try it out.

MiniRead Exercise B
Answers will vary. Samples are provided.

1. Carefree
2. **A.** The Frogs have an easy life in the swamp, but they are not satisfied.
   B. They ask for a king to rule over them. Jupiter sends a log, but the Frogs insist on a real king.
   C. Jupiter finally sends a stork, which eats the Frogs.
3. You should be careful what you ask for; it might be worse than what you already have.

Lesson 9: Understanding Plot

MiniRead Exercise A
Answers will vary. Samples are provided.

1. Andre and Mike are caught out in a storm with no shelter.
2. Mike's foot is caught beneath a large tree limb, and a tornado is headed toward them.
3. A camp counselor rescues them and takes them back to the lodge.
4. *Illustrations and sentences will vary. Sentences should be based on the answers for questions 1–3.*

MiniRead Exercise B
Answers will vary. Samples are provided.

1. Luisa's parents are getting a divorce.
2. Luisa is afraid that she will not see her dad anymore.
3. Luisa's father promises her that he will still be a part of her life.
4. *Illustrations and sentences will vary. Sentences should be based on the answers for questions 1-3.*

Lesson 10: Comparing and Contrasting

MiniRead Exercise A

Answers will vary. Sample responses are based on a comparison of setting.

1. **Gym before:** paint peeling off the walls and bleachers; water stains on the ceiling tiles; smelled like sweat

   Gym after: shiny, black trash bags covering the walls; Christmas lights twinkling; stars hanging from the ceiling; sweat smell not as bad

   Both: visible water stains; the bleachers covered with peeling paint

2. Although the gym in "The Great Cover-Up" is ugly and smelled disgusting, Ani and the other council members are able to transform it into a dreamland. They do this by using trash bags to cover the walls, stringing up Christmas lights, hanging stars from the ceiling, and using cleaning supplies to get rid of the smell.

MiniRead Exercise B

1. **Rick:** younger and shorter than Steve; not as good of a basketball player as his brother; awkward when he was young; plays pro basketball

   Steve: older and taller than Rick; better basketball player; patient; willing to teach his younger brother; does not play pro basketball; is proud of his younger brother who does.

   Both: competitive; argumentative; good at sports; loves to played basketball

2. In "Success Story," two brothers, Steve and Rick, have much in common—they both love to play basketball and are very competitive. However, although Steve is the better player, he is willing to teach Rick all he knows so that Rick can one day play pro basketball.

Rikki-tikki-tavi

Based on the story by Rudyard Kipling

This is the story of a great war. Rikki-tikki-tavi fought this war in an English family's home in India. He had some help, but he did the real fighting.

Rikki-tikki was a mongoose. His name came from the sound he made going into battle: *Rikk-tikk-tikki-tikki-tchk!*

When Rikki was small, a flood swept him away from his home and family. A little boy named Teddy found him half-dead and brought him home. Teddy and his mother warmed the mongoose till he woke up.

Although the mother had a soft spot for animals, she wasn't sure she wanted a wild animal in her house. But Teddy's father convinced her that a mongoose was the perfect house pet. After all, deadly snakes lived right in their garden, and mongooses were snake killers.

Rikki-tikki soon felt better, and he spent the rest of the day and the next morning exploring Teddy's house. In the yard he heard the sad voices of two tailorbirds, Darzee and his wife. The birds were crying because a cobra named Nag had eaten one of their babies. Just then, Nag himself appeared. He was a huge black cobra, five feet long.

"I am Nag," he said. "Look, and be afraid!"

Though Rikki had never met a cobra, he knew that a mongoose's job was to kill snakes. Nag knew that, too, and the cobra was afraid.

Rikki-tikki replied, "Well. Do you think you should eat baby birds?"

Nag then played a trick on Rikki-tikki.

Notes

"Let's talk," he said. "If you eat eggs, why shouldn't I eat birds?"

"Behind you! Look behind you!" cried Darzee.

Rikki-tikki jumped high up in the air. He just missed being struck by Nag's wife Nagaina, who had slithered up behind him. Rikki landed on Nagaina's back and bit her, but she struggled free.

When a mongoose's eyes grow red, it means he is angry. Now Rikki-tikki's eyes grew very red. But Nag and Nagaina were gone.

Teddy ran down the path to pet Rikki-tikki. But as Teddy bent down, something moved in the dust. It was Karait, a small but deadly snake. Rikki's eyes glowed red.

Teddy shouted to his parents. His father ran out with a stick. But Rikki-tikki had already killed Karait.

Teddy's father beat the dead Karait.

"Why is he doing that?" thought Rikki-tikki. "I have already killed the snake."

The family treated Rikki like a hero. He enjoyed the attention. But he did not forget about Nag and Nagaina.

That night, Rikki wandered around inside the house. He met Chuchundra the muskrat, a little ratlike animal. Chuchundra was very scared.

"Don't kill me!" cried Chuchundra.

"Why would I kill you?" said Rikki-tikki scornfully.

"I don't know," said Chuchundra. "Maybe Nag will think I am you some dark night, and he will kill me. My cousin Chua, the rat, told me—"

"Told you what?" said Rikki-tikki.

Chuchundra was terrified, but he told Rikki that Nag and Nagaina were planning an attack that very night.

Notes

Just then, Rikki-tikki heard a soft *scratch-scratch* coming from the bathroom. Rikki-tikki moved quietly into the bathroom. There he heard Nag and Nagaina whispering in the drainpipe.

"Go in quietly, and kill the big man first," said Nagaina.

"Are you sure we should kill the people?" said Nag.

"Of course. The mongoose will leave if we kill them. Then we can be king and queen of the garden, and we will have a safe hatching ground for our eggs," said Nagaina. She and Nag had eggs that were almost ready to hatch.

Nag slipped through the drain into the bathroom. His head came first, then his five feet of scaly body. Rikki-tikki was angry, but also afraid. He stayed very still for an hour. Then, he moved slowly toward Nag. He knew he had to kill Nag with his first bite. Rikki jumped on Nag's head. Nag shook him every which way. Though Rikki was dizzy and hurt all over, he held on tightly.

Then Rikki felt a blast. The fight had awakened Teddy's father, who shot Nag.

The man picked up Rikki. He shouted, "It's the mongoose again! This time, he has saved our lives!"

Exhausted, Rikki-tikki dragged himself to Teddy's bedroom.

When morning came, Rikki-tikki knew he had a job to finish. Nagaina was still alive. Rikki went to Darzee for help. Darzee told Rikki that Nagaina was by the trash heap, crying over Nag's body. Her eggs were in the melon garden. But the foolish Darzee refused to help Rikki get rid of the cobra's eggs. Darzee didn't think it was fair to destroy eggs.

Notes

Darzee's wife had more common sense. She didn't want young cobras around. She helped Rikki by fluttering around, pretending her wing was broken. Nagaina couldn't resist such an easy target, so she pursued the bird.

Meanwhile, Rikki-tikki found Nagaina's twenty-five soft, white eggs. He had crushed all but one when he heard Darzee's wife screaming:

"Rikki-tikki, I led Nagaina toward the house. Now she is going in! Hurry! She is going to kill!"

Holding the last egg in his mouth, Rikki-tikki hurried to the porch.

There, Teddy and his parents sat at the breakfast table. They were as still as stones, hardly daring to breathe. Nagaina was coiled up on the floor by Teddy's chair.

Rikki-tikki came up and cried, "Turn round and fight, Nagaina!"

"I will fight you soon," she said, but she didn't turn away from Teddy's bare leg.

Rikki-tikki's eyes were blood red. "Look what I have here," he said. "Your last egg! I have smashed all the others."

Nagaina spun around. Teddy's father grabbed Teddy and pulled him across the table to safety.

"Tricked! *Rikk-tck-tck!*" laughed Rikki-tikki. "*Rikki-tikki-tck-tck!* Now, come and fight with me."

Nagaina looked at her egg. "Give me the egg, Rikki-tikki. I will go away and never come back," she said, lowering her hood.

"Yes, you will go away—to the trash heap. Fight!" said Rikki-tikki.

They circled each other in a deadly dance. But Rikki had forgotten the egg. Nagaina quickly caught her last egg in her mouth and raced away with it. Rikki-tikki followed her and caught her tail in his sharp little teeth. Together they disappeared down a rat hole.

Darzee, who was watching the battle, cried, "A mongoose has no chance against a snake down there. Brave Rikki is dead!"

But suddenly, the grass moved again. There was Rikki-tikki. He dragged himself out of the hole.

"It is all over," Rikki said. "Nagaina is dead."

Then he curled up right there and slept until late afternoon. He didn't even hear the Coppersmith, a little bird whose job it was to shout out the good news.

That night at the house, Rikki ate a feast. He was amused by all the fuss.

"Just think, he saved our lives and Teddy's life," said Teddy's mother.

"What are they worried about?" Rikki-tikki wondered. "The cobras are all dead. And if any more come, I'm here."

Rikki-tikki was proud in his own way, and he had a right to be. From then on, he protected the yard. No cobra ever again dared to enter it.

Three Skeleton Key

Based on the short story by George G. Toudouze

Notes

My most terrifying experience? Well, working in a lighthouse is mostly quite boring. You have to keep the light in order and write reports. However, in my thirty-five years of service, I certainly had a few frightening experiences.

When I was young, I took a job in a newly built lighthouse off the coast of Guiana. The lighthouse was very isolated. It was about twenty miles from land. The pay was high, though, and I wanted to save money before I married.

The lighthouse stood on a small rock named Three Skeleton Key. It had earned its name from the story of three men who had escaped from prison in a stolen canoe. Their canoe wrecked on the rock, and the men eventually died of hunger and thirst. When the men were discovered, nothing remained but three heaps of bones. The story was that the three skeletons danced over the small rock, screaming. . . .

Three Skeleton Key was an island of black rock. It was about one hundred fifty feet long, perhaps forty feet wide. The rocks were dangerously smooth. One wrong step, and you'd fall into the sea. The sea was full of sharks.

Still, it was a nice life there. During the day, we would clean the rooms and the light itself. At night, we would sit on the balcony and watch the strong white bar of light shine over the sea. My fellow keepers were named Le Gleo and Itchoua. We liked our life on the key.

One night, Itchoua called Le Gleo and me from our rooms. We climbed to the balcony and stood beside him.

Itchoua pointed out to the sea. There we saw a big ship headed straight towards us. It was an odd course, we thought. Ships were a rare sight in our waters. Our lighthouse existed to warn ships away from the rocks, so most ships steered clear of us.

Le Gleo cried out, "What's wrong with the ship's crew? Are they all drunk or insane? Can't they see us?"

Itchoua looked at us sharply and said, "See us? I'm sure they do—if there *is* a crew aboard!"

Then we understood the ship's odd behavior. For some reason, the ship's crew had abandoned it. Then, the ship had sailed by itself, guided by the wind.

We kept watching as the ship sailed on. In the light of our lantern, the ship seemed strong. Itchoua cried out, "Why was the ship abandoned? Nothing is smashed. There's no sign of fire. And, it doesn't look like it's sinking."

For the next four hours, the ship played around us. It zigzagged, stopped, and then suddenly sailed forward.

When dawn broke, we got out our binoculars to inspect the ship.

Just then, the wind rose, and the ship changed course. It headed straight for us again. This time, it came very close. We knew it could not turn in time.

All this time, we kept our binoculars aimed at the ship. We suddenly cried out together, "The rats!"

Now we knew why the ship was sailing without a crew. The crew had been driven out by rats. The rats of the sea are large, strong, intelligent, and brave. If you harm one, his sharp cry will bring crowds of his fellows to tear your flesh. They will not stop until nothing is left of you but bones.

Notes

Notes

At times, the rats will attack a ship's crew. They either drive them from the ship or eat them alive. Studying the ship, I turned sick. Its lifeboats were all in place. Its crew had not abandoned ship.

The ship came for us at full speed. It crashed on a sharp point of rock and then split in two. It sank like a stone.

But the rats did not drown. They sprang along the masts and onto the rocks right before the ship sank. Then they noticed us—fresh meat.

We barely had time to jump back. We closed the door leading to the balcony, and we went down the stairs. We shut every window tightly. It didn't take long for the horrible group of rats to run up the tower. They scratched at the glass. There were so many rats that it seemed as if a fur coat covered the tower. Just a few millimeters of glass separated our faces from their beady eyes, sharp claws, and teeth. We were sealed alive in our own lighthouse. We were prisoners of a horde of starving rats.

When night came, we lit the light. As the light turned, it blinded thousands of rats crowded against the glass. Their cries were so loud we had to shout to hear one another. We couldn't sleep all night.

The next day we were calmer. We had fun by teasing the rats. We would place our faces against the glass. The rats couldn't understand the invisible barrier that separated us from them. But, the day after that, we realized how serious our position was. The air in the lighthouse smelled of rats. Of course, we couldn't open the windows to get fresh air.

The morning of the fourth day, I saw that the wooden frame of my window had been eaten away from the outside. I called Le Gleo and Itchoua. They helped me seal the window over with a sheet of tin. When we had finished, Itchoua pointed at the tin plate, "If that gives way," he said, "they can change the name of the place to Six Skeleton Key."

The next six days and seven nights, the only fun thing to do was watch clusters of rats fall from the rock. The rats would fall a hundred and twenty feet into the water. There the sharks could eat them. It didn't seem to matter, though. There were still so many rats left.

We thought often of those three prisoners who had died on the rock. We imagined our bones joining theirs. The darkness of our prison increased our gloom. We had to seal every window with tin. The only light came in through the lantern room at the very top of the tower.

Le Gleo had nightmares where he saw the three skeletons of the prisoners dancing around him. His crazy descriptions were so clear that Itchoua and I began to see the three skeletons, too.

There was only one thing left to do. We decided not to light the lantern on the ninth night. This is never done unless the light keepers are dead. The light is necessary to warn ships away from the rock. But, that night, Three Skeleton Key was dark.

At two in the morning, the sheet of metal sealing Itchoua's window gave way. Itchoua just had time to leap to his feet and cry for help. The three of us fought the maddened rats that flowed through the open window.

They bit. We struck them down with our knives. Then, we went back up the stairs, fighting off the rats that leaped on us. We found ourselves on the floor of the lantern room. We had no food or drink. We were bleeding all over. Our clothes were shredded.

Notes

(Notes)

Le Gleo stared at Itchoua and me. Then he looked at the rats and began laughing horribly, "Hee! Hee! The Three Skeletons! Hee! Hee! The Three Skeletons are now *six* skeletons! *Six* skeletons!"

He threw his head back and laughed. I did the only thing I could—I swung the back of my hand across his face. His laughing stopped. Then he began to cry like a child.

As morning arrived, the patrol came to find out why our lighthouse was dark. Through my binoculars, I could see the horrified faces of the patrol officers and crew. I learned later that they thought we had been eaten alive.

The crew were about to leave when Itchoua managed to signal them. They signaled back; we were rescued.

The patrol boat came back at noon, along with a supply ship, two small coast-guard boats, and the fireboat.

The fireboat's powerful jet of water knocked many rats from the tower into the sea. There the sharks gulped them down. Yet more rats swam out to the fireboat. The men were forced to fight the rats with their bare hands. At last, all but one of the boats left. All that night, Le Gleo raved about skeletons while Itchoua and I burned with fever.

The next afternoon, I saw a tugboat towing a huge barge filled with meat. The tugboat dragged the barge close to the island. The rats swam out and boarded it. The tug dragged the barge about a mile from shore. There the barge was soaked in gasoline and set ablaze.

As the barge burned, the rats tried to escape. A patrol boat bombed them. The sharks finished off the rest.

A small boat from the patrol boat took us off to the hospital. Le Gleo's mind had cracked; he went completely crazy. He was locked up in an insane asylum, the poor man! Itchoua's bites were infected; he died within a week.

As for me—when they aired out the lighthouse and repaired the damage done by the rats, I returned to Three Skeleton Key. Why not? I liked the place. To be honest, it was the most pleasant job I ever had.

Eeking Out a Life
Based on the newspaper article by Matt Surman

Notes

Sunny Jim was once a rat alone in the wilderness. Who knows what dangers he faced?

Was he chased by hungry owls? Did sewer rats go after him? Did he search for a child who lost him?

His new owners can only guess. Hayley Huttenmaier and her fiancé Nachshon Rose rescued the little rat.

Rose was out walking when he found him. The rat ran past him and hid. Gradually he emerged and sat on Rose's shoe.

Clearly the white and brownish-gray rat was a pet. He was clean and friendly and tiny. So Rose carried him home. Huttenmaier and Rose already had two dogs and three cats.

Now Sunny Jim lives inside a cabinet. He has a little room with brick walls. He has toys, a soft bed, and plenty of food.

Huttenmaier believes a child lost the rat. They placed an ad, but no one has called. Rose doesn't want to give Sunny back. He believes the rat was unwanted by its owner, or that parents made their child abandon the little rat.

Is owning him dangerous? Experts agree he's not a danger.

According to Louis Stack, pet rats are like little dogs. "You can watch TV with them sitting on your shoulder."

Stack belongs to the American Fancy Rat and Mouse Association. Its members raise and show rats the way people show dogs.

Sunny's owners are happy to give him a safe home. Maybe they'll get him a friend some day. Then there'll be a Rat Pack.

"Eeking Out a Life" by Matt Surman adapted from *The Los Angeles Times,* July 8, 2000. Copyright © 2000 by **The Los Angeles Times.** Retold by Holt, Rinehart and Winston. Reproduced by permission of the publisher.

Cellular Telephone Owner's Manual

Changing the Battery

There are two ways to remove and replace your battery.

Standard Method

1. Turn off your telephone.
2. Press the latch button on the back of the battery. Then, slide the battery down until it stops.
3. Carefully take out the battery.
4. To replace the battery, line up a new battery on the grooves. Slide it upward in the direction of the arrows until it clicks into place.

Quick-Change Method

This method lets you replace the battery during a phone call.

1. Tell the person you're talking to that you are going to change the battery.
2. Remove the battery from the cell phone.
3. Put in the extra battery. (Be sure it has been charged up and is ready to use.)
4. Press PWR (power). This will return you to your telephone call. You have five seconds to press PWR before your call is disconnected.

The quick-change method allows you to replace the battery during a telephone call. This is useful if you see the "low battery" message during a call.

It is a good idea to practice this method before trying it during a real phone call.

Mother and Daughter

Based on the short story by Gary Soto

Notes

Yollie's mother, Mrs. Moreno, was a large woman. She wore a muumuu and butterfly-shaped glasses. She liked to water her lawn in the evening and wave at cars passing by. Now and then a driver would shout *"Mamacita!"* But most of the time they just stared and wondered how she got so large.

Mother and daughter usually got along. They watched bargain matinees together, and played croquet in the summer and checkers in the winter. Mrs. Moreno encouraged Yollie to study hard. She wanted her daughter to be a doctor.

"Tienes que estudiar mucho," Mrs. Moreno would say. "You have to study a lot, then you can get a good job and take care of me."

"Yes, Mama," Yollie would respond, her face buried in a book.

Everyone thought Yollie's mother was funny. Her brother Raul, a nightclub owner, thought she was funny enough to go into show business.

But there was nothing funny about Yollie needing a new outfit for the eighth-grade fall dance. They couldn't afford one. The little money Mrs. Moreno had saved was for Yollie's college education.

The best Mrs. Moreno could do was buy Yollie a pair of black shoes with velvet bows and fabric dye to color her white summer dress black.

"We can color your dress so it will look brand-new," her mother said. She poured the black liquid into a tub.

Notes

Yollie didn't want to watch. She *knew* it wouldn't work. But to her surprise, the dress came out shiny black. It looked brand-new. She smiled at her mother, who hugged Yollie and said, "See, what did I tell you?"

The dance was important to Yollie because she was in love with Ernie Castillo, the third-best speller in the class. She bathed, dressed, and did her hair and nails. Then she jumped into the car.

Mrs. Moreno let Yollie out in front of the school. She waved and told her to have a good time.

Yollie ran into her best friend, Janice. They didn't say it, but each thought the other was the most beautiful girl at the dance. All the boys would want to dance with them.

The evening was warm but thick with clouds. Paper lanterns in the trees made the evening seem romantic. Everyone danced, sipped punch, and stood in groups of threes and fours, talking.

Yollie kept smoothing her dress down when the wind picked it up. She had her eye on Ernie. It turned out that Ernie had his eye on Yollie, too. He ate a handful of cookies nervously, then asked her for a dance.

"Sure," she said. She almost threw herself into his arms.

As they danced, rain began falling. Yollie loved the sound of the raindrops ticking against the leaves. She leaned her head on Ernie's shoulder. He felt warm and tender. Yollie could tell he was in love with her.

It began to pour. The girls hurried to the restrooms. One girl cried because her velvet dress was wet. Yollie felt sorry for her and helped her dry the dress off with paper towels.

Notes

Yollie went to a mirror. Her mother's makeup had washed away. She combed her damp hair. She couldn't wait to get back to Ernie.

Yollie looked down, and shame spread across her face. A black puddle was forming at her feet. The dye was falling from her dress like black tears. Yollie saw that her dress was gray. She looked around. Everyone would laugh. They would know that she dyed an old dress because she couldn't afford a new one. She hurried from the restroom with her head down. She raced home, crying as the rain mixed with her tears.

When she arrived home, her mother was on the couch eating cookies and watching TV.

"How was the dance, *m'ija?*"

Yollie ran to her bedroom. She undressed and threw the dress on the floor.

Her mother came into the room, "What's wrong, baby?"

"The dress. It's cheap! It's no good!" Yollie kicked the dress at her mother and watched it land in her hands. Mrs. Moreno studied it closely but couldn't see what was wrong. "What's the matter? It's just a bit wet."

"The dye came out, that's what."

Mrs. Moreno looked at her hands and saw the grayish dye. Poor baby, she thought. She wanted to tell her daughter how sorry she was. But she knew it wouldn't help. She walked back to the living room and cried.

The next morning, mother and daughter stayed away from each other. Yollie sat in her room. Her mother watered her plants with a Pepsi bottle.

"Drink, my children," she said loud enough for Yollie to hear. "Water is all you need. My daughter needs clothes, but I don't have any money."

Notes

Yollie was embarrassed about what she had said to her mother last night. It wasn't her mother's fault that they were poor.

When they sat down together for lunch, they both felt awkward. But Mrs. Moreno had made a fresh stack of tortillas and cooked up a pan of *chile verde.* That broke the ice. She licked her thumb and smacked her lips.

"You know, honey, we have to figure a way to make money," Yollie's mother said. "You and me. We don't have to be poor. Maybe we could invent something."

"What can we make?" asked Yollie. She took another tortilla.

The mother looked around for ideas, but then shrugged. "Let's forget it. It's better to get an education. If you have spare time then maybe you can invent something."

The phone rang. Yollie leaned over from her chair to answer it. It was Ernie wondering why she had left. He was glad to find out that she wasn't mad at him. He asked if she would like to go to a movie.

"I'll ask," Yollie said, smiling. She covered the phone with her hand and counted to ten. Then she said, "My mom says it's OK. What are we going to see?"

After Yollie hung up, her mother climbed onto a chair to reach the top shelf in the hall closet. She reached behind a stack of towels and pushed her chubby hand into a cigar box. There she kept a secret stash of money.

"I've been saving a little money every month," said Mrs. Moreno. "For you, *m'ija.*" Her mother held up five twenties. The green money smelled sweeter than flowers. They drove to Macy's and bought a blouse, shoes, and a skirt that would not bleed in rain or any other weather.

The Smallest Dragonboy

Based on the short story by Anne McCaffrey

(Notes)

Keevan couldn't keep up with the other candidates. Beterli was the oldest boy, and he led the group. Keevan was sure that Beterli had set a fast pace just to embarrass him. Keevan would arrive at the end of the group. He'd be out of breath, and the instructor would be angry.

Dragonriders* had to be on time. This was true even for candidates. The Weyrleader of Benden Weyr did not put up with laziness. A good record was especially important now. It was near hatching time. The candidates were waiting hopefully for the glowing eggs. The eggs were hardening on the hot sands of the Hatching Ground cave. Baby dragons would crack their spotted shells and stagger out to choose their lifetime companions.

Just the thought of that great moment made Keevan's breath catch in his throat. To be chosen—to be a dragonrider! He could sit on his winged dragon. The dragon would be his friend for life. They would use a special type of communication—telepathy—so that they could read each other's thoughts. They would understand each other without having to speak to each other. The dragon would be Keevan's friend in good times and in fighting times. They would fly without effort over the lands of Pern!

But Keevan worried that he'd never become a dragonrider because he was too small. People were always

---

* A guide to the meanings of many of the fictional terms in "The Smallest Dragonboy" appears at the end of the story.

Adaptation of "The Smallest Dragonboy" by Anne McCaffrey. Copyright © 1973, 2001 by Anne McCaffrey. First appeared in *Science Fiction Tales.* Retold by Holt, Rinehart and Winston. Reproduced by permission of **Anne McCaffrey and agent, Virginia Kidd.**

calling him "babe." Keevan had to work twice as hard as any other boy his age to prove himself.

Notes

Keevan certainly never dreamed of Impressing a bronze. Maybe he had a chance to Impress a green dragon. Green dragons were small and fast, and there were more of them. But to fly a bronze? A bronze rider could hope to become a Weyrleader!

They arrived at the Hatching Ground. "Impression time is close, candidates," the instructor was saying. All the candidates were surrounding him. "See the stretch marks on this promising egg." The stretch marks *were* larger than yesterday.

"I'd say the great opening day is nearly here," the instructor went on. Then his face became serious. "As we well know, there are only forty eggs and seventy-two candidates. Some of you may be disappointed on the great day."

Some of the boys laughed nervously. Everyone started to walk among the eggs. Beterli stepped up to "his" egg, daring anyone to come near it. Keevan smiled, because he had already touched it without Beterli seeing.

"I don't know why you're allowed in this Impression, Keevan. There are enough of us without a babe," Beterli said, shaking his head.

"I'm of age." Keevan kept his voice calm. He told himself not to be bothered by Beterli's words.

Beterli stood on his toe tips. "You can't even see over an egg. Hatching Day, you'd better get in front, or the dragons won't see you at all."

"You'd better make sure a dragon sees *you* this time, Beterli," Keevan replied. "You're almost too old, aren't you?"

Notes

Beterli's face went red. He took a step forward, his hand half raised. Keevan stood his ground, but if Beterli came any closer, he would call the instructor. No one fought on the Hatching Ground. Surely Beterli knew that.

Fortunately, at that moment, the instructor called the boys together. He led them from the Hatching Ground to start on evening chores. One of the chores was to bring black rock to the kitchen ovens.

After the chores were done, people of the Weyr began to gather for the evening meal. The dragonriders came in from the Feeding Ground. Tonight Keevan's father, K'last, was at the main dragonrider table.

K'last and another dragonrider, L'vel, were discussing the age of the candidates. L'vel thought that only the older boys should be candidates. But K'last insisted that any boy over twelve had the right to stand in the Hatching Ground.

"Only a dragon knows what he wants in a rider. We certainly can't tell. Time and again people are surprised by the dragons' choices," K'last smiled and looked around the table. "The dragons never seem to make mistakes, though."

"Now, K'last, just look at the list of boys for this Impression. Seventy-two boys and only forty eggs. Drop off the twelve youngest, and there's still plenty for the hatchlings to choose from."

"Half the Weyr-bred lads have already been through several Impressions," one of the bronze riders said. "Let's drop some of *them* this time. Give the new ones a chance."

Everyone argued all through dinner. When the evening meal was over, no decision had been made. The Weyrleader promised to consider the matter, though.

Notes

Not many candidates slept that night. The boys were feeling unsure of themselves as they were called out of bed for morning chores. Keevan's foster mother, Mende, had to tell Keevan twice that he was being clumsy.

"What is the matter with you, boy?" she asked when he missed the bin and dropped black rock all over the ground.

"They're going to keep me from this Impression."

"What?" Mende stared at him. "Who?"

"You heard them talking at dinner last night. The babes won't be allowed at the hatching."

Mende looked at him a moment longer. Then, she touched his arm gently. "There's lots of talk around a supper table, Keevan. And it ends with supper. I've heard the same nonsense before every hatching. Nothing is ever changed, though."

"There's always a first time," Keevan answered.

"That'll be enough of that, Keevan. Finish your job. All my fosterlings make dragonriders."

"The first time?" Keevan was bold enough to ask as he went off to get rock.

If Beterli hadn't been getting rock at the same time, things might have turned out differently, Keevan thought later. Keevan was gathering a second load of rock when Beterli arrived.

"Have you heard the news, babe?" Beterli asked. He was grinning from ear to ear.

"The eggs are cracking?" Keevan nearly dropped the loaded shovel.

"No! Guess again!" Beterli was much too pleased with himself.

Notes

"I don't have time for guessing games," Keevan said, pretending not to care. He began to shovel black rock as fast as he could.

Beterli grabbed the shovel from Keevan's hands. "Guess!" he said.

"Give me my shovel, Beterli!" Keevan stood up tall, but he still didn't come to Beterli's shoulders. Other boys suddenly appeared around them.

He grabbed the shovel from Beterli. The older boy tried to get it back. But Keevan held the handle tightly.

With a sudden movement, Beterli rammed the handle into Keevan's chest. He knocked Keevan over. Keevan felt a sharp pain behind his left ear, a terrible pain in his left shin, and then he felt nothing.

The next morning, Mende's voice woke him. Keevan thought he had overslept, so he tried to throw back the covers. But he couldn't move. He was tucked firmly into his bed. And then the tight bandage on his head and the ache in his leg brought back recent events.

"Hatching?" he cried.

"No, lovey," Mende said in a kind voice. Her hand was cool and gentle on his forehead. "Though some people won't be at any hatching ever again." Her voice was stern when she told him that Beterli had been dropped.

"Am I still a candidate?" Keevan asked.

"Well, you are and you aren't, lovey," Mende said. "Is the numbweed making you feel better?" Keevan nodded.

At any other time, Keevan would have liked being taken care of like this. But now he lay in bed worrying. Beterli had been dropped. Would the others think it was his fault? But everyone was there! Beterli had started the fight. Keevan's worry increased.

Eventually the numbweed made Keevan sleepy. He let go of his fears.

Then, he heard a hum. It began to grow. Keevan realized that the hatching had started. But he was flat in bed!

He sat up. The numbweed made it hard to move. Carefully, he took a step. The broken leg dragged. It hurt, but what was pain to a dragonman?

No one had said he couldn't go to the Impression. "You are and you aren't" were Mende's words.

The humming got louder and faster. Keevan knew he must hurry. But if he hurried down the ramp, he'd fall flat on his face.

He decided to go flat on his rear end, like a crawling child. Then he scrambled down the ramp. He waited a moment at the bottom to catch his breath. Somehow he managed to push himself up, even though he was dizzy.

Then he heard the crowd. He heard oohs, soft cheers, and excited whispers. An egg had cracked, and the dragon had chosen his rider. Keevan went even faster. If he didn't get there soon, there'd be no hatching left for him.

Finally, Keevan staggered onto the Hatching Ground. No one noticed him. And Keevan couldn't see anything but the backs of the candidates. Suddenly, a large gap appeared in the wall of candidates, and Keevan saw the eggs. There didn't seem to be *any* left uncracked. He could see the lucky boys standing beside the dragons.

Suddenly he wished he'd stayed in bed. Now everyone would see his shameful failure. So he scrambled to reach the shadowy walls of the Hatching Ground. He mustn't be seen.

(**Notes**)

Notes

He didn't notice, therefore, that the remaining boys began to come toward him. Keevan collapsed, sobbing, onto the sand. He didn't see how confused the Weyrfolk were. He didn't hear the whispers of people guessing what would come next.

The Weyrleader and Weyrwoman had joined the crowd of boys moving toward the entrance.

"I've never seen anything like it," the Weyrleader was saying. "Only thirty-nine riders chosen. And the bronze is trying to leave the Hatching Ground. It hasn't made an Impression yet!"

The Weyrwoman replied. "The hatchling makes no choice because the right boy isn't here."

"There's only Beterli and K'last's young son missing. And there's a full wing of likely boys to choose from. . . ."

"None are acceptable, it seems. Where is the dragon going? He's not going to the entrance after all. Oh, what is over there, in the shadows?"

Keevan heard the sounds of voices nearing him. He wanted to dig himself into the sand.

Don't worry! Please don't worry! The thought was urgent, but it wasn't his own.

Someone kicked sand over Keevan and knocked roughly against him.

"Go away. Let me alone!" he cried.

Why? was the hurt-sounding question put in his mind. There was no voice, but the question was there. It was perfectly clear in his mind.

Keevan could not believe it. He lifted his head and stared into the glowing eyes of a small bronze dragon. The dragon was trying hard to stand up.

Keevan dragged himself to his knees. He wasn't aware of the pain in his legs. He didn't even see the ring of boys who'd been passed over. Resentfully, they all watched him Impress the dragon. The Weyrfolk watched. They were amused and surprised at the dragon's choice.

Why? asked the dragon again. *Don't you like me?* His eyes showed fear. His voice was so sad that Keevan staggered forward and threw his arms around the dragon's neck. Keevan stroked him and without words, he assured the hatchling over and over again that he was the most perfect, most beautiful, and most beloved dragon in all the Weyrs of Pern.

"What's his name, K'van?" asked Lessa, the Weyrwoman. She smiled warmly at the new dragonrider. Keevan stared at her for a while. Then he gave her a big smile. She had shortened his name, making him a dragonrider forever.

My name is Heth, the dragon thought. Then he hiccuped. *I'm hungry.*

"Dragons are born hungry," said Lessa, laughing. "F'lar, give the boy a hand. He can barely manage his own legs, much less a dragon's."

K'van remembered his stick and drew himself up. "We'll be just fine, thank you."

"You may be the smallest dragonrider ever, young K'van," F'lar, the Weyrleader, said, "but you're one of the bravest!"

And Heth agreed! Heth's and K'van's hearts leaped with pride and joy. K'van wondered if his heart would burst right out of his body. He looped an arm around Heth's neck. The pair, the smallest dragonboy and the hatchling who wouldn't choose anyone else, walked out of the Hatching Ground together forever.

Notes

Notes

Key Terms

Benden Weyr: the name of a specific cave colony inside the cone of an old volcano on the planet Pern.

Dragonriders: people who ride dragons on the planet Pern. They help protect the other people who live on the planet.

Hatching Ground: a place on the planet Pern where dragons hatch from their eggs.

Impression: a ceremony in which a newborn dragon chooses its own rider. It is the most important event in Pern society.

Pern: an imaginary planet somewhere in outer space. Pern is threatened by the dangerous Red Star, which periodically rains deadly threadlike plant spores on the planet.

Weyrs: cave colonies inside the cones of old volcanoes on the planet Pern.

Weyr-bred: raised in a Weyr.

Weyrfolk: people who live in a Weyr.

Weyrleader: the male leader of a Weyr.

Weyrwoman: the female leader of a Weyr.

Antaeus

Based on the short story by Borden Deal

Notes

It was during the wartime. Lots of people were coming North for jobs in factories. Kids were sometimes thrown into new groups and new lives that were completely different from anything they had ever known before. I remember this one kid, T. J., who came from down South. His family moved into our building.

Our building was just like all the others there. Families were crowded into a few rooms. There were about twenty-five or thirty kids about my age in that one building. Of course, there were a few of us who formed a gang. I was the one who brought T. J. into the gang.

The building right next door to us was a factory. It was a low building with a flat, tarred roof. The roof had a wall all around it. No one paid any attention to the roof because it was higher than any of the other buildings around. So my gang used the roof as a headquarters. We could get up there by crossing over to the fire escape from our own roof on a plank. It was a secret place for us.

I remember the day I first took T. J. up there to meet the gang. He was a healthy kid with lots of white hair. He talked more slowly than any of us. You noticed the difference in the way he talked right away.

We climbed up over the wall and dropped down on the roof. The gang was there.

"Hi, " I said. I pointed to T. J. "He just moved into the building yesterday." The gang said "Hi."

Notes

For a moment, no one had anything to say. T. J. looked around at the rooftop and down at the black tar under his feet. "Where I come from," he said, "we played out in the woods. Don't you have woods around here? Don't you have fields to grow things in—no watermelons or anything?"

"No," I said. "Why do you want to grow something? The folks can buy everything they need at the store."

He looked at me again with that strange look. "In Alabama," he said, "I had my own acre of cotton and my own acre of corn. It was mine to plan and make every year."

Blackie said, "Who wants to have their own acre of cotton and corn? That's just work. What can you do with an acre of cotton and corn?"

T. J. explained, but we didn't understand anything. We thought T. J. was strange and different. We were all attracted by his self-confidence.

He moved his foot against the black tar. "We could make our own field right here," he said softly. "When spring comes, we could grow watermelons."

"You'd have to be a good farmer to make these tar roofs grow any watermelons," I said. We all laughed.

But, T. J. was serious. He said we could carry dirt up to the roof and spread it out even. We could water the seeds in the dirt. Then we'd have a crop.

I slapped T. J. on the shoulder. "That's a wonderful idea," I said. Everybody smiled at him. "Our own private roof garden." We decided that we would get the dirt from an empty lot near our school.

T. J. kept the project going all through the winter months. He kept talking about the watermelons and the cotton we

Notes

could grow. He got the other kids in the gang to help him carry the dirt to the roof after school.

When I think about it now, I don't see how he kept us on the project. It was hard work. We had to carry the boxes of dirt all the way up the stairs to the roof. We also had to make sure no grown-ups saw what we were doing. But T. J. kept the vision bright within us.

During the cold months, the earth just lay there. It was lifeless. But one day it rained. After the rain there was a softness to the air. The earth was alive and warm.

T. J. smelled the air. "It's spring," he said.

We all tried to sniff the air the way T. J. did. It was the first time in my life that spring and earth meant something to me. I looked at T. J. and understood the dream that lay beyond his plan. He was a new Antaeus, preparing his own bed of strength.

"It's planting time," he said. "We'll have to find some seed."

"There are stores over on Sixth Street," I said. "We could probably get some grass seed there."

T. J. looked at the earth and then at us. "You really want to grow some grass," he said. "I've never tried to grow grass."

"But it's pretty," Blackie said. "We could play on it. It's like having our own lawn."

"Well," T. J. said. He looked at the rest of us. "I was thinking of growing vegetables. But we'll plant grass."

He was smart. He knew where to give in. And I don't think it made any difference to him. He just wanted to grow something, even if it was grass.

"Of course," T. J. said. "I do think we should also plant a row of watermelons."

Notes

"All right," I said.

Things went very quickly then. We stole seed from the open bins at the store. T. J. showed us how to prepare the earth and sow the grass seed. The earth looked rich and black with moisture. It seemed the grass grew overnight.

We couldn't walk or play on the grass as we had expected to. It was too delicate. But that was fine. It was enough to look at the grass and realize that it was the work of our own hands. We measured how much the grass grew each day.

T. J. was trying to find some watermelon seeds. He finally got his hands on a seed catalog. "We can order them now," he said. "Look!" We all crowded around.

"What are you boys doing up here?" an adult voice said behind us.

It surprised us. No one else had ever come up here before. We turned around and saw three men. They weren't policemen or night watchmen. They were three men in business suits. They walked toward us.

"What are you boys doing up here?" the one in the middle said again.

We stood still.

The men stared at the grass behind us. "What's this?" the man said. "How did you get it up here?"

"We planted it," T. J. said.

The men kept looking at the grass as if they didn't believe it. It was a thick carpet over the earth now.

"Yes, sir," T. J. said proudly. "We carried that earth up here and planted that grass." He showed them the seed catalog. "And we're planning to plant some watermelons."

The man look at him. "What do you think you're doing? Do you want to go to jail?"

Notes

T. J. looked shaken. The rest of us were silent. We were afraid of the men. We had grown up aware of adult authority. We knew the power of policemen, night watchmen, and teachers. This man sounded like all the others. But it was a new thing to T. J.

One man said to another man beside him, "Make sure that all that dirt is taken away tomorrow."

T. J. came forward. "That's our earth," he said. The man looked at him coldly. "But it's my building."

The men walked away. T. J. stood and looked after them. He was angry.

He turned to us. "We won't let them do it," he said. "We'll stay up here all day tomorrow and the day after that. We won't let them do it."

We just looked at him. We knew there was no stopping the men. We started moving slowly to the fire escape.

"They can't touch it," T. J. said. "I won't let them lay a dirty hand on it!"

He picked up the dirt and threw it over the wall of the roof. We began to do the same. We destroyed the grass that we had grown.

It took less time than you would think. When it was finally over, we were all still. We looked down at the black tar. It felt harsh under the soles of our shoes.

T. J. stood for a moment. Then, he started moving to the fire escape.

We followed him. But T. J. was quick. He went down the fire escape and disappeared toward the street. He didn't look back.

They did not find him for two weeks.

Notes

Then the Nashville police caught him. He was walking along the railroad track. He was heading South, heading home.

As for us, we never again climbed the fire escape to the roof.

The Highwayman

by Alfred Noyes

Part 1

1   The wind was a torrent of darkness among the gusty trees,
    The moon was a ghostly galleon[1] tossed upon cloudy seas,
    The road was a ribbon of moonlight over the purple moor,
    And the highwayman came riding——

5   Riding——riding——
    The highwayman came riding, up to the old inn door.

(In Other Words) In the moonlit night, a highwayman rode his horse through the dark countryside. Finally, he came to an old country inn.

    He'd a French cocked hat on his forehead, a bunch of lace at
       his chin,
    A coat of the claret[2] velvet, and breeches of brown doeskin.
    They fitted with never a wrinkle. His boots were up to the
       thigh.

10   And he rode with a jeweled twinkle,
          His pistol butts a-twinkle,
    His rapier hilt[3] a-twinkle, under the jeweled sky.

(In Other Words) His clothes were elegant, and they fit perfectly. His guns and sword had jewels on their handles.

1. **galleon:** large sailing ship.
2. **claret** (KLAR iht): purplish red, like claret wine.
3. **rapier** (RAY pee uhr) **hilt:** sword handle.

Notes

Over the cobbles he clattered and clashed in the dark inn
    yard.
And he tapped with his whip on the shutters, but all was
    locked and barred,
He whistled a tune to the window, and who should be
15   waiting there
But the landlord's black-eyed daughter,
        Bess, the landlord's daughter
Plaiting⁴ a dark red love knot into her long black hair.

In Other Words He rode up to the inn and knocked, but
it was locked up. When he whistled, the innkeeper's
daughter came to the window. She had been braiding
her hair.

And dark in the dark old inn yard a stable wicket⁵ creaked
Where Tim the ostler⁶ listened. His face was white and
20   peaked.
His eyes were hollows of madness, his hair like moldy hay,
But he loved the landlord's daughter,
        The landlord's red-lipped daughter,
Dumb as a dog he listened, and he heard the robber say—

In Other Words The strange man who took care of
horses at the inn waited to hear the conversation. He
was very jealous because he loved the same girl.

25   "One kiss, my bonny sweetheart, I'm after a prize tonight,
But I shall be back with the yellow gold before the morning
    light

4. **plaiting:** braiding.
5. **wicket:** small door or gate.
6. **ostler** (AHS luhr): person who takes care of horses; groom.

Notes

Yet, if they press me sharply, and harry[7] me through the day
Then look for me by moonlight,
     Watch for me by moonlight,
I'll come to thee by moonlight, though hell should bar the
30   way."

In Other Words The highwayman told his girlfriend that he was going to rob another stagecoach that night. He planned to come back that same night, but the soldiers might give him trouble. If so, then he would be back the next night.

He rose upright in the stirrups.[8] He scarce could reach her
     hand,
But she loosened her hair in the casement.[9] His face burnt
     like a brand
As the black cascade of perfume came tumbling over his
     breast;
And he kissed its waves in the moonlight,
35   (Oh, sweet black waves in the moonlight!)
Then he tugged at his rein[10] in the moonlight, and galloped
     away to the west.

In Other Words He tried to kiss her goodbye, but the window was too high. So she let her hair down, and he kissed it. Then, he rode off.

---

7. **harry:** harass or push along.
8. **stirrups:** foot supports attached to a horse saddle.
9. **casement:** window that opens outward on hinges.
10. **rein:** strap attached to bit in the mouth of a horse used to control the horse.

(Notes) | # Part 2

He did not come in the dawning. He did not come at noon;
And out of the tawny sunset, before the rise of the moon,
When the road was a gypsy's ribbon, looping the purple
    moor,
40   A redcoat troop came marching——
        Marching——marching——
King George's men came marching, up to the old inn door.

> **(In Other Words)** He didn't come back that night, and he didn't show up the next day. However, soldiers came to the inn.

They said no word to the landlord. They drank his ale
    instead.
But they gagged his daughter, and bound her, to the foot of
    her narrow bed.
Two of them knelt at her casement, with muskets at their
45   side!
There was death at every window;
        And hell at one dark window;
For Bess could see, through her casement, the road that *he*
    would ride.

> **(In Other Words)** The soldiers drank the innkeeper's beer. They also tied his daughter to the foot of her bed. Two soldiers with guns watched out her window for the highwayman.

They had tied her up to attention, with many a sniggering
    jest;[11]

11. **sniggering jest:** a snickered joke.

Notes

They had bound a musket[12] beside her, with the muzzle
50   beneath her breast!
"Now, keep good watch!" and they kissed her. She heard the
      dead man say——

Look for me by moonlight;
      Watch for me by moonlight;
I'll come to thee by moonlight, though hell should bar the way!

(In Other Words) The soldiers had tied the innkeeper's daughter so that a gun was pointed at her chest. They teased her and kissed her and told her to watch for the highwayman. She knew he was riding into a death trap.

She twisted her hands behind her; but all the knots held
55   good!
She writhed[13] her hands till her fingers were wet with sweat
      or blood!
They stretched and strained in the darkness, and the hours
      crawled by like years,
Till, now, on the stroke of midnight,
      Cold, on the stroke of midnight,
The tip of one finger touched it! The trigger at least was
60   hers!

(In Other Words) She tried for hours to loosen the ropes, but they were very tight. Finally, at midnight, she could reach the trigger of the gun.

The tip of one finger touched it; she strove[14] no more for the rest!

---

12. **musket:** a gun used by soldiers.
13. **writhed** (ry*th*d): twisted back and forth.
14. **strove:** past tense of strive; try hard.

The Highwayman   **489**

Notes

Up, she stood up to attention, with the muzzle beneath her
    breast.

She would not risk their hearing; she would not strive again;

For the road lay bare in the moonlight;

65   Blank and bare in the moonlight;

And the blood of her veins, in the moonlight, throbbed to
    her love's refrain.

In Other Words She had reached the trigger. That was all she needed. She didn't want the soldiers to know what she had done. She watched the road for the highwayman.

Tlot-tlot; tlot-tlot! Had they heard it? The horse hoofs ringing
    clear;

Tlot-tlot, tlot-tlot, in the distance? Were they deaf that they
    did not hear?

Down the ribbon of moonlight, over the brow of the hill,

70   The highwayman came riding,

        Riding, riding!

The redcoats looked to their priming![15] She stood up, straight
    and still.

In Other Words She heard the highwayman coming on his horse. The soldiers got their guns ready. She stood up.

Tlot-tlot, in the frosty silence! *Tlot-tlot,* in the echoing night!

Nearer he came and nearer. Her face was like a light!

Her eyes grew wide for a moment; she drew one last deep

75   breath,

15. **priming:** explosive for firing a gun.

Then her fingers moved in the moonlight,

    Her musket shattered the moonlight,

Shattered her breast in the moonlight and warned him——

    with her death.

(**In Other Words**) The highwayman came nearer. She took a deep breath and pulled the trigger. The shot killed her, but it warned him, as she had planned.

He turned. He spurred to the west; he did not know who stood

Bowed, with her head o'er the musket, drenched with her own blood!

80

Not till the dawn he heard it, his face grew gray to hear

How Bess, the landlord's daughter,

    The landlord's black-eyed daughter,

Had watched for her love in the moonlight, and died in the darkness there.

(**In Other Words**) The highwayman quickly turned around and rode in the other direction. He didn't hear until dawn that his girlfriend had shot herself to warn him.

85   Back, he spurred like a madman, shouting a curse to the sky,

With the white road smoking behind him and his rapier brandished high.

Blood-red were his spurs in the golden noon; wine-red was his velvet coat;

When they shot him down on the highway,

    Down like a dog on the highway,

Notes

90 And he lay in his blood on the highway, with the bunch of
lace at his throat.

In Other Words He rode back like a madman, cursing. The soldiers shot him on the highway. He lay there in his own blood, still in his fine clothes.

And still of a winter's night, they say, when the wind is in the trees,
When the moon is a ghostly galleon tossed upon cloudy seas,
When the road is a ribbon of moonlight over the purple moor,
A highwayman comes riding——
95   *Riding——riding——*
A highwayman comes riding, up to the old inn door.

Over the cobbles he clatters and clangs in the dark inn yard;
He taps with his whip on the shutters, but all is locked and barred.
He whistles a tune to the window, and who should be waiting there
100 *But the landlord's black-eyed daughter,*
Bess, the landlord's daughter,
Plaiting a dark red love knot into her long black hair.

In Other Words The legend of Bess and the highwayman lives on. On some winter nights when the moon is up and the wind blows, the ghost of the highwayman rides again. He rides to the inn and knocks on the window. The innkeeper's daughter is still waiting for him and is still braiding her hair.

Gentlemen of the Road
Based on the article by Mara Rockliff

Notes

Highwaymen were bandits. They robbed travelers in seventeenth- and eighteenth-century England. Why did people once think of them as gentlemen?

Many people in England became rich in those centuries. The rich dressed in silks and velvets. They lived in huge houses. They traveled to London for parties. They spent summers by the sea. But the poor lived in filth. In the worst years, 74 percent of the children in London died before the age of five.

New toll roads ran through the countryside. Rich people traveled on these good roads. The highwaymen could stop travelers and rob them.

The highwaymen called themselves gentlemen of the road. How did they get this reputation?

Some people saw them as Robin Hoods. (They gave some of what they stole to the poor.)

These bandits looked like gentlemen. Many began poor. But once they got money, they dressed in style.

Some highwaymen tried to act like gentlemen as well. They were polite to ladies. They sometimes asked their victims' forgiveness. Some bandits let their victims keep precious items. Others took only what they felt they needed and returned the rest.

Even when caught and sentenced to hang, some highwaymen acted bravely. With the noose around their necks, some threw themselves off the scaffold. They did not wait for the wagon they stood on to be pulled from under them. In songs and stories, this last act made them look brave in the face of death.

The Fall of the House of Poe
Based on the article by Mara Rockliff

Notes

How would you feel if your favorite place were torn down? Terrible, right?

If Edgar Allan Poe were alive today, he might feel terrible about the loss of a boardinghouse[1] where he once lived in New York City. Some people want to tear it down.

New York University now owns the building. For years it has held classrooms and offices. But in 1999, NYU officials decided to tear it down. A new law school building would replace it.

Loyal Poe fans objected. They wrote letters. They passed around petitions. At a rally, hundreds of people chanted, "No, no, Poe won't go."

NYU representatives said Poe had lived in the boardinghouse for as little as six months. He had written no important works there. One spokesperson for NYU said, "This is not a building that remembers Poe."

Eight other buildings where Poe lived in New York City are gone. Protesters found he and his wife had lived in this one the longest. Those months may have been his happiest. He was at the top of his career. He was writing and editing his own magazine. He also had published *The Raven and Other Poems.*

On September 29, 2000, after checking all the facts, State Supreme Court Judge Robert E. Lippmann dismissed the case. He found no legal reason to stop NYU from tearing down the Poe house. An NYU spokesman added, "The Tell-Tale Heart does not beat beneath the floorboards of this building." Preservation groups planned to appeal the judge's decision.

1. **boardinghouse:** a house where people live and pay for their rooms and meals.

It Just Keeps Going and Going . . .

Based on the article by Joan Burditt

Notes

It is a human-made monster. No one can escape it. It can reach around the entire planet. This monster is called the Brain, Crusher, Grog, and the Creeper. It reproduces fast. It shuts down entire systems. It's a computer virus.

Experts disagree on how serious these viruses really are. In fact, information and opinions on viruses are spreading as fast as the viruses themselves. Viruses are self-replicating. That means they make copies of themselves over and over.

A model by computer scientist Eugene Kaspersky shows how a computer virus works.

A teacher finds mistakes in an exam answer key. So he tosses it at the trash can and leaves. Later, a cleaner sees the answer key on the floor. He puts it back on the desk. A sticky note is now stuck to the key. The note says, "Copy two times, and put copies in other teachers' boxes."

The next day, the teacher calls in sick. A substitute takes over for the teacher. She sees the answer key with the note stuck to it. She leaves the note on. Then, she copies and passes out the answer key.

The other teachers give the key and note to the office clerk. She then makes more copies and passes them out. By the end of the day, the school is out of paper. The teachers' boxes are filled with useless answer keys.

Notes

This example shows what happens with a computer virus. The difference between the model and a computer virus is in the intent. The teacher didn't plan to create a monster. The whole mess was just a series of causes and effects. On the other hand, people create computer viruses to cause trouble. The virus destroys correct information. It costs billions of dollars in lost work time every year.

People working on antivirus programs are making it easier to find a virus before it spreads. Still, watch what you put in your computer . . . and in your trash.

Echo and Narcissus

Based on the myth retold by Roger Lancelyn-Green

Notes

Echo was one of many nymphs, or fairies, who lived in the Greek mountains. She was very beautiful, but she always talked too much. Once she made Hera,[1] queen of the gods, very angry.

Here's what happened. Zeus,[2] king of the gods, lived on Mount Olympus with the other gods. Sometimes Zeus descended from Olympus to spend time on earth with the nymphs. That made Hera, his wife, jealous. She would come down to earth to search for him.

Each time, Hera met Echo, who talked on and on and on. Finally, Hera realized that Echo was purposely detaining her with endless stories and gossip. While Echo talked, Zeus hurried back to Mount Olympus. He pretended he'd been there all along.

Furious with Echo, Hera thought of a fitting punishment. "From now on," she commanded, "you can only repeat what others say. You will never be able to speak first."

Echo wept at her cruel punishment. She was sad and lonely, but soon she had another misfortune. She fell in love with a handsome young hunter named Narcissus.

Many nymphs loved Narcissus, but he scorned them all. He loved only himself.

When Echo saw Narcissus, she fell madly in love. Since she could not speak, she followed him secretly.

1. **Hera** (HIRH uh).
2. **Zeus** (zoos).

"Narcissus" (retitled "Echo and Narcissus") adapted from *Tales the Muses Told* by Roger Lancelyn-Green. Copyright © 1965 by Richard G. Lancelyn-Green. Retold by Holt, Rinehart and Winston. Published by The Bodley Head. Reproduced by permission of **Random House UK Ltd.**

Notes

One day Narcissus became lost. "Is anybody here?" he called. Echo repeated, "Here!"

Narcissus looked around but saw no one. "Whoever you are, come to me!"

And Echo responded, "Come to me!"

Whatever he said, Echo repeated. Then, he cried, "Let us meet!"

Happily, she came running from her hiding place. When she tried to hug him, he shoved her away. He told her he would rather die than have her touch him.

"I would have you touch me!" poor Echo repeated.

"I'll never let you kiss me," he told her.

"Kiss me! Kiss me!" Echo sank to the ground.

Narcissus hurried away. "Kissing you would kill me!" he called back furiously.

"Kill me!" Echo begged. Her heart was broken.

Aphrodite,[3] goddess of love, granted Echo's wish. Echo pined away and died. But we can still hear her voice among the rocks when someone calls.

Aphrodite decided to punish Narcissus. He had insulted her by scorning Echo and the other nymphs. "He shall love only himself and die," she said.

One day Narcissus came to a pool in the mountains. Thirsty, he lay down to drink.

He was surprised to see a beautiful face in the water looking up at him. He thought it was a water nymph and fell immediately in love.

"I love you! Be mine!" he cried.

But when he reached into the water, the face disappeared. When the water grew still again, his beloved's face returned.

3. **Aphrodite** (af ruh DYT ee).

Narcissus had no idea he was seeing his own reflection. (Maybe it was the first time a pool reflected the face of someone looking into it.)

He was enchanted and couldn't leave. Helplessly, he lay each day gazing at his beloved's face. Like Echo, he could not have the love he wanted. He, too, pined away and died from a broken heart.

His last words were, "Farewell, my love, farewell." Whispering, Echo repeated them.

In the spring, a new flower appeared where Narcissus had died. It was the first narcissus—with white petals around a yellow center.

And so we know why there are echoes and how the first narcissus flower came to be.

Notes

After Twenty Years

Based on the short story by O. Henry

Notes

The policeman walked up the street. He always walked boldly.

There were few people out that night. It was too cold, windy, and rainy.

The officer studied the street carefully. With his strong body and bold walk, he could turn heads. Lights were on at a few stores. Most stores had been closed for hours, though.

The policeman slowed down. A man leaned against the doorway of a dark hardware store. He had an unlit cigar in his mouth.

"It's all right, Officer," he said quickly. "I'm just waiting for a friend. We decided to meet here twenty years ago. There used to be a restaurant here."

"It was torn down five years ago," said the policeman.

The man struck a match and lit his cigar. The light showed a pale face with a square jaw. He had a little white scar near his right eyebrow. He wore a large diamond pin in his scarf.

"Twenty years ago tonight," said the man, "I ate here with Jimmy Wells. We were raised together here in New York. We were like brothers. The next morning, I was leaving for the West to make my fortune. Jimmy didn't want to leave New York. We agreed to meet here in twenty years."

The policeman said, "Twenty years is a long time. Haven't you heard from your friend?"

"Well, yes, we wrote for a time," said the man. "But after a year or two, we stopped. The West is a big place, and I kept moving around. I know Jimmy will meet me if he's alive."

The man pulled out a watch. It was decorated with small diamonds.

"Three minutes to ten," he said. "It was exactly ten o'clock when we left here twenty years ago."

"Did pretty well out West, didn't you?" asked the policeman.

"You bet! I hope Jimmy has done half as well. He was a good man—a bit slow, though. It takes the West to make a man really sharp."

"I'll be leaving," said the policeman. "I hope your friend comes soon. Are you going to leave if he's not here by ten?"

"No!" said the other. "I'll give him at least half an hour. If he's alive, he will be here by then. Goodbye, Officer."

"Good night, sir," said the policeman.

A light, cold rain fell. The wind had increased. The man smoked and waited for his friend.

In about twenty minutes, a tall man crossed the street. He was wearing a long coat with the collar turned up to his ears. He went directly to the man in the door.

"Is that you, Bob?" he asked.

"Is that you, Jimmy Wells?" cried the man in the door.

"Bless my heart!" said the tall man.

He grasped Bob's hands. "I was sure you'd come. Twenty years is a long time! The old restaurant is gone, Bob. How has the West treated you, old man?"

"Very well. I have everything I ever wanted. You've changed a lot, Jimmy. You seem two or three inches taller."

"Oh, I grew a bit after I was twenty."

"Are you doing well in New York, Jimmy?"

"Okay. I work for the city. Come on, Bob. We'll go to a place I know and have a long talk about old times."

Notes

Notes

The two men walked up the street, arm in arm. The man from the West talked a lot about his success. The other man listened with interest.

A brightly lit drugstore stood at the corner. When they came into the light, each man turned to look at the other's face.

The man from the West stopped suddenly. He released his arm.

"You're not Jimmy Wells," he snapped. "Even twenty years can't change a man's nose from a Roman to a pug."[1]

"It sometimes changes a good man into a bad one," said the tall man. "You've been under arrest for ten minutes, 'Silky' Bob. The police department in Chicago thought you might have come here. They want to talk to you. Before we go to the station, here's a note I was asked to give you. It's from Patrolman Wells."

The man from the West unfolded the little piece of paper. By the time he had read the note, his hand shook.

Bob: I was at the place on time. When you struck the match to light your cigar, I saw it was the face of the man wanted in Chicago. Somehow I couldn't arrest you myself. Instead, I went around and got a plainclothes man to do the job.

Jimmy

---

1. **"...change a man's nose from a Roman to a pug":** A Roman nose has a bridge that is high and noticeable. A pug nose is short and wide. It usually turns up at the end.

What's *Really* in a Name?
Based on the article by Joan Burditt

Notes

Patsy seemed like a movie star before she became one. She was my sister's friend. She was only in the sixth grade, but she seemed almost grown up to seven-year-old me.

As an adult, Patsy was on television and in movies. Once I looked for her name in the credits. It wasn't there. My sister said Patsy used a *pseudonym,* a made-up or fake name.

I felt confused. Why did she need a new name?

Writers may use fake names called pen names. Mark Twain's real name was Samuel Clemens. Archibald Lynn Joscelyn writes westerns under the name of Al Cody. The romance writer Elaine Carr is really a man named Charles Mason.

Writers may use pen names to sell books. William Sydney Porter had a criminal record. As an ex-convict, he might have had trouble getting his books published. So he wrote stories under the name of O. Henry.

Many people want names that are easy to remember. Which has a better ring—Charles Lutwidge Dodgson or Lewis Carroll? Reginald Dwight or Elton John? Norma Jean Baker or Marilyn Monroe?

Why am I troubled about Patsy's name change? I thought Patsy changed her name to get rid of her past. Her old friends, the neighborhood, even me. Patsy, Norma Jean, Reginald—they probably all had good reasons for choosing new names. But I hope they held on to their roots. I agree with writer James Baldwin. He said, "Know from whence[1] you came. If you know from whence you came, there are absolutely no limitations to where you can go."

1. **whence:** where.

Bargain

Based on the short story by A. B. Guthrie

Notes

Mr. Baumer and I had closed his store and were walking to the post office to mail the bills. We saw Freighter Slade standing alone in front of the saloon. Mr. Baumer held out a bill to Slade.

"What do you want, Dutchie?" Slade said.

"Twenty-one dollars and fifty cents—for the things you bought."

"You know what I do with bills, Dutchie?" Slade crumpled the envelope and dropped it. Then he took Mr. Baumer's nose between two fingers and twisted it hard. He turned and went into the bar.

Mr. Baumer picked up the bill and smoothed it. He didn't say anything, and I felt embarrassed for him. After he mailed the bills, we walked home together.

"Study, Al," he told me. "It's important to know how to read and write and do math."

I'd been working for Mr. Baumer in the summer and after school since my dad died.

The store wasn't big, but it had groceries on one side and clothing and cloth on the other. In the back were kerosene,[1] whiskey, buckets, and tools. It would have closed long ago if Mr. Baumer hadn't been so stubborn and worked so hard.

The next afternoon, Mr. Baumer was sitting at his desk. He was a small, bent man with a little belly. The only thing unusual about him was his chin, which looked like a little

1. **kerosene** (kehr uh SEEN): a thin, petroleum-based oil used as fuel.

"Bargain" adapted from *The Big It and Other Stories* by A. B. Guthrie. Copyright © 1960 by A. B. Guthrie. Retold by Holt, Rinehart and Winston. All rights reserved. Reproduced by permission of **Houghton Mifflin Company**.

Notes

pink hill. Carefully he touched his nose. When he saw me, he sighed, "That Slade."

"It's useless sending him a bill, Mr. Baumer. He can't even read, and he doesn't pay anybody."

"I think he hates me for coming from another country. I came here at sixteen, I learned to read and write, and now I own a business."

"He hates everybody."

"But he doesn't pinch everybody's nose—or call them Dutchie."

"You shouldn't have sold Slade anything unless he paid first."

"I know," he answered. "A man makes mistakes."

"I think you'd better forget Slade's bill."

"But it's not about money anymore, Al."

"Then, what is it?"

He thought a little. "It is the thing. You see, it's the thing."

I didn't know what he meant. "Slade steals whiskey and other things from the merchandise he carries," he continued.

"All the freighters steal whiskey," I told him. The fifty-mile trip from the train took at least two days with one overnight stop. Freighters would drill a hole in a whiskey barrel and take some. Then they'd say that the missing whiskey had evaporated.

"Even Moore, who carries your freight, steals whiskey."

"Yes," Mr. Baumer said. I watched his eyes—thinking.

For a month nothing happened. Early in October, Mr. Baumer and I were walking to the post office with his bills. It was dark, and I didn't see Slade right away. He was standing in front of the bar just like last time.

Notes

When he saw Slade, Mr. Baumer asked me to find Slade's bill. The next thing I knew, Mr. Baumer was falling, dropping the envelopes. Slade had hit him hard on his back, saying, "How're you, Dutchie?" Meanwhile, Dr. King and another man had come along and were watching. Then Slade slugged Mr. Baumer, knocking him flat.

Before he could get up, Slade crushed Mr. Baumer's right hand with his boot heel.

Dr. King saw what had happened. He looked Mr. Baumer over and said to Slade, "I think you've broken his hand."

"He's lucky I didn't kill him," said Slade. "If you don't stay away from me, Dutchie, I'll give you more of the same!"

The next day Mr. Baumer's hand was in a sling, and he couldn't work much. I told him I would get the law after Slade, but he said the law wasn't good at settling plain fights.

"Well, I'd do something."

"Yes, you would, Al."

Six weeks before Christmas, Mr. Baumer hired Slade to carry his freight. I could hardly believe it. Ed Hempel, the new clerk, told me that Mr. Baumer had sent him to find Slade and that he'd seen them talking in the store. Then Mr. Baumer told Moore he'd changed to Slade.

Mr. Baumer never said anything to me about hiring Slade. I felt really bad because I couldn't look up to him anymore, even though I wanted to.

Slade brought in several loads for Mr. Baumer. Before Christmas the weather turned very cold. One afternoon it was 42 degrees below zero.

That day Moore came into the store to tell us Slade was dead. "I guess your new man froze to death."

"He knows too much to freeze," Mr. Baumer said.

"He's sure frozen now. He's in the wagon outside. I found him doubled up in the snow with no fire. I had an extra man, so I brought your load in. But your stuff will have to wait."

I went to look at Slade. His body was bent, as if he had frozen leaning forward in a chair.

Mr. Connor, the undertaker, took Slade's body away.

It was beginning to get dark, so Mr. Baumer told Colly, Ed, and me to unload the wagon. One of the last things we unloaded was a barrel.

"Mr. Baumer, we'll never sell all this, will we?"

"Sure we will, Al. I got it cheap—a bargain."

I looked at the barrel again. In big letters were the words "Wood Alcohol—Deadly Poison."

"Hurry. It's late." For a second I saw a hard look in his eyes. I saw, you might say, that hilly chin reflected in his eyes. "Then we go home, Al. It's good to know how to read."

Yeh-Shen

Based on a version of the Chinese folk tale told by Ai-Ling Louie

(Notes)

Long ago, a chief named Wu lived in a cave in China with his two wives. Each of them had a baby daughter. But then Chief Wu and one of his wives got sick and died.

The little orphan daughter, named Yeh-Shen, grew up in her stepmother's home. She was as bright and lovely as her stepsister was plain. Her stepmother was jealous of Yeh-Shen and gave her the hardest work to do.

Yeh-Shen's only friend was a golden-eyed fish. She shared the little food she had with the fish, and it grew large.

When the stepmother heard of this friendship, she was very angry that Yeh-Shen had kept a secret from her. She went down to the pond and lured the fish to the bank. There she killed it and took it home to cook for dinner.

When Yeh-Shen found her pet was gone, she fell to the ground and cried into the pond.

"Ah, poor child!" a voice said.

An old man in ragged clothes was looking down at her. He told her that her stepmother had killed the fish. Yeh-Shen gasped. The old man went on. "I have come to bring you a gift. Listen. The bones of your fish are filled with a powerful spirit. Whenever you really need something, kneel before the bones. Let them know your heart's desire. But do not waste their gifts."

With that, the old man rose into the sky. Yeh-Shen sadly went to the trash to get her friend's bones.

Adaptation of *Yeh-Shen: A Cinderella Story from China,* retold by Ai-Ling Louie. Text copyright © 1982 by Ai-Ling Louie. Retold by Holt, Rinehart and Winston. All rights reserved. Reproduced by permission of **Philomel Books, an imprint of Penguin Putnam Books for Young Readers, a Member of Penguin Group (USA) Inc., 345 Hudson St., New York, NY 10014.** Electronic format by permission of **McIntosh and Otis, Inc.**

Yeh-Shen was often left alone after that. The sad girl took comfort in speaking to the bones of her fish. She was often hungry, and she would ask the bones for food.

The spring festival time came near, when young men and women hoped to meet the person they would marry. Yeh-Shen longed to go. However, her stepmother wanted to find a husband for her own daughter first.

On the holiday the stepmother and her daughter dressed in their best clothes and set out for the festival. They made Yeh-Shen stay home to guard the fruit trees.

As soon as she was alone, Yeh-Shen went to kneel before the bones of her fish. "Oh, dear friend," she said. "I long to go to the festival, but I have no nice clothes."

At once, she found herself dressed in a sky blue dress and a feathered cloak. On her feet were golden slippers. When she walked in them, her feet were as light as air.

"Be sure not to lose the golden shoes," said the spirit of the bones. Yeh-Shen promised to be careful and went off to join the festival.

All day at the festival, people round Yeh-Shen whispered, "Look at that beautiful girl! Who is she?" Then she heard her stepsister: "Mother, she looks like Yeh-Shen!"

Yeh-Shen quickly ran off. As she ran she lost one of her golden slippers. When it fell off, her fine clothes turned back to rags. Only one thing remained—a tiny golden shoe.

Yeh-Shen ran to the bones of her fish and returned the slipper. The bones were silent. Yeh-Shen realized she'd lost her only friend. She hid the little shoe in her bed and went outside, where she cried until she fell asleep with her arms around a fruit tree.

Notes

Notes

Meantime, a villager found the shoe and sold it to a merchant. The merchant gave it to the king of T'o Han. The king marveled at the tiny slipper's beauty. He decided to find the woman who owned it.

All the women from the area were called to try on the shoe, but no one claimed it. Under cover of darkness, Yeh-Shen finally dared to come. She tiptoed across the floor of the building holding the shoe, and looked carefully. Recognizing it, she took it to return to the fish bones, so her friend would speak to her again.

The king was about to have her arrested. Then he noticed her lovely face shining from within her ragged clothes. He also saw she had the tiniest feet he had ever seen.

The king waved to his men. The girl in rags was allowed to leave with the golden slipper. Quietly, the king's men followed her home.

Yeh-Shen was about to hide both shoes in her bed when there was a pounding on the door. Yeh-Shen found the king at her door. He spoke to her kindly and asked her to try on the shoes. As soon as she put them on, her rags once more became the feathered cloak and beautiful sky blue gown.

The king knew he'd found his true love.

Not long after this, Yeh-Shen was married to the king. The king would not allow her to bring her wicked stepmother and stepsister to his palace. And one day, it is said, they were crushed to death in a shower of flying stones.

Names/Nombres

Based on the essay by Julia Alvarez

Notes

When we came to New York City, our names changed right away. The immigration officer asked my father, *Mister Elbures,* if he had anything to declare. My father shook his head no. We were waved through. I was afraid of being turned away if I corrected the man's pronunciation. But I said our name to myself. I opened my mouth wide for the blast of the *a.* I trilled my tongue for the *r, All-vah-rrr-es!*

At the hotel, my mother was *Missus Alburest.* I was *little girl,* as in, "Hey, little girl, stop riding the elevator up and down. It's not a toy."

We moved into our new apartment building. The manager there called my father *Mister Alberase.* The neighbors who became mother's friends called her *Jew-lee-ah* instead of *Hoo-lee-ah.* I was known as *Hoo-lee-tah* at home. But at school I was *Judy* or *Judith.* Once an English teacher called me *Juliet.*

Getting used to my new names took a while. I wanted to correct my teachers and new friends. But my mother said it didn't matter. "You know what your friend Shakespeare said, 'A rose by any other name would smell as sweet.'"[1] Because I wrote stories and poems, my family called any famous author "my friend."

By high school, I was a popular kid. My friends called me *Jules* or *Hey Jude.* One group of friends called me *Alcatraz.*

---

1. **"A rose . . . as sweet":** Julia's mother is quoting from the play *Romeo and Juliet.*

Notes

My "Wanted" poster would read *JUDY ALCATRAZ.* Who would ever trace her to me?

My older sister, *Mauricia,* had the hardest time. She and I were the family's Americans. We had been born in New York City. Then our parents had gotten homesick and gone "home." My mother told of how she had almost changed my sister's name.

Some of the new mothers were talking about their babies' names. Among the Sallys and Johns, my mother was shy about her baby's rich, noisy name. She gave her baby's name as *Maureen.*

"Why did you give her an Irish name?" one woman asked. "There are so many pretty Spanish names."

My mother blushed. She said her mother-in-law had just died. Her husband wanted to call the first daughter for his mother, *Mauran.* My mother thought the name was ugly. She added part of her own mother's name, *Felicia,* to *Mauran.*

"Her name is *Mao-ree-shee-ah,*" my mother told the women.

"Why, that's a beautiful name," the new mothers cried. "*Moor-ee-sha,*" they said. *Moor-ee-sha* it was when we returned to the States eleven years later. Sometimes she was called *Maria* or *Marsha* by mistake.

My little sister, Ana, had the easiest time of all. She was plain *Anne.* She turned out to be the family's pale, blond "American beauty." Her boyfriends sometimes called her *Anita* or *Anita Banana.*

By her college years in the late sixties, using names from other countries was popular. Once a roommate answered when I called Ana.

Notes

"Can I speak to Ana?" I asked, saying her name the American way.

"Ana? Oh, you must mean *Ah-nah*!"

As time passed, I no longer cared about my name being pronounced right. I just wanted to be Judy. I wanted to fit in with the Sallys and Janes in my class. But my accent and looks gave me away. People would say, "So where are you from, Judy?"

"New York," I said. After all, I had been born blocks away.

"I mean, *originally.*"

"From the Caribbean," I answered.

"Really? I've been to Bermuda. We went last April. I got the worst sunburn! So, are you from Portoriko?"[2]

"No," I sighed. "From the Dominican Republic."

"Where's that?"

"South of Bermuda."

I knew they didn't mean to hurt me. Still, I did not like being seen as different.

"Say your name in Spanish, oh, please say it!" I made mouths drop one day by saying my twelve names: "Julia Altagracia María Teresa Álvarez Tavares Perello Espaillat Julia Pérez Rochet González."

My different background was really clear when my whole family attended school events. Aunts, uncles, and the many little cousins came to my graduation. They sat in the first row to try to understand the fast American speakers. But then they spoke loudly among themselves.

Introducing them to my friends was hard. These relatives had long names. There were so many of them. Their connections to me were hard to understand. There was my

2. **Portoriko:** This spelling makes fun of the schoolmates' pronunciation of Puerto Rico.

Notes

aunt Tía[3] Josefina, who was really a much older cousin. One uncle Tío José brought my godmother, Tía Amelia. My friends usually had only "Mom and Dad" to introduce.

After the graduation, my family waited outside. My friends and I signed yearbooks with nicknames like "Beans" and "Pepperoni" and "Alcatraz." We hugged and cried. We promised to keep in touch.

Our goodbyes went on too long. I heard my father's voice calling, "*Hoo-lee-tah!*"

Back home, my large family gave me a party. The cake said *Happy Graduation, Julie.* There were many gifts. My parents gave me the biggest gift—a typewriter for writing my stories and poems.

The family said that someday my name would be well known. I laughed, wondering which one I would go by.

---

3. **Tía** (TEE uh): Spanish for "Aunt." Tío is "Uncle."

Amigo Brothers

Based on the story by Piri Thomas

Antonio Cruz and Felix Vargas were both seventeen. They had been best friends for so long they felt like brothers. They lived in the same apartment house on the Lower East Side of Manhattan. Antonio was light-skinned, tall, and thin. Felix was dark, short, and muscular.

Both dreamed of becoming the world lightweight boxing champion. They trained together. Early mornings, they ran along the river together.

Both had won four boxing medals. Their styles were different, though. Antonio had a longer reach and was a better boxer, but Felix was a more powerful slugger.

In just two weeks, they would fight each other. The winner would represent their club in the Golden Gloves Championship Tournament.

As they ran one morning, Felix said they needed to stop and talk. Their match was less than a week away. They leaned against the railing, looking out at the river.

"I don't know how to say this, bro," Felix began.

"I've been worrying about our fight, too, panin.[1] I don't sleep. I think about pulling punches so I don't hurt you."

"Me, too," said Felix. "I want to win fair and square. Let's make a promise, OK? When we fight, we've gotta be like strangers."

"Sí,"[2] Antonio agreed.

(Notes)

---

1. **panin** (pah NEEN): Puerto Rican Spanish slang for "pal" or "buddy."
2. **sí**: Spanish for "yes."

Notes

"Listen, Tony, I think we shouldn't see each other until the fight. I'm going to Aunt Lucy's in the Bronx. I'll train up there."

Felix suggested they split right there. After the fight, he said, they'd be together again like nothing ever happened. They hugged and went their separate ways.

The night before the fight, Antonio went up to the roof. The only way not to hurt Felix, he thought, was to knock him out quickly. He worried about what the fight would do to their friendship.

That night, Felix watched a boxing movie, imagining himself as the hero. It was Felix the Champion against Antonio the Challenger. He hoped for a quick, clean knockout, too.

On the day of the tournament, fans filled Tompkins Square Park. In their dressing rooms, Antonio put on white trunks, black socks, and black shoes. Felix wore light blue trunks, red socks, and white shoes.

There were six matches before their fight. Finally, it was time. The crowd roared as they entered the ring.

Bong! Bong! Bong! "Ladies and Gentlemen, Señores[3] and Señoras.[4] For the main event we have two young Puerto Rican boxers. Felix Vargas at 134 pounds and Antonio Cruz at 133 pounds."

The referee told them to fight cleanly. "Now shake hands and come out fighting."

The bell sounded for round one. Felix punched a hard straight left, but Antonio slipped away. Antonio's three fast lefts snapped Felix's head back. Felix knew then that Antonio wasn't pulling any punches. Both would fight to win.

3. **Señores** (seh NYAW rehs): Spanish for "gentlemen."
4. **Señoras** (seh NYAW rahs): Spanish for "ladies."

Antonio danced around, punching again and again. Felix moved in closer so he could reach Antonio. At the end of the round, he trapped Antonio against the ropes and smashed his abdomen. Two hard lefts to his head set Felix's ear ringing.

Bong! Both boxers froze mid-punch as round one ended.

Felix's right ear rang as he moved to his corner. Antonio had red marks on his midribs. "Remember," Antonio's trainer told him, "Felix always goes for the body."

Felix's trainer warned him, too. "You gotta get in close, or he'll chop you up from way back."

Bong! Bong! Round two. Felix rushed in and landed a solid right to the head. Hurt, Antonio hit back hard and fast. Felix returned a left to Antonio's head and a right to the body.

Antonio waited while Felix danced around. Then, Felix rushed in and slugged Antonio. Antonio hit him hard on the chin, and lights exploded inside Felix's head. His legs folded, but he managed to fight off Antonio's attack. Felix came back with a powerful right.

Antonio smashed Felix's right eye, which puffed up right away. Toe to toe, the boxers battered each other. Right, left, right, left. The crowd stood and roared.

A sudden right to the chin turned Antonio's legs to jelly. Felix hit wildly until Antonio punched him hard on the nose.

Then Felix landed a fierce blow. Antonio dropped, then staggered to his feet. He slugged Felix hard, and Felix went down flat on his back.

He got up in a fog. The crowd roared wildly as the bell sounded the end of round two.

Notes

Notes

Both fighters were hurting, but the doctor said they were OK to continue.

Bong!—the last round. So far the fight seemed even, but there could be no tie. There had to be a winner.

Antonio charged, driving Felix against the ropes. They pounded each other fiercely. Felix's eye was closed, and blood poured from Antonio's nose. The crowd watched in silence.

The bell sounded the end of the fight. But the boxers kept on pounding each other. The referee and trainers pulled them apart, and someone poured cold water over them.

Felix and Antonio looked around and hurried toward each other. The audience cried out in alarm. Would they fight to the death? Then they cheered as the amigo brothers hugged.

"Ladies and Gentlemen, Señores and Señoras. The winner and champion is . . . " The announcer turned to point to the winner.

But he stood alone in the ring. The champions had already left, arm in arm.

from Barrio Boy

Based on the autobiography by Ernesto Galarza

Notes

One morning, my mother and I walked to Lincoln School. The school was half a block long. It was a new, three-story building, painted yellow. It had a shingled roof, different from the red tile roof of my school in Mazatlán. I saw other differences. None of them made me feel better.

My mother and I walked together into the school. She held my hand.

We had carefully planned my first day at school. Mrs. Dodson had told us how to find it. We had walked past it several times. Friends in the barrio explained that the head of the school was called a *principal*. They said the principal was a lady, not a man. They also said there was always someone at school who spoke Spanish.

We found Miss Nettie Hopley's office. There was a sign on the door. It was in both Spanish and English. It said "Principal."

Miss Hopley was at a desk to one side. She sat in a chair with wheels.

She half turned in the chair. We didn't know what she said to us next. She gave us a big smile. We said nothing. She said more words we did not understand, but she had a friendly voice and a sparkle in her eyes. She showed us to the table. I almost tiptoed. I made sure my mother was between me and this gringo lady. In seconds, I had to decide if she was a friend or a menace. We sat down.

Then Miss Hopley stood up. She was very tall, with a shapely figure. She seemed like a giant. I decided I liked her.

Notes

She walked to the office door and called a name. A boy of about ten entered. He sat down at the table. He was brown like us. He was plump. His shiny black hair was combed straight back.

Miss Hopley sat down with us. She asked us questions. We answered. The boy translated. My name was Ernesto. My mother's name was Henriqueta. My birth certificate was in San Blas. Here was my last report card from my school in Mazatlán. Miss Hopley wrote things in a book. My mother signed a card.

As long as my mother stayed, I felt safe. Once the questions were over, my mother left. Then, Miss Hopley took my hand. She led me to Miss Ryan's first grade.

Miss Ryan took me to a seat at the front of the room. I shrank into my seat and watched her carefully. Because I was so small, she seemed very tall.

During the next few weeks, I became less afraid of Miss Ryan. She would bend over my desk to help me with English words. She'd often make happy announcements to the whole class. "Ito can read a sentence," she'd say. And small Japanese Ito would slowly read aloud. "Come, Skipper, come. Come and run." The class would listen in wonder.

There were many other first-graders learning English. They too had moments of glory like Ito's. I had my own the day I could say *butterfly*. I had been saying boo-ter-flee. "Children," said Miss Ryan. "Ernesto has learned how to say *butterfly*!" And I said the word just as Miss Ryan had. Soon I could read a sentence. "Come butterfly, come fly with me."

First-graders who didn't know English got private lessons. Miss Ryan and I would read about sheep and a scared chicken. She'd help me say words like *pasture*, *bow-wow-wow, hay,* and *pretty.* To my Mexican ear, these words had too many sounds and letters.

Miss Ryan would make me watch her lips. Then I'd close my eyes as she said words I found hard to read. It felt like together we were learning the secrets of English and grieving over the tale of Bo-Peep.

I graduated with honors from the first grade. The main reason was that I had fallen in love with Miss Ryan. We all loved her. We sensed that she was on our side.

Students from Lincoln were from many different races. They all came from the lower part of town. I had three friends in the second grade. Kazushi was Japanese. Matti was a skinny Italian boy. And Manuel was a fat Portuguese. He'd never get into a fight. Instead, he'd force you to the ground and sit on you. There were students from all over the world, as well as from the United States.

Miss Hopley and her teachers never let us forget why we were at Lincoln. Foreigners were to become good Americans. American-born students were to accept the rest of us. Off the school grounds, we insulted each other as adults did. On the playground, we would be sent to the principal's office for calling someone a wop, a chink, a dago, or a greaser. But our teachers helped us see that racial hatred was wrong.

At Lincoln, we became American, but we didn't have to give up our own culture. The teachers called us the names our parents did. No one was ever scolded for speaking his first language on the playground. We told stories about our countries. Miss Hopley showed wonder over these stories. Her eyes would open wide until they popped slightly.

She said I should become a proud American. But she also made it clear that there was no shame in being Mexican.

A Mason-Dixon Memory

Based on the essay by Clifton Davis

(**Notes**)

Dondré Green glanced nervously around the ballroom. Important people were there to raise money for a minority golf scholarship. I was the entertainer. Dondré was an eighteen-year-old from Monroe, Louisiana. He was the evening's honored guest.

Dondré attended a mainly white Southern high school. Dondré, a senior, was black.

He stepped up to the microphone. The audience stood and clapped. Then, Dondré said:

"I love golf," he said. "For the past two years, I've been a member of the St. Frederick High School golf team. And though I was the only black member, I've always felt at home playing at the mostly white country clubs across Louisiana."

Dondré then told us how that feeling changed on April 17, 1991.

"Our team had driven from Monroe. When we arrived at the Caldwell Parish Country Club in Columbia, we walked to the putting green," Dondré said.

A man from the club spoke to the team's coach. Then, Coach Murphy returned to his players.

"I want to see the seniors," he said.

"I don't know how to tell you this," Murphy told the four seniors. "But the Caldwell Parish Country Club is reserved for whites only. I want you seniors to decide what our response should be. If we leave, we forfeit¹ the tournament. If we stay, Dondré can't play."

1. **forfeit** (FAWR fiht): to lose or give up something as a penalty.

"A Mason-Dixon Memory" by Clifton Davis, slightly adapted from *Reader's Digest*, March 1993. Copyright © 1993 by Mel White. Retold by Holt, Rinehart and Winston. Reproduced by permission of **Mel White.**

Listening to Dondré's story, I remembered a similar experience.

In 1959 I was thirteen years old. My mother, my stepfather, and I lived in a small black ghetto in Long Island, New York. Our eighth-grade class was to visit Washington, D.C., and Glen Echo Amusement Park in Maryland.

Because our family was poor, I had to raise money for the trip myself. I sold candy bars, delivered newspapers, and mowed lawns. Three days before the deadline, I had made enough. I was going!

I was the only nonwhite in our part of the train to Washington. At the hotel in D.C., I roomed with Frank Miller, a businessman's son. Together, we dropped water balloons out our hotel window. We soon became close friends.

Every morning, we boarded the school bus for an adventure. We visited the Lincoln Memorial. We read Lincoln's Gettysburg Address. The speech was about the bloodiest fight in the Civil War. It said: ". . . we here highly resolve that these dead shall not have died in vain—that this nation, under God, shall have a new birth of freedom. . . ." Lincoln's face seemed very sad. The next morning, I knew why.

"Clifton," a chaperone said, "could I see you?"

My friends turned pale. They thought we'd been caught throwing water balloons.

"Do you know about the Mason-Dixon line?" she asked.

"No," I said.

"Before the Civil War," she said, "the Mason-Dixon line was the dividing line between slave states and free states. Today the Mason-Dixon line is an invisible border between

Notes

the North and the South. Things change when you leave Washington, D.C., and enter Maryland."

She then told me that Glen Echo Amusement Park, in Maryland, did not allow Negroes inside.

Back in our room, Frank said, "What happened, Clifton? Are we in trouble?"

I just lay on my bed and began to cry. Frank was shocked. Junior-high boys didn't cry too often.

Suddenly, I knew how it felt to be a "nigger." Never before had I been kept out of a place because of my race.

"Clifton," Frank whispered, "what is the matter?"

"They won't let me go to Glen Echo Park tonight because I'm a Negro."

"Phew!" Frank said. "I thought it was serious!"

I stared at him. "It *is* serious. They don't let Negroes into the park. I can't go with you!" I shouted. "That's pretty serious to me."

I was ready to punch Frank in the face. Then he said, "Then I won't go either."

For a minute, we didn't move. Then, Frank grinned. I will never forget that moment. Soon, eleven white boys had joined me in the room. They had all wanted to go to the amusement park. But they all decided, "We won't go." We had started a small revolution. My heart began to race. I was not alone. I felt grateful and proud.

Dondré Green's teammates were like my friends. Standing by their friend cost them a lot. But when it was time to decide, no one stopped to think. "Let's get out of here," one of his teammates whispered. And they left, just like that. Not only the seniors, but the younger players, too.

Dondré was amazed by his friends' response. The people of Louisiana also surprised him. They passed a new law. Now, private groups cannot invite a team and then bar a team member because of race.

As he spoke to us, Dondré's eyes filled with tears. "I love my coach and my teammates for sticking by me," he said. "It goes to show that there are always good people who will not give in to bigotry.² The kind of love they showed me that day will conquer hatred every time."

Suddenly the banquet crowd was standing and clapping.

In Washington, D.C., my friends showed that kind of love. A chaperone appeared with tickets to a Senators-Tigers game. Everyone cheered. We'd never been to a professional baseball game before.

On the way to the game, we stopped by the Lincoln Memorial. Everyone grew silent. I stared at Mr. Lincoln. His eyes still looked sad and tired.

I remembered the words of his speech: ". . . we here highly resolve . . . that this nation, under God, shall have a new birth of freedom. . . ."

Lincoln's words were telling us that freedom is not free.

Everyone should be let into amusement parks and country clubs. When they are not, the war for freedom begins again. Sometimes the war is fought with fists and guns. More often the best weapon is a simple act of love and courage.

Lincoln's words always remind me of my eleven white friends. I like to think that when we stopped that night, Mr. Lincoln smiled at last. As Dondré said, "The kind of love they showed me that day will conquer hatred every time."

Notes

2. **bigotry** (BIHG uh tree): hatred toward people who are different in race, religion, politics, or other beliefs.

Buddies Bare Their Affection for Ill Classmate

Based on a newspaper article from the *Austin American-Statesman*

Notes

Oceanside, California, March 19 — In Mr. Alter's class, nearly all the boys are bald. Thirteen fifth-graders shaved their heads for a sick buddy. They didn't want him to feel different.

Eleven-year-old Scott Sebelius explained. "People can't tell who's who. They don't know who has cancer."

Ian O'Gorman is the one with cancer. His disease is called lymphoma. First, doctors removed a tumor. Then, he started chemotherapy.[1]

"I had tubes up my nose," Ian said. "And I had butterflies in my stomach."

Ian has eight more weeks of chemotherapy. It will make all his hair fall out. Before that happens, he chose to shave his head. His friends astonished[2] him by shaving theirs, too.

It was ten-year-old Kyle Hanslik's idea. All the boys went to the barbershop together.

Ian's father choked back tears. He is moved by the boys' support. Jim Alter, Ian's teacher, shaved his head, too.

On March 2 Ian left the hospital. He is pale and twenty pounds lighter. But he's eager to play baseball and basketball. He thinks he can start on Monday.

1. **chemotherapy** (KEE moh THEHR uh pee): the use of chemical agents to treat disease.
2. **astonished** (uh STAHN ihsht): to be suddenly surprised.

The Origin of the Seasons
Based on the myth retold by Olivia Coolidge

(**Notes**)

Demeter was the great earth mother. She stood tall. Her hair was the color of wheat. She was the goddess of the harvest and taught the farmers everything they knew. Demeter's daughter was named Persephone.

Persephone was the young girl of spring. She lived in a land where the spring is long and lovely. There she played and laughed with other girls. One day Hades heard Persephone's laughter. Hades was the god of the dead, but even he was touched by Persephone's beauty. He wanted to marry her. So, Hades went up to Olympus to get permission from Zeus, the chief god. Zeus agreed that Hades could take Persephone as his wife.

One day Persephone was gathering flowers with her friends. Persephone wandered away from the other girls. As she looked a little ahead, she noticed the most beautiful flower. She stretched out her hand to reach for the flower. Suddenly, the earth opened in front of her. Then, she found herself caught in a stranger's arms. Persephone screamed and tried to get free. Her armful of flowers fell to earth. However, Hades was far stronger than she. He swept her into his golden chariot, took the reins of his coal-black horses, and was gone. The earth made a rumbling sound as it closed behind them. The other girls ran to find Persephone. They went to the place where they had seen her last, but they couldn't find her anywhere. All they saw were roses and lilies scattered over the grass.

"The Origin of the Seasons" adapted from *Greek Myths* by Olivia Coolidge. Copyright © 1949 and renewed © 1977 by Olivia E. Coolidge. All rights reserved. Retold by Holt, Rinehart and Winston. Reproduced by permission of **Houghton Mifflin Company.**

Notes

When Demeter heard the news of her daughter's disappearance, she was overcome with sadness. She searched everywhere. She asked everyone she met if they had seen her daughter. Neither gods nor men had seen Persephone. Demeter finally asked the god Phoebus Apollo. He sees all things from his chariot in the heavens.

"Yes, I have seen your daughter," said the god. "Hades has taken her, and Zeus agreed to it."

When she heard this, Demeter became very upset. With Zeus on Hades' side, she knew that she would never be able to rescue Persephone. Demeter decided to disguise herself as an old woman and wander the earth.

While she wandered, Demeter forgot all about her duties as the harvest goddess. No fruit, vegetables, or wheat grew anymore. The gods looked down on the earth. They realized that people might starve to death unless Demeter helped things grow again.

At last Zeus sent Iris, the rainbow, to seek out Demeter. He wanted Iris to ask Demeter to save the people on earth. Dazzling Iris swept down from Olympus. She offered Demeter beautiful gifts from the other gods. But Demeter would not listen. She said that she would not let fruit grow on the earth until Persephone was returned to her.

At last Zeus saw that he must send a messenger to bring back Persephone to her mother. The messenger went to the land of the dead. He found Hades sitting upon his throne. Persephone sat pale and sad beside him. She hadn't had anything to eat or drink since she'd been in the land of the dead. She sprang up with joy when she saw Zeus's messenger. Hades looked gloomy because he really loved Persephone. He knew he couldn't disobey Zeus, though. So,

Notes

he came up with a trick. He pressed Persephone to eat with him before she left. Persephone really wanted to get out of there, but Hades begged her to take a pomegranate. Persephone didn't want to delay her trip by arguing. She thought it would be easier to say Yes. So, she ate seven of the seeds. Then, Zeus's messenger took her with him. Persephone finally came back to earth.

When Demeter saw Zeus's messenger with her daughter, she rushed forward. Persephone, too, rushed forward. She threw her arms around her mother's neck. For a long time, they held each other. But then Demeter asked the girl, "Did you eat or drink anything with Hades?" The girl replied, "I took a pomegranate and ate seven of its seeds."

"Oh, no!" said the goddess. "My daughter, what have you done? The Fates have said that if you ate anything in the land of the dead, you must return to Hades. However, you didn't eat the whole pomegranate. You ate only seven of its seeds. Therefore, you must live in the land of the dead for seven months of the year. For the other five months, you may live with me."

And that's what the Fates decided. Even Zeus could not change their minds. For seven months every year, Persephone lives in the land of the dead. At this time, Demeter is sad and misses her daughter. The trees lose their leaves. The cold comes. The earth lies still and dead. After seven months, Persephone returns. Her mother is glad, and the earth is happy. The wheat springs up. It is bright, fresh, and green in the fields. Flowers bloom, birds sing, and young animals are born. The heavens smile for joy.

The Flight of Icarus

Based on the myth retold by Sally Benson

(Notes)

> **Cast of Characters**
>
> **King Minos:** King of Crete.
> **Theseus:** Hero from Athens held captive by Minos.
> Daedalus helped him escape from Crete.
> **Daedalus:** Built the labyrinth for Minos.
> **Icarus:** Daedalus's young son.

After Theseus escaped, King Minos was angry. He locked Daedalus, the builder of his labyrinth, in a tower. Icarus, Daedalus's young son, helped his father escape.

Because Crete is an island, Daedalus and Icarus were still prisoners. They tried—and failed—to escape by ship.

Daedalus said, "I will try the air." He told Icarus to bring him feathers. Daedalus shaped wax into wings and covered them with the feathers.

When Daedalus tried out the wings, the wind lifted him up. Excitedly, he made a pair of wings for Icarus. Icarus tried them out and was able to fly.

"Now we will escape," said Daedalus. "Don't fly low, or your wings will become wet and heavy. Don't fly high, or the sun will melt the wax."

Together they began their flight across the sea.

Icarus loved the freedom of flight. He flew higher, closer and closer to the blazing sun. The wax began to melt—small feathers and then large feathers dropped off. Wildly, Icarus beat his wings, but there were no feathers to hold him up. He plunged into the sea and drowned.

Daedalus gathered his son's body in his arms and flew to land. There he buried Icarus.

Then, Daedalus flew to the island of Sicily where he built a temple for the god Apollo. His wings were hung in the temple as a gift to the god. Daedalus mourned for Icarus, who had not listened to his father's words and had flown too close to the sun.

Notes

Sir Gawain and the Loathly Lady

Based on the retelling by Betsy Hearne

Notes

One day in spring, King Arthur was hunting with all his knights. Suddenly a deer ran by in the distance. King Arthur told his knights that he would chase the deer by himself. King Arthur went after the deer until he killed it. He was about to call for his knights when he heard a voice behind him.

"Well done, King Arthur!"

King Arthur turned to see a strange knight. The knight was fully armed. He was standing only a few yards away.

"You have done me wrong many years and given away my northern lands," said the strange knight. "I have your life in my hands. What will you do now?"

"Sir Knight, what is your name?" asked the king.

"My name is Gromer Somer Joure."

"Spare my life, Sir Gromer, and I'll give you whatever I can. It is shameful to kill me here. I have only my hunting gear, but you're armed for battle."

"I'll spare your life if you promise me something. You will meet me here on this day one year from now. None of your knights will come with you. On that day, you must tell me the answer to this riddle: What do women want? If you do not bring the answer to my riddle, you will lose your head."

"I promise," said the king. "Now let me go."

The knight laughed. "Do not think of playing false, King Arthur."

"I won't. I'm a true knight." The king began to blow his bugle for his knights to find him. Sir Gromer turned his

"Sir Gawain and the Loathly Lady" adapted from *The Oryx Multicultural Folktale Series: Beauties and Beasts* by Betsy Hearne. Copyright © 1993 by The Oryx Press. Retold by Holt, Rinehart and Winston. Reproduced by permission of **Greenwood Publishing Group, Inc., Westport, CT,** for Oryx Press.

Notes

horse and was gone as quickly as he had come. The knights found their king alone with the deer he had killed.

The king told his favorite knight, Sir Gawain, what had happened.

"Don't worry," said Gawain. "Get your horse ready to ride into strange country. Ask everyone you meet the answer to the riddle. I will ride another way, and I will write all the answers in a book."

So, Gawain rode one way, and the king another. Each one asked every man and woman they found, "What do women want?"

Some said they loved beautiful clothes. Some said they loved to be praised. Some said they loved a handsome man. Some said one thing, and others said another. Gawain had so many answers that he made a great book to hold them. After many months of traveling, he came back to King Arthur's court. The king was there already with his book. Each looked over the other's work. But no answer seemed right.

King Arthur decided that he needed to look a little more. He had only a month left. So, he rode away to Ingleswood Forest.

There he met a lady. King Arthur was amazed. She was the ugliest creature that he had ever seen. Her face seemed almost like that of an animal. She had a pushed-in nose and a few yellow teeth in her mouth. Her body was twisted. She had a hunched back. But she rode cheerfully on her horse. Her voice was sweet and soft.

"I am glad that I have met with you, King Arthur," Dame Ragnell said. "Speak with me. Your life is in my hands. I know of your situation. I warn you that you will not find your answer if I do not tell you."

Notes

"What do you want with me, lady?" said the king. He was surprised that she was so bold.

"I will make you a deal," said Dame Ragnell slowly. "If your life is saved another way, you don't need to grant my wish. If my answer saves your life, grant me Sir Gawain as my husband. Choose now."

"I cannot grant you Sir Gawain," said the king. "That's his choice. He is not mine to give."

"Well," she said. "Then go home again and speak to Sir Gawain. Even though I'm ugly, I'm in good spirits. Through me, he may save your life."

They said goodbye to each other. The king returned to Carlyle with a heavy heart. The first man he met was Sir Gawain. "How did it go?" Gawain asked.

"Couldn't be worse," said the king. "I'm afraid that I'll die at Sir Gromer's hand."

"No," said Gawain. "I would rather die myself. I will do anything to help you."

"Gawain, I met today with the ugliest lady that I ever saw. She said she would save my life if you became her husband."

"Is that all?" asked Gawain. "Then I shall marry her and marry her again! I don't care if she's as ugly as the devil. You are my king, and I am your friend. It is my duty to save your life. If I don't, I'm a big coward."

"Thank you, Gawain," said King Arthur. "You have saved my life."

The day soon came when the king was to meet Dame Ragnell and take his answer to Sir Gromer. The king rode about a mile when he met Dame Ragnell. He told her that Gawain had agreed to marry her.

Notes

"Now you will know the answer to your riddle," began Dame Ragnell. "There is one thing that every woman wants: We want to rule over men. Then, all is ours. Now go and tell that to your knight. You will not be harmed."

The king went off to meet Sir Gromer and tell him the answer to the riddle.

When he heard King Arthur's answer, Sir Gromer was silent. He was angry. Then he cried out, "I hope to God that the one who told you the answer will burn in a fire. She's my sister, Dame Ragnell. She wasted my time. Go where you like, King Arthur."

Now King Arthur had to follow through with his promise to Dame Ragnell. He was ashamed to bring the ugly lady to the court. When they arrived at Carlyle, everyone wondered where she came from. They had never seen such an ugly creature.

When he saw the king and Dame Ragnell coming, Sir Gawain stepped forward and said, "I am ready to follow through with my promise."

"God have mercy," said the Dame Ragnell when she saw Gawain. "For your sake I wish I were a pretty woman because you're such a good person."

At the wedding, Dame Ragnell dressed better than anyone else. But all her fine clothes could not hide her ugliness. When the party began, only Dame Ragnell ate with an appetite. All the other ladies and gentlemen sat like stones. After the wedding party, Sir Gawain and Lady Ragnell went to the bedroom that had been prepared for them.

"Ah, Gawain," said the lady. "Since we are married, be polite and come to bed. If I were pretty, you would be happy. For Arthur's sake, kiss me at least."

Notes

Sir Gawain turned to the lady. But instead of the ugly lady, he saw the loveliest lady he had ever seen.

"What are you?" cried Gawain.

"Sir, I am your wife, of course. Why are you so mean?"

"Lady, I am sorry," said Gawain. "Now you are a beautiful lady, and today you were the ugliest woman that I've ever seen." And he took her in his arms and kissed her with great joy.

"Sir," she said, "You have half-broken the spell on me. So, you will have me, but my beauty won't stay. You may see me pretty by night and ugly by day. Or else, see me ugly by night and pretty by day.

"The choice is too hard!" cried Gawain. "I don't know what I should say. The choice is in your hands!"

"Thank you, Gawain," said the lady. "Now I know I am truly loved. I can be pretty for you both day and night. I was shaped by witchcraft by my stepmother. According to her spell, I was to be the ugliest creature until the best knight of England married me and let me have control. Kiss me, Sir Gawain. Be happy." The two thanked God for their good fortune.

King Arthur came himself to call them to breakfast the next day. He wondered why Gawain stayed so late with his ugly bride. Sir Gawain rose and took the hand of the lady. He opened the door to greet the king.

Dame Ragnell stood by the fire, with her pale lovely skin and red hair spilling down to her knees. "Look," said Gawain to the king. "This is my wife, Dame Ragnell. She once saved your life." And Gawain told the king about the stepmother's spell.

From then on, Dame Ragnell was always the prettiest lady at every party. Sir Gawain loved her all his life.

StreetWheelie Productions

StreetWheelie Productions

2323 South Robertson Boulevard

Beverly Hills, CA 90210

Notes

June 7, 2002

Miss Samantha Lancaster

1920 Ygnacio Valley Road

Walnut Creek, CA 94598

Dear Sam:

We at StreetWheelie Productions are pleased to offer you a part in our production. Your contract is included with this letter. I know that contracts can be difficult to read. So, it is important that you and your parents understand this contract completely. Then, you should sign it. We have listed the issues below.

<u>Your Responsibilities</u>

- Transportation: You are responsible for getting to and from work.
- Work Schedule: You are responsible for keeping track of the filming schedule. Check your e-mail for updates.
- Arrival Time: You must arrive on time for work. You should report to the makeup person one hour before you are supposed to start filming.
- Appearance: You may not change your hairstyle or hair color during filming.
- Equipment: You must bring your own bike to all filming.

Notes

- Parental Supervision: A parent must be present during filming.

Wages

- You will be paid a minimum hourly wage.
- You will receive a check at the end of each week.
- You cannot work more than eight hours a day.
- You can take a one-hour break each day. You will get paid for this break.

Bonus:

- You will receive a bonus (extra money) on the last day of work.
- You will receive this extra money only if you did a good job. You must fulfill all your responsibilities.
- This bonus will equal the total amount you made during the filming. In other words, this bonus will double your money.

If you have any questions, call Juanita Diaz, our lawyer. Her phone number is on the contract. We look forward to having you on the project.

Sincerely,

Cassandra Rice

Cassandra Rice, Casting Director